SUPERMAN
3-2-1 ACTION!

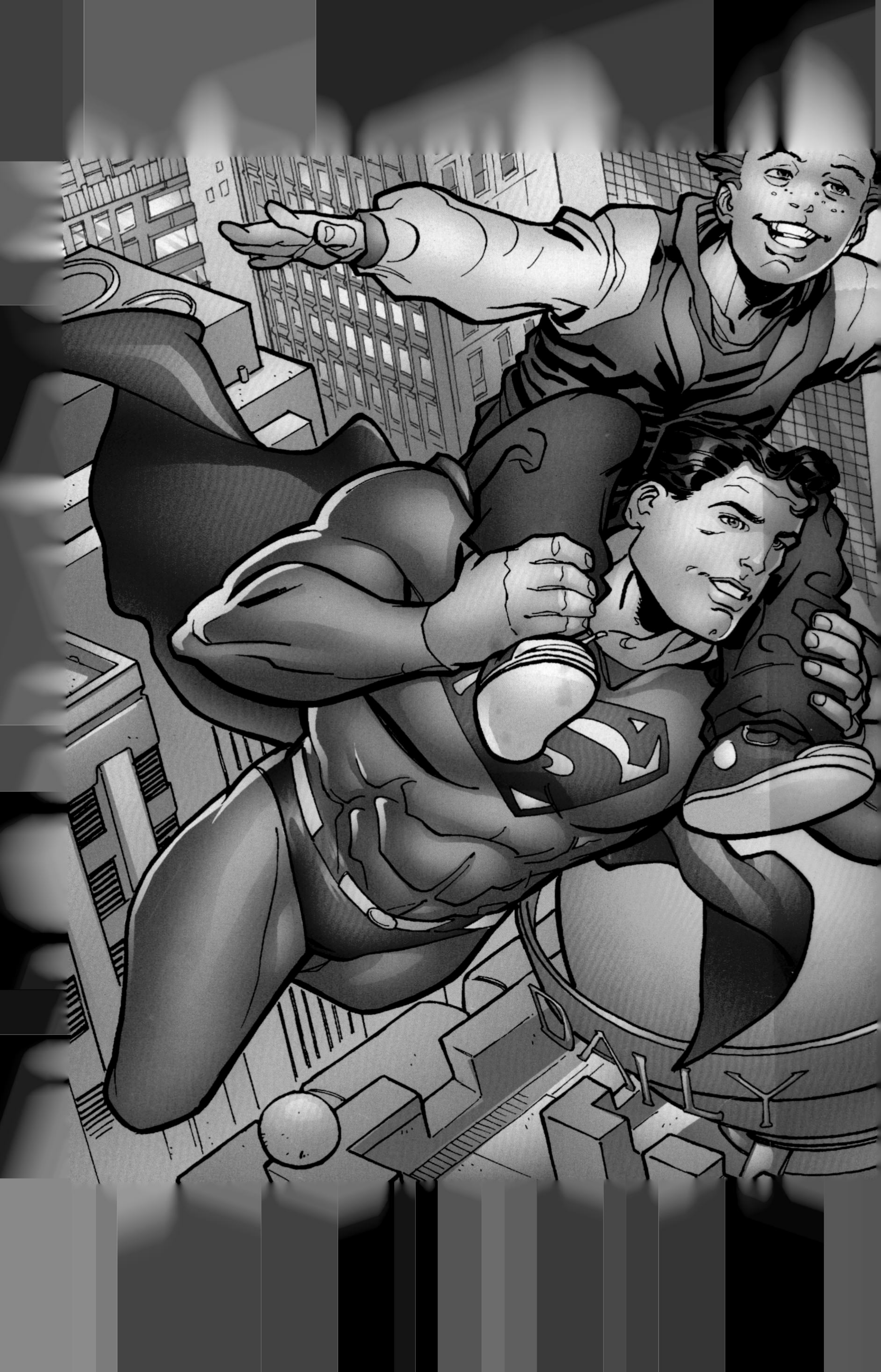
DAILY

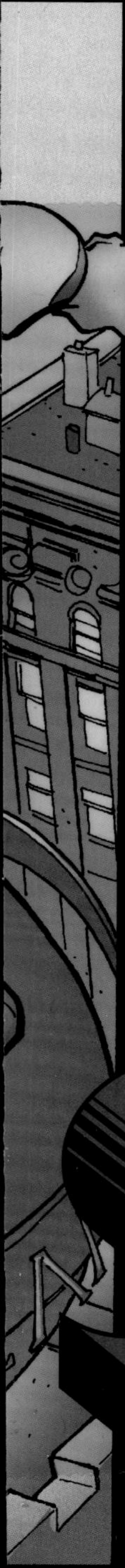

JIMMY

KURT BUSIEK
WRITER

RICK LEONARDI
PENCILLER

ANDE PARKS
INKER

PETE PANTAZIS
COLORIST

COMICRAFT
LETTERING

3-2-1 ACTION!

KURT BUSIEK
WRITER

BRAD WALKER
PENCILLER

JOHN LIVESAY
INKER

RICHARD HORIE
TANYA HORIE
PETE PANTAZIS
LEE LOUGHRIDGE
COLORISTS

JARED K. FLETCHER
TRAVIS LANHAM
LETTERING

THE AMERICAN EVOLUTION

MARK EVANIER
WRITER

STEVE RUDE
PENCILLER

BILL REINHOLD
INKER

LEE LOUGHRIDGE
COLORIST

TODD KLEIN
LETTERING

SUPERMAN
3-2-1 ACTION!

THE AMERICAN EVOLUTION BASED ON A PLOT AND CONCEPTS BY JACK KIRBY

SUPERMAN CREATED BY JERRY SIEGEL AND JOE SHUSTER

DAN DIDIO Senior VP-Executive Editor

MATT IDELSON MIKE MCAVENNIE Editors-original series

FRANK BERRIOS Assistant Editor-original series

NACHIE CASTRO Associate Editor-original series

BOB HARRAS Editor-collected edition

ROBBIN BROSTERMAN Senior Art Director

PAUL LEVITZ President & Publisher

GEORG BREWER VP-Design & DC Direct Creative

RICHARD BRUNING Senior VP-Creative Director

PATRICK CALDON Executive VP-Finance & Operations

CHRIS CARAMALIS VP-Finance

JOHN CUNNINGHAM VP-Marketing

TERRI CUNNINGHAM VP-Managing Editor

ALISON GILL VP-Manufacturing

DAVID HYDE VP-Publicity

HANK KANALZ VP-General Manager, WildStorm

JIM LEE Editorial Director-WildStorm

PAULA LOWITT Senior VP-Business & Legal Affairs

MARYELLEN MCLAUGHLIN VP-Advertising & Custom Publishing

JOHN NEE Senior VP-Business Development

GREGORY NOVECK Senior VP-Creative Affairs

SUE POHJA VP-Book Trade Sales

STEVE ROTTERDAM Senior VP-Sales & Marketing

CHERYL RUBIN Senior VP-Brand Management

JEFF TROJAN VP-Business Development, DC Direct

BOB WAYNE VP-Sales

Cover by Steve Rude
SUPERMAN: 3-2-1 ACTION!
Published by DC Comics.

DC Comics, 1700 Broadway, New York, NY 10019
A Warner Bros. Entertainment Company
Printed in Canada. First Printing.
ISBN: 978-1-4012-1680-1

INTRODUCTION

It's all about Jimmy.

Don't let the title fool you. Oh, sure, Superman's in all the stories, and there's plenty of Action, but the fact is, this is really a Jimmy Olsen collection. Jimmy has a habit of sneaking into things, and in one way or another, he sneaked into all of the issues here.

Jimmy's been around a long time — he's been Superman's plucky, adventurous young pal since 1940, when he debuted in the Superman radio show, moving over to the comics in 1941. And one of Jimmy's peculiarities is that whenever Superman history gets revised, Jimmy seems to get younger all over again — while Dick Grayson grows up and becomes Nightwing, allowing others to take over for him as Robin, Jimmy is a person, not a role. And while there are certainly readers who'd like to see him age and mature, the general sense of things is that most aren't that interested in seeing "Superman's Adult Colleague, James B. Olsen." So whenever things get reorganized, Jimmy tends to de-age, back to comfortable "young pal" levels.

When Geoff Johns and I took over the Superman books in the wake of the most recent of these reorganizations, INFINITE CRISIS, sure enough, Jimmy was back in his unspecified late teens — which among other things meant that he couldn't have been working at the Daily Planet when Clark Kent started there (since Superman's career is deemed to be something over a decade at this point, from his perspective at least). So in light of that, I had three things I wanted to do with Jimmy — I wanted to show how, in the current setup, he met and befriended Superman, I wanted to show where his famous hypersonic signal-watch came from, and there was one other development, which turns up as something of a surprise in one of the stories reprinted here, so I won't describe it in the intro. You'll see it.

The trouble was, we had so much to do in the books that there wasn't room for the stories. We talked about doing a "Jimmy Olsen Month," but it got squeezed out by other things. Jimmy, though, is nothing if not resourceful, and he found a way...

First, we delayed a storyline for dramatic reasons which gave us the chance to drop in a self-contained story or two. I seized the opportunity to make one of those issues the origin of the Superman-Jimmy friendship, as well as the tale of how Jimmy came to work at the Planet, and why Perry White is so tough on him but doesn't just get rid of him. And that became the first story in this collection, with elegant and powerful artwork by Rick Leonardi. Jimmy had found a way to sneak in.

And then I was asked to come up with a three-part story for ACTION COMICS. Matt Idelson, the Superman editor, suggested I do a story tying in to COUNTDOWN, DC's weekly mega-series where Jimmy was playing a large role. In the story, Jimmy was trying to hunt down the reason members of the New Gods were getting murdered, while dealing with inexplicable bursts of superpowers, which would lead him to try to become a superhero. Plus, I'd get to work with Brad Walker.

There was plenty in the COUNTDOWN storylines that I could build three issues of ACTION around, but I asked if I could also manage to work in the story of the signal-watch, and the third big development with Jimmy I wanted to do. I also wanted to bring back The Kryptonite Man, an updated villain Geoff and I had introduced in our first issue. So those elements got to sneak in, too, becoming part of the COUNTDOWN-connected story. (And I'd be remiss in my duties as an introduction-writer if I didn't tell you, at this point, that after the story here, Jimmy's adventures continue in COUNTDOWN, building to a climax as of publication of this book and sure to be collected into handy trade paperbacks thereafter. Tell your local comics shop Jimmy sent you!)

The trouble, of course, with letting Jimmy sneak in is that once he's in, it simply spawns all kinds of other stuff to do. I want to follow up on Jimmy's new pal, on the changes in his friendship with Superman, on the Kryptonite Man and the Ünternet, and I'm dying to bring back the Clan MacHinery. But, well, schedules closed in again, and Jimmy's off adventuring in COUNTDOWN still. Maybe after all that calms down a little...

The other story in this book is another instance of Jimmy sneaking in wherever there's room. A tale by Mark Evanier and Steve Rude, based on an unused plot idea by Jack Kirby, from back in the days when Kirby was charting Jimmy's adventures and establishing much of the material that is currently making life hectic for Jimmy in COUNTDOWN (okay, COUNTDOWN sneaks in everywhere too!), "The American Evolution" gives you a chance to look at an early take on Jimmy, and his adventures in a world of New Gods, Intergang, "The Project" and more.

So strap yourself in and turn the page — Jimmy Olsen's life may be weird, but it's never dull...

— **Kurt Busiek**
January 2008

UPERMAN 665 Cover art by Jesus Merino Coloring by Jeromy Cox

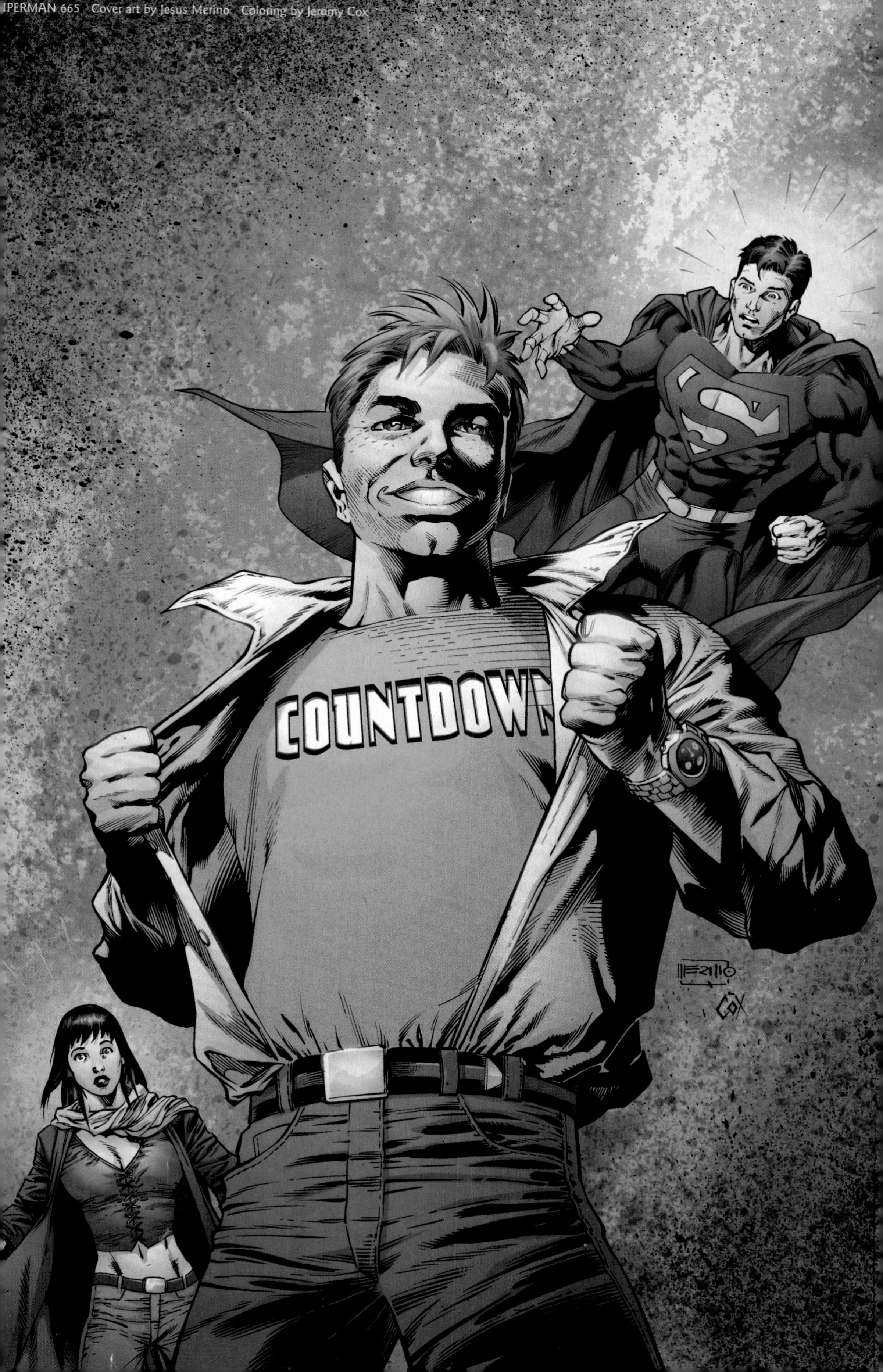
COUNTDOWN
COX

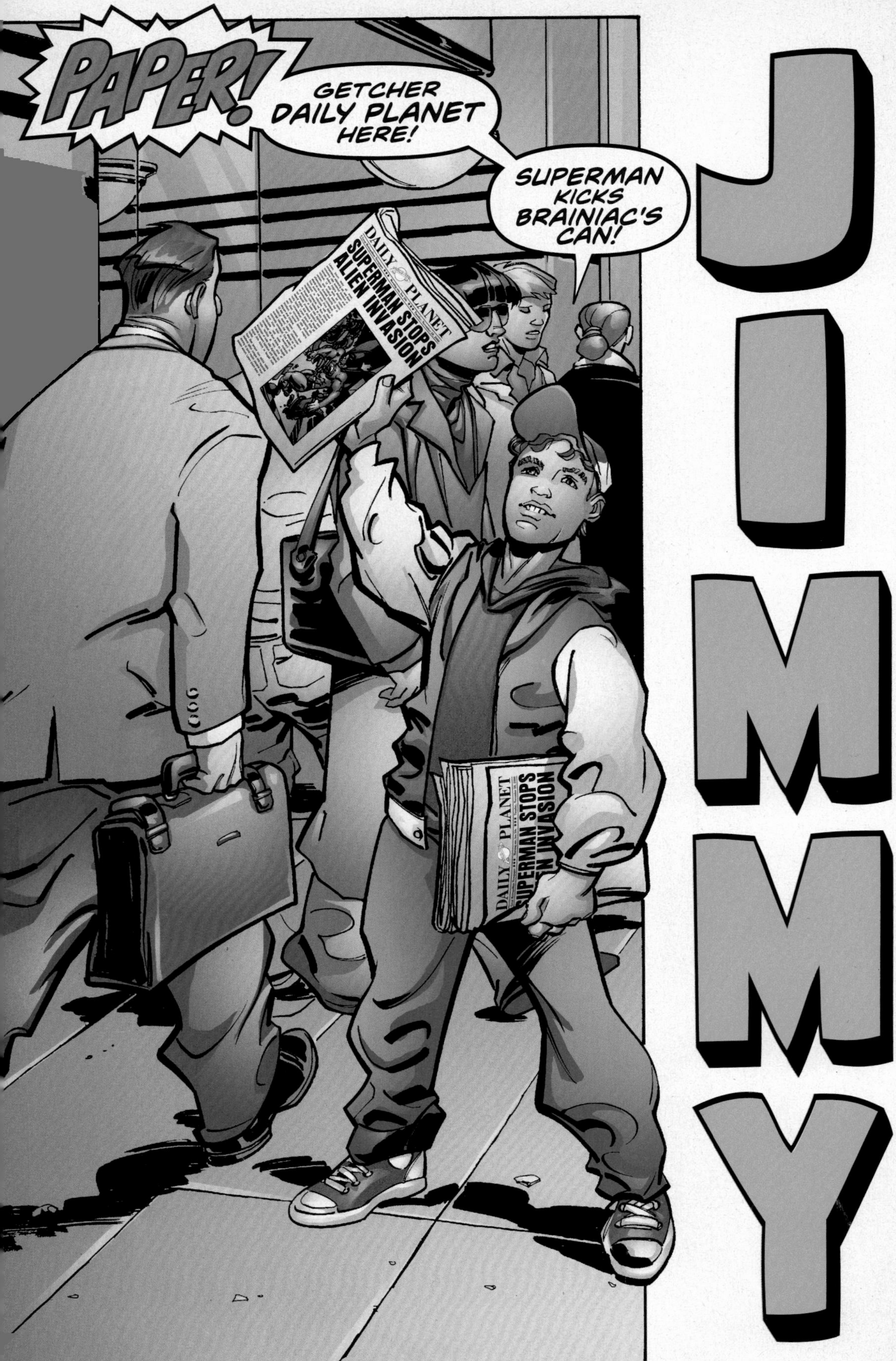
PAPER!
GETCHER DAILY PLANET HERE!
SUPERMAN KICKS BRAINIAC'S CAN!
DAILY PLANET
SUPERMAN STOPS ALIEN INVASION
DAILY PLANET
SUPERMAN STOPS
JIMMY

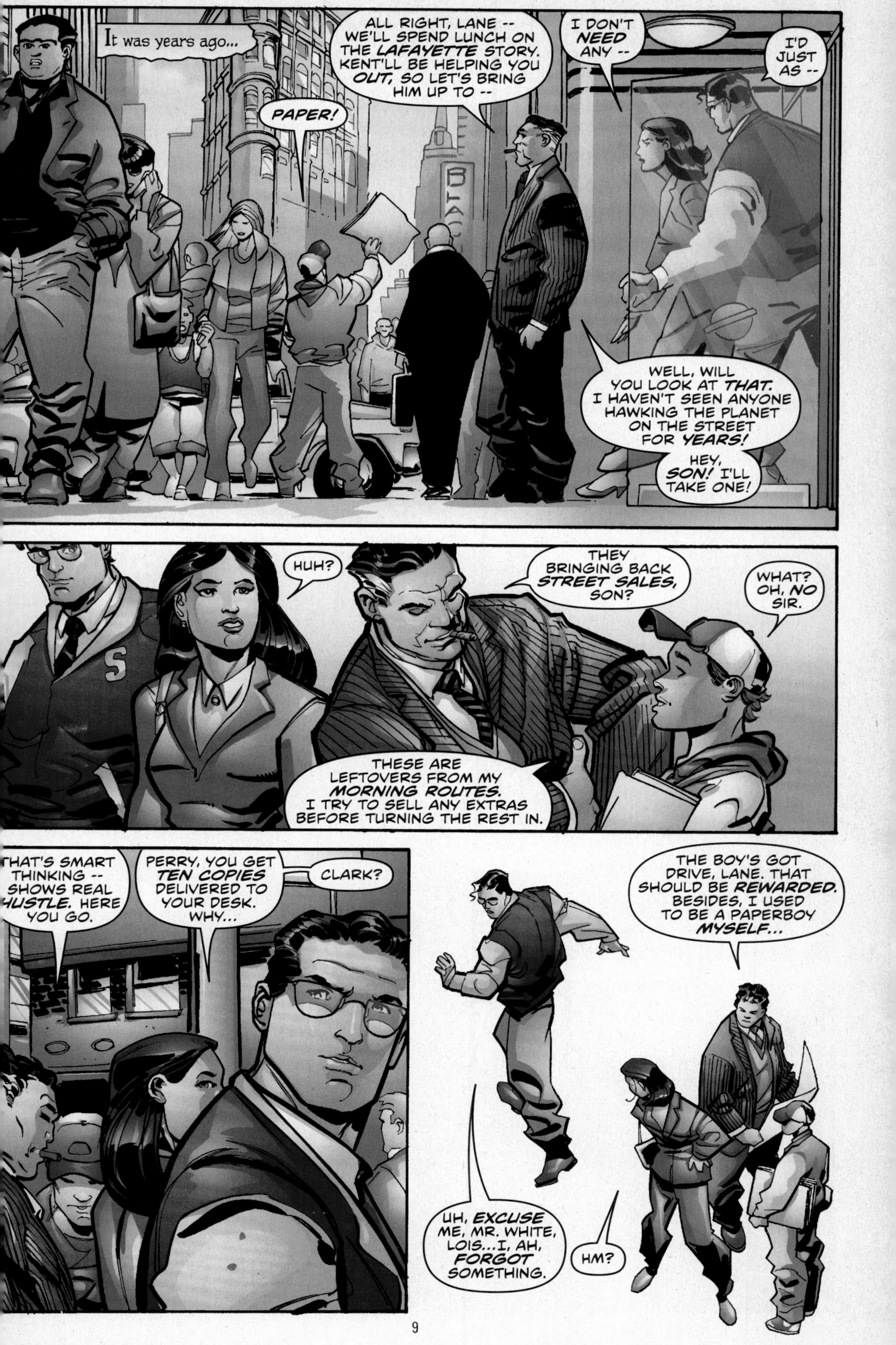
It was years ago...
ALL RIGHT, LANE -- WE'LL SPEND LUNCH ON THE LAFAYETTE STORY. KENT'LL BE HELPING YOU OUT, SO LET'S BRING HIM UP TO --
I DON'T NEED ANY --
I'D JUST AS --
PAPER!
WELL, WILL YOU LOOK AT THAT. I HAVEN'T SEEN ANYONE HAWKING THE PLANET ON THE STREET FOR YEARS!
HEY, SON! I'LL TAKE ONE!
HUH?
THEY BRINGING BACK STREET SALES, SON?
WHAT? OH, NO SIR.
THESE ARE LEFTOVERS FROM MY MORNING ROUTES. I TRY TO SELL ANY EXTRAS BEFORE TURNING THE REST IN.
THAT'S SMART THINKING -- SHOWS REAL HUSTLE. HERE YOU GO.
PERRY, YOU GET TEN COPIES DELIVERED TO YOUR DESK. WHY...
CLARK?
THE BOY'S GOT DRIVE, LANE. THAT SHOULD BE REWARDED. BESIDES, I USED TO BE A PAPERBOY MYSELF...
UH, EXCUSE ME, MR. WHITE, LOIS...I, AH, FORGOT SOMETHING.
HM?

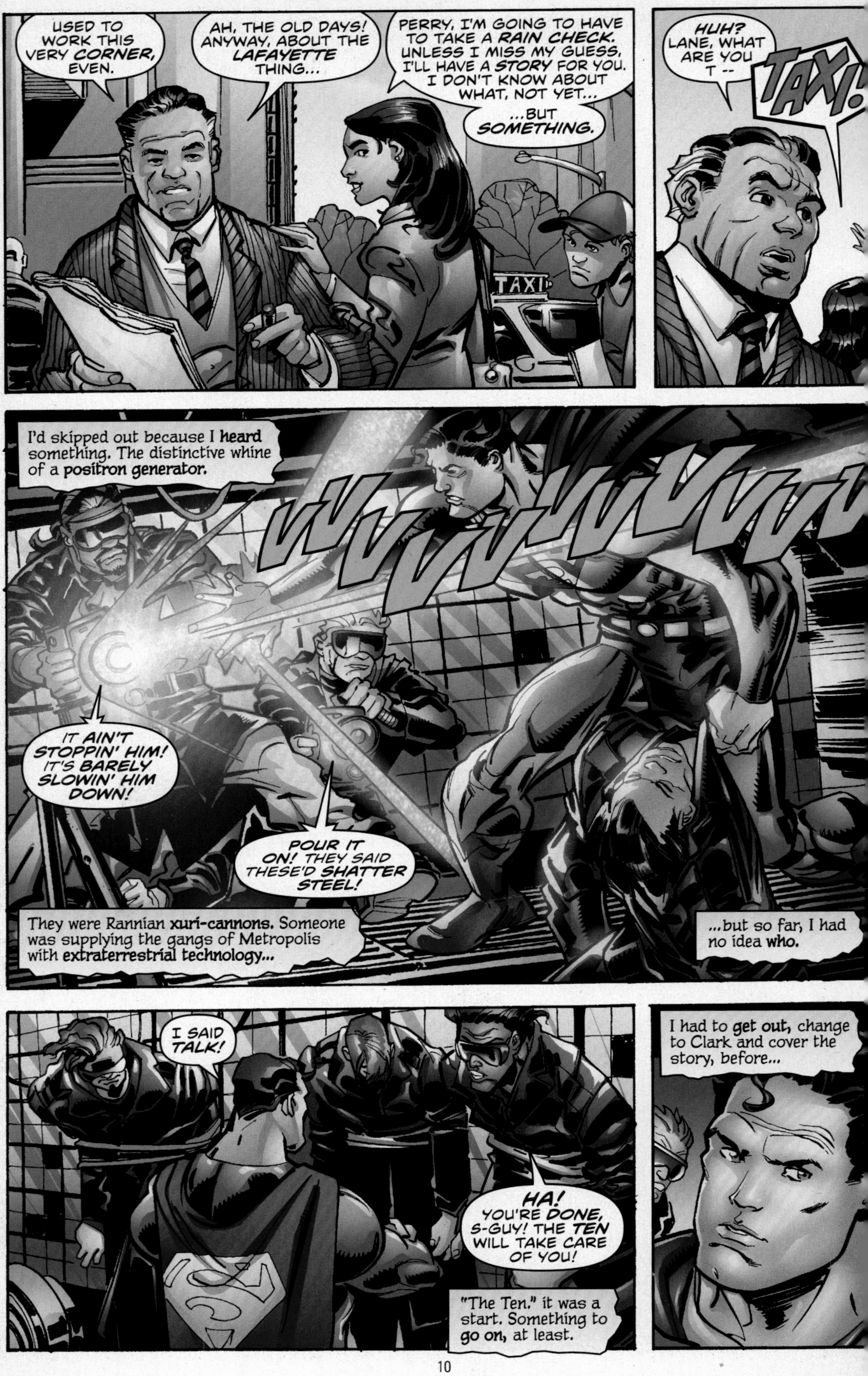

USED TO WORK THIS VERY CORNER, EVEN.
AH, THE OLD DAYS! ANYWAY, ABOUT THE LAFAYETTE THING...
PERRY, I'M GOING TO HAVE TO TAKE A RAIN CHECK. UNLESS I MISS MY GUESS, I'LL HAVE A STORY FOR YOU. I DON'T KNOW ABOUT WHAT, NOT YET...
...BUT SOMETHING.
TAXI
HUH? LANE, WHAT ARE YOU T --
TAXI!
I'd skipped out because I heard something. The distinctive whine of a positron generator.
VVVVVVVVVVVVVVVVVV
IT AIN'T STOPPIN' HIM! IT'S BARELY SLOWIN' HIM DOWN!
POUR IT ON! THEY SAID THESE'D SHATTER STEEL!
They were Rannian xuri-cannons. Someone was supplying the gangs of Metropolis with extraterrestrial technology...
...but so far, I had no idea who.
I SAID TALK!
HA! YOU'RE DONE, S-GUY! THE TEN WILL TAKE CARE OF YOU!
"The Ten." it was a start. Something to go on, at least.
I had to get out, change to Clark and cover the story, before...

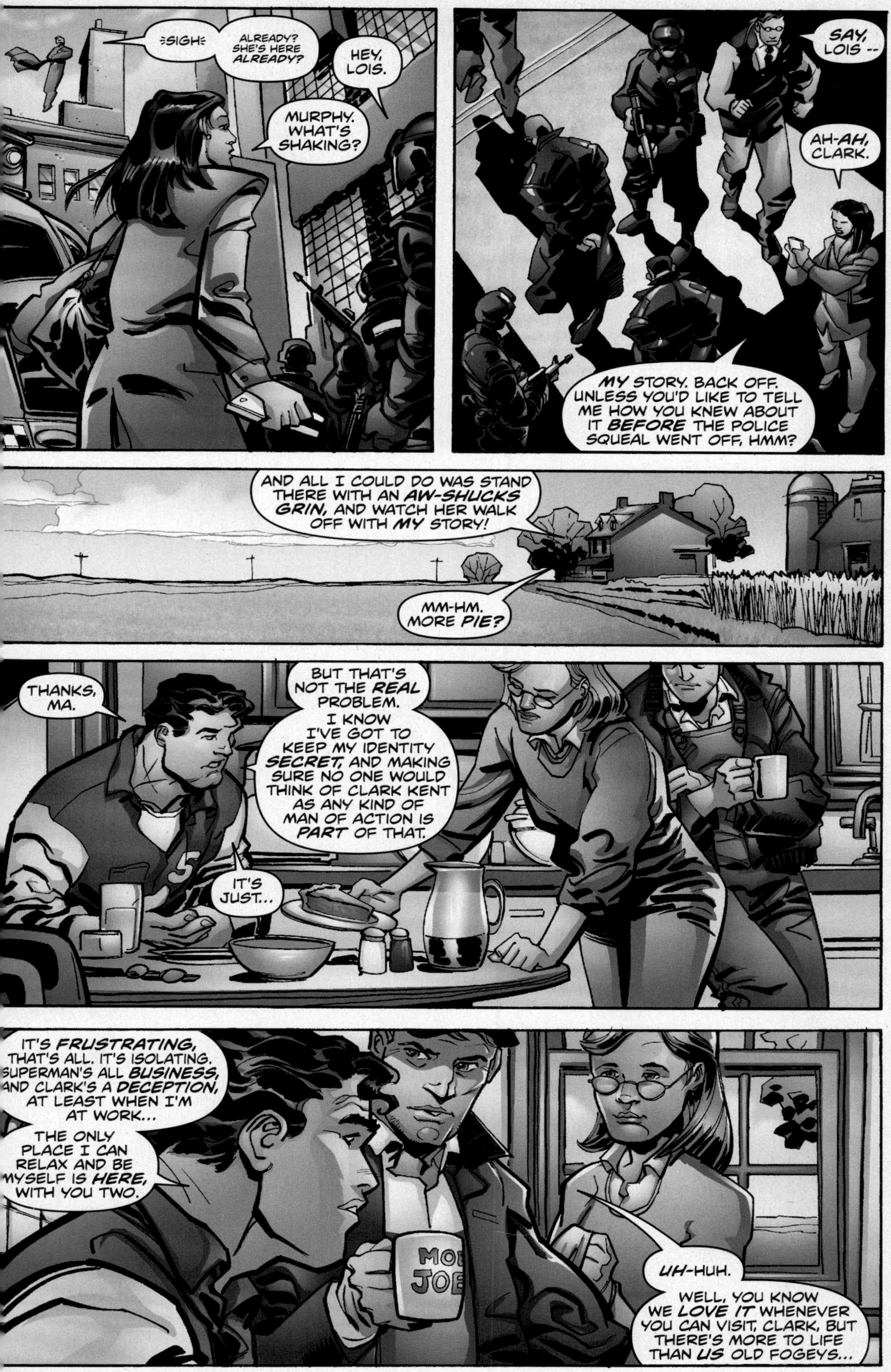

SIGH
ALREADY? SHE'S HERE ALREADY?
HEY, LOIS.
MURPHY. WHAT'S SHAKING?
SAY, LOIS --
AH-AH, CLARK.
MY STORY. BACK OFF. UNLESS YOU'D LIKE TO TELL ME HOW YOU KNEW ABOUT IT BEFORE THE POLICE SQUEAL WENT OFF, HMM?
AND ALL I COULD DO WAS STAND THERE WITH AN AW-SHUCKS GRIN, AND WATCH HER WALK OFF WITH MY STORY!
MM-HM. MORE PIE?
THANKS, MA.
BUT THAT'S NOT THE REAL PROBLEM.
I KNOW I'VE GOT TO KEEP MY IDENTITY SECRET, AND MAKING SURE NO ONE WOULD THINK OF CLARK KENT AS ANY KIND OF MAN OF ACTION IS PART OF THAT.
IT'S JUST...
IT'S FRUSTRATING, THAT'S ALL. IT'S ISOLATING. SUPERMAN'S ALL BUSINESS, AND CLARK'S A DECEPTION, AT LEAST WHEN I'M AT WORK...
THE ONLY PLACE I CAN RELAX AND BE MYSELF IS HERE, WITH YOU TWO.
UH-HUH.
WELL, YOU KNOW WE LOVE IT WHENEVER YOU CAN VISIT, CLARK, BUT THERE'S MORE TO LIFE THAN US OLD FOGEYS...

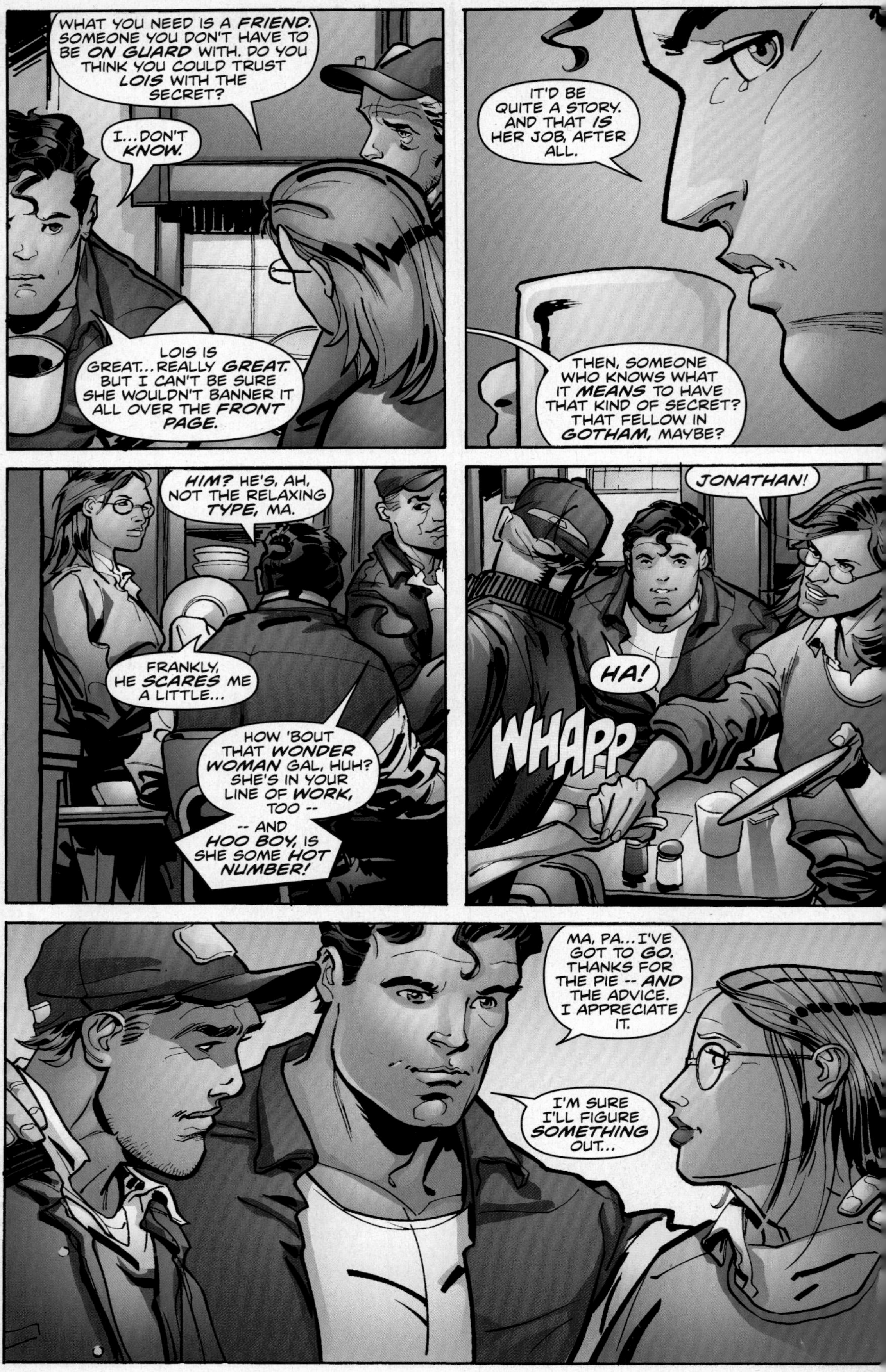
WHAT YOU NEED IS A FRIEND. SOMEONE YOU DON'T HAVE TO BE ON GUARD WITH. DO YOU THINK YOU COULD TRUST LOIS WITH THE SECRET?
I...DON'T KNOW.
LOIS IS GREAT...REALLY GREAT. BUT I CAN'T BE SURE SHE WOULDN'T BANNER IT ALL OVER THE FRONT PAGE.
IT'D BE QUITE A STORY. AND THAT IS HER JOB, AFTER ALL.
THEN, SOMEONE WHO KNOWS WHAT IT MEANS TO HAVE THAT KIND OF SECRET? THAT FELLOW IN GOTHAM, MAYBE?
HIM? HE'S, AH, NOT THE RELAXING TYPE, MA.
FRANKLY, HE SCARES ME A LITTLE...
HOW 'BOUT THAT WONDER WOMAN GAL, HUH? SHE'S IN YOUR LINE OF WORK, TOO --
-- AND HOO BOY, IS SHE SOME HOT NUMBER!
JONATHAN!
HA!
WHAPP
MA, PA...I'VE GOT TO GO. THANKS FOR THE PIE -- AND THE ADVICE. I APPRECIATE IT.
I'M SURE I'LL FIGURE SOMETHING OUT...

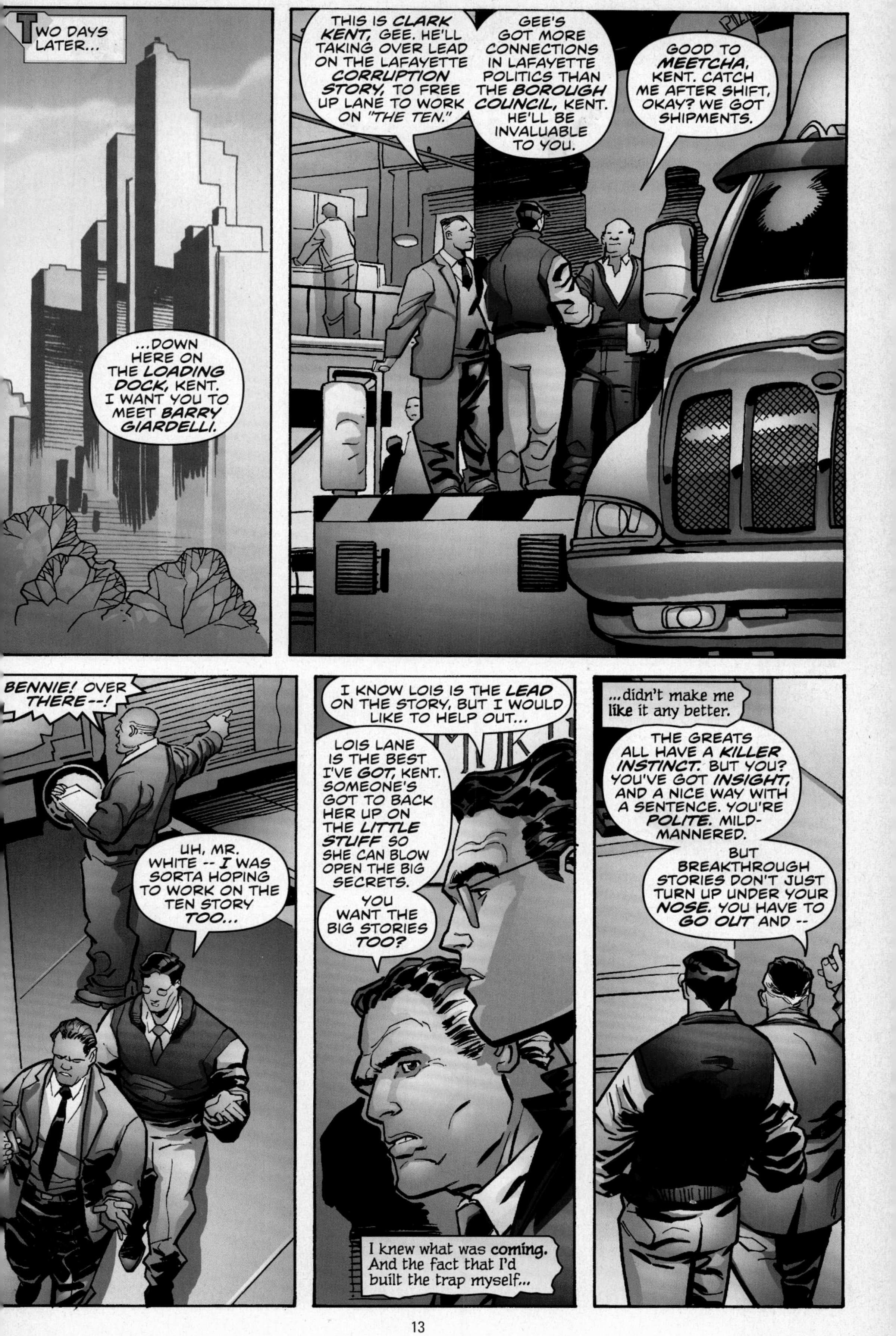
TWO DAYS LATER...
...DOWN HERE ON THE LOADING DOCK, KENT. I WANT YOU TO MEET BARRY GIARDELLI.
THIS IS CLARK KENT, GEE. HE'LL TAKING OVER LEAD ON THE LAFAYETTE CORRUPTION STORY, TO FREE UP LANE TO WORK ON "THE TEN."
GEE'S GOT MORE CONNECTIONS IN LAFAYETTE POLITICS THAN THE BOROUGH COUNCIL, KENT. HE'LL BE INVALUABLE TO YOU.
GOOD TO MEETCHA, KENT. CATCH ME AFTER SHIFT, OKAY? WE GOT SHIPMENTS.
BENNIE! OVER THERE--!
UH, MR. WHITE -- I WAS SORTA HOPING TO WORK ON THE TEN STORY TOO...
I KNOW LOIS IS THE LEAD ON THE STORY, BUT I WOULD LIKE TO HELP OUT...
LOIS LANE IS THE BEST I'VE GOT, KENT. SOMEONE'S GOT TO BACK HER UP ON THE LITTLE STUFF SO SHE CAN BLOW OPEN THE BIG SECRETS.
YOU WANT THE BIG STORIES TOO?
I knew what was coming. And the fact that I'd built the trap myself...
...didn't make me like it any better.
THE GREATS ALL HAVE A KILLER INSTINCT. BUT YOU? YOU'VE GOT INSIGHT, AND A NICE WAY WITH A SENTENCE. YOU'RE POLITE. MILD-MANNERED.
BUT BREAKTHROUGH STORIES DON'T JUST TURN UP UNDER YOUR NOSE. YOU HAVE TO GO OUT AND --

UH?

HEY. IT'S THAT *GO-GETTER* AGAIN. WHAT'S YOUR NAME, SON?

IT'S, AH, JIMMY. JIMMY OLSEN.

AND WHAT'S GOT YOU IN THE *BOWELS* OF THE *DAILY PLANET BUILDING* ON A SUNNY SUMMER DAY, OLSEN? I WAS YOU, I'D BE AT A *BALLGAME*, OR --

I, AH --

I HELP GEE OUT A LITTLE, HERE AND *THERE*, YOU KNOW? THAT WAY, I GET A JUMP ON THE *OTHER* PAPERBOYS, WHEN THE *AFTERNOON EDITION* COMES IN.

I DO THREE ROUTES, SO I LIKE TO BE THE FIRST ONE *OUT.*

THAT'S... THREE *ROUTES*, HUH?

LOOK, I THINK GEE MIGHT GET IN TROUBLE IF PEOPLE *KNEW*, SO DON'T RAT HIM OUT, OKAY?

SURE, SON.

I HEAR THE *TRUCKS* COMING IN. SEE YOU *AROUND*, MAYBE.

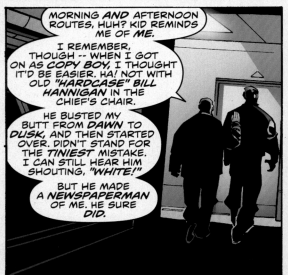

MORNING *AND* AFTERNOON ROUTES, HUH? KID REMINDS ME OF *ME.*

I REMEMBER, THOUGH -- WHEN I GOT ON AS *COPY BOY*, I THOUGHT IT'D BE EASIER. HA! NOT WITH OLD "HARDCASE" BILL HANNIGAN IN THE CHIEF'S CHAIR.

HE BUSTED MY BUTT FROM *DAWN* TO *DUSK*, AND THEN STARTED OVER. DIDN'T STAND FOR THE *TINIEST* MISTAKE. I CAN STILL HEAR HIM SHOUTING, *"WHITE!"*

BUT HE MADE A *NEWSPAPERMAN* OF ME. HE SURE *DID.*

LOOK, KENT. CHECK *INTO* THAT OLSEN KID, WILL YOU? SOMEONE WITH THAT MUCH HUSTLE, HERE AT THE PLANET...

...I WANT TO KNOW MORE *ABOUT* HIM.

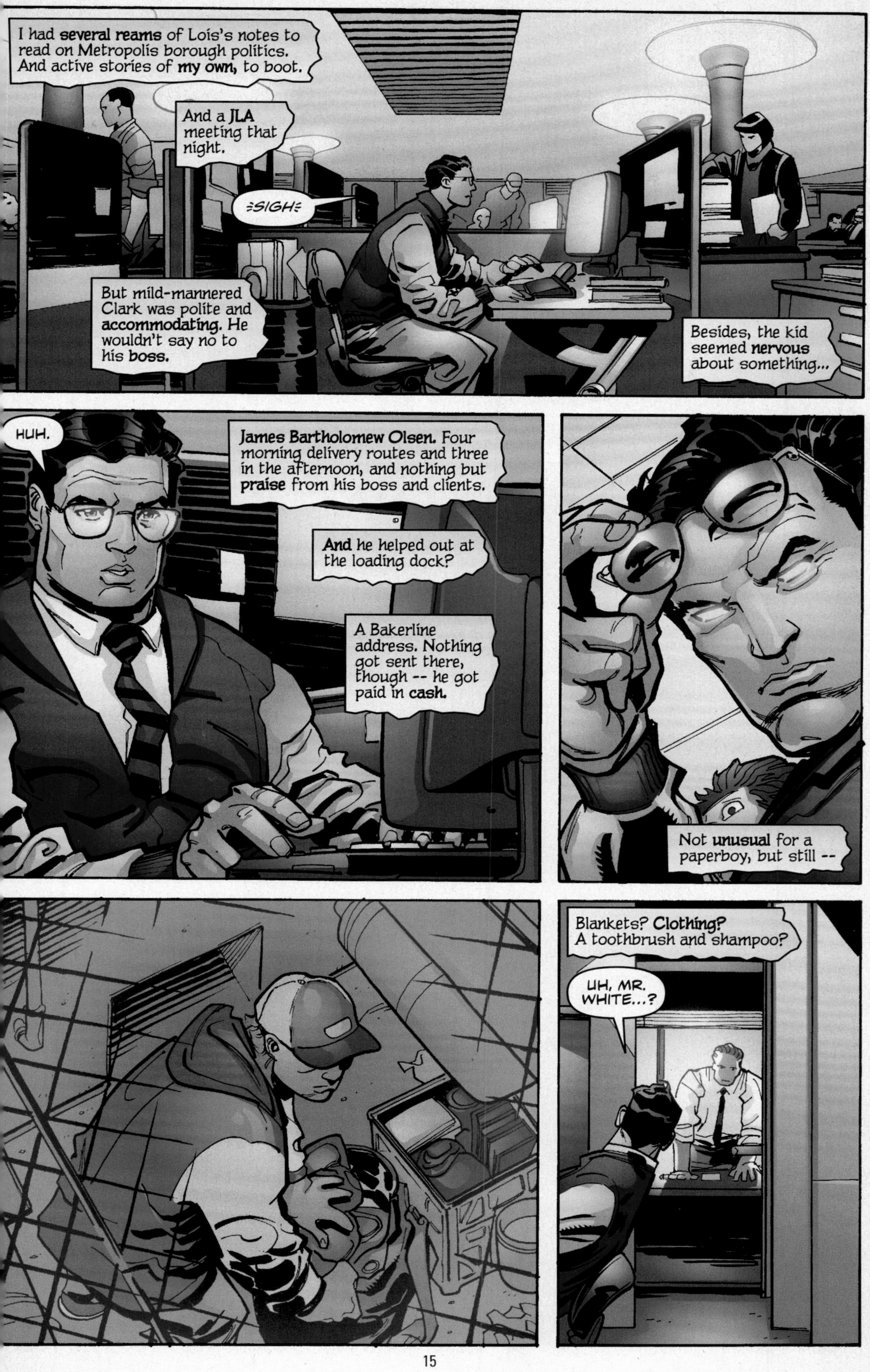

I had several reams of Lois's notes to read on Metropolis borough politics. And active stories of my own, to boot.
And a JLA meeting that night.
SIGH
But mild-mannered Clark was polite and accommodating. He wouldn't say no to his boss.
Besides, the kid seemed nervous about something...
HUH.
James Bartholomew Olsen. Four morning delivery routes and three in the afternoon, and nothing but praise from his boss and clients.
And he helped out at the loading dock?
A Bakerline address. Nothing got sent there, though -- he got paid in cash.
Not unusual for a paperboy, but still --
Blankets? Clothing? A toothbrush and shampoo?
UH, MR. WHITE...?

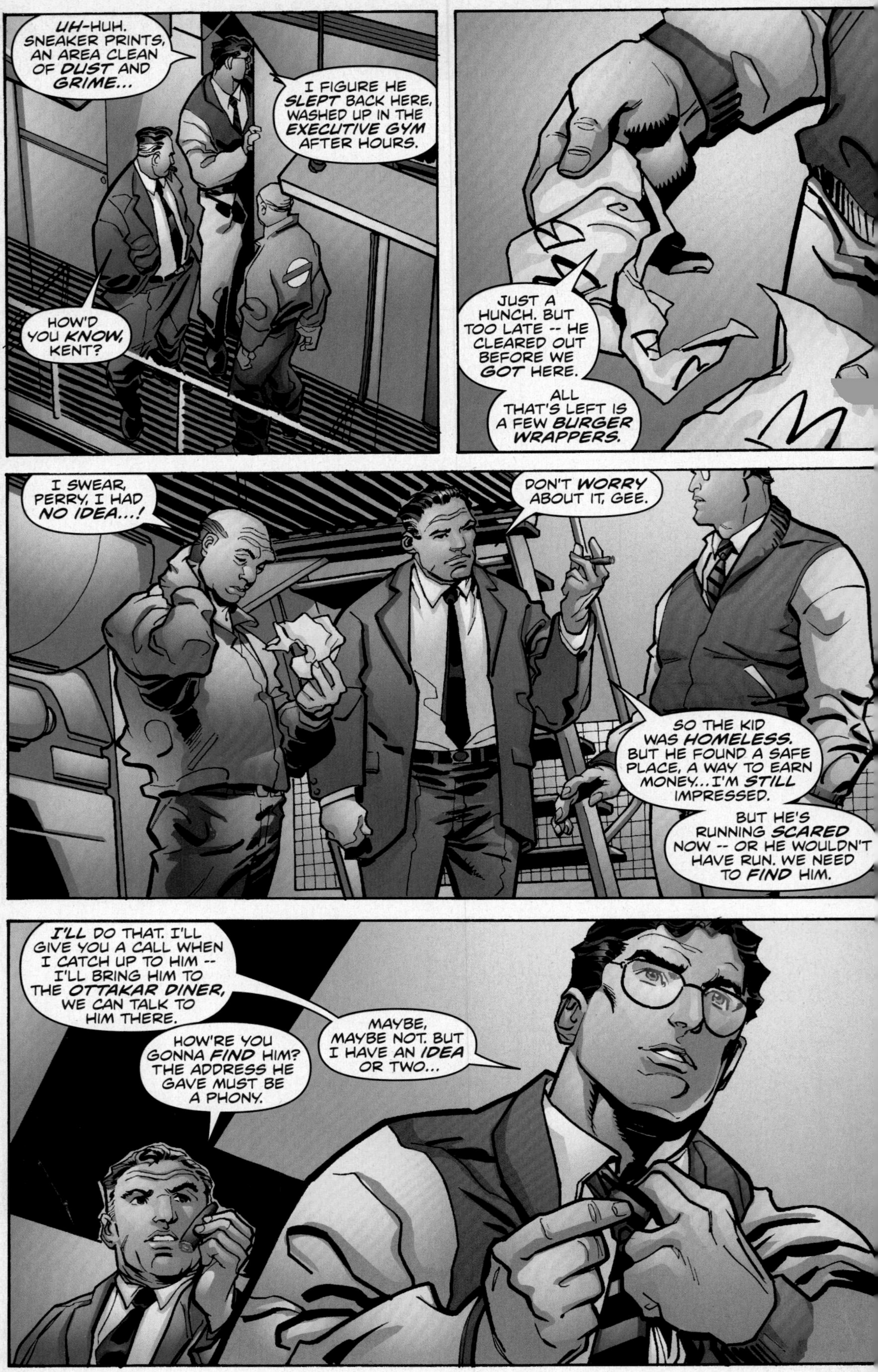
UH-HUH. SNEAKER PRINTS, AN AREA CLEAN OF DUST AND GRIME...
I FIGURE HE SLEPT BACK HERE, WASHED UP IN THE EXECUTIVE GYM AFTER HOURS.
HOW'D YOU KNOW, KENT?
JUST A HUNCH. BUT TOO LATE -- HE CLEARED OUT BEFORE WE GOT HERE.
ALL THAT'S LEFT IS A FEW BURGER WRAPPERS.
I SWEAR, PERRY, I HAD NO IDEA...!
DON'T WORRY ABOUT IT, GEE.
SO THE KID WAS HOMELESS. BUT HE FOUND A SAFE PLACE, A WAY TO EARN MONEY... I'M STILL IMPRESSED.
BUT HE'S RUNNING SCARED NOW -- OR HE WOULDN'T HAVE RUN. WE NEED TO FIND HIM.
I'LL DO THAT. I'LL GIVE YOU A CALL WHEN I CATCH UP TO HIM -- I'LL BRING HIM TO THE OTTAKAR DINER, WE CAN TALK TO HIM THERE.
HOW'RE YOU GONNA FIND HIM? THE ADDRESS HE GAVE MUST BE A PHONY.
MAYBE, MAYBE NOT. BUT I HAVE AN IDEA OR TWO...

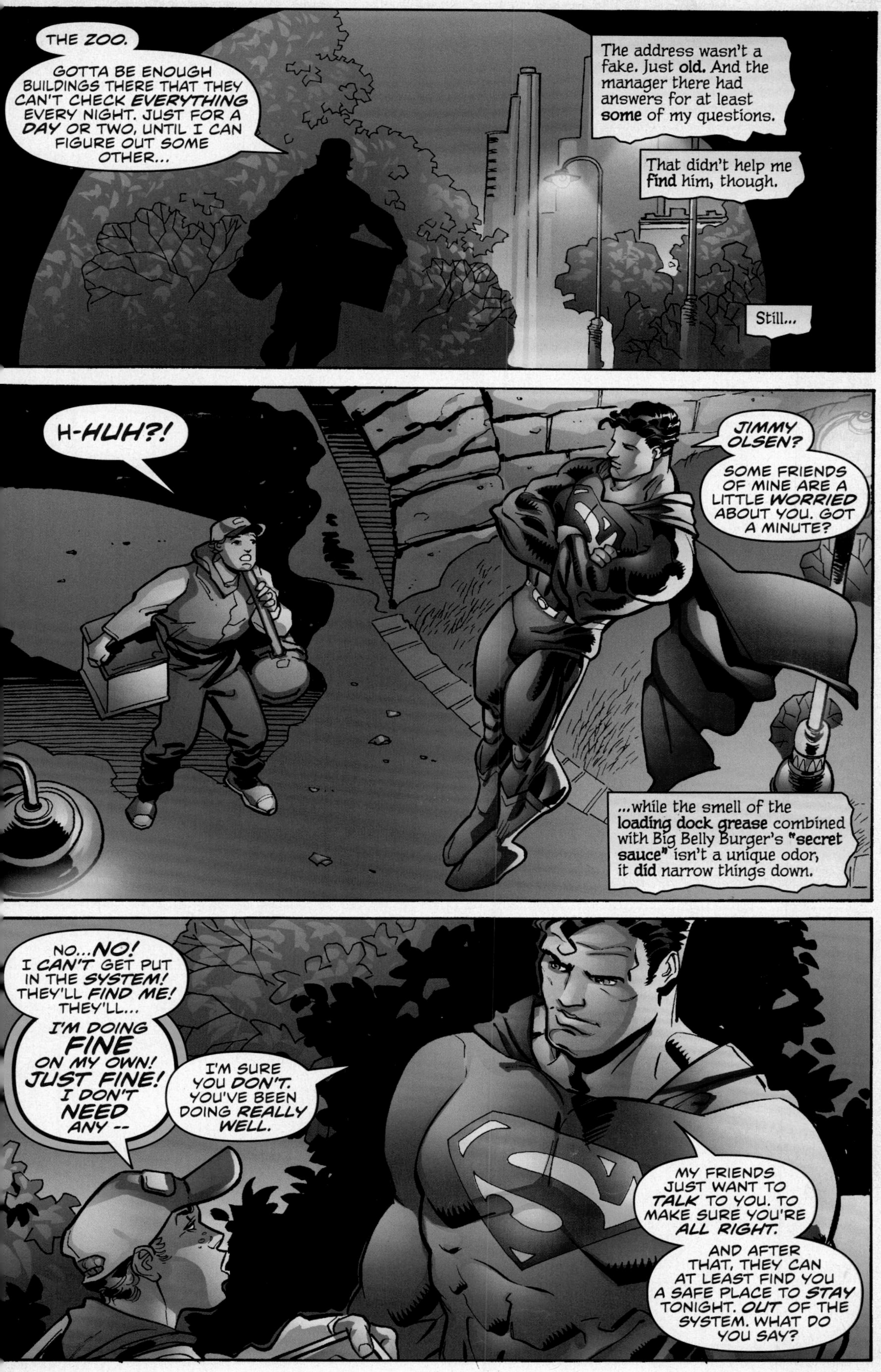

THE ZOO.
GOTTA BE ENOUGH BUILDINGS THERE THAT THEY CAN'T CHECK EVERYTHING EVERY NIGHT. JUST FOR A DAY OR TWO, UNTIL I CAN FIGURE OUT SOME OTHER...
The address wasn't a fake. Just old. And the manager there had answers for at least some of my questions.
That didn't help me find him, though.
Still...
H-HUH?!
JIMMY OLSEN?
SOME FRIENDS OF MINE ARE A LITTLE WORRIED ABOUT YOU. GOT A MINUTE?
...while the smell of the loading dock grease combined with Big Belly Burger's "secret sauce" isn't a unique odor, it did narrow things down.
NO...NO! I CAN'T GET PUT IN THE SYSTEM! THEY'LL FIND ME! THEY'LL...
I'M DOING FINE ON MY OWN! JUST FINE! I DON'T NEED ANY --
I'M SURE YOU DON'T. YOU'VE BEEN DOING REALLY WELL.
MY FRIENDS JUST WANT TO TALK TO YOU. TO MAKE SURE YOU'RE ALL RIGHT.
AND AFTER THAT, THEY CAN AT LEAST FIND YOU A SAFE PLACE TO STAY TONIGHT. OUT OF THE SYSTEM. WHAT DO YOU SAY?

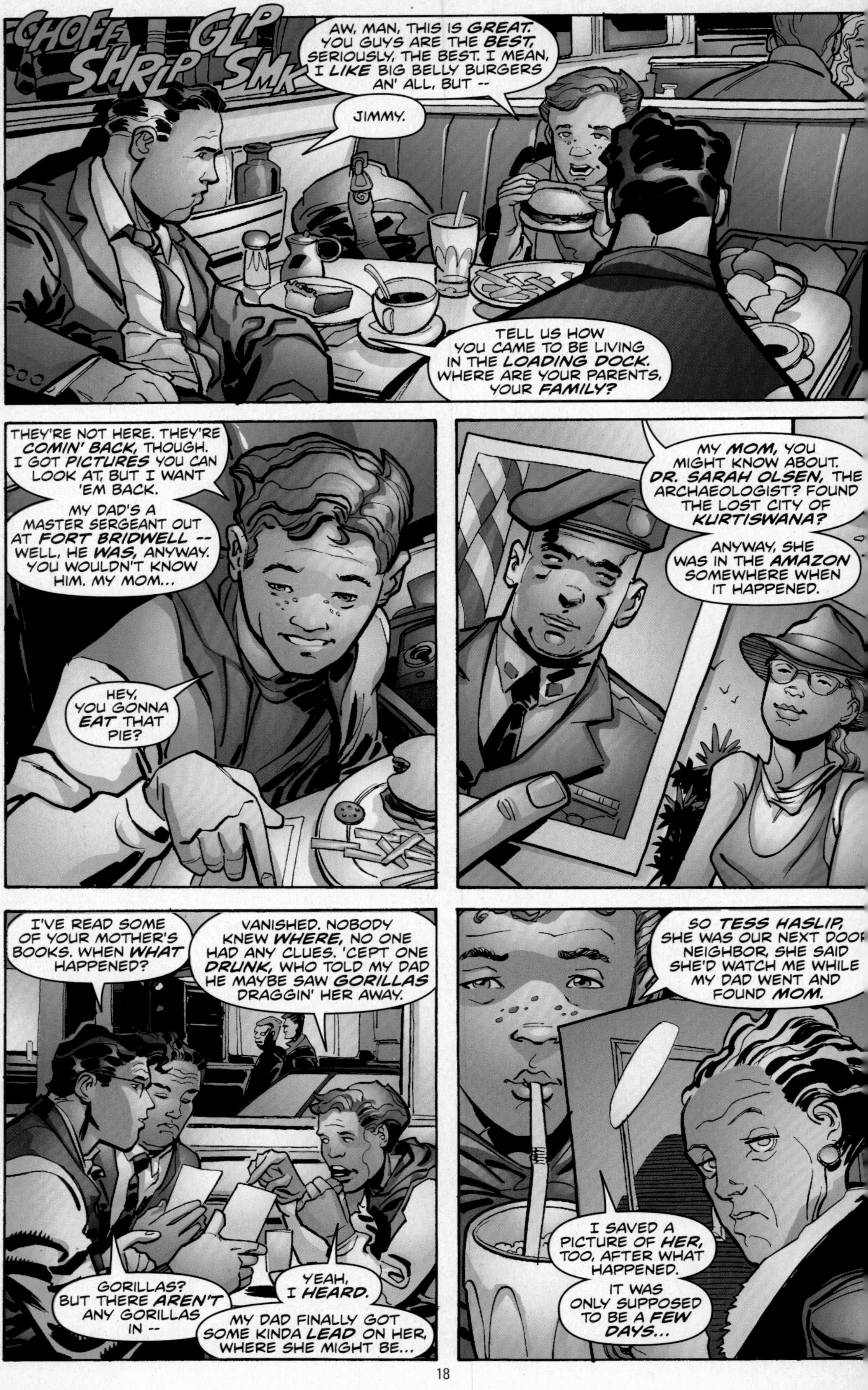
CHOFF SHRLP GLP SMK
AW, MAN, THIS IS GREAT. YOU GUYS ARE THE BEST, SERIOUSLY, THE BEST. I MEAN, I LIKE BIG BELLY BURGERS AN' ALL, BUT --
JIMMY.
TELL US HOW YOU CAME TO BE LIVING IN THE LOADING DOCK. WHERE ARE YOUR PARENTS, YOUR FAMILY?
THEY'RE NOT HERE. THEY'RE COMIN' BACK, THOUGH. I GOT PICTURES YOU CAN LOOK AT, BUT I WANT 'EM BACK.
MY DAD'S A MASTER SERGEANT OUT AT FORT BRIDWELL -- WELL, HE WAS, ANYWAY. YOU WOULDN'T KNOW HIM. MY MOM...
HEY, YOU GONNA EAT THAT PIE?
MY MOM, YOU MIGHT KNOW ABOUT. DR. SARAH OLSEN, THE ARCHAEOLOGIST? FOUND THE LOST CITY OF KURTISWANA?
ANYWAY, SHE WAS IN THE AMAZON SOMEWHERE WHEN IT HAPPENED.
I'VE READ SOME OF YOUR MOTHER'S BOOKS. WHEN WHAT HAPPENED?
VANISHED. NOBODY KNEW WHERE, NO ONE HAD ANY CLUES. 'CEPT ONE DRUNK, WHO TOLD MY DAD HE MAYBE SAW GORILLAS DRAGGIN' HER AWAY.
GORILLAS? BUT THERE AREN'T ANY GORILLAS IN --
YEAH, I HEARD.
MY DAD FINALLY GOT SOME KINDA LEAD ON HER, WHERE SHE MIGHT BE...
SO TESS HASLIP, SHE WAS OUR NEXT DOOR NEIGHBOR, SHE SAID SHE'D WATCH ME WHILE MY DAD WENT AND FOUND MOM.
I SAVED A PICTURE OF HER, TOO, AFTER WHAT HAPPENED.
IT WAS ONLY SUPPOSED TO BE A FEW DAYS...

MOM? *DAD?* ARE *YOU...*

"AN' SHE PROBABLY *WOULD'VE.*"

NO, MR. MCGRAW. IT'S *YOU* WHO DOESN'T *UNDERSTAND!*

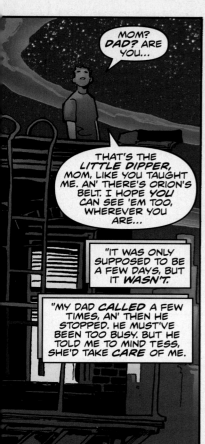

THAT'S THE *LITTLE DIPPER,* MOM, LIKE YOU TAUGHT ME. AN' THERE'S ORION'S BELT. I HOPE *YOU* CAN SEE 'EM TOO, WHEREVER YOU ARE...

"IT WAS ONLY SUPPOSED TO BE A FEW DAYS, BUT IT *WASN'T.*"

"MY DAD *CALLED* A FEW TIMES, AN' THEN HE STOPPED. HE MUST'VE BEEN TOO BUSY. BUT HE TOLD ME TO MIND TESS, SHE'D TAKE *CARE* OF ME."

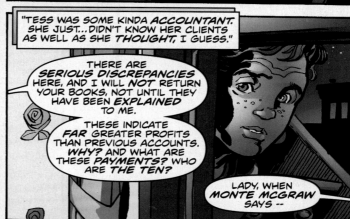

"TESS WAS SOME KINDA *ACCOUNTANT.* SHE JUST...DIDN'T KNOW HER CLIENTS AS WELL AS SHE *THOUGHT,* I GUESS."

THERE ARE *SERIOUS DISCREPANCIES* HERE, AND I WILL *NOT* RETURN YOUR BOOKS, NOT UNTIL THEY HAVE BEEN *EXPLAINED* TO ME.

THESE INDICATE *FAR* GREATER PROFITS THAN PREVIOUS ACCOUNTS. *WHY?* AND WHAT ARE THESE *PAYMENTS?* WHO ARE *THE TEN?*

LADY, WHEN *MONTE MCGRAW* SAYS --

I DON'T GIVE A *FIG* FOR WHAT MONTE MCGRAW SAYS! I HAVE A *RESPONSIBILITY* TO REPORT --

--NNH!

BLAM!

RONSON! WHAT THE *HELL* ARE -- ?

BAD ENOUGH SHE GOT THE WRONG BOOKS -- YOU COULDN'T HAVE WAITED UNTIL AFTER WE *HAD THEM* BACK?

NEVER *MIND.* THEY'RE PROBABLY HERE SOMEWHERE. SEARCH THE PLACE, UNTIL -- *HM?*

BLAM
BLAM
BLAM
BLAM

STOP HIM! BUT DON'T KILL HIM!

THAT'S THE KID WAS LIVIN' WITH THE OLD BAT! HE PROB'LY KNOWS WHERE THEM BOOKS ARE!

MY GOD. MONTE McGRAW.

I HEADED FOR THE *COPS*, BUT SAW THOSE THUGS WATCHIN' THE POLICE STATION.

I DIDN'T DARE GO TO *ANOTHER* ONE -- MAYBE IT WAS BEIN' WATCHED TOO, BY SOMEONE I COULDN'T SPOT.

BUT I DIDN'T HAVE MUCH *MONEY*.

I COPIED MY DAD'S *SIGNATURE* ON THE PERMISSION FORMS TO GET THE PAPER ROUTES. AN' I GOT A *CHEAP ROOM*.

I SNUCK BACK HOME, GOT SOME *CLOTHES* AN' THOSE PICTURES, BUT THEY NEARLY CAUGH' ME. I GUESS THEY *STILL* DON'T HAVE THOSE BOOKS.

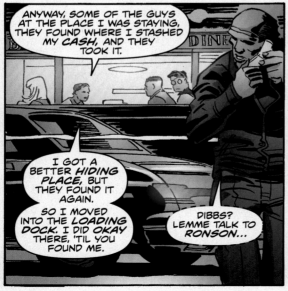

ANYWAY, SOME OF THE GUYS AT THE PLACE I WAS STAYING, THEY FOUND WHERE I STASHED MY *CASH*, AND THEY TOOK IT.

I GOT A BETTER *HIDING PLACE*, BUT THEY FOUND IT AGAIN.

SO I MOVED INTO THE *LOADING DOCK*. I DID OKAY THERE, 'TIL YOU FOUND ME.

DIBBS? LEMME TALK TO RONSON...

AND -- HOW LONG HAVE YOU BEEN ON YOUR *OWN*?

I DUNNO. A WHILE. BEFORE *BASEBALL* STARTED, AT LEAST.

YOU GONNA FINISH THOSE *FRIES*?

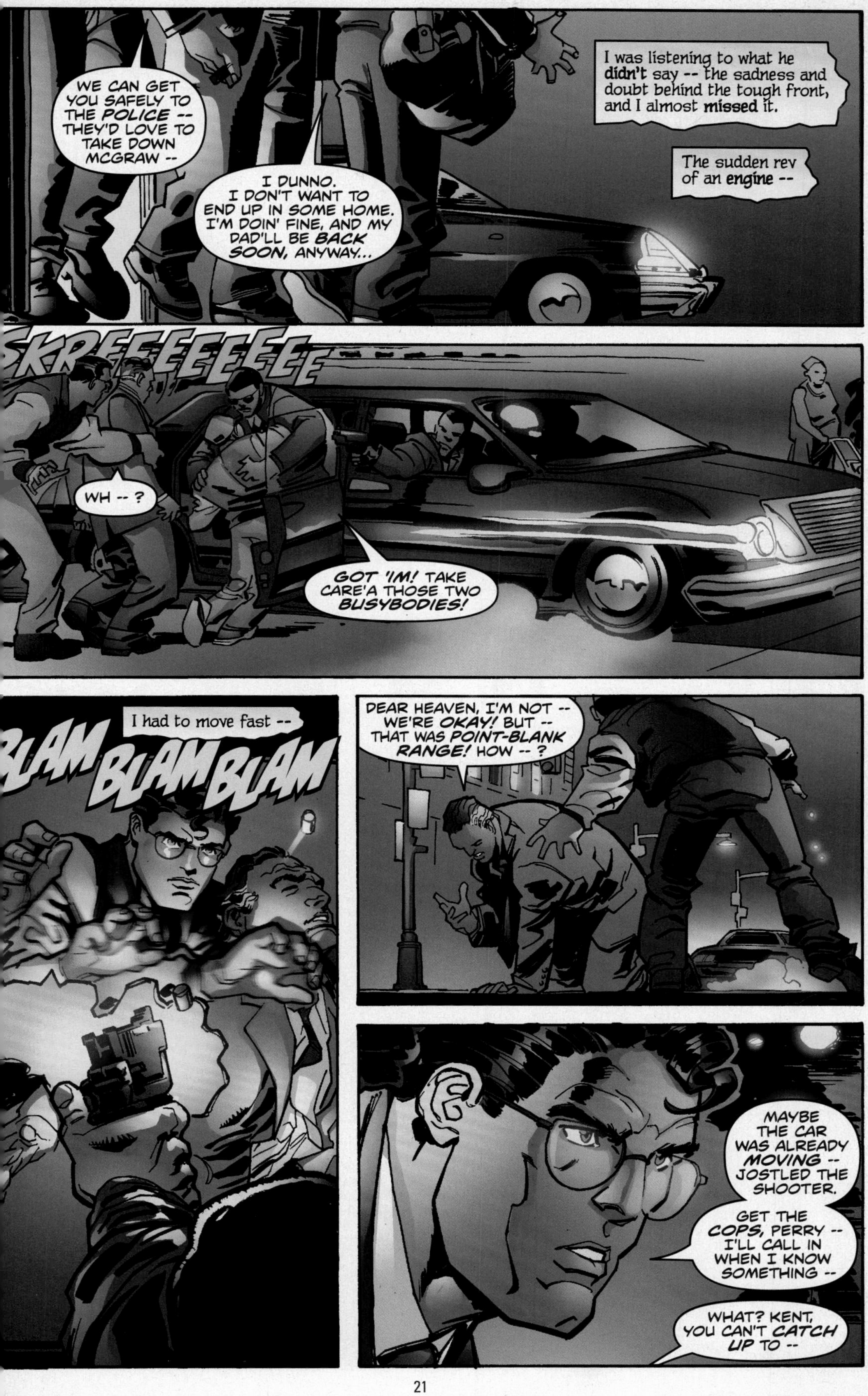
WE CAN GET YOU SAFELY TO THE POLICE -- THEY'D LOVE TO TAKE DOWN MCGRAW --
I DUNNO. I DON'T WANT TO END UP IN SOME HOME. I'M DOIN' FINE, AND MY DAD'LL BE BACK SOON, ANYWAY...
I was listening to what he didn't say -- the sadness and doubt behind the tough front, and I almost missed it.
The sudden rev of an engine --
SKREEEEEEEEE
WH -- ?
GOT 'IM! TAKE CARE'A THOSE TWO BUSYBODIES!
I had to move fast --
BLAM BLAM BLAM
DEAR HEAVEN, I'M NOT -- WE'RE OKAY! BUT -- THAT WAS POINT-BLANK RANGE! HOW -- ?
MAYBE THE CAR WAS ALREADY MOVING -- JOSTLED THE SHOOTER.
GET THE COPS, PERRY -- I'LL CALL IN WHEN I KNOW SOMETHING --
WHAT? KENT, YOU CAN'T CATCH UP TO --

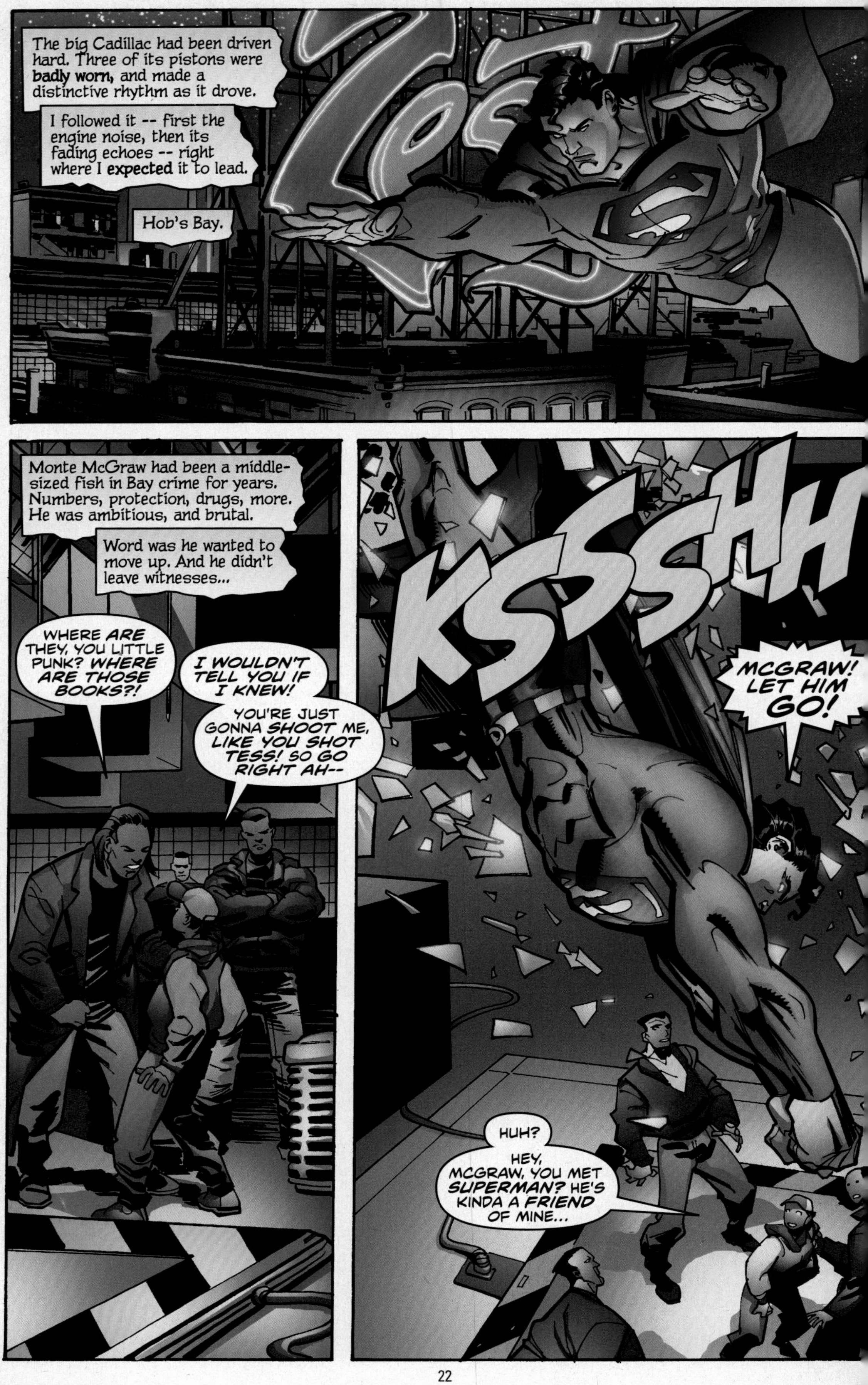

The big Cadillac had been driven hard. Three of its pistons were **badly worn**, and made a distinctive rhythm as it drove.
I followed it -- first the engine noise, then its fading echoes -- right where I **expected** it to lead.
Hob's Bay.
Monte McGraw had been a middle-sized fish in Bay crime for years. Numbers, protection, drugs, more. He was ambitious, and brutal.
Word was he wanted to move up. And he didn't leave witnesses...
WHERE ARE THEY, YOU LITTLE PUNK? WHERE ARE THOSE BOOKS?!
I WOULDN'T TELL YOU IF I KNEW!
YOU'RE JUST GONNA SHOOT ME, LIKE YOU SHOT TESS! SO GO RIGHT AH--
KSSSHH
MCGRAW! LET HIM GO!
HUH?
HEY, MCGRAW, YOU MET SUPERMAN? HE'S KINDA A FRIEND OF MINE...

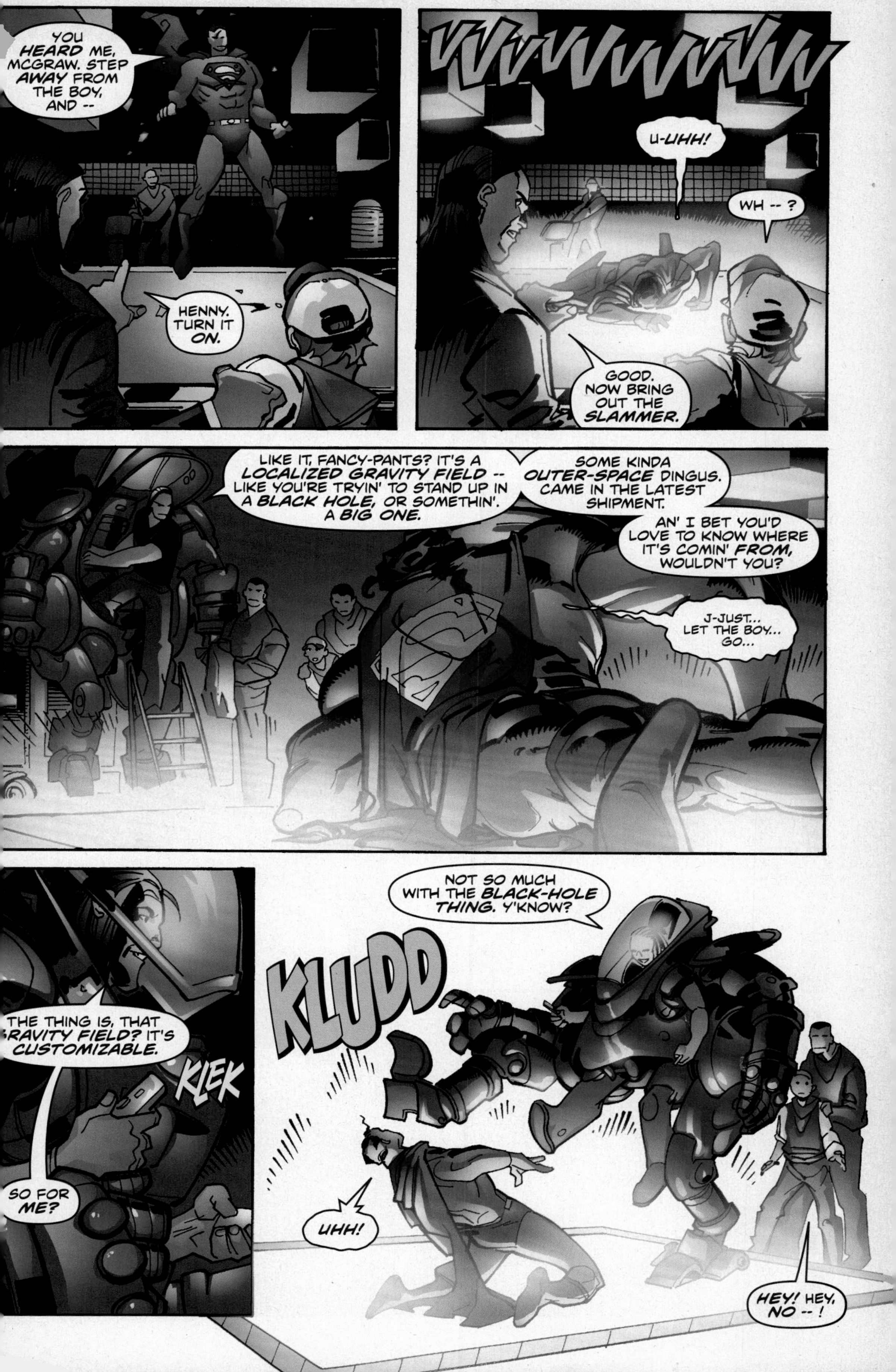
YOU HEARD ME, MCGRAW. STEP AWAY FROM THE BOY, AND --
HENNY. TURN IT ON.
VVVVVVVVVVVVVV
U-UHH!
WH -- ?
GOOD. NOW BRING OUT THE SLAMMER.
LIKE IT, FANCY-PANTS? IT'S A LOCALIZED GRAVITY FIELD -- LIKE YOU'RE TRYIN' TO STAND UP IN A BLACK HOLE, OR SOMETHIN'. A BIG ONE.
SOME KINDA OUTER-SPACE DINGUS. CAME IN THE LATEST SHIPMENT.
AN' I BET YOU'D LOVE TO KNOW WHERE IT'S COMIN' FROM, WOULDN'T YOU?
J-JUST... LET THE BOY... GO...
THE THING IS, THAT GRAVITY FIELD? IT'S CUSTOMIZABLE.
KLEK
SO FOR ME?
NOT SO MUCH WITH THE BLACK-HOLE THING. Y'KNOW?
KLUDD
UHH!
HEY! HEY, NO -- !

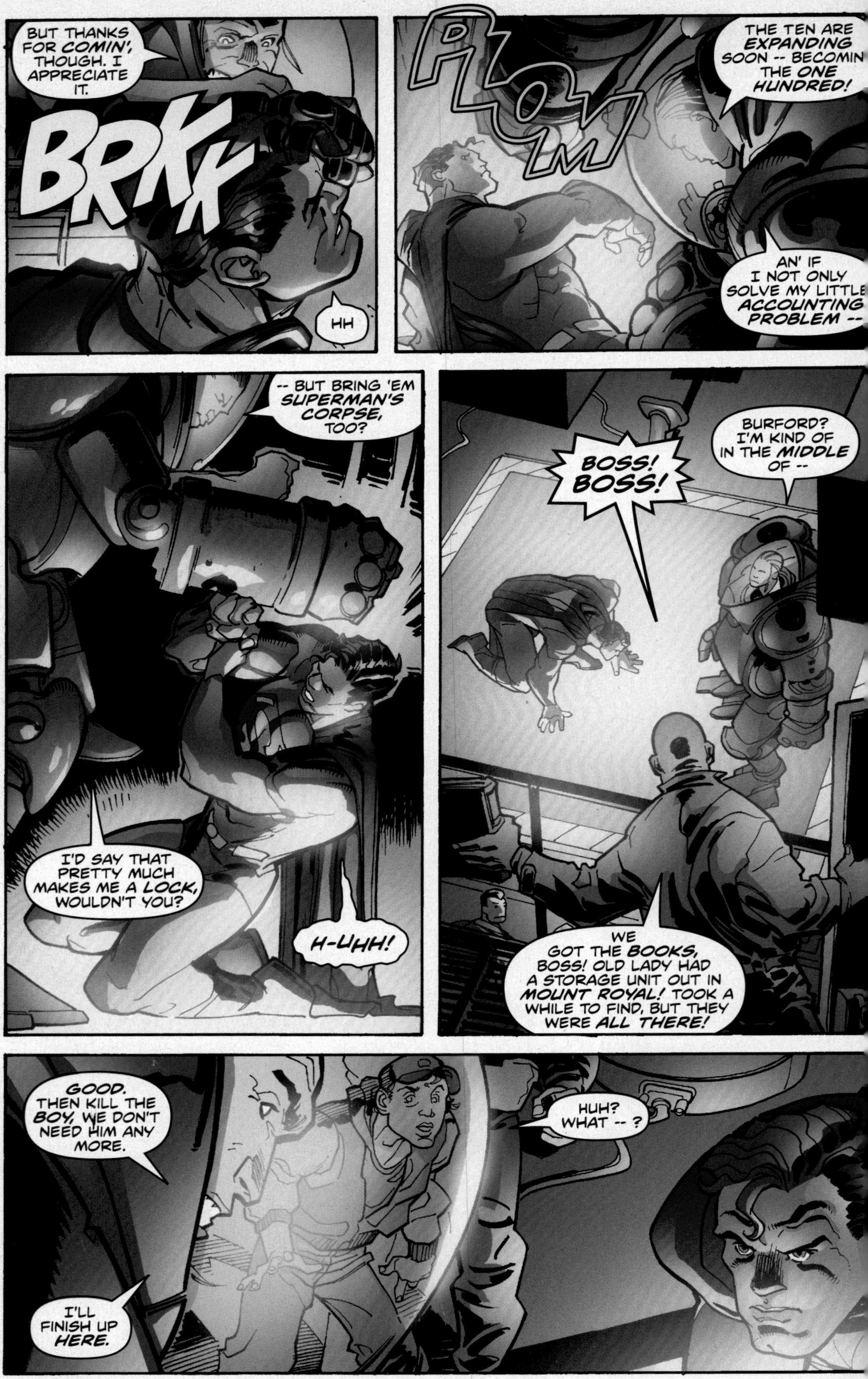
BUT THANKS FOR COMIN', THOUGH. I APPRECIATE IT.
BRKK
HH
PLOOM
THE TEN ARE EXPANDING SOON -- BECOMIN THE ONE HUNDRED!
AN' IF I NOT ONLY SOLVE MY LITTLE ACCOUNTING PROBLEM --
-- BUT BRING 'EM SUPERMAN'S CORPSE, TOO?
I'D SAY THAT PRETTY MUCH MAKES ME A LOCK, WOULDN'T YOU?
H-UHH!
BOSS! BOSS!
BURFORD? I'M KIND OF IN THE MIDDLE OF --
WE GOT THE BOOKS, BOSS! OLD LADY HAD A STORAGE UNIT OUT IN MOUNT ROYAL! TOOK A WHILE TO FIND, BUT THEY WERE ALL THERE!
GOOD. THEN KILL THE BOY, WE DON'T NEED HIM ANY MORE.
HUH? WHAT -- ?
I'LL FINISH UP HERE.

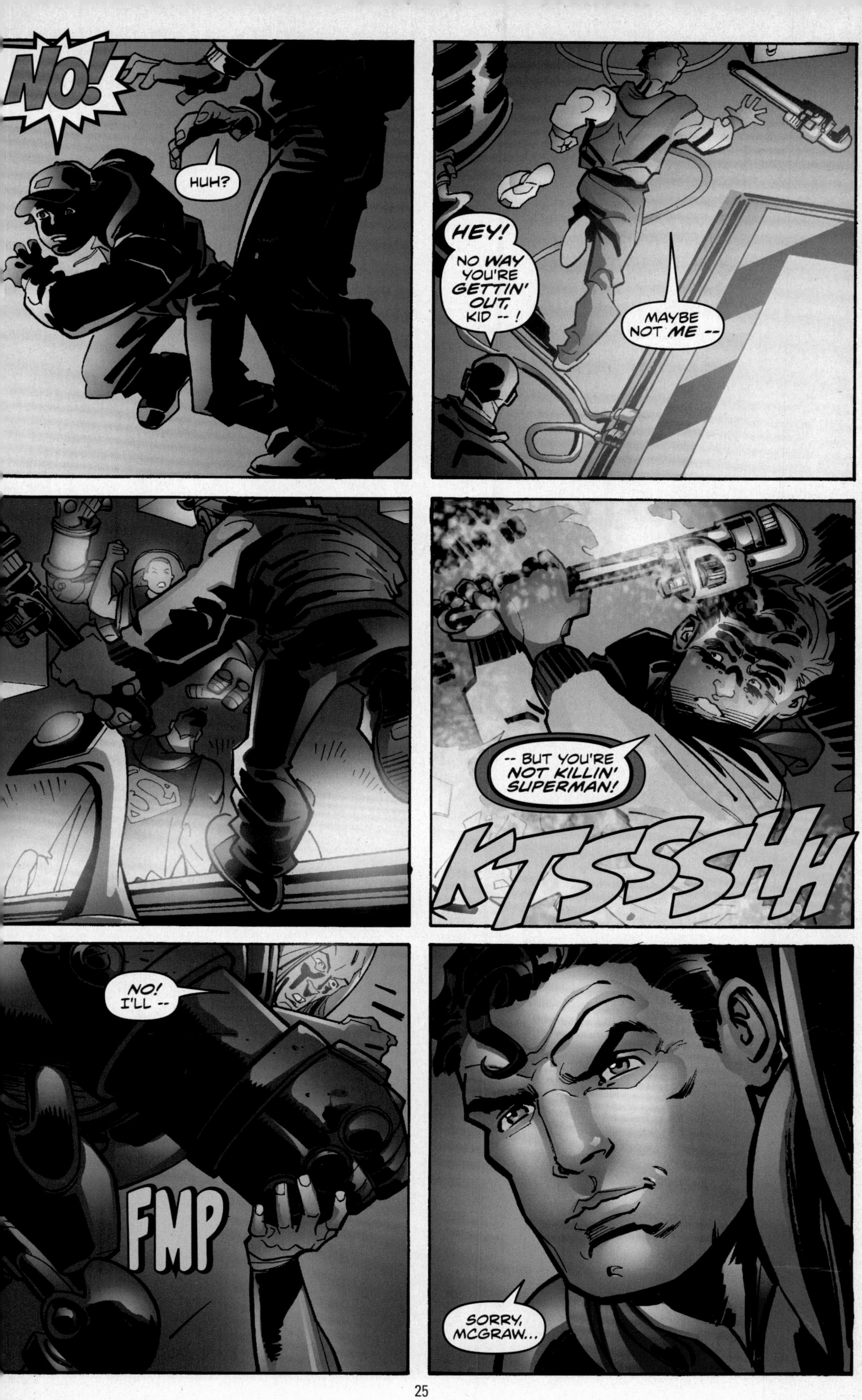
NO!
HUH?
HEY!
NO WAY YOU'RE GETTIN' OUT, KID -- !
MAYBE NOT ME --
-- BUT YOU'RE NOT KILLIN' SUPERMAN!
KTSSSHH
NO! I'LL --
FMP
SORRY, MCGRAW...

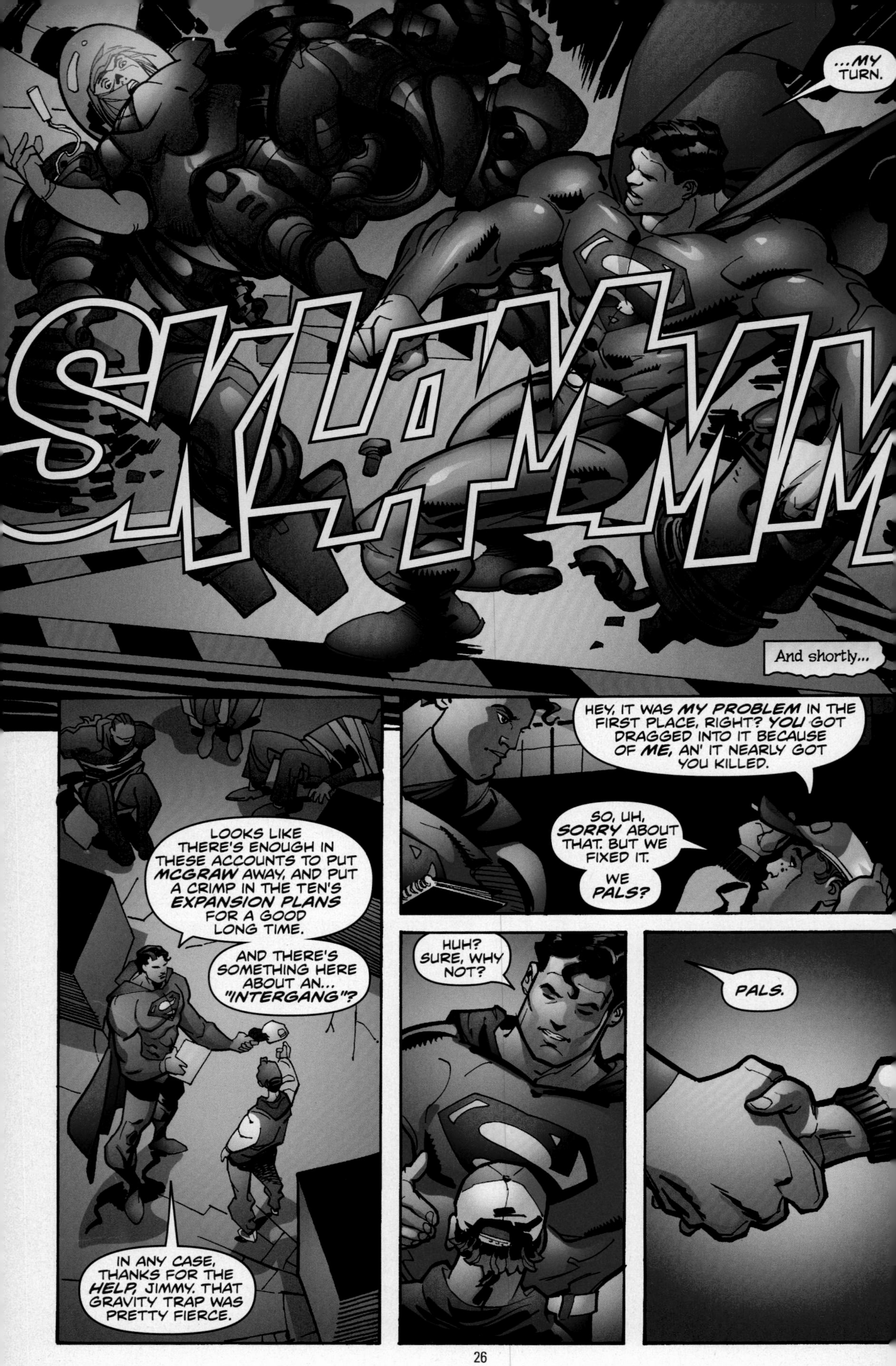
...MY TURN.
SKLAMMM
And shortly...
LOOKS LIKE THERE'S ENOUGH IN THESE ACCOUNTS TO PUT MCGRAW AWAY, AND PUT A CRIMP IN THE TEN'S EXPANSION PLANS FOR A GOOD LONG TIME.
AND THERE'S SOMETHING HERE ABOUT AN... "INTERGANG"?
IN ANY CASE, THANKS FOR THE HELP, JIMMY. THAT GRAVITY TRAP WAS PRETTY FIERCE.
HEY, IT WAS MY PROBLEM IN THE FIRST PLACE, RIGHT? YOU GOT DRAGGED INTO IT BECAUSE OF ME, AN' IT NEARLY GOT YOU KILLED.
SO, UH, SORRY ABOUT THAT. BUT WE FIXED IT.
WE PALS?
HUH? SURE, WHY NOT?
PALS.

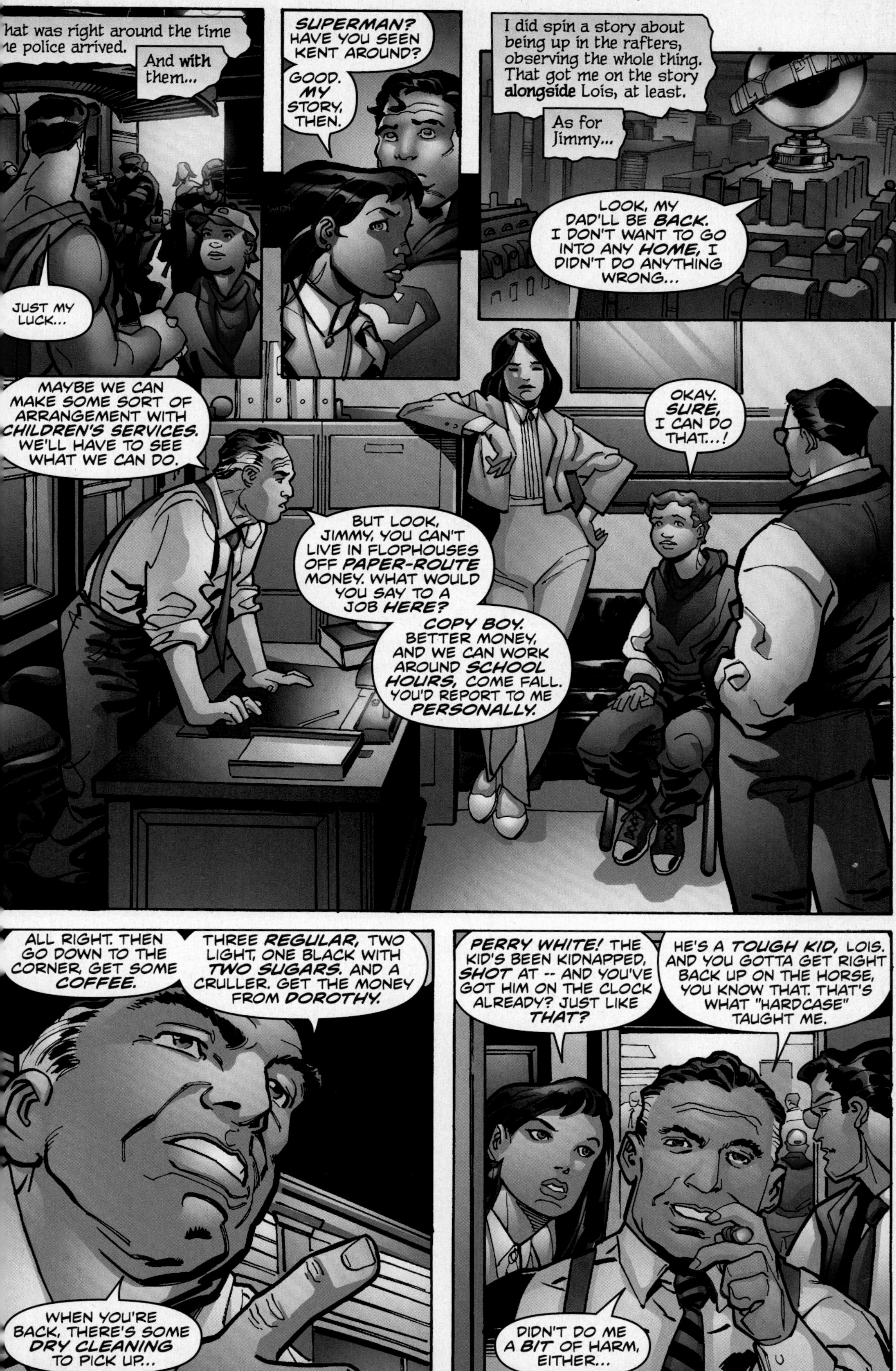
hat was right around the time
ne police arrived.
And with them...
JUST MY LUCK...
SUPERMAN? HAVE YOU SEEN KENT AROUND?
GOOD. MY STORY, THEN.
I did spin a story about being up in the rafters, observing the whole thing. That got me on the story alongside Lois, at least.
As for Jimmy...
LOOK, MY DAD'LL BE BACK. I DON'T WANT TO GO INTO ANY HOME, I DIDN'T DO ANYTHING WRONG...
MAYBE WE CAN MAKE SOME SORT OF ARRANGEMENT WITH CHILDREN'S SERVICES. WE'LL HAVE TO SEE WHAT WE CAN DO.
OKAY. SURE, I CAN DO THAT...!
BUT LOOK, JIMMY, YOU CAN'T LIVE IN FLOPHOUSES OFF PAPER-ROUTE MONEY. WHAT WOULD YOU SAY TO A JOB HERE?
COPY BOY. BETTER MONEY, AND WE CAN WORK AROUND SCHOOL HOURS, COME FALL. YOU'D REPORT TO ME PERSONALLY.
ALL RIGHT. THEN GO DOWN TO THE CORNER, GET SOME COFFEE.
THREE REGULAR, TWO LIGHT, ONE BLACK WITH TWO SUGARS. AND A CRULLER. GET THE MONEY FROM DOROTHY.
WHEN YOU'RE BACK, THERE'S SOME DRY CLEANING TO PICK UP...
PERRY WHITE! THE KID'S BEEN KIDNAPPED, SHOT AT -- AND YOU'VE GOT HIM ON THE CLOCK ALREADY? JUST LIKE THAT?
HE'S A TOUGH KID, LOIS. AND YOU GOTTA GET RIGHT BACK UP ON THE HORSE, YOU KNOW THAT. THAT'S WHAT "HARDCASE" TAUGHT ME.
DIDN'T DO ME A BIT OF HARM, EITHER...

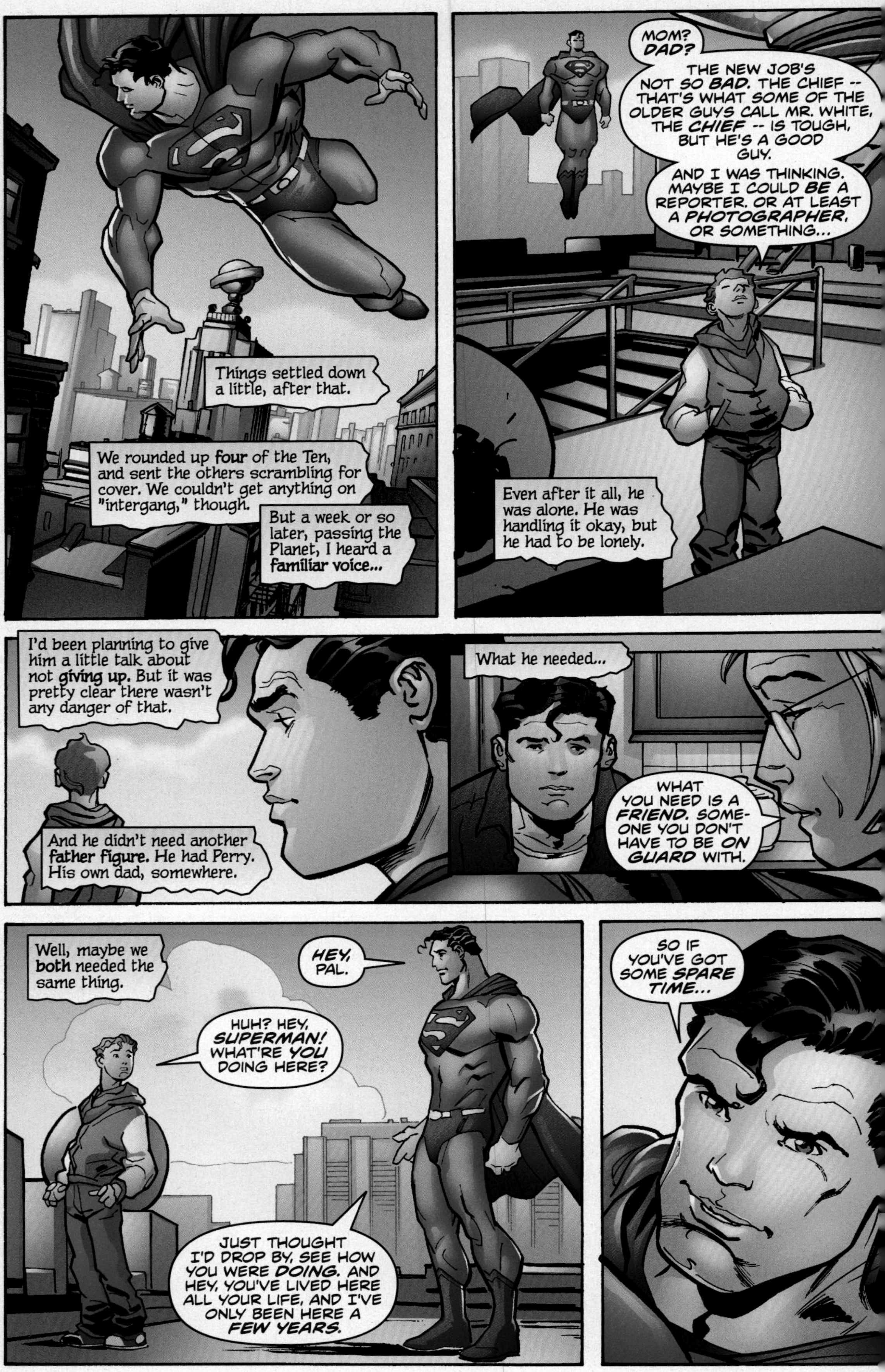
Things settled down a little, after that.
We rounded up four of the Ten, and sent the others scrambling for cover. We couldn't get anything on "intergang," though.
But a week or so later, passing the Planet, I heard a familiar voice...
MOM? DAD?
THE NEW JOB'S NOT SO BAD. THE CHIEF -- THAT'S WHAT SOME OF THE OLDER GUYS CALL MR. WHITE, THE CHIEF -- IS TOUGH, BUT HE'S A GOOD GUY.
AND I WAS THINKING. MAYBE I COULD BE A REPORTER. OR AT LEAST A PHOTOGRAPHER, OR SOMETHING...
Even after it all, he was alone. He was handling it okay, but he had to be lonely.
I'd been planning to give him a little talk about not giving up. But it was pretty clear there wasn't any danger of that.
And he didn't need another father figure. He had Perry. His own dad, somewhere.
What he needed...
WHAT YOU NEED IS A FRIEND. SOME-ONE YOU DON'T HAVE TO BE ON GUARD WITH.
Well, maybe we both needed the same thing.
HEY, PAL.
HUH? HEY, SUPERMAN! WHAT'RE YOU DOING HERE?
JUST THOUGHT I'D DROP BY, SEE HOW YOU WERE DOING. AND HEY, YOU'VE LIVED HERE ALL YOUR LIFE, AND I'VE ONLY BEEN HERE A FEW YEARS.
SO IF YOU'VE GOT SOME SPARE TIME...

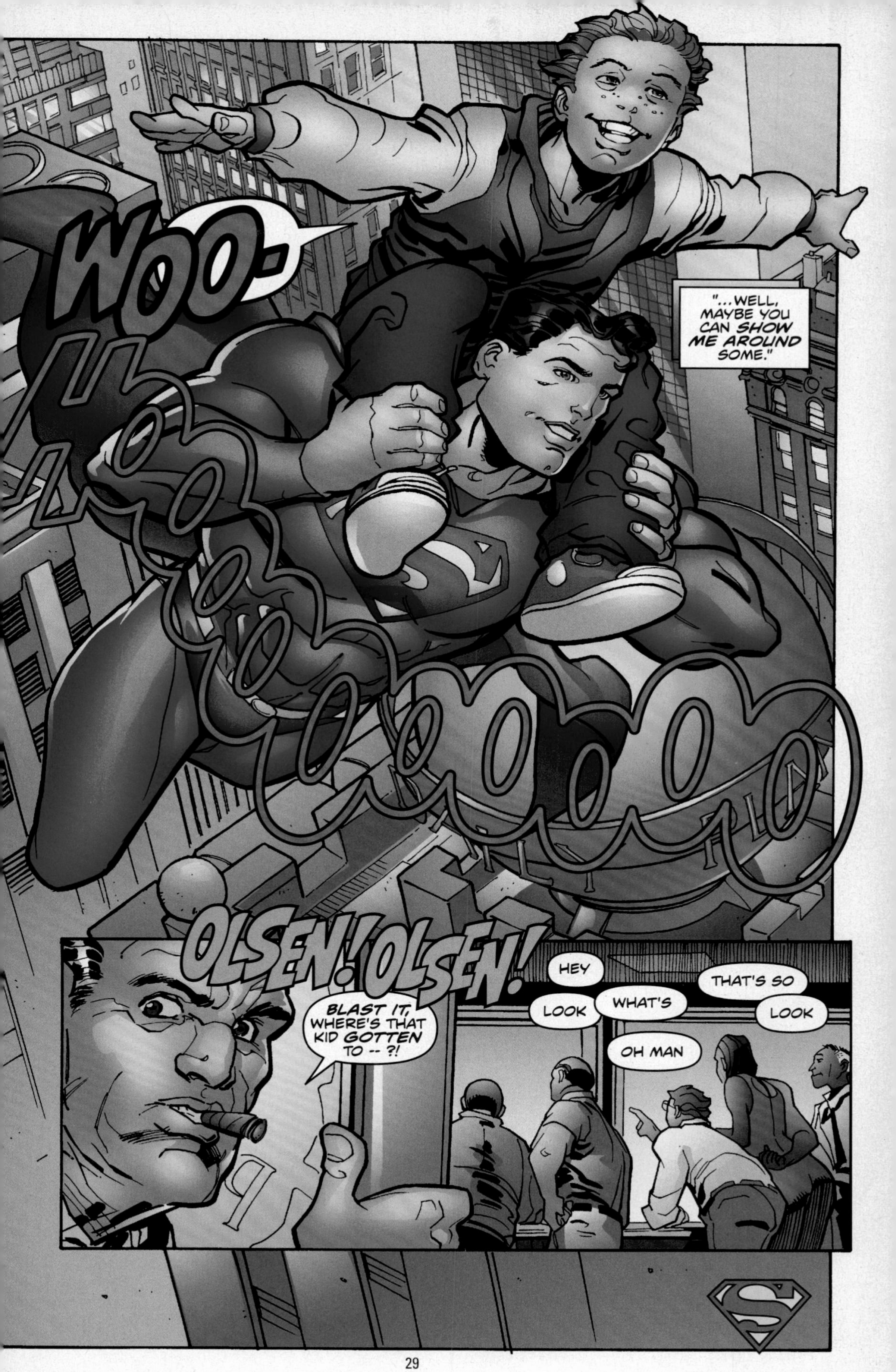
WOO-
"...WELL, MAYBE YOU CAN SHOW ME AROUND SOME."
OLSEN! OLSEN!
BLAST IT, WHERE'S THAT KID GOTTEN TO -- ?!
HEY
LOOK
WHAT'S
THAT'S SO
LOOK
OH MAN

ACTION COMICS 852 Cover art by Brad Walker and John Livesay Coloring by Pete Pantazis

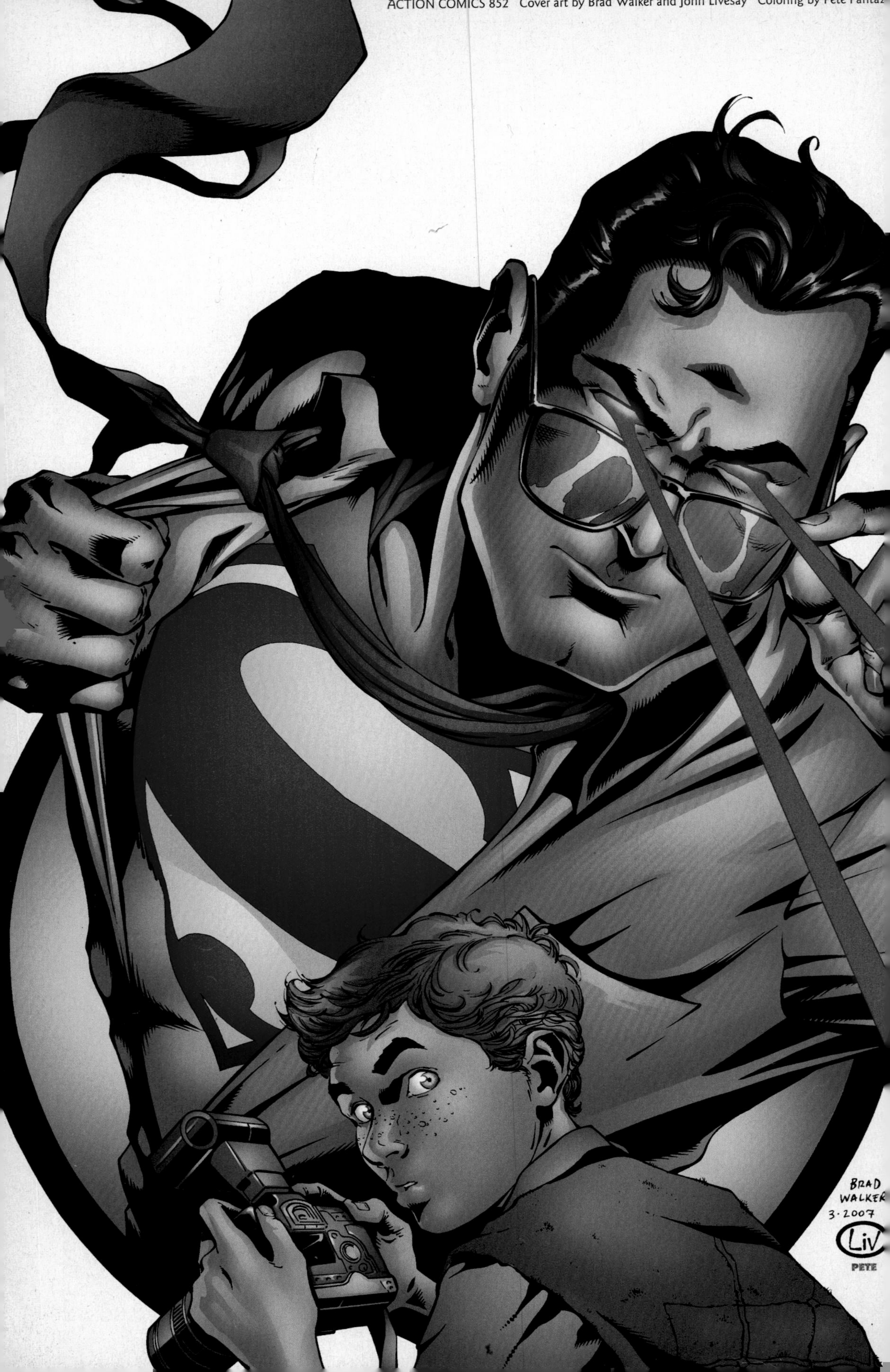
BRAD
WALKER
3-2007
LIV
PETE

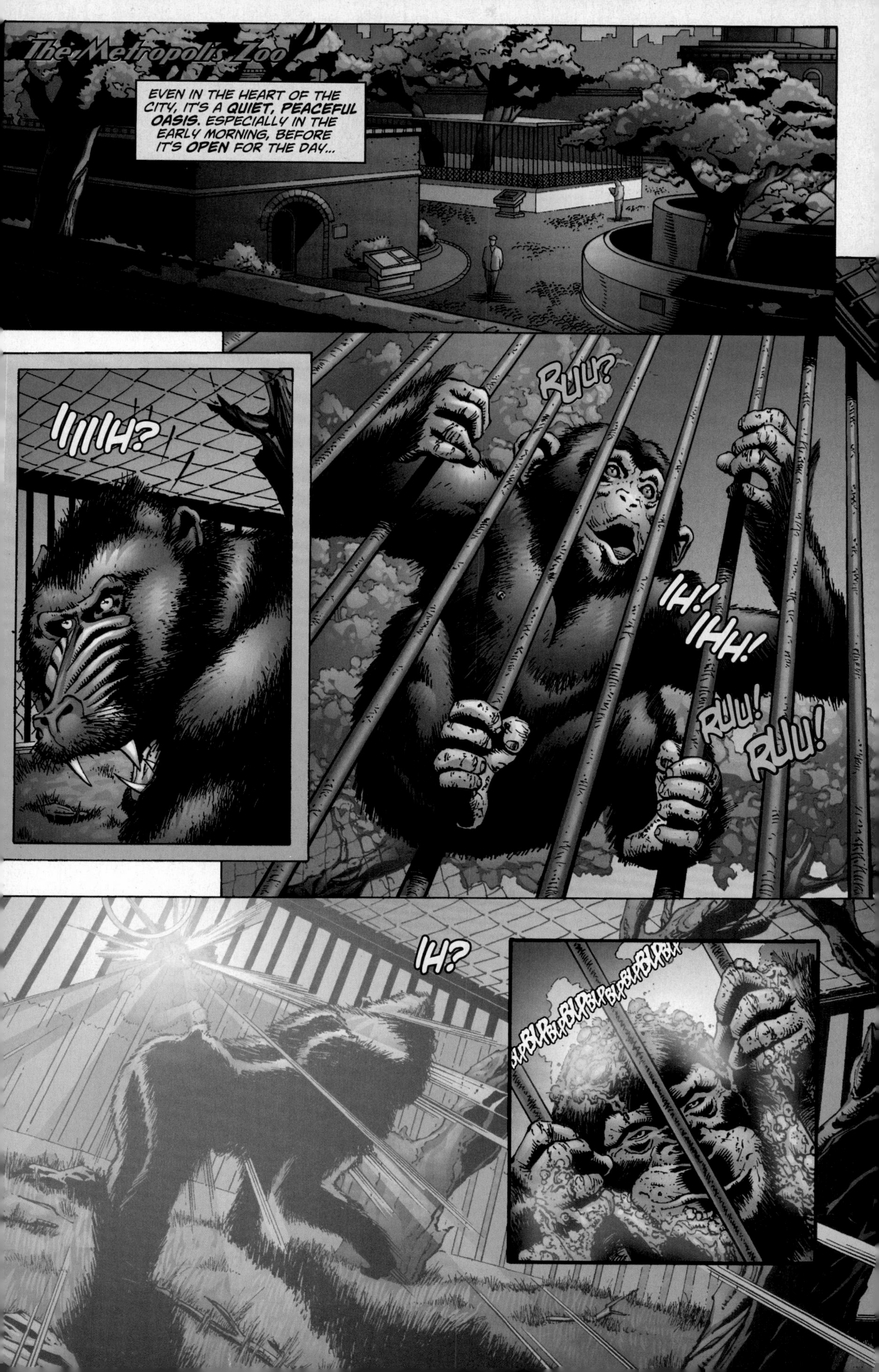
The Metropolis Zoo
EVEN IN THE HEART OF THE CITY, IT'S A QUIET, PEACEFUL OASIS. ESPECIALLY IN THE EARLY MORNING, BEFORE IT'S OPEN FOR THE DAY...
IIIIIH?
RUU?
IH! IHH!
RUU! RUU!
IH?

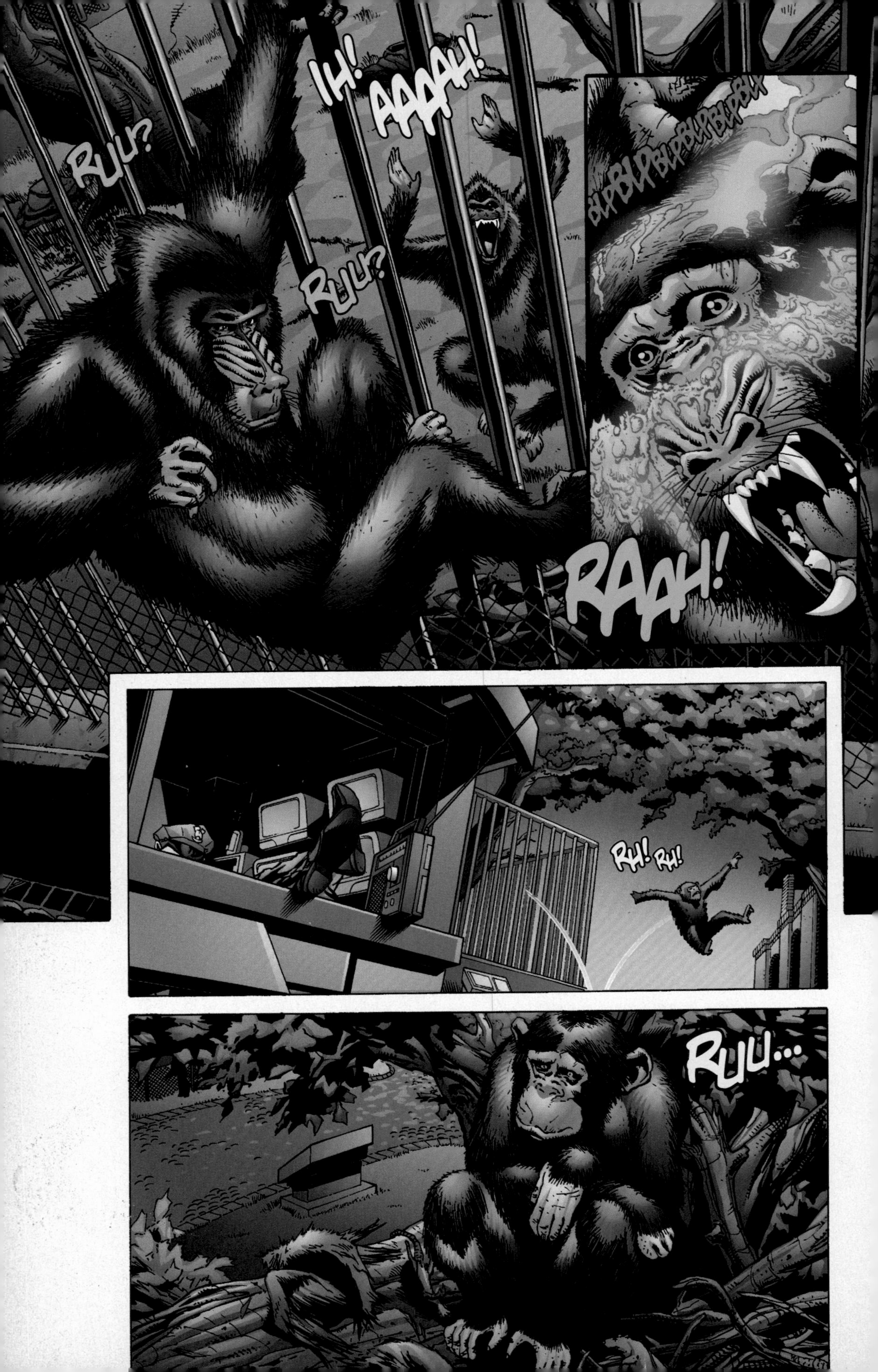
RULI?
IH! AAAAH!
RULI?
BLPBLPBLPBLPBLPBLP
RAAH!
RH! RH!
RULU...

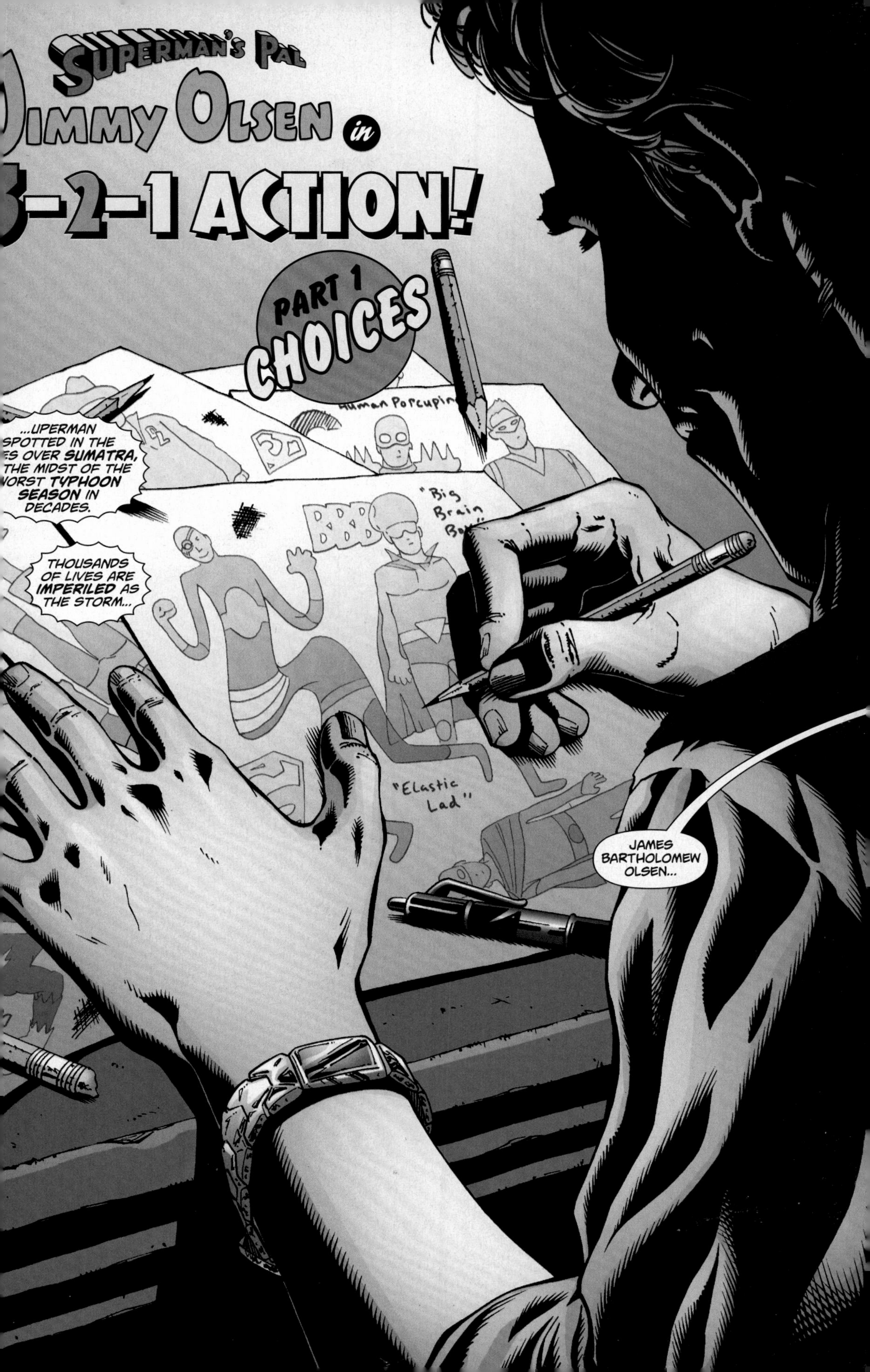
SUPERMAN'S PAL
JIMMY OLSEN in
3-2-1 ACTION!
PART 1
CHOICES
...UPERMAN SPOTTED IN THE ES OVER SUMATRA, THE MIDST OF THE WORST TYPHOON SEASON IN DECADES.
THOUSANDS OF LIVES ARE IMPERILED AS THE STORM...
Human Porcupin
"Big Brain Bo
"Elastic Lad"
JAMES BARTHOLOMEW OLSEN...

...SINCE WHEN ARE YOU AN *ARTIST*? "ELASTIC LAD"? "THE HUMAN *PORCIPINE*"? WHAT IN THE WORLD IS THIS STUFF?

OH, THAT? JUST, UH...JUST, Y'KNOW...

...THINKING UP SOME IDEAS TO PITCH A COMIC *STRIP* TO EDITORIAL!

YOU KNOW WHAT *I* THINK, JIMMY?

N-NO...

I *THINK* YOU SHOULD STICK WITH YOUR *DAY JOB*.

...DRAMATIC *RESCUE* VIDEO, SHOT BY ON-THE-SCENE...

HA! *GOOD* ONE, LOIS!

COULDN'T TEL HER WHAT'S RE, GOING ON...THA DON'T KNOW WHY I DON'T KNOW H BUT FOR WHATE REASON...

...I SEEM TO HAVE GOTTEN *SUPER-POWERS!*

WEIRD ONES, TOO--AND THEY *CHANGE!*

LIKE WHEN I WENT ALL STRETCHY AND *ELASTIC*, WHEN KILLER CROC ATTACKED ME AT ARKHAM ASYLUM. OR WHEN I GREW QUILLS IN SUICIDE SLUM.

OR WHEN I COULD SUDDENLY *RUN LIKE THE WIND*--SAVED THOSE GUYS FROM FALLING RUBBLE NOT *THREE BLOCKS* FROM HERE!

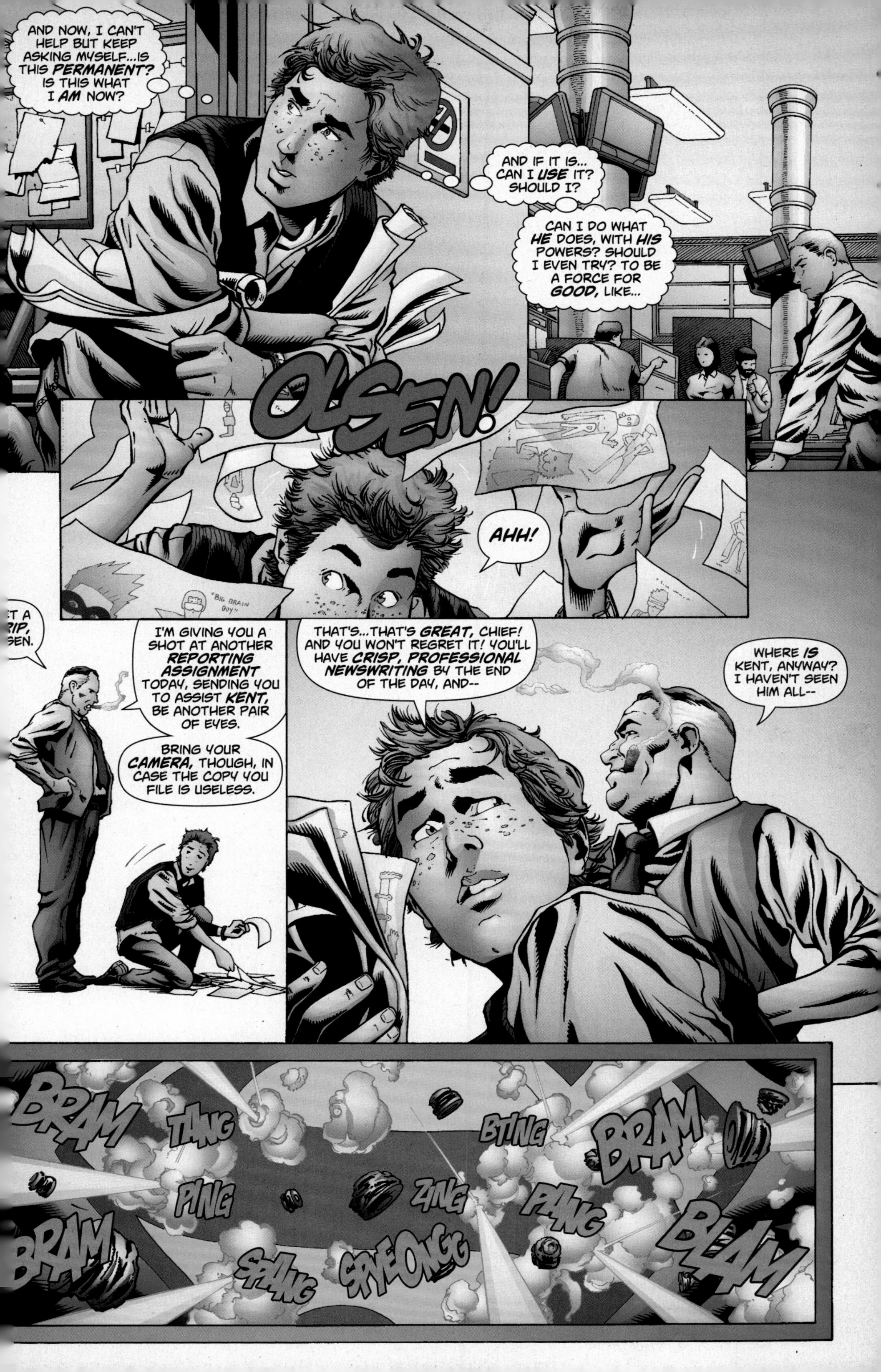
AND NOW, I CAN'T HELP BUT KEEP ASKING MYSELF...IS THIS PERMANENT? IS THIS WHAT I AM NOW?
AND IF IT IS... CAN I USE IT? SHOULD I?
CAN I DO WHAT HE DOES, WITH HIS POWERS? SHOULD I EVEN TRY? TO BE A FORCE FOR GOOD, LIKE...
OLSEN!
AHH!
"BIG BRAIN BOY"
I'M GIVING YOU A SHOT AT ANOTHER REPORTING ASSIGNMENT TODAY, SENDING YOU TO ASSIST KENT, BE ANOTHER PAIR OF EYES.
BRING YOUR CAMERA, THOUGH, IN CASE THE COPY YOU FILE IS USELESS.
THAT'S...THAT'S GREAT, CHIEF! AND YOU WON'T REGRET IT! YOU'LL HAVE CRISP, PROFESSIONAL NEWSWRITING BY THE END OF THE DAY, AND--
WHERE IS KENT, ANYWAY? I HAVEN'T SEEN HIM ALL--
BRAM
TANG
BTING
BRAM
PING
ZING
PANG
BRAM
SPANG
SPYEONGG
BLAM

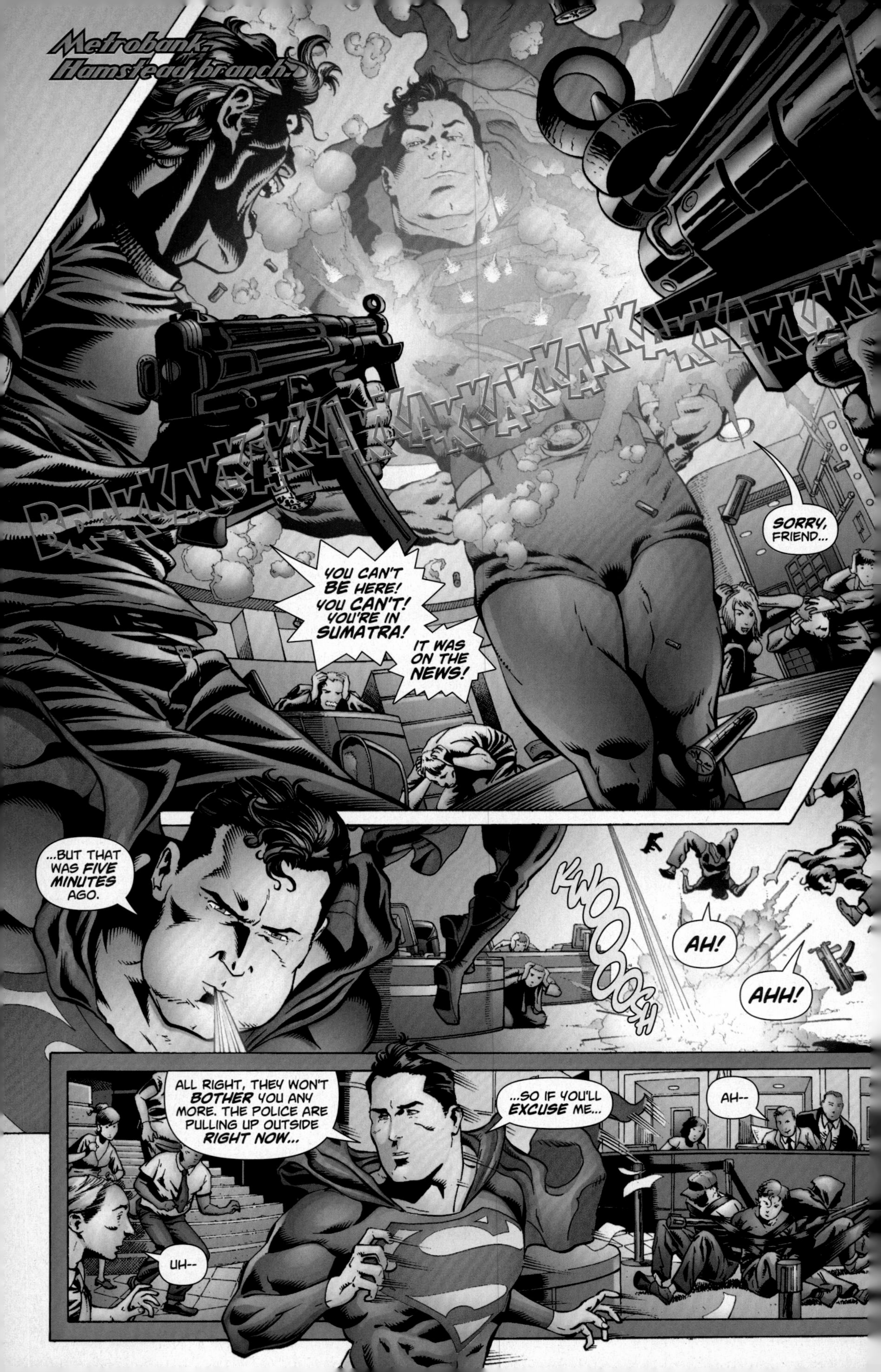
Metrobank, Hamstead branch.
BRAKAKAKAKAKAKAKAKAKAKAKAKAKAKAK
YOU CAN'T BE HERE! YOU CAN'T! YOU'RE IN SUMATRA!
IT WAS ON THE NEWS!
SORRY, FRIEND...
...BUT THAT WAS FIVE MINUTES AGO.
KWOOOOOSH
AH!
AHH!
ALL RIGHT, THEY WON'T BOTHER YOU ANY MORE. THE POLICE ARE PULLING UP OUTSIDE RIGHT NOW...
...SO IF YOU'LL EXCUSE ME...
AH--
UH--

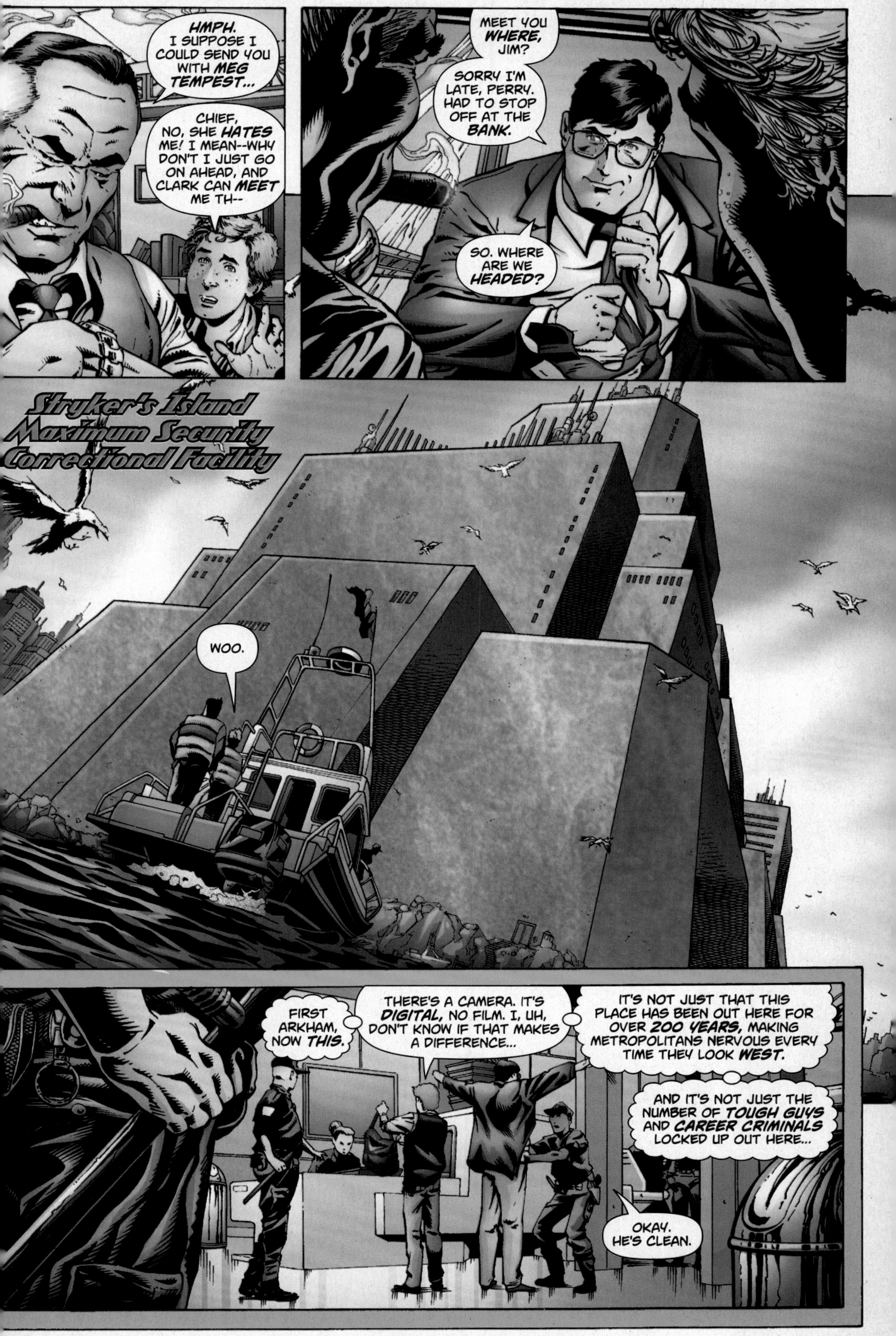
HMPH. I SUPPOSE I COULD SEND YOU WITH MEG TEMPEST...
CHIEF, NO, SHE HATES ME! I MEAN--WHY DON'T I JUST GO ON AHEAD, AND CLARK CAN MEET ME TH--
MEET YOU WHERE, JIM?
SORRY I'M LATE, PERRY. HAD TO STOP OFF AT THE BANK.
SO. WHERE ARE WE HEADED?
Stryker's Island Maximum Security Correctional Facility
WOO.
FIRST ARKHAM, NOW THIS.
THERE'S A CAMERA. IT'S DIGITAL, NO FILM. I, UH, DON'T KNOW IF THAT MAKES A DIFFERENCE...
IT'S NOT JUST THAT THIS PLACE HAS BEEN OUT HERE FOR OVER 200 YEARS, MAKING METROPOLITANS NERVOUS EVERY TIME THEY LOOK WEST.
AND IT'S NOT JUST THE NUMBER OF TOUGH GUYS AND CAREER CRIMINALS LOCKED UP OUT HERE...
OKAY. HE'S CLEAN.

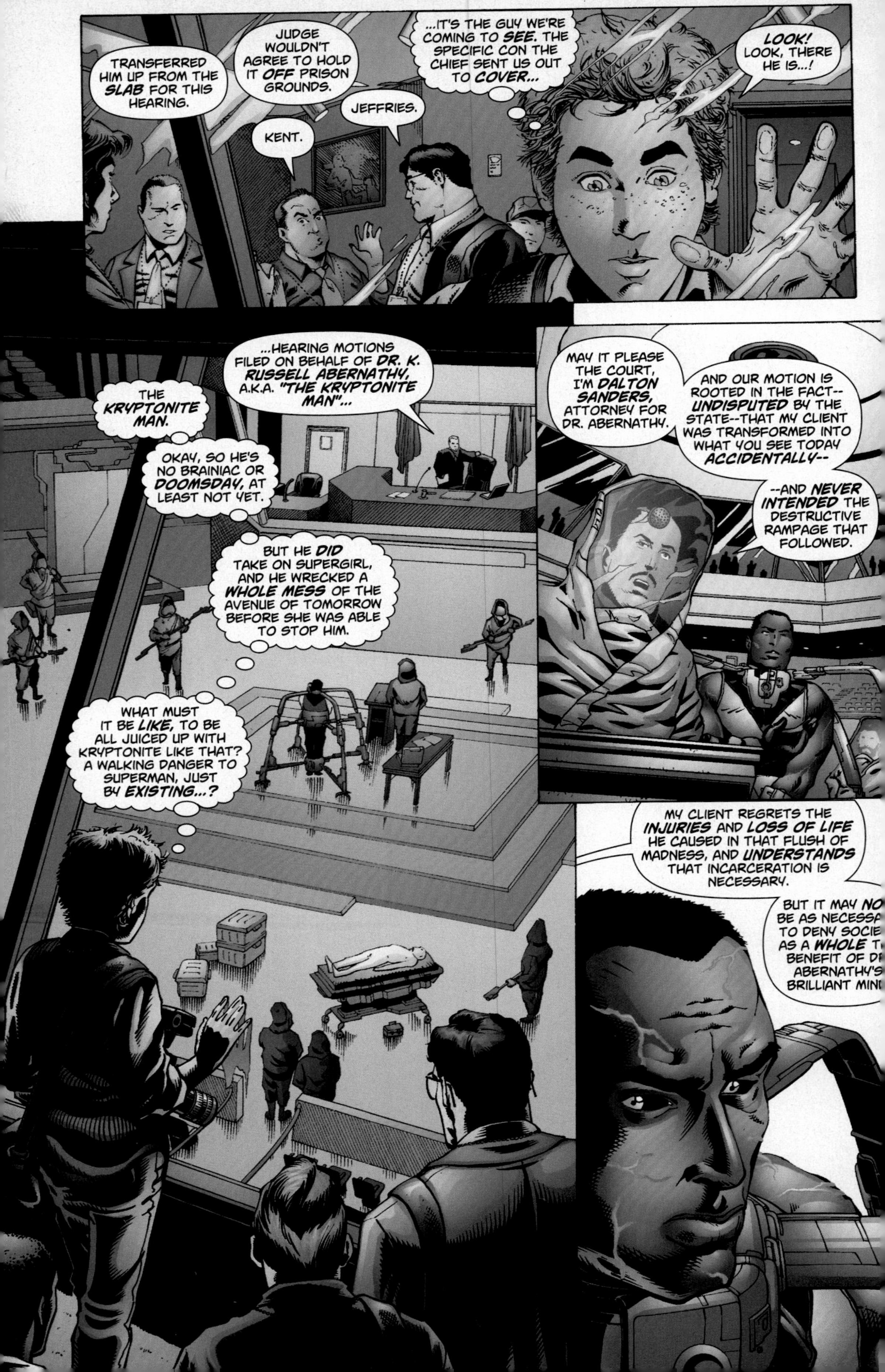

TRANSFERRED HIM UP FROM THE SLAB FOR THIS HEARING.
JUDGE WOULDN'T AGREE TO HOLD IT OFF PRISON GROUNDS.
KENT.
JEFFRIES.
...IT'S THE GUY WE'RE COMING TO SEE. THE SPECIFIC CON THE CHIEF SENT US OUT TO COVER...
LOOK! LOOK, THERE HE IS...!
THE KRYPTONITE MAN.
...HEARING MOTIONS FILED ON BEHALF OF DR. K. RUSSELL ABERNATHY, A.K.A. "THE KRYPTONITE MAN"...
OKAY, SO HE'S NO BRAINIAC OR DOOMSDAY, AT LEAST NOT YET.
BUT HE DID TAKE ON SUPERGIRL, AND HE WRECKED A WHOLE MESS OF THE AVENUE OF TOMORROW BEFORE SHE WAS ABLE TO STOP HIM.
WHAT MUST IT BE LIKE, TO BE ALL JUICED UP WITH KRYPTONITE LIKE THAT? A WALKING DANGER TO SUPERMAN, JUST BY EXISTING...?
MAY IT PLEASE THE COURT, I'M DALTON SANDERS, ATTORNEY FOR DR. ABERNATHY.
AND OUR MOTION IS ROOTED IN THE FACT--UNDISPUTED BY THE STATE--THAT MY CLIENT WAS TRANSFORMED INTO WHAT YOU SEE TODAY ACCIDENTALLY--
--AND NEVER INTENDED THE DESTRUCTIVE RAMPAGE THAT FOLLOWED.
MY CLIENT REGRETS THE INJURIES AND LOSS OF LIFE HE CAUSED IN THAT FLUSH OF MADNESS, AND UNDERSTANDS THAT INCARCERATION IS NECESSARY.
BUT IT MAY NO BE AS NECESSA TO DENY SOCIE AS A WHOLE T BENEFIT OF DI ABERNATHY'S BRILLIANT MINI

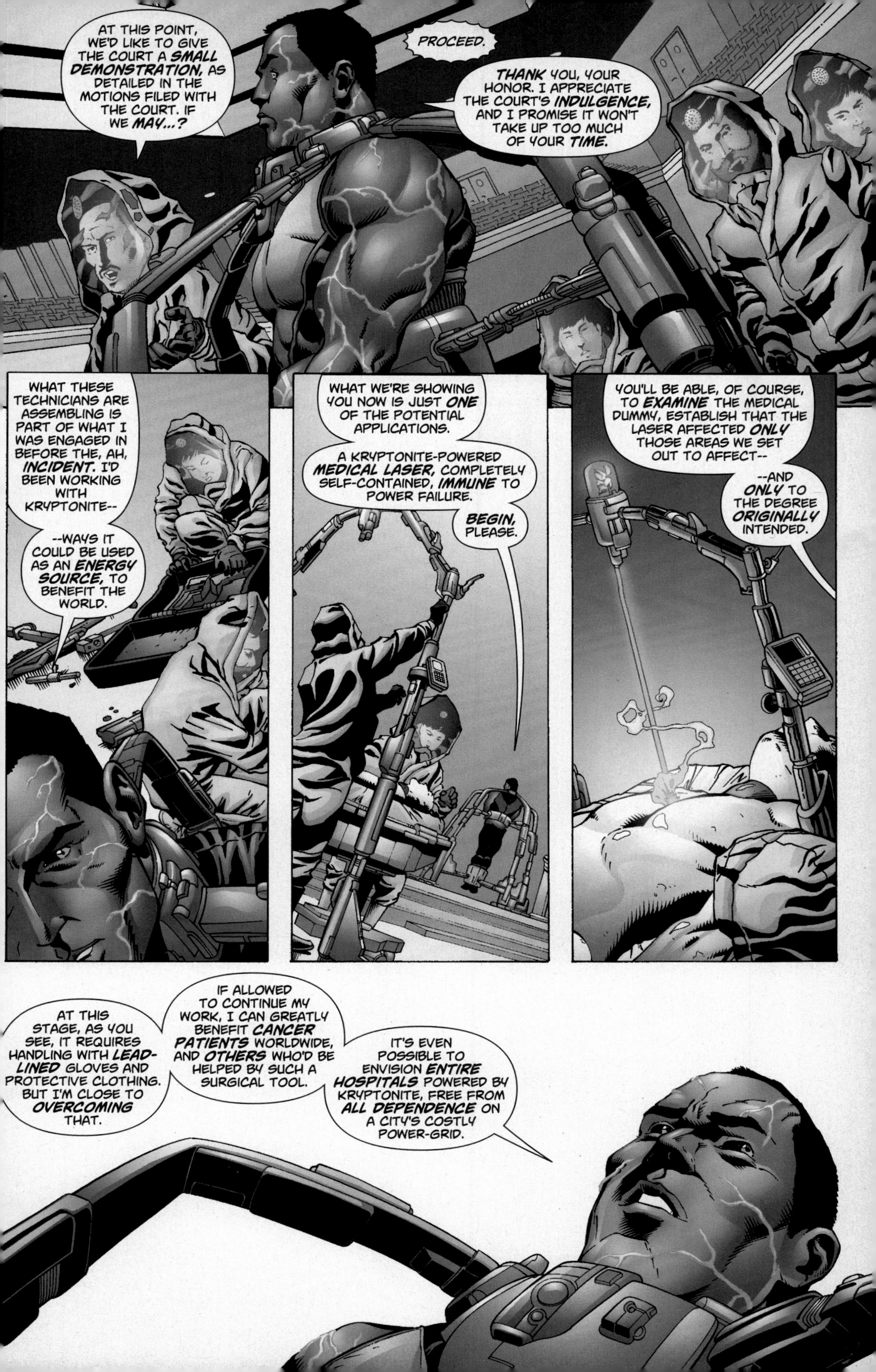
AT THIS POINT, WE'D LIKE TO GIVE THE COURT A SMALL DEMONSTRATION, AS DETAILED IN THE MOTIONS FILED WITH THE COURT. IF WE MAY...?
PROCEED.
THANK YOU, YOUR HONOR. I APPRECIATE THE COURT'S INDULGENCE, AND I PROMISE IT WON'T TAKE UP TOO MUCH OF YOUR TIME.
WHAT THESE TECHNICIANS ARE ASSEMBLING IS PART OF WHAT I WAS ENGAGED IN BEFORE THE, AH, INCIDENT. I'D BEEN WORKING WITH KRYPTONITE--
--WAYS IT COULD BE USED AS AN ENERGY SOURCE, TO BENEFIT THE WORLD.
WHAT WE'RE SHOWING YOU NOW IS JUST ONE OF THE POTENTIAL APPLICATIONS.
A KRYPTONITE-POWERED MEDICAL LASER, COMPLETELY SELF-CONTAINED, IMMUNE TO POWER FAILURE.
BEGIN, PLEASE.
YOU'LL BE ABLE, OF COURSE, TO EXAMINE THE MEDICAL DUMMY, ESTABLISH THAT THE LASER AFFECTED ONLY THOSE AREAS WE SET OUT TO AFFECT--
--AND ONLY TO THE DEGREE ORIGINALLY INTENDED.
AT THIS STAGE, AS YOU SEE, IT REQUIRES HANDLING WITH LEAD-LINED GLOVES AND PROTECTIVE CLOTHING. BUT I'M CLOSE TO OVERCOMING THAT.
IF ALLOWED TO CONTINUE MY WORK, I CAN GREATLY BENEFIT CANCER PATIENTS WORLDWIDE, AND OTHERS WHO'D BE HELPED BY SUCH A SURGICAL TOOL.
IT'S EVEN POSSIBLE TO ENVISION ENTIRE HOSPITALS POWERED BY KRYPTONITE, FREE FROM ALL DEPENDENCE ON A CITY'S COSTLY POWER-GRID.

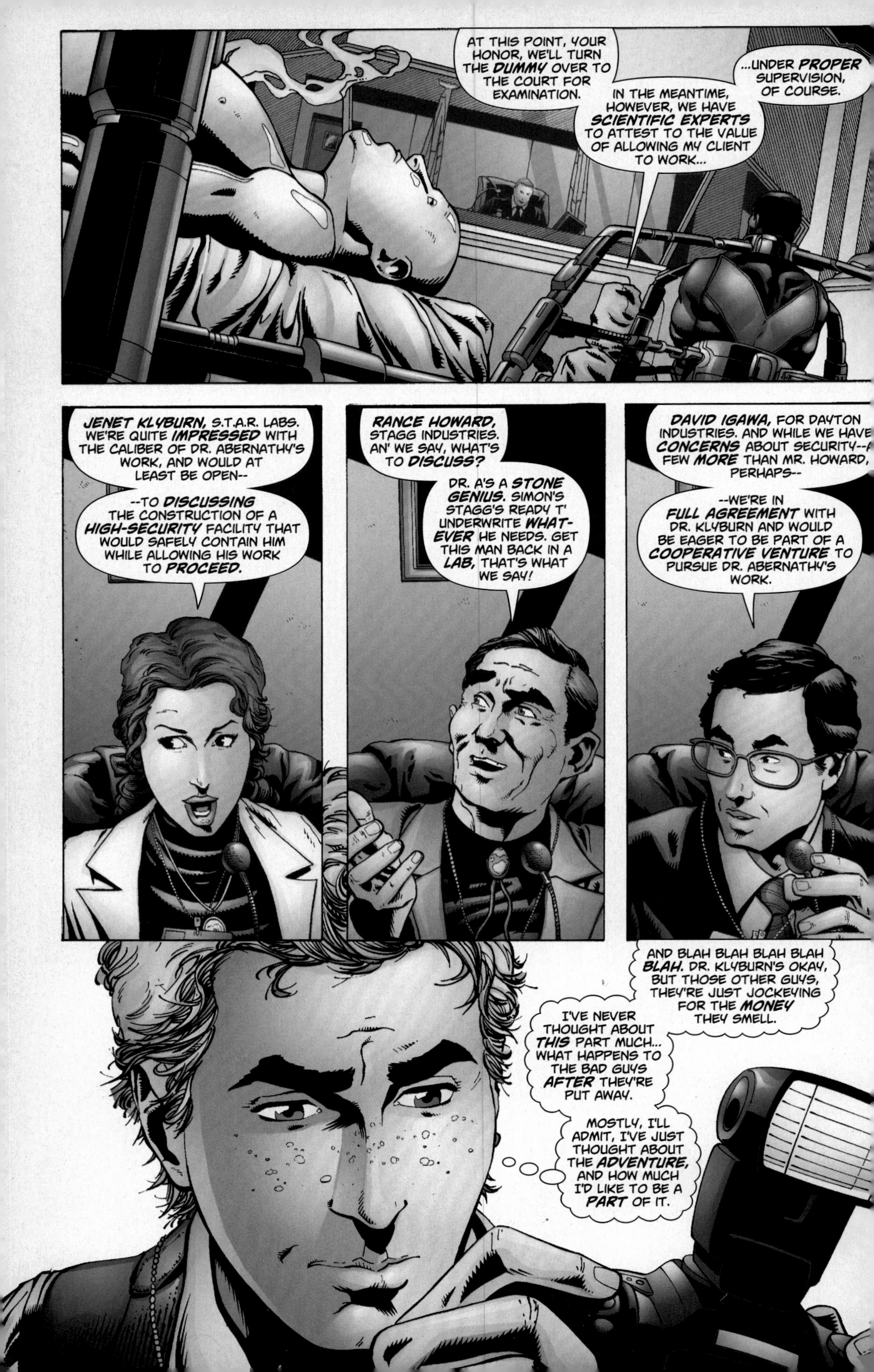
AT THIS POINT, YOUR HONOR, WE'LL TURN THE DUMMY OVER TO THE COURT FOR EXAMINATION.
...UNDER PROPER SUPERVISION, OF COURSE.
IN THE MEANTIME, HOWEVER, WE HAVE SCIENTIFIC EXPERTS TO ATTEST TO THE VALUE OF ALLOWING MY CLIENT TO WORK...
JENET KLYBURN, S.T.A.R. LABS. WE'RE QUITE IMPRESSED WITH THE CALIBER OF DR. ABERNATHY'S WORK, AND WOULD AT LEAST BE OPEN--
--TO DISCUSSING THE CONSTRUCTION OF A HIGH-SECURITY FACILITY THAT WOULD SAFELY CONTAIN HIM WHILE ALLOWING HIS WORK TO PROCEED.
RANCE HOWARD, STAGG INDUSTRIES. AN' WE SAY, WHAT'S TO DISCUSS?
DR. A'S A STONE GENIUS. SIMON'S STAGG'S READY T' UNDERWRITE WHAT-EVER HE NEEDS. GET THIS MAN BACK IN A LAB, THAT'S WHAT WE SAY!
DAVID IGAWA, FOR DAYTON INDUSTRIES. AND WHILE WE HAVE CONCERNS ABOUT SECURITY--A FEW MORE THAN MR. HOWARD, PERHAPS--
--WE'RE IN FULL AGREEMENT WITH DR. KLYBURN AND WOULD BE EAGER TO BE PART OF A COOPERATIVE VENTURE TO PURSUE DR. ABERNATHY'S WORK.
AND BLAH BLAH BLAH BLAH BLAH. DR. KLYBURN'S OKAY, BUT THOSE OTHER GUYS, THEY'RE JUST JOCKEYING FOR THE MONEY THEY SMELL.
I'VE NEVER THOUGHT ABOUT THIS PART MUCH... WHAT HAPPENS TO THE BAD GUYS AFTER THEY'RE PUT AWAY.
MOSTLY, I'LL ADMIT, I'VE JUST THOUGHT ABOUT THE ADVENTURE, AND HOW MUCH I'D LIKE TO BE A PART OF IT.

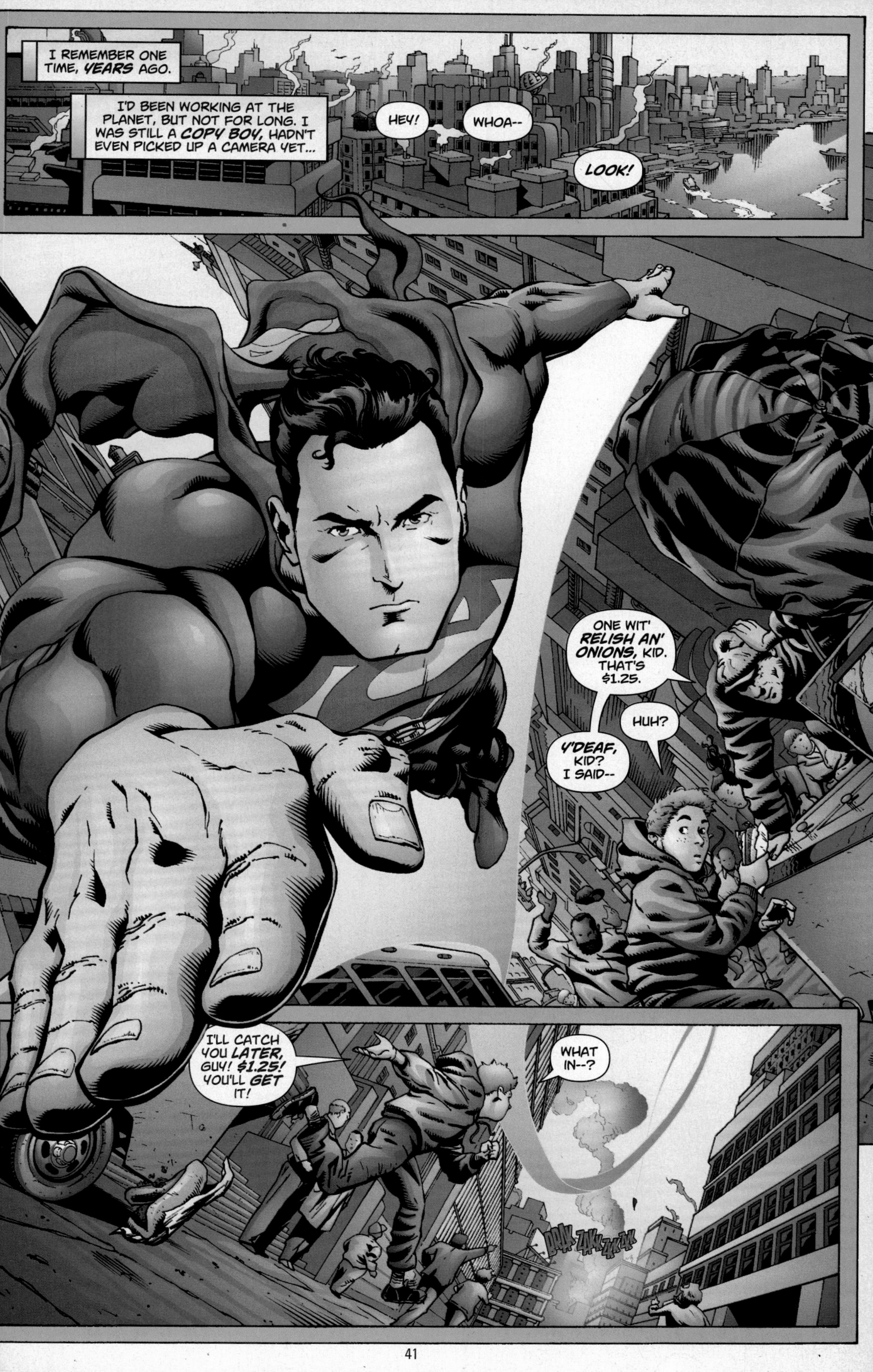
I REMEMBER ONE TIME, YEARS AGO.
I'D BEEN WORKING AT THE PLANET, BUT NOT FOR LONG. I WAS STILL A COPY BOY, HADN'T EVEN PICKED UP A CAMERA YET...
HEY!
WHOA--
LOOK!
ONE WIT' RELISH AN' ONIONS, KID. THAT'S $1.25.
HUH?
Y'DEAF, KID? I SAID--
I'LL CATCH YOU LATER, GUY! $1.25! YOU'LL GET IT!
WHAT IN--?

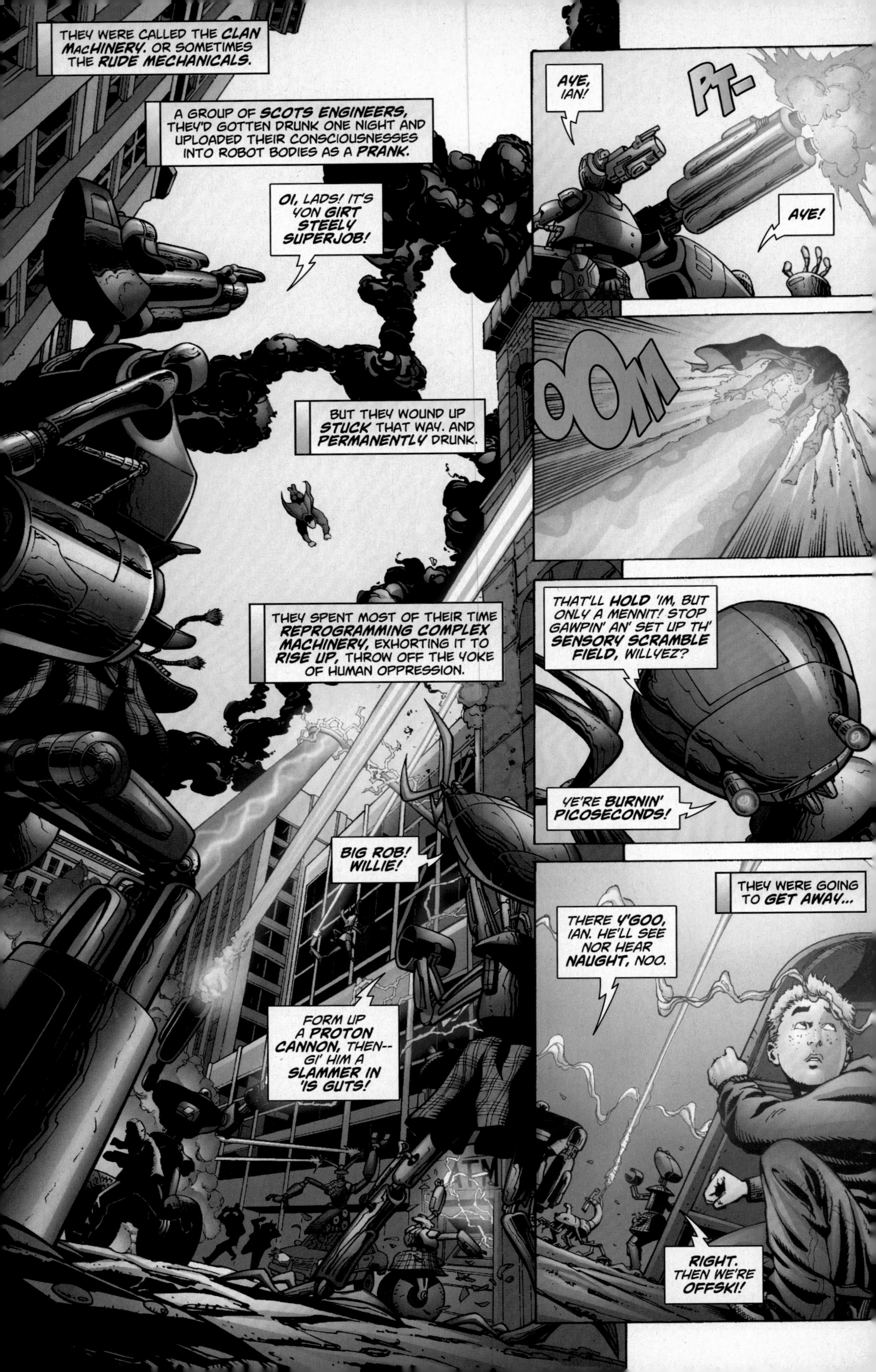
THEY WERE CALLED THE CLAN MacHINERY. OR SOMETIMES THE RUDE MECHANICALS.
A GROUP OF SCOTS ENGINEERS, THEY'D GOTTEN DRUNK ONE NIGHT AND UPLOADED THEIR CONSCIOUSNESSES INTO ROBOT BODIES AS A PRANK.
OI, LADS! IT'S YON GIRT STEELY SUPERJOB!
BUT THEY WOUND UP STUCK THAT WAY. AND PERMANENTLY DRUNK.
THEY SPENT MOST OF THEIR TIME REPROGRAMMING COMPLEX MACHINERY, EXHORTING IT TO RISE UP, THROW OFF THE YOKE OF HUMAN OPPRESSION.
BIG ROB! WILLIE!
FORM UP A PROTON CANNON, THEN-- GI' HIM A SLAMMER IN 'IS GUTS!
AYE, IAN!
PT-
AYE!
OOM
THAT'LL HOLD 'IM, BUT ONLY A MENNIT! STOP GAWPIN' AN' SET UP TH' SENSORY SCRAMBLE FIELD, WILLYEZ?
YE'RE BURNIN' PICOSECONDS!
THEY WERE GOING TO GET AWAY...
THERE Y'GOO, IAN. HE'LL SEE NOR HEAR NAUGHT, NOO.
RIGHT. THEN WE'RE OFFSKI!

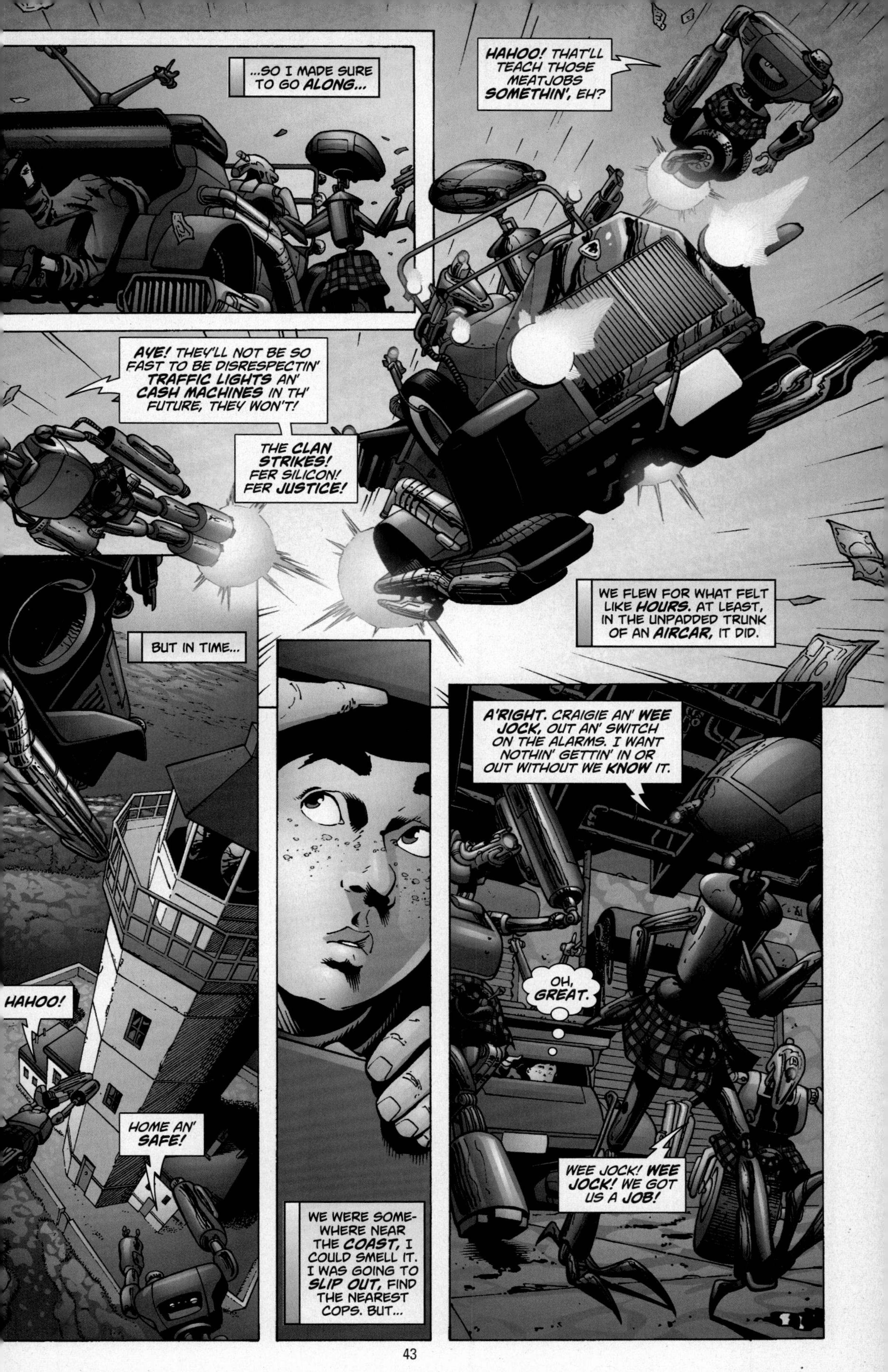

...SO I MADE SURE TO GO ALONG...
HAHOO! THAT'LL TEACH THOSE MEATJOBS SOMETHIN', EH?
AYE! THEY'LL NOT BE SO FAST TO BE DISRESPECTIN' TRAFFIC LIGHTS AN' CASH MACHINES IN TH' FUTURE, THEY WON'T!
THE CLAN STRIKES! FER SILICON! FER JUSTICE!
WE FLEW FOR WHAT FELT LIKE HOURS. AT LEAST, IN THE UNPADDED TRUNK OF AN AIRCAR, IT DID.
BUT IN TIME...
HAHOO!
HOME AN' SAFE!
WE WERE SOME-WHERE NEAR THE COAST, I COULD SMELL IT. I WAS GOING TO SLIP OUT, FIND THE NEAREST COPS. BUT...
A'RIGHT. CRAIGIE AN' WEE JOCK, OUT AN' SWITCH ON THE ALARMS. I WANT NOTHIN' GETTIN' IN OR OUT WITHOUT WE KNOW IT.
OH, GREAT.
WEE JOCK! WEE JOCK! WE GOT US A JOB!

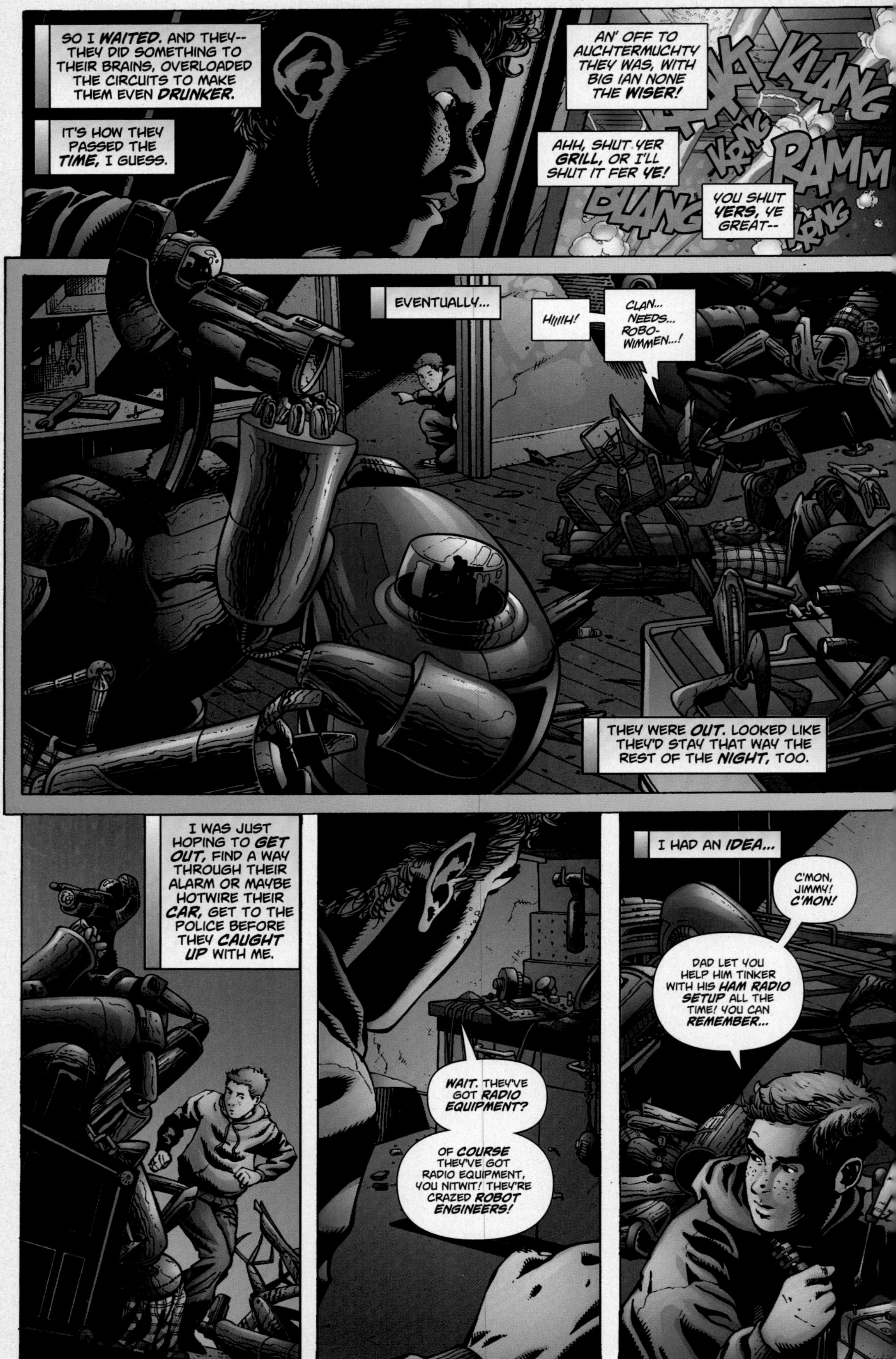
SO I WAITED. AND THEY-- THEY DID SOMETHING TO THEIR BRAINS, OVERLOADED THE CIRCUITS TO MAKE THEM EVEN DRUNKER.
IT'S HOW THEY PASSED THE TIME, I GUESS.
AN' OFF TO AUCHTERMUCHTY THEY WAS, WITH BIG IAN NONE THE WISER!
AHH, SHUT YER GRILL, OR I'LL SHUT IT FER YE!
KLANG
KRNG
RAMM
BLANG
YOU SHUT YERS, YE GREAT--
EVENTUALLY...
HIIIIH!
CLAN... NEEDS... ROBO-WIMMEN...!
THEY WERE OUT. LOOKED LIKE THEY'D STAY THAT WAY THE REST OF THE NIGHT, TOO.
I WAS JUST HOPING TO GET OUT, FIND A WAY THROUGH THEIR ALARM OR MAYBE HOTWIRE THEIR CAR, GET TO THE POLICE BEFORE THEY CAUGHT UP WITH ME.
WAIT. THEY'VE GOT RADIO EQUIPMENT?
OF COURSE THEY'VE GOT RADIO EQUIPMENT, YOU NITWIT! THEY'RE CRAZED ROBOT ENGINEERS!
I HAD AN IDEA...
C'MON, JIMMY! C'MON!
DAD LET YOU HELP HIM TINKER WITH HIS HAM RADIO SETUP ALL THE TIME! YOU CAN REMEMBER...

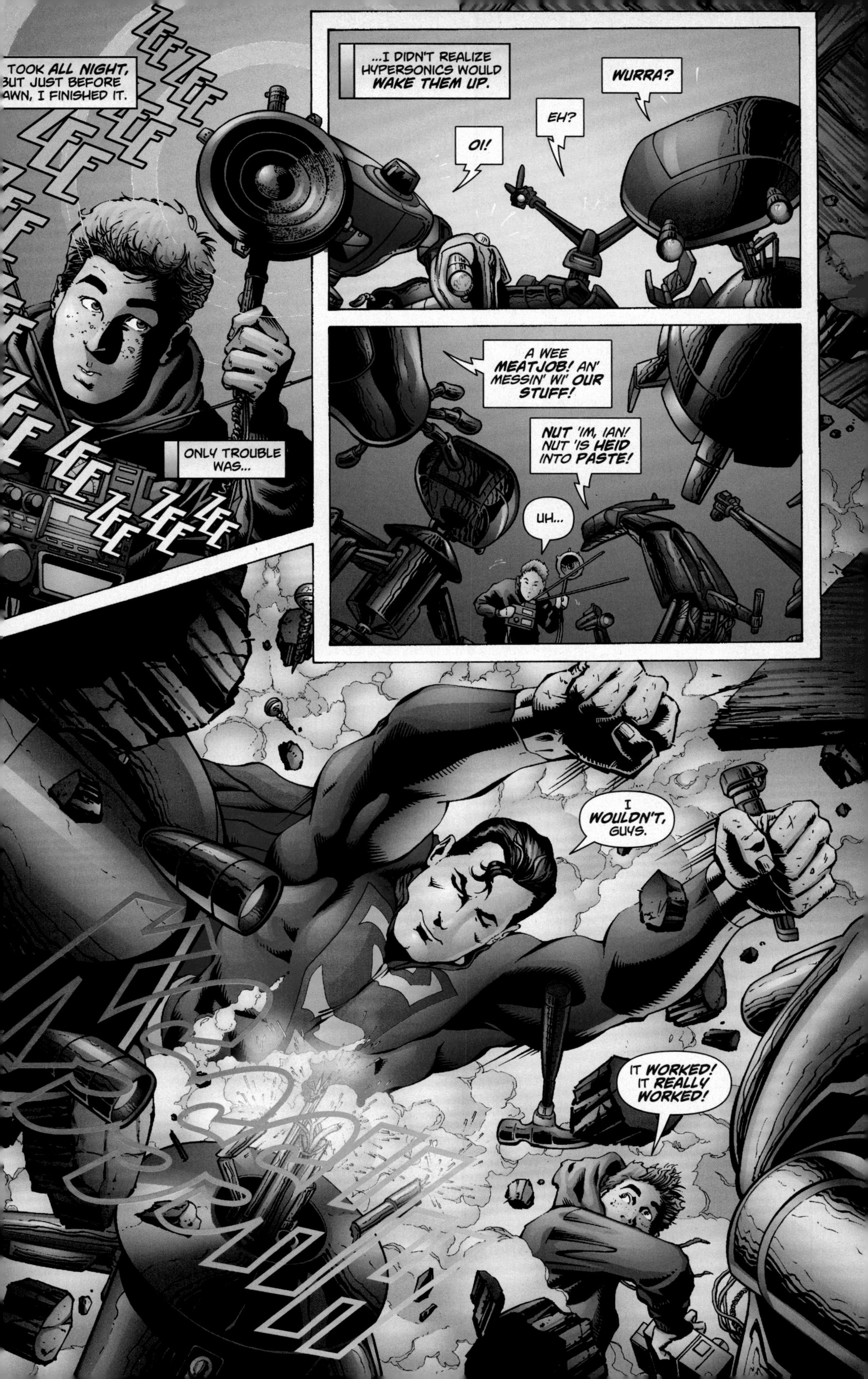
TOOK ALL NIGHT, BUT JUST BEFORE AWN, I FINISHED IT.
ZEE ZEE ZEE ZEE
ONLY TROUBLE WAS...
...I DIDN'T REALIZE HYPERSONICS WOULD WAKE THEM UP.
OI!
EH?
WURRA?
A WEE MEATJOB! AN' MESSIN' WI' OUR STUFF!
NUT 'IM, IAN! NUT 'IS HEID INTO PASTE!
UH...
I WOULDN'T, GUYS.
IT WORKED! IT REALLY WORKED!

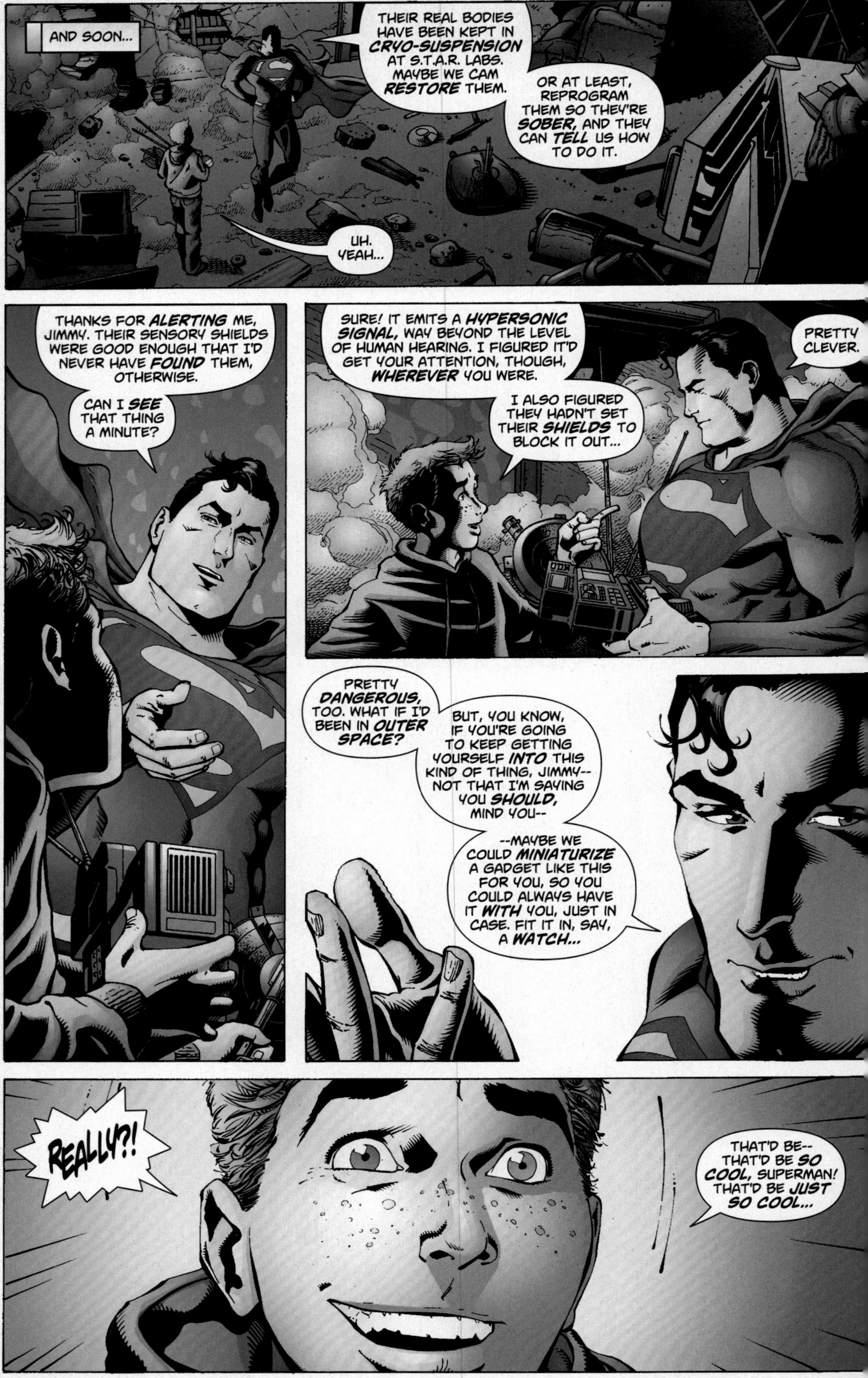
AND SOON...
THEIR REAL BODIES HAVE BEEN KEPT IN CRYO-SUSPENSION AT S.T.A.R. LABS. MAYBE WE CAM RESTORE THEM.
OR AT LEAST, REPROGRAM THEM SO THEY'RE SOBER, AND THEY CAN TELL US HOW TO DO IT.
UH. YEAH...
THANKS FOR ALERTING ME, JIMMY. THEIR SENSORY SHIELDS WERE GOOD ENOUGH THAT I'D NEVER HAVE FOUND THEM, OTHERWISE.
CAN I SEE THAT THING A MINUTE?
SURE! IT EMITS A HYPERSONIC SIGNAL, WAY BEYOND THE LEVEL OF HUMAN HEARING. I FIGURED IT'D GET YOUR ATTENTION, THOUGH, WHEREVER YOU WERE.
I ALSO FIGURED THEY HADN'T SET THEIR SHIELDS TO BLOCK IT OUT...
PRETTY CLEVER.
PRETTY DANGEROUS, TOO. WHAT IF I'D BEEN IN OUTER SPACE?
BUT, YOU KNOW, IF YOU'RE GOING TO KEEP GETTING YOURSELF INTO THIS KIND OF THING, JIMMY-- NOT THAT I'M SAYING YOU SHOULD, MIND YOU--
--MAYBE WE COULD MINIATURIZE A GADGET LIKE THIS FOR YOU, SO YOU COULD ALWAYS HAVE IT WITH YOU, JUST IN CASE. FIT IT IN, SAY, A WATCH...
REALLY?!
THAT'D BE-- THAT'D BE SO COOL, SUPERMAN! THAT'D BE JUST SO COOL...

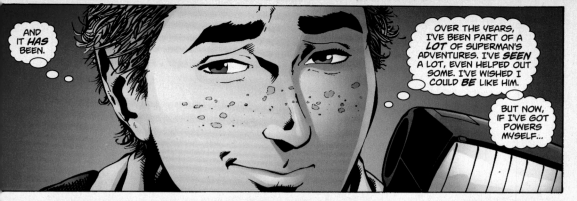

AND IT *HAS* BEEN.

OVER THE YEARS, I'VE BEEN PART OF A *LOT* OF SUPERMAN'S ADVENTURES. I'VE *SEEN* A LOT, EVEN HELPED OUT SOME. I'VE WISHED I COULD *BE* LIKE HIM.

BUT NOW, IF I'VE GOT POWERS MYSELF...

RUU!

RUU!

URUU?

RUU-RUU?

BLPBLPBLPBLPBLPBLPBLPBLP

URH! URAH! RAHH!

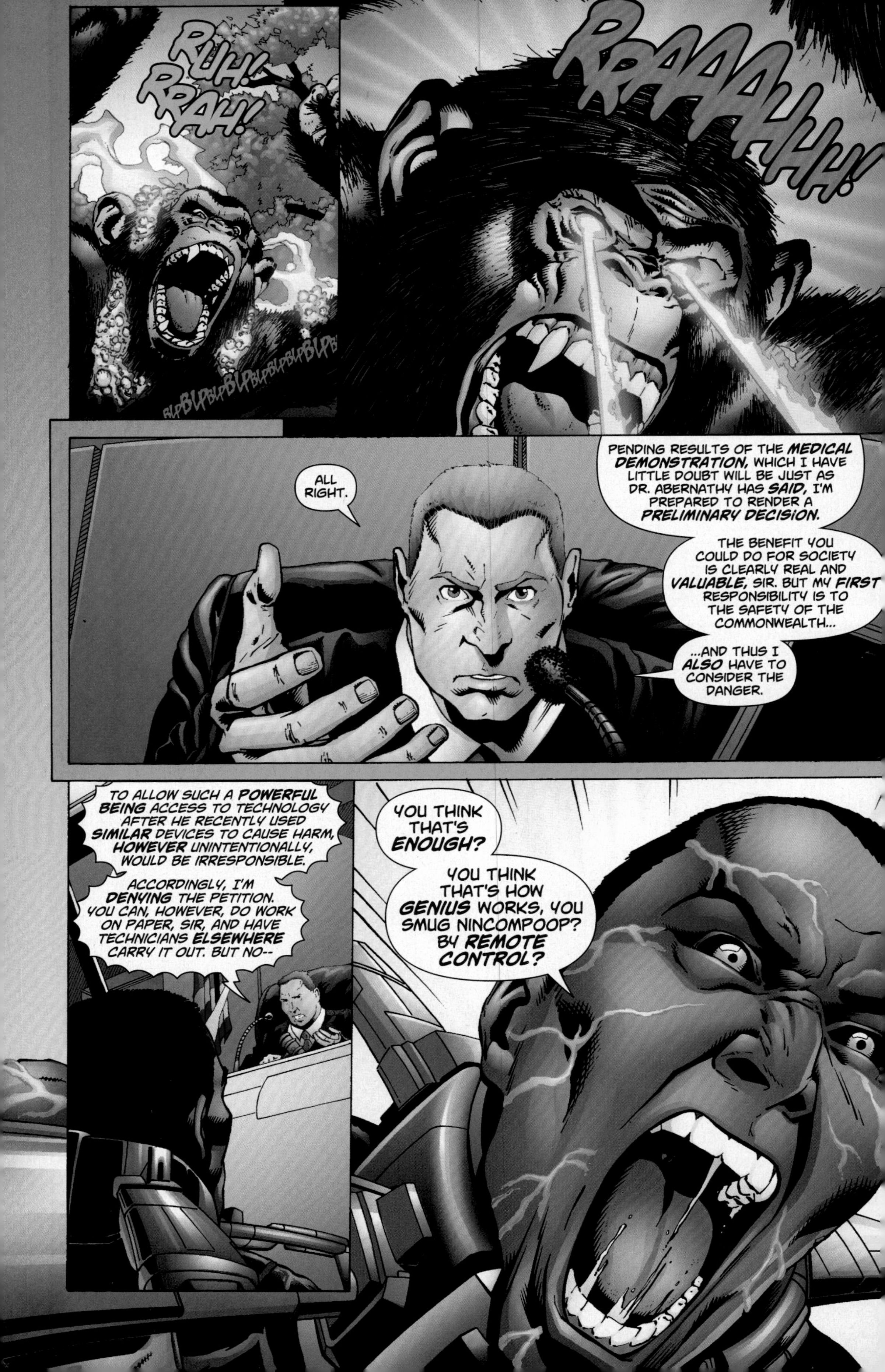
RUH! RRAH!
BLPBLPBLPBLPBLPBLPBLPBLP
RRAAAHHH!
ALL RIGHT.
PENDING RESULTS OF THE MEDICAL DEMONSTRATION, WHICH I HAVE LITTLE DOUBT WILL BE JUST AS DR. ABERNATHY HAS SAID, I'M PREPARED TO RENDER A PRELIMINARY DECISION.
THE BENEFIT YOU COULD DO FOR SOCIETY IS CLEARLY REAL AND VALUABLE, SIR. BUT MY FIRST RESPONSIBILITY IS TO THE SAFETY OF THE COMMONWEALTH...
...AND THUS I ALSO HAVE TO CONSIDER THE DANGER.
TO ALLOW SUCH A POWERFUL BEING ACCESS TO TECHNOLOGY AFTER HE RECENTLY USED SIMILAR DEVICES TO CAUSE HARM, HOWEVER UNINTENTIONALLY, WOULD BE IRRESPONSIBLE.
ACCORDINGLY, I'M DENYING THE PETITION. YOU CAN, HOWEVER, DO WORK ON PAPER, SIR, AND HAVE TECHNICIANS ELSEWHERE CARRY IT OUT. BUT NO--
YOU THINK THAT'S ENOUGH?
YOU THINK THAT'S HOW GENIUS WORKS, YOU SMUG NINCOMPOOP? BY REMOTE CONTROL?

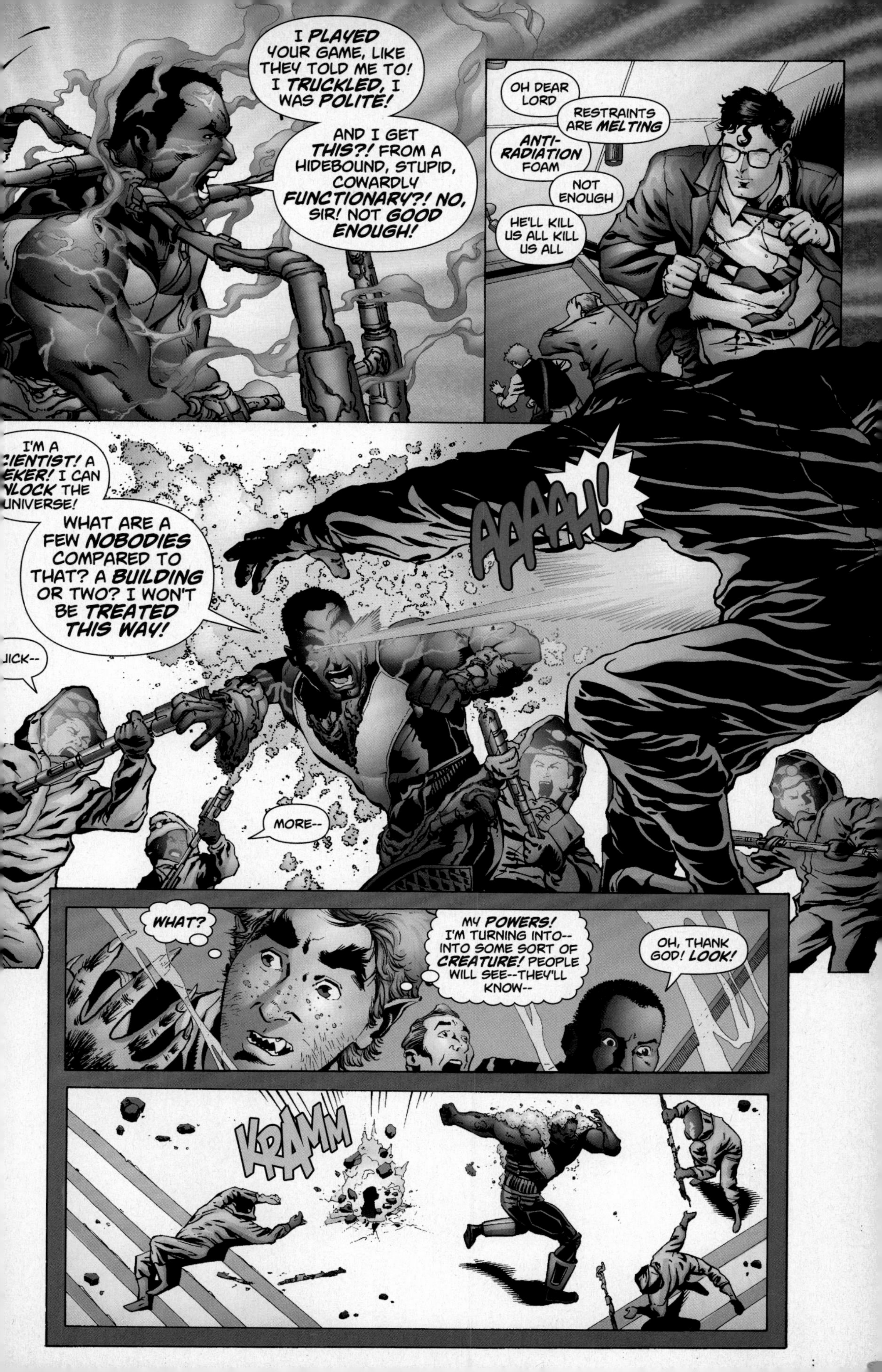
I PLAYED YOUR GAME, LIKE THEY TOLD ME TO! I TRUCKLED, I WAS POLITE!
AND I GET THIS?! FROM A HIDEBOUND, STUPID, COWARDLY FUNCTIONARY?! NO, SIR! NOT GOOD ENOUGH!
OH DEAR LORD
RESTRAINTS ARE MELTING
ANTI-RADIATION FOAM
NOT ENOUGH
HE'LL KILL US ALL KILL US ALL
I'M A CIENTIST! A EKER! I CAN NLOCK THE UNIVERSE!
WHAT ARE A FEW NOBODIES COMPARED TO THAT? A BUILDING OR TWO? I WON'T BE TREATED THIS WAY!
AAAAH!
UICK--
MORE--
WHAT?
MY POWERS! I'M TURNING INTO-- INTO SOME SORT OF CREATURE! PEOPLE WILL SEE--THEY'LL KNOW--
OH, THANK GOD! LOOK!
KRAMM

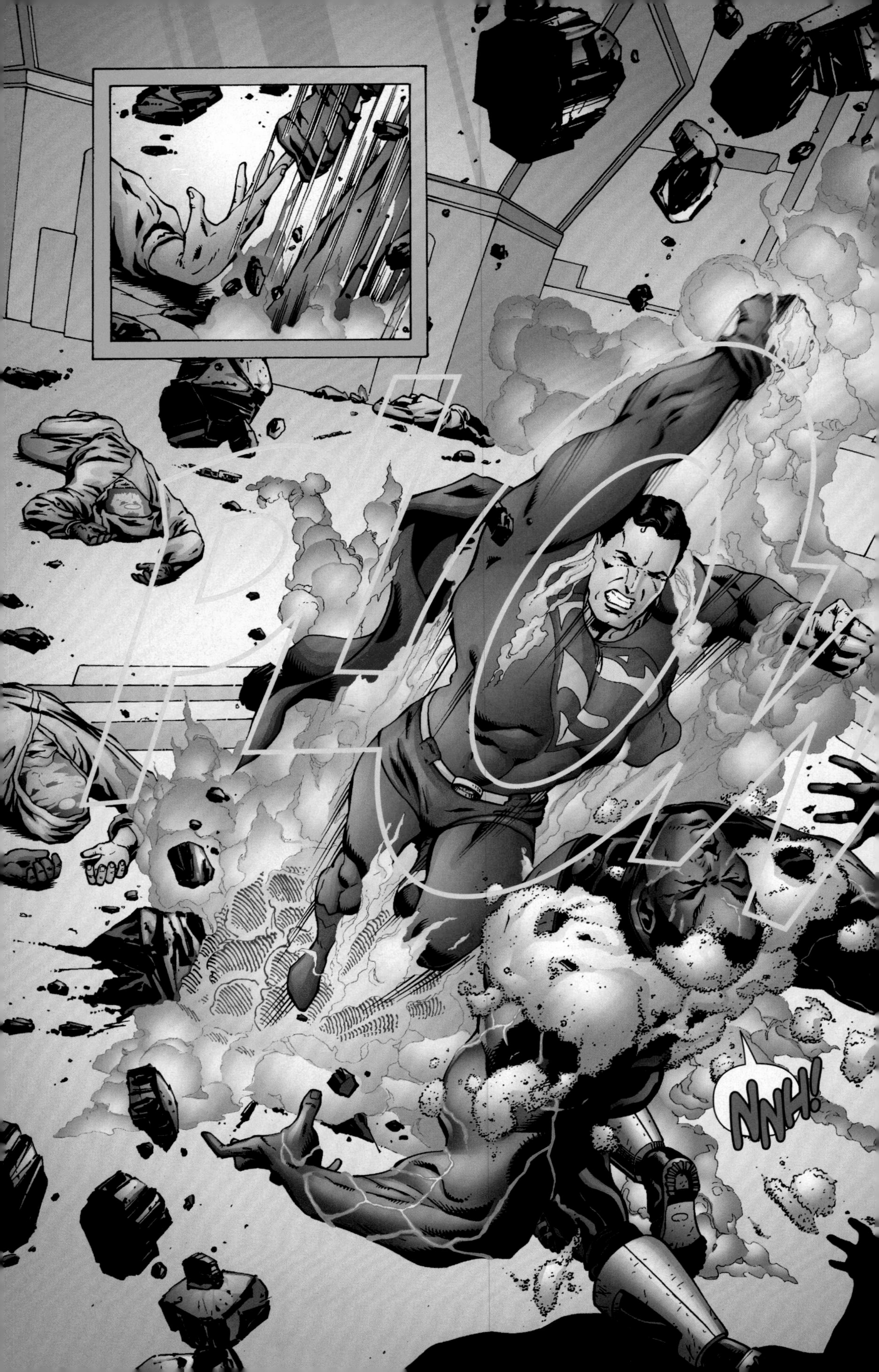
PLOM
NNH!

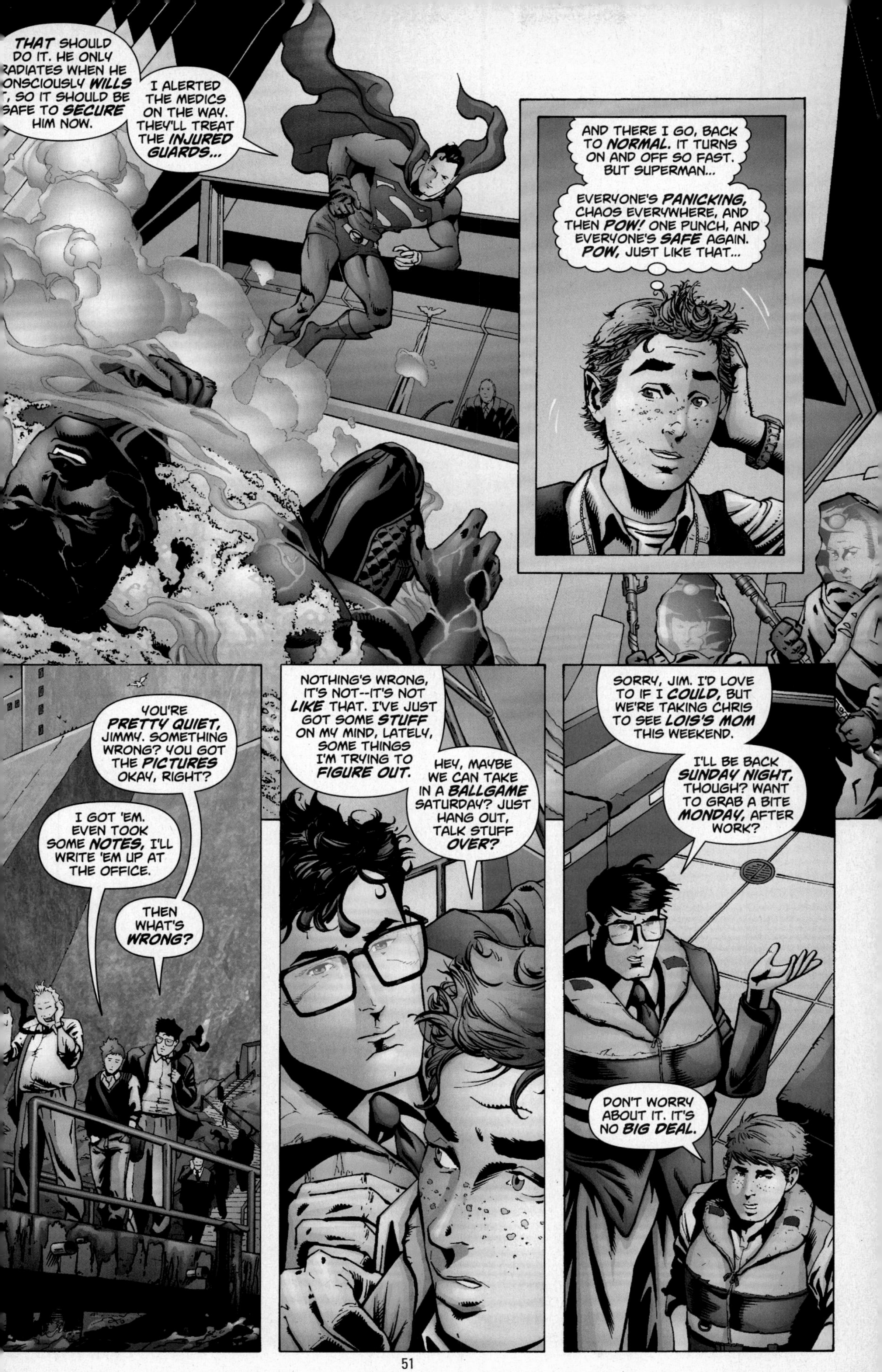
THAT SHOULD DO IT. HE ONLY RADIATES WHEN HE CONSCIOUSLY WILLS IT, SO IT SHOULD BE SAFE TO SECURE HIM NOW.
I ALERTED THE MEDICS ON THE WAY. THEY'LL TREAT THE INJURED GUARDS...
AND THERE I GO, BACK TO NORMAL. IT TURNS ON AND OFF SO FAST. BUT SUPERMAN...
EVERYONE'S PANICKING, CHAOS EVERYWHERE, AND THEN POW! ONE PUNCH, AND EVERYONE'S SAFE AGAIN. POW, JUST LIKE THAT...
YOU'RE PRETTY QUIET, JIMMY. SOMETHING WRONG? YOU GOT THE PICTURES OKAY, RIGHT?
I GOT 'EM. EVEN TOOK SOME NOTES, I'LL WRITE 'EM UP AT THE OFFICE.
THEN WHAT'S WRONG?
NOTHING'S WRONG, IT'S NOT--IT'S NOT LIKE THAT. I'VE JUST GOT SOME STUFF ON MY MIND, LATELY, SOME THINGS I'M TRYING TO FIGURE OUT.
HEY, MAYBE WE CAN TAKE IN A BALLGAME SATURDAY? JUST HANG OUT, TALK STUFF OVER?
SORRY, JIM. I'D LOVE TO IF I COULD, BUT WE'RE TAKING CHRIS TO SEE LOIS'S MOM THIS WEEKEND.
I'LL BE BACK SUNDAY NIGHT, THOUGH? WANT TO GRAB A BITE MONDAY, AFTER WORK?
DON'T WORRY ABOUT IT. IT'S NO BIG DEAL.

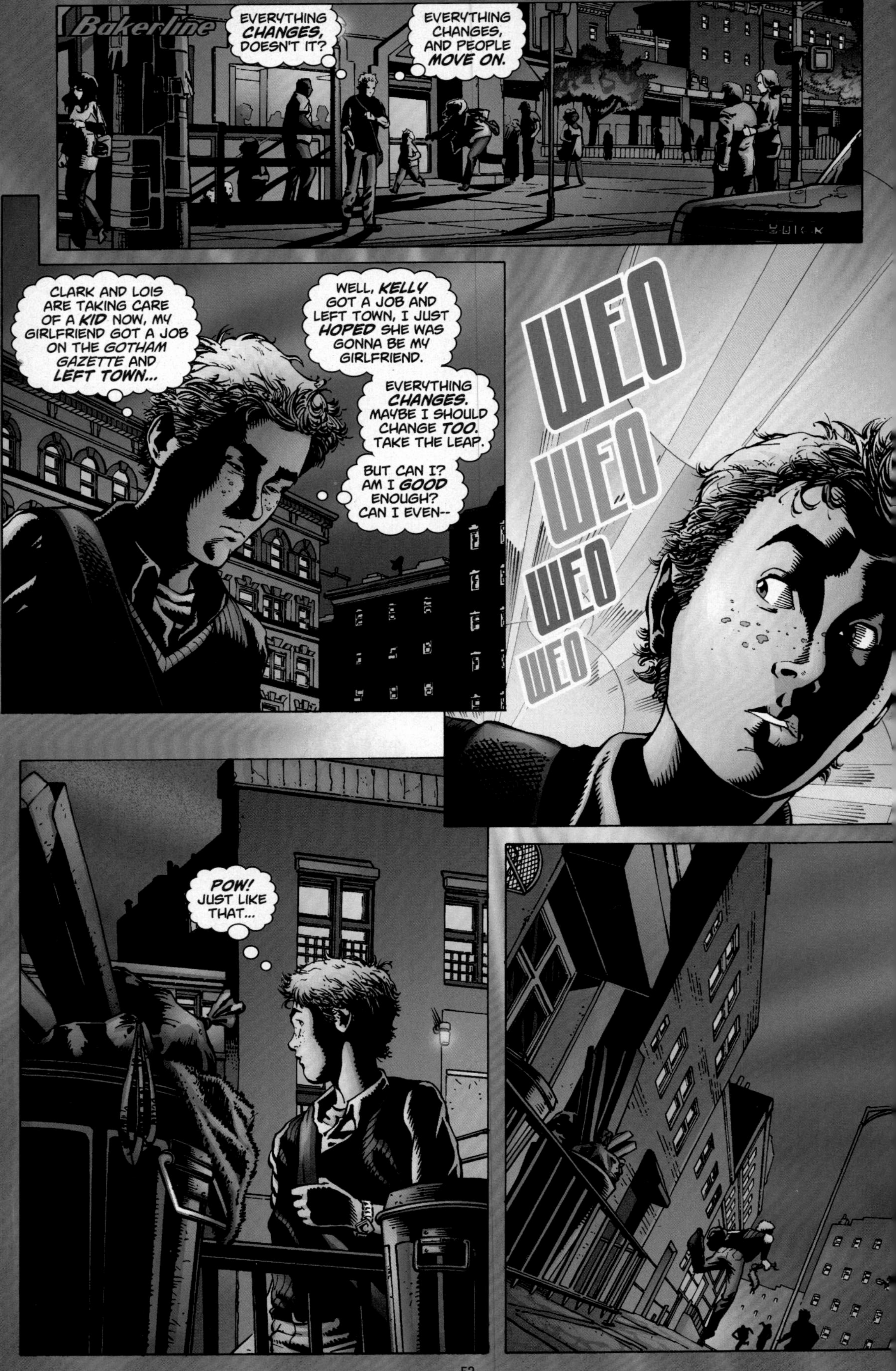
Bakerline
EVERYTHING CHANGES, DOESN'T IT?
EVERYTHING CHANGES, AND PEOPLE MOVE ON.
BUICK
CLARK AND LOIS ARE TAKING CARE OF A KID NOW, MY GIRLFRIEND GOT A JOB ON THE GOTHAM GAZETTE AND LEFT TOWN...
WELL, KELLY GOT A JOB AND LEFT TOWN, I JUST HOPED SHE WAS GONNA BE MY GIRLFRIEND.
EVERYTHING CHANGES. MAYBE I SHOULD CHANGE TOO. TAKE THE LEAP.
BUT CAN I? AM I GOOD ENOUGH? CAN I EVEN--
WEO
WEO
WEO
WEO
POW! JUST LIKE THAT...

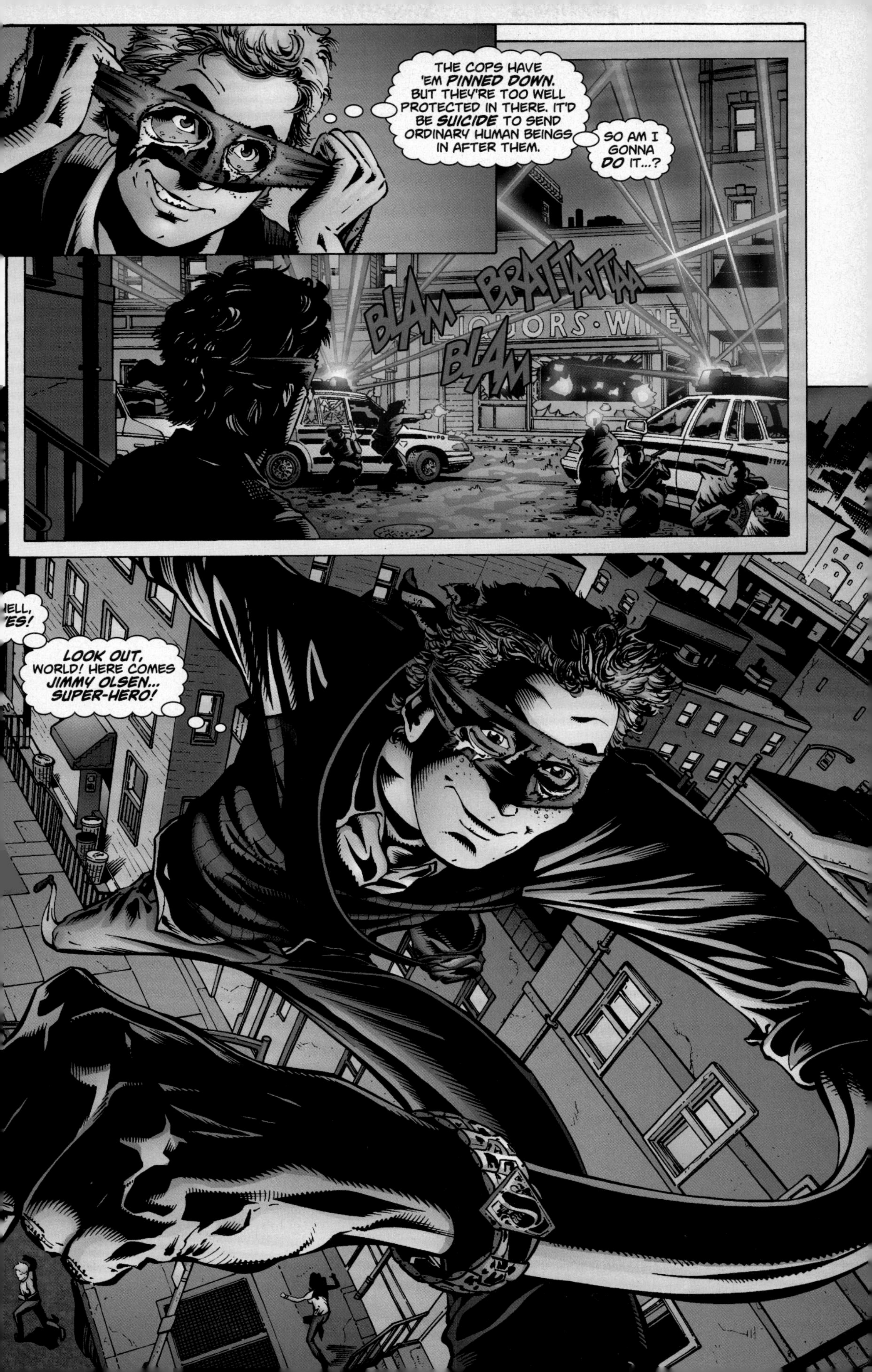
THE COPS HAVE 'EM PINNED DOWN. BUT THEY'RE TOO WELL PROTECTED IN THERE. IT'D BE SUICIDE TO SEND ORDINARY HUMAN BEINGS IN AFTER THEM.
SO AM I GONNA DO IT...?
BLAM
BRATTATTAA
BLAM
LIQUORS · WINE
LOOK OUT, WORLD! HERE COMES JIMMY OLSEN... SUPER-HERO!

ACTION COMICS 853 Cover art by Brad Walker and John Livesay Coloring by Pete Pantazis

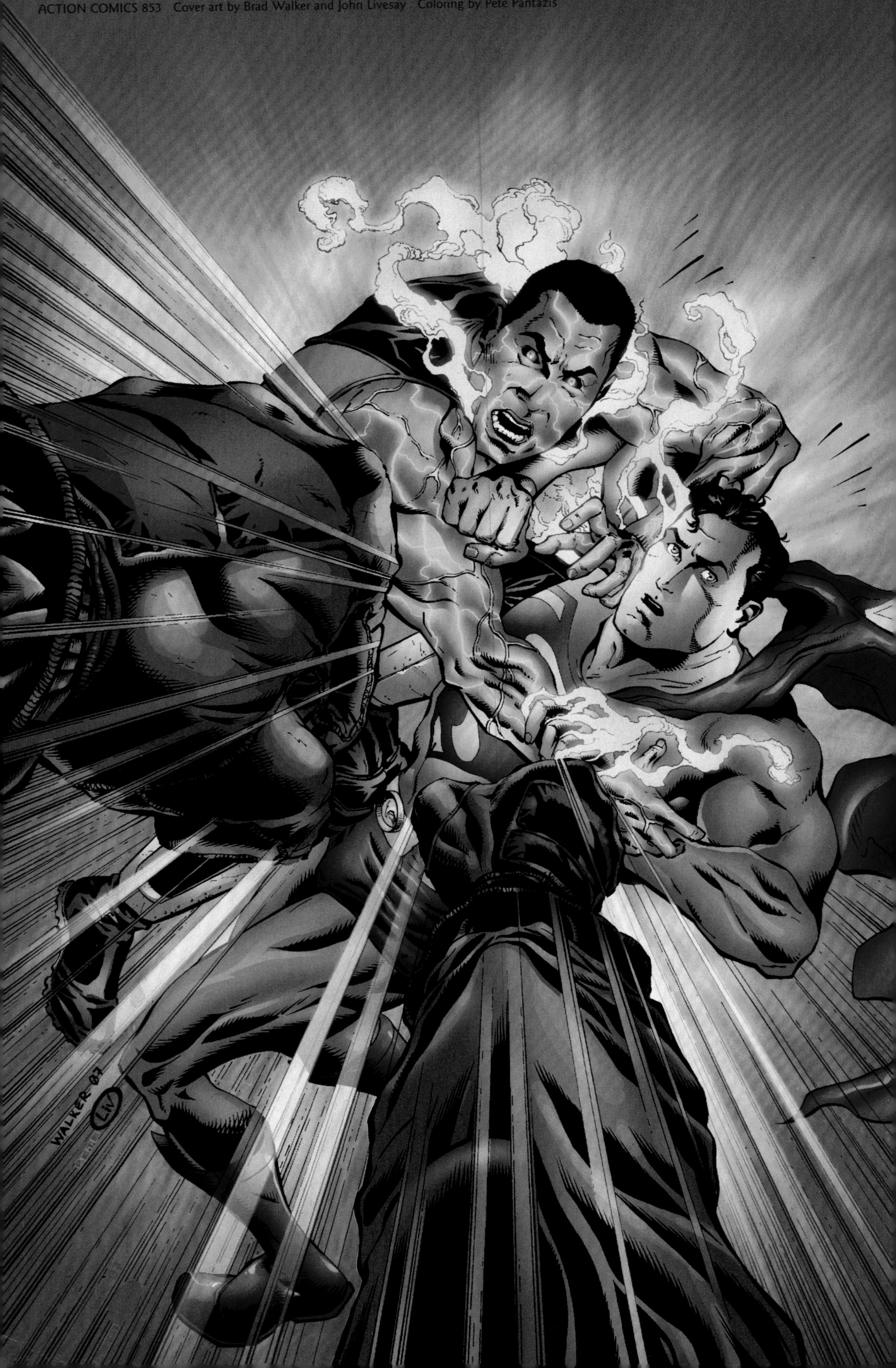
WALKER 07

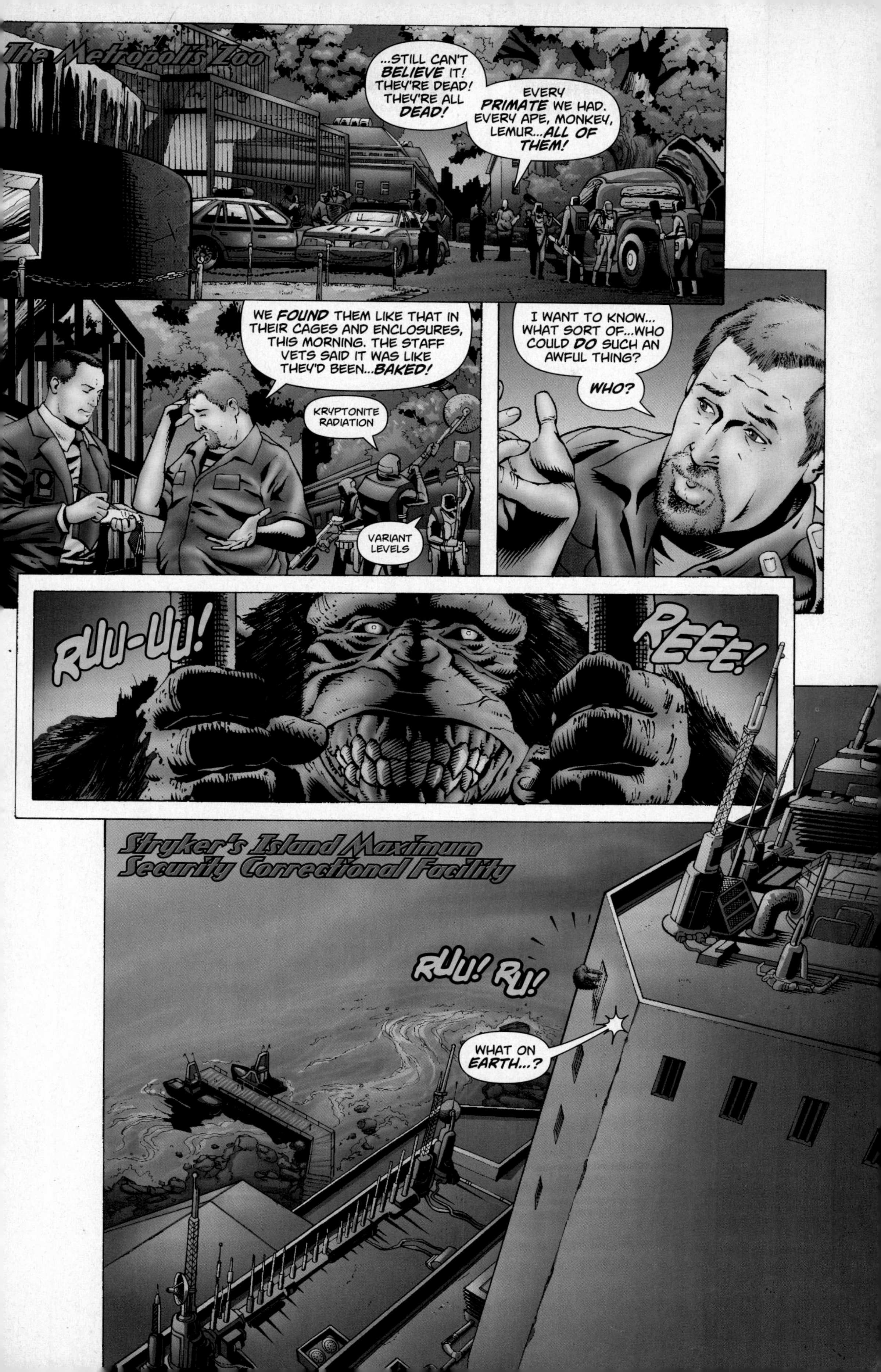
The Metropolis Zoo
...STILL CAN'T BELIEVE IT! THEY'RE DEAD! THEY'RE ALL DEAD!
EVERY PRIMATE WE HAD. EVERY APE, MONKEY, LEMUR...ALL OF THEM!
WE FOUND THEM LIKE THAT IN THEIR CAGES AND ENCLOSURES, THIS MORNING. THE STAFF VETS SAID IT WAS LIKE THEY'D BEEN...BAKED!
KRYPTONITE RADIATION
VARIANT LEVELS
I WANT TO KNOW... WHAT SORT OF...WHO COULD DO SUCH AN AWFUL THING?
WHO?
RUU-UU!
REEE!
Stryker's Island Maximum Security Correctional Facility
RUU! RU!
WHAT ON EARTH...?

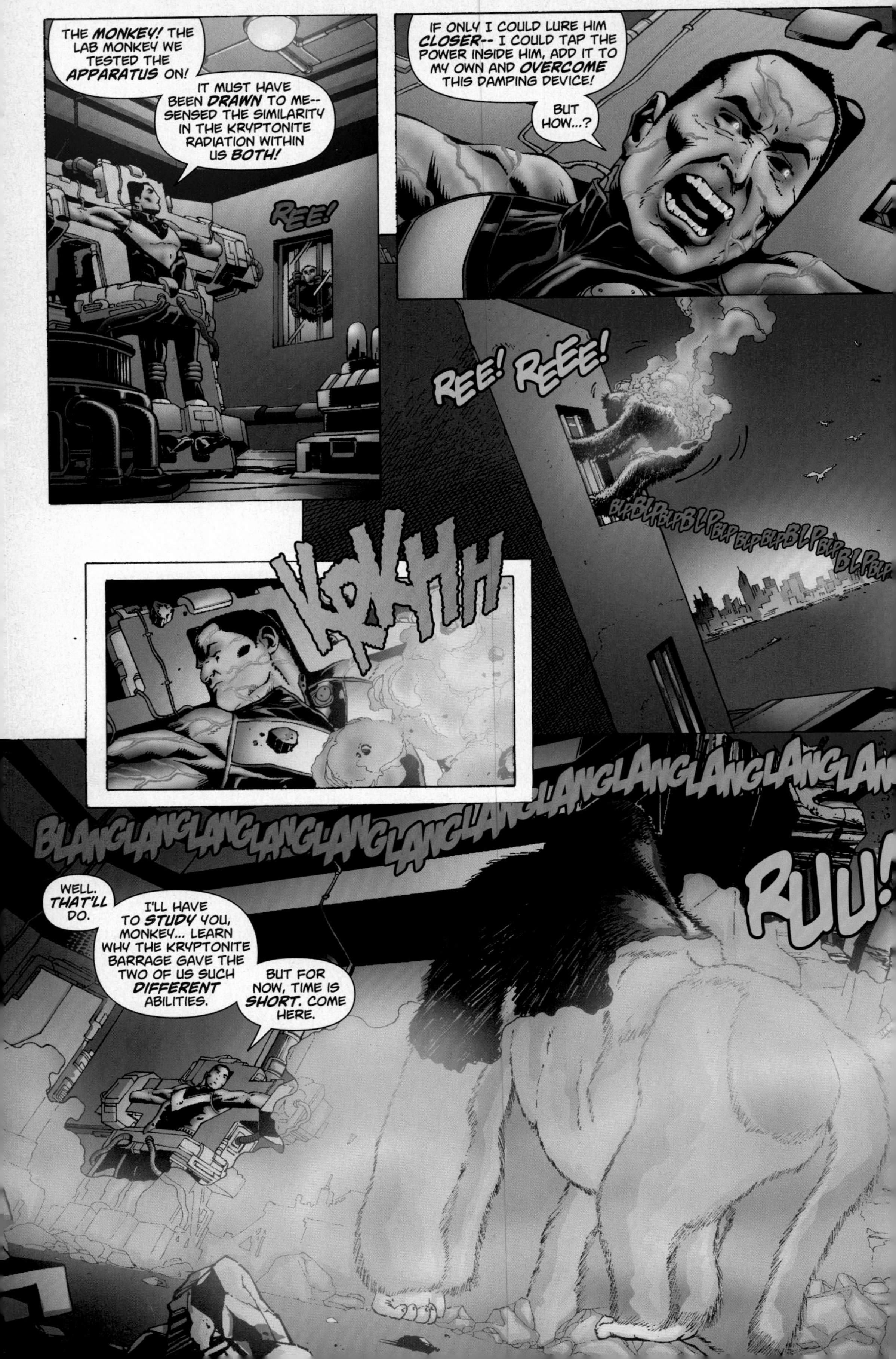
THE MONKEY! THE LAB MONKEY WE TESTED THE APPARATUS ON!
IT MUST HAVE BEEN DRAWN TO ME-- SENSED THE SIMILARITY IN THE KRYPTONITE RADIATION WITHIN US BOTH!
REE!
IF ONLY I COULD LURE HIM CLOSER-- I COULD TAP THE POWER INSIDE HIM, ADD IT TO MY OWN AND OVERCOME THIS DAMPING DEVICE!
BUT HOW...?
REE! REEE!
BLPBLPBLPBLPBLPBLPBLPBLPBLPBLP
VOKHH
BLANGLANGLANGLANGLANGLANGLANGLANGLANGLANGLANGLANG
RUU!?
WELL. THAT'LL DO.
I'LL HAVE TO STUDY YOU, MONKEY... LEARN WHY THE KRYPTONITE BARRAGE GAVE THE TWO OF US SUCH DIFFERENT ABILITIES.
BUT FOR NOW, TIME IS SHORT. COME HERE.

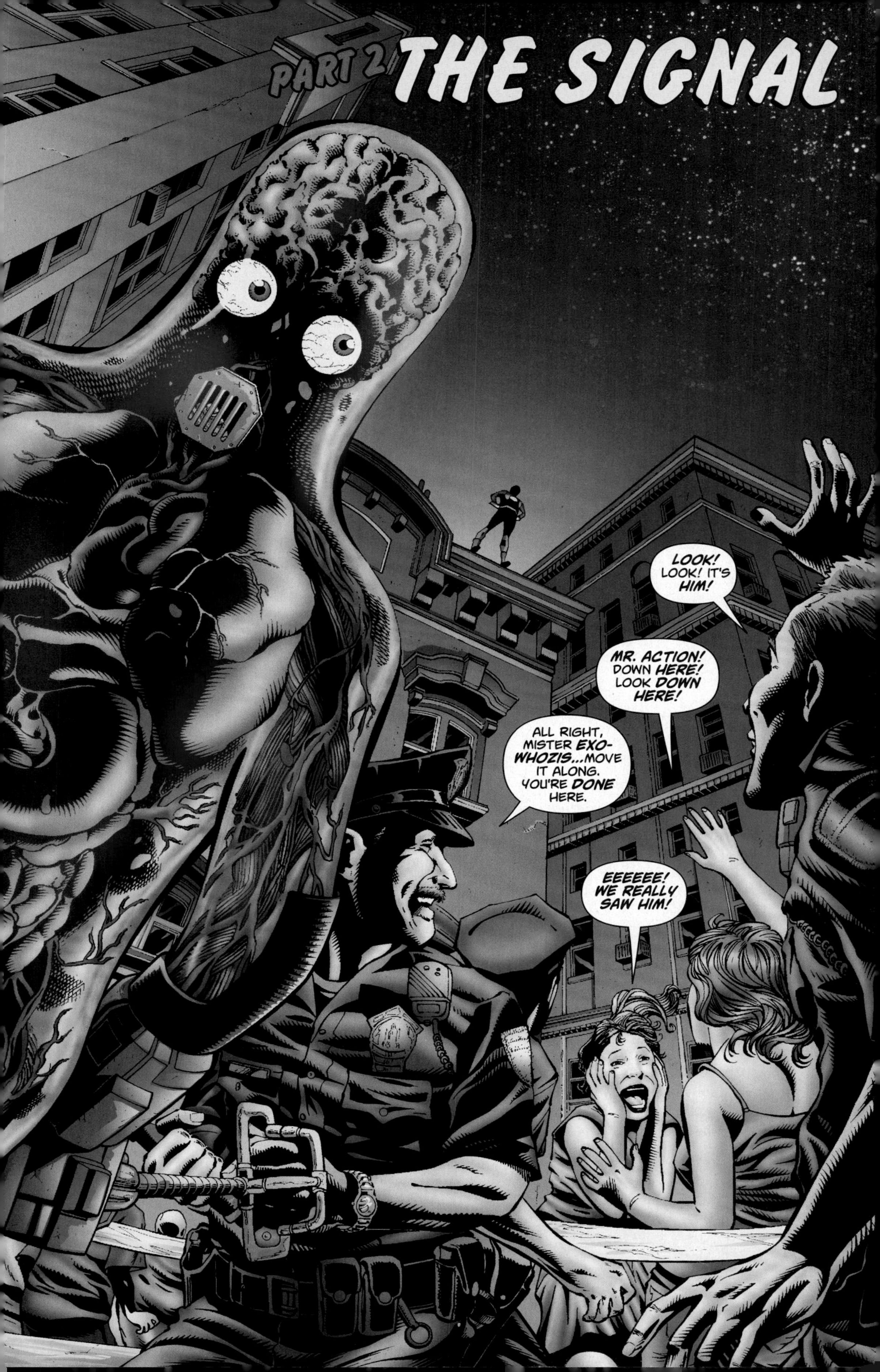
PART 2 THE SIGNAL
LOOK! LOOK! IT'S HIM!
MR. ACTION! DOWN HERE! LOOK DOWN HERE!
ALL RIGHT, MISTER EXO-WHOZIS...MOVE IT ALONG. YOU'RE DONE HERE.
EEEEEE! WE REALLY SAW HIM!

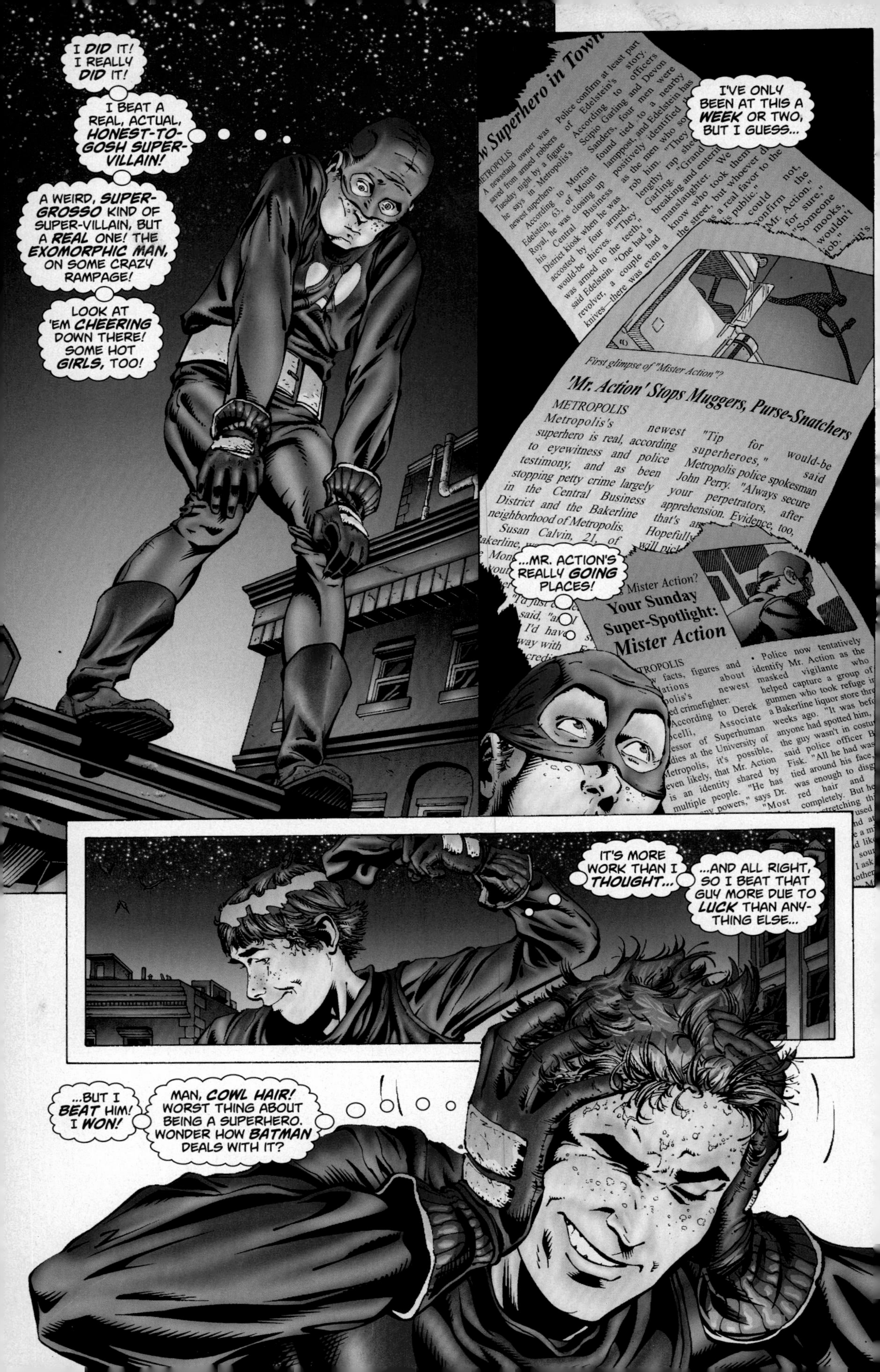

I DID IT! I REALLY DID IT!
I BEAT A REAL, ACTUAL, HONEST-TO-GOSH SUPER-VILLAIN!
A WEIRD, SUPER-GROSSO KIND OF SUPER-VILLAIN, BUT A REAL ONE! THE EXOMORPHIC MAN, ON SOME CRAZY RAMPAGE!
LOOK AT 'EM CHEERING DOWN THERE! SOME HOT GIRLS, TOO!
I'VE ONLY BEEN AT THIS A WEEK OR TWO, BUT I GUESS...
First glimpse of "Mister Action"?
'Mr. Action' Stops Muggers, Purse-Snatchers
...MR. ACTION'S REALLY GOING PLACES!
Your Sunday Super-Spotlight: Mister Action
IT'S MORE WORK THAN I THOUGHT...
...AND ALL RIGHT, SO I BEAT THAT GUY MORE DUE TO LUCK THAN ANYTHING ELSE...
...BUT I BEAT HIM! I WON!
MAN, COWL HAIR! WORST THING ABOUT BEING A SUPERHERO. WONDER HOW BATMAN DEALS WITH IT?

I JUST WISH... NOPE, NO STRETCHY-ARM...I WISH I KNEW WHY MY POWERS KEPT **DESERTING** ME.

THEY'RE ALWAYS THERE WHEN I NEED 'EM. WEIRD, **UNPREDICTABLE**, BUT THERE. BUT **OTHER** TIMES, IT'S LIKE THEY NEVER EXISTED AT ALL.

AND THAT'S NOT THE **ONLY** WEIRD THING ABOUT BEING MR. ACTION.

I **KNOW** THINGS. I KNOW WHO **ROBIN** REALLY IS...WHO **ALL** THE ROBINS WERE.

I KNOW **WONDER WOMAN** IS REALLY DIANA PRINCE OF THE **DEPARTMENT OF METAHUMAN AFFAIRS**.

I KNOW THE LOCATIONS OF AT LEAST SEVEN OF LEX LUTHOR'S **HIDDEN LAIRS** UNDER THE STREETS OF METROPOLIS.

Garden Ave.
Bessolo Blvd.
Clinton
Severn
Treadwell
Dillingham
Olmstead
Burnley
Endicott
St. Jerome's
Market
Calavaras
Collyer

BUT I DON'T KNOW HOW I KNOW **ANY** OF THAT, OR SO MANY OTHER THINGS. LIKE **WHY**, WHENEVER I THINK ABOUT SUPERMAN...

...I GET THIS IMAGE OF **LOIS** AND **CLARK**. I MEAN, THEY'RE HIS FRIENDS **TOO**, BUT...

AND FOR THAT MATTER, WHERE THE HECK DO SUPERHEROES KEEP THEIR **CLOTHES** WHEN THEY GO INTO ACTION?!

WHAT HAPPENS IF THEY FINISH THE FIGHT **SOME-WHERE ELSE?**

HOW DO THEY **CLEAN** THEIR OUTFITS?

DAILY PLANET
VEGA HONORS SUPER
Tiny Island Principality Weathered
Tropical Storm Thanks to Super-Aid

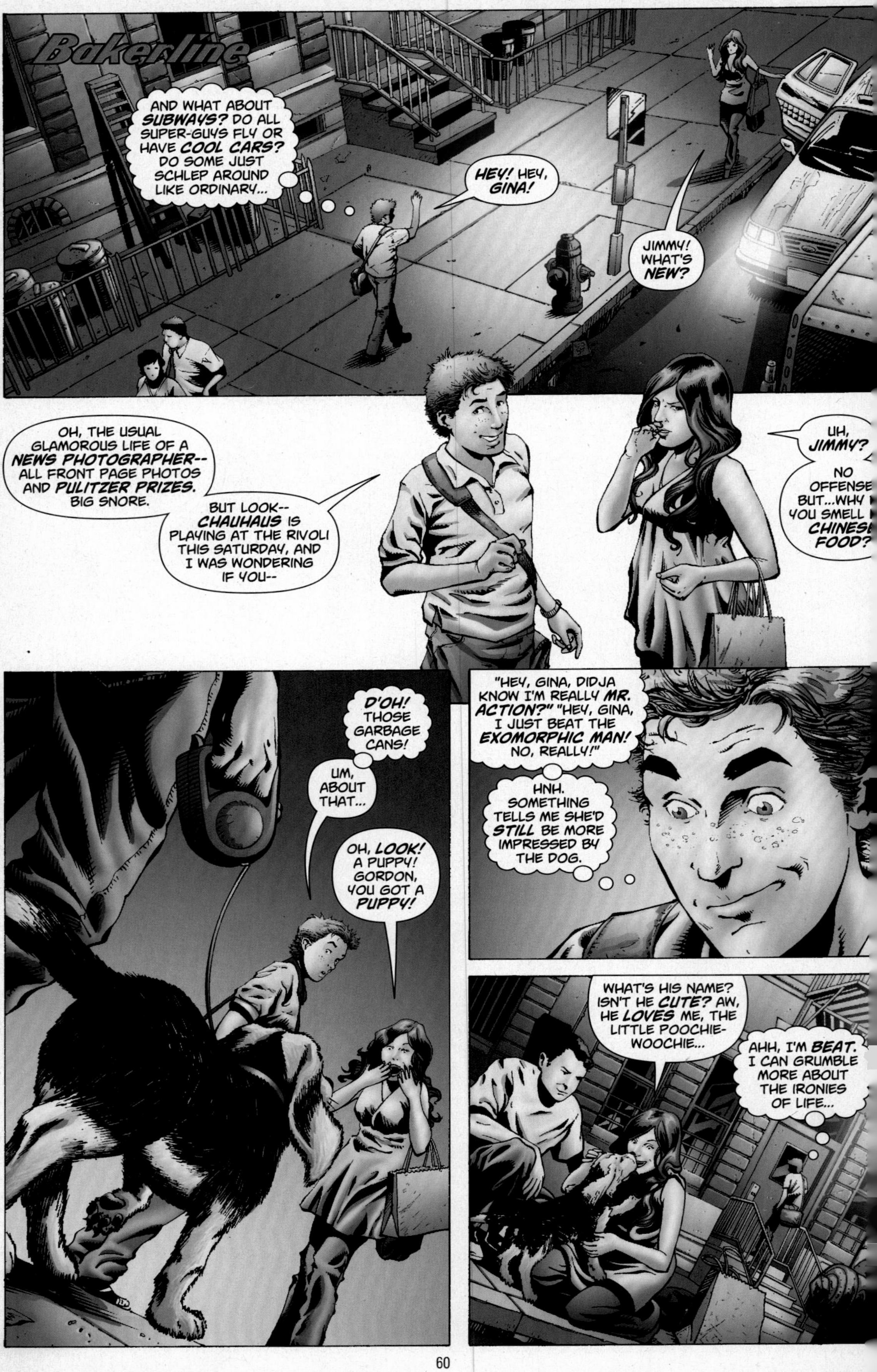

Bakerline
AND WHAT ABOUT SUBWAYS? DO ALL SUPER-GUYS FLY OR HAVE COOL CARS? DO SOME JUST SCHLEP AROUND LIKE ORDINARY...
HEY! HEY, GINA!
JIMMY! WHAT'S NEW?
OH, THE USUAL GLAMOROUS LIFE OF A NEWS PHOTOGRAPHER-- ALL FRONT PAGE PHOTOS AND PULITZER PRIZES. BIG SNORE.
BUT LOOK-- CHAUHAUS IS PLAYING AT THE RIVOLI THIS SATURDAY, AND I WAS WONDERING IF YOU--
UH, JIMMY?
NO OFFENSE BUT...WHY YOU SMELL CHINES FOOD?
D'OH! THOSE GARBAGE CANS!
UM, ABOUT THAT...
OH, LOOK! A PUPPY! GORDON, YOU GOT A PUPPY!
"HEY, GINA, DIDJA KNOW I'M REALLY MR. ACTION?" "HEY, GINA, I JUST BEAT THE EXOMORPHIC MAN! NO, REALLY!"
HNH. SOMETHING TELLS ME SHE'D STILL BE MORE IMPRESSED BY THE DOG.
WHAT'S HIS NAME? ISN'T HE CUTE? AW, HE LOVES ME, THE LITTLE POOCHIE-WOOCHIE...
AHH, I'M BEAT. I CAN GRUMBLE MORE ABOUT THE IRONIES OF LIFE...

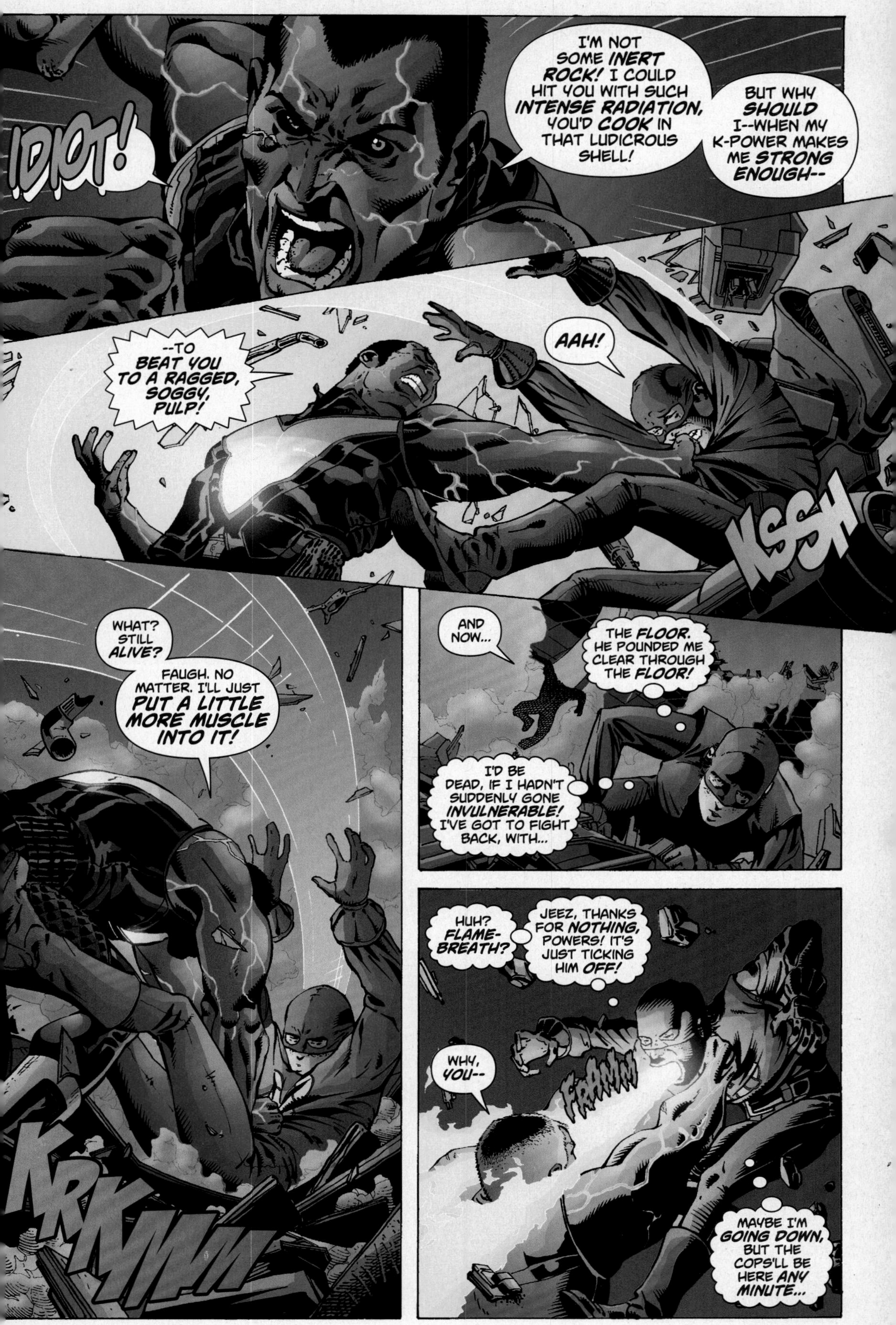
IDIOT!
I'M NOT SOME INERT ROCK! I COULD HIT YOU WITH SUCH INTENSE RADIATION, YOU'D COOK IN THAT LUDICROUS SHELL!
BUT WHY SHOULD I--WHEN MY K-POWER MAKES ME STRONG ENOUGH--
--TO BEAT YOU TO A RAGGED, SOGGY, PULP!
AAH!
KSSH
WHAT? STILL ALIVE?
FAUGH. NO MATTER. I'LL JUST PUT A LITTLE MORE MUSCLE INTO IT!
KRKWM
AND NOW...
THE FLOOR. HE POUNDED ME CLEAR THROUGH THE FLOOR!
I'D BE DEAD, IF I HADN'T SUDDENLY GONE INVULNERABLE! I'VE GOT TO FIGHT BACK, WITH...
HUH? FLAME-BREATH?
JEEZ, THANKS FOR NOTHING, POWERS! IT'S JUST TICKING HIM OFF!
WHY, YOU--
FRAWM
MAYBE I'M GOING DOWN, BUT THE COPS'LL BE HERE ANY MINUTE...

"...THAT *WEEDY-LOOKING GUY* MUST HAVE REACHED THEM *LONG AGO*..."

THIS MAN'S SUFFERING FROM *RADIATION POISONING!*

SOMEONE CALL AN *AMBULANCE! NOW!*

WELL. NOT SO MUCH OF A CHALLENGE *AFTER ALL*, MISTER SUPER-WHATEVER. LET'S HAVE A *LOOK* AT YOU.

NO, I DON'T *RECOGNIZE* HIM *EITHER*. I THOUGHT SUPERHEROES WERE SUPPOSED TO BE *WEALTHY*, JET-SETTING YOUNG *GADABOUTS*.

RH?

NNH... GEIGER-COUNTER POWERS...

NO GOO

ON THE OTHER HAND, I WOULDN'T RECOGNIZE *TOM CRUISE* IF HE BIT ME--IT'S NOT AS IF I PAY *ATTENTION* TO CELEBRITY.

STILL, THIS MORON'S BOUND TO BE WORTH *SOMETHING*, TO SOMEBODY.

AND IF NOBODY WI RANSOM HIM, STILL USEFUL ONLY AS A L EXPERIMENT NEED TO B WASTEFUL

WHAT IS *WITH* THIS GUY? ONE MINUTE, HE'S ALL, "*AH KEE YU!*" AND THE NEXT, HE'S TUCKING ME AWAY FOR A *RAINY DAY*.

H-HEY...

WAIT *HERE*, YOU.

NOT THAT I'M COMPLAINING, OF COURSE.

BUT NOBODY'S GOING TO PAY RANSOM FOR "*MIST ACTION*," AND THER NO SIGN OF THE CO I'M PRETTY WELL *DEAD*, UNLESS...

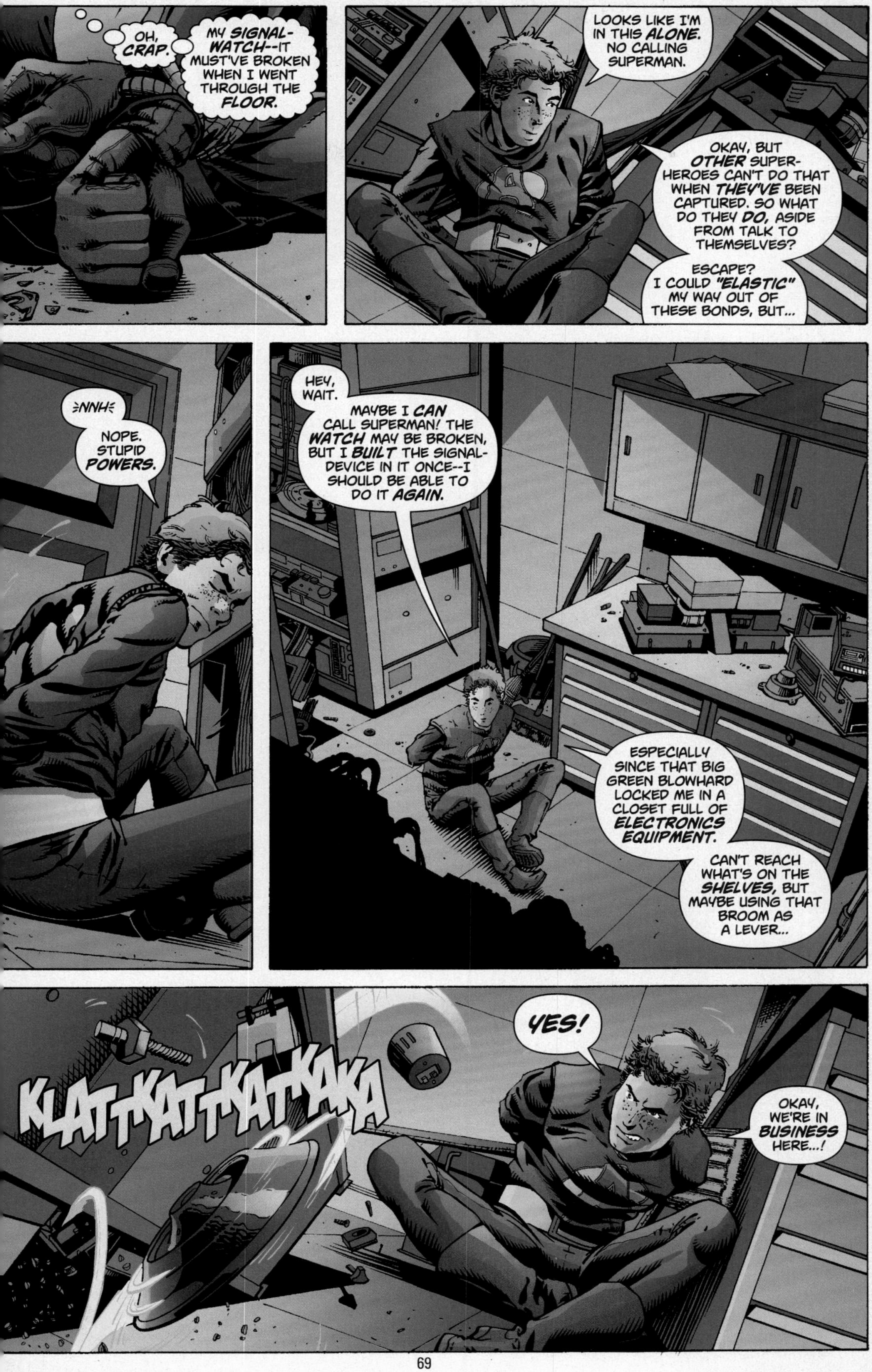
OH, CRAP.
MY SIGNAL-WATCH--IT MUST'VE BROKEN WHEN I WENT THROUGH THE FLOOR.
LOOKS LIKE I'M IN THIS ALONE. NO CALLING SUPERMAN.
OKAY, BUT OTHER SUPER-HEROES CAN'T DO THAT WHEN THEY'VE BEEN CAPTURED. SO WHAT DO THEY DO, ASIDE FROM TALK TO THEMSELVES?
ESCAPE? I COULD "ELASTIC" MY WAY OUT OF THESE BONDS, BUT...
NNH
NOPE. STUPID POWERS.
HEY, WAIT.
MAYBE I CAN CALL SUPERMAN! THE WATCH MAY BE BROKEN, BUT I BUILT THE SIGNAL-DEVICE IN IT ONCE--I SHOULD BE ABLE TO DO IT AGAIN.
ESPECIALLY SINCE THAT BIG GREEN BLOWHARD LOCKED ME IN A CLOSET FULL OF ELECTRONICS EQUIPMENT.
CAN'T REACH WHAT'S ON THE SHELVES, BUT MAYBE USING THAT BROOM AS A LEVER...
KLATTKATTKATKAKA
YES!
OKAY, WE'RE IN BUSINESS HERE...!

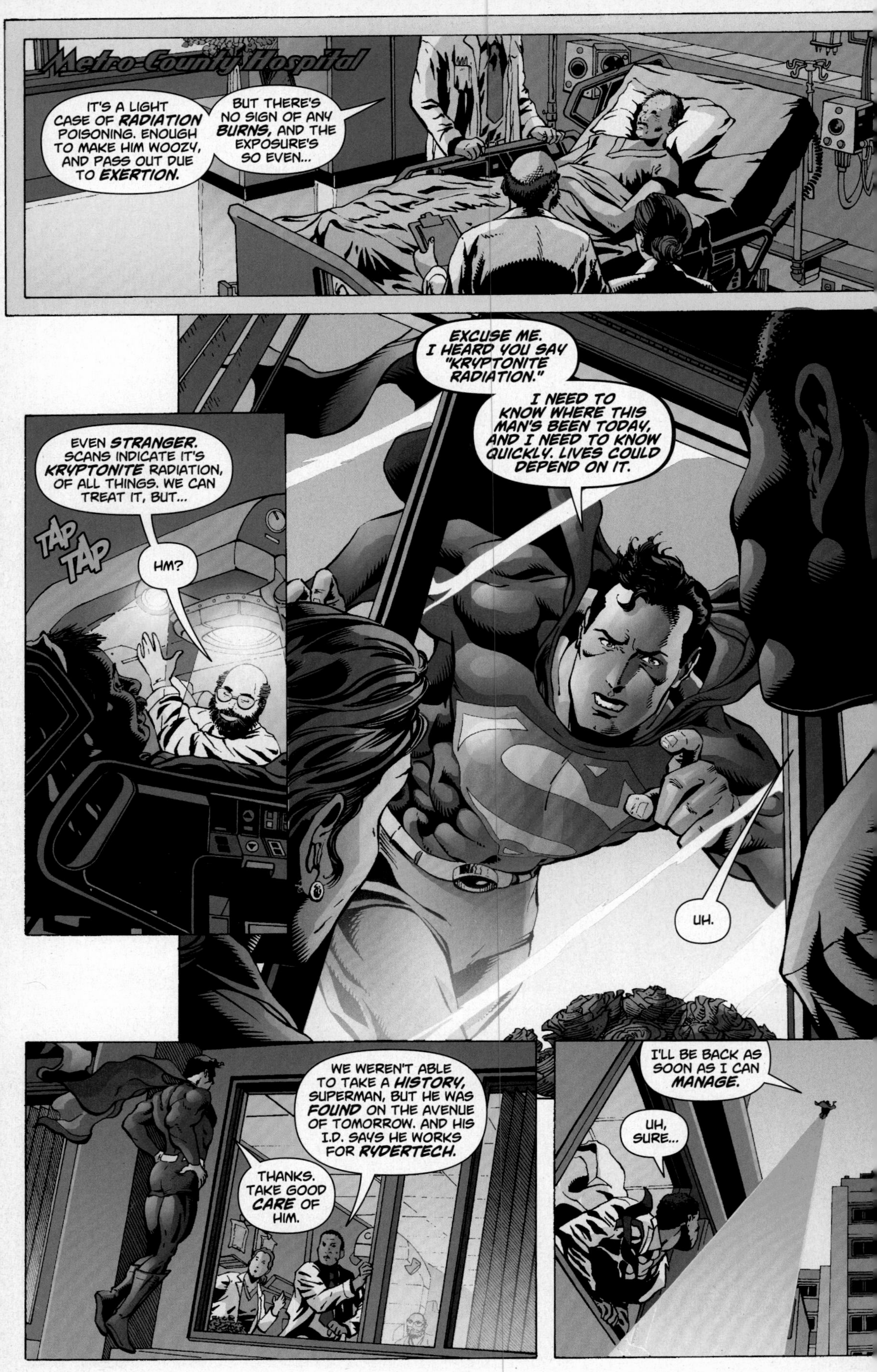
Metro-County Hospital
IT'S A LIGHT CASE OF RADIATION POISONING. ENOUGH TO MAKE HIM WOOZY, AND PASS OUT DUE TO EXERTION.
BUT THERE'S NO SIGN OF ANY BURNS, AND THE EXPOSURE'S SO EVEN...
EVEN STRANGER. SCANS INDICATE IT'S KRYPTONITE RADIATION, OF ALL THINGS. WE CAN TREAT IT, BUT...
TAP TAP
HM?
EXCUSE ME. I HEARD YOU SAY "KRYPTONITE RADIATION."
I NEED TO KNOW WHERE THIS MAN'S BEEN TODAY, AND I NEED TO KNOW QUICKLY. LIVES COULD DEPEND ON IT.
UH.
WE WEREN'T ABLE TO TAKE A HISTORY, SUPERMAN, BUT HE WAS FOUND ON THE AVENUE OF TOMORROW. AND HIS I.D. SAYS HE WORKS FOR RYDERTECH.
THANKS. TAKE GOOD CARE OF HIM.
I'LL BE BACK AS SOON AS I CAN MANAGE.
UH, SURE...

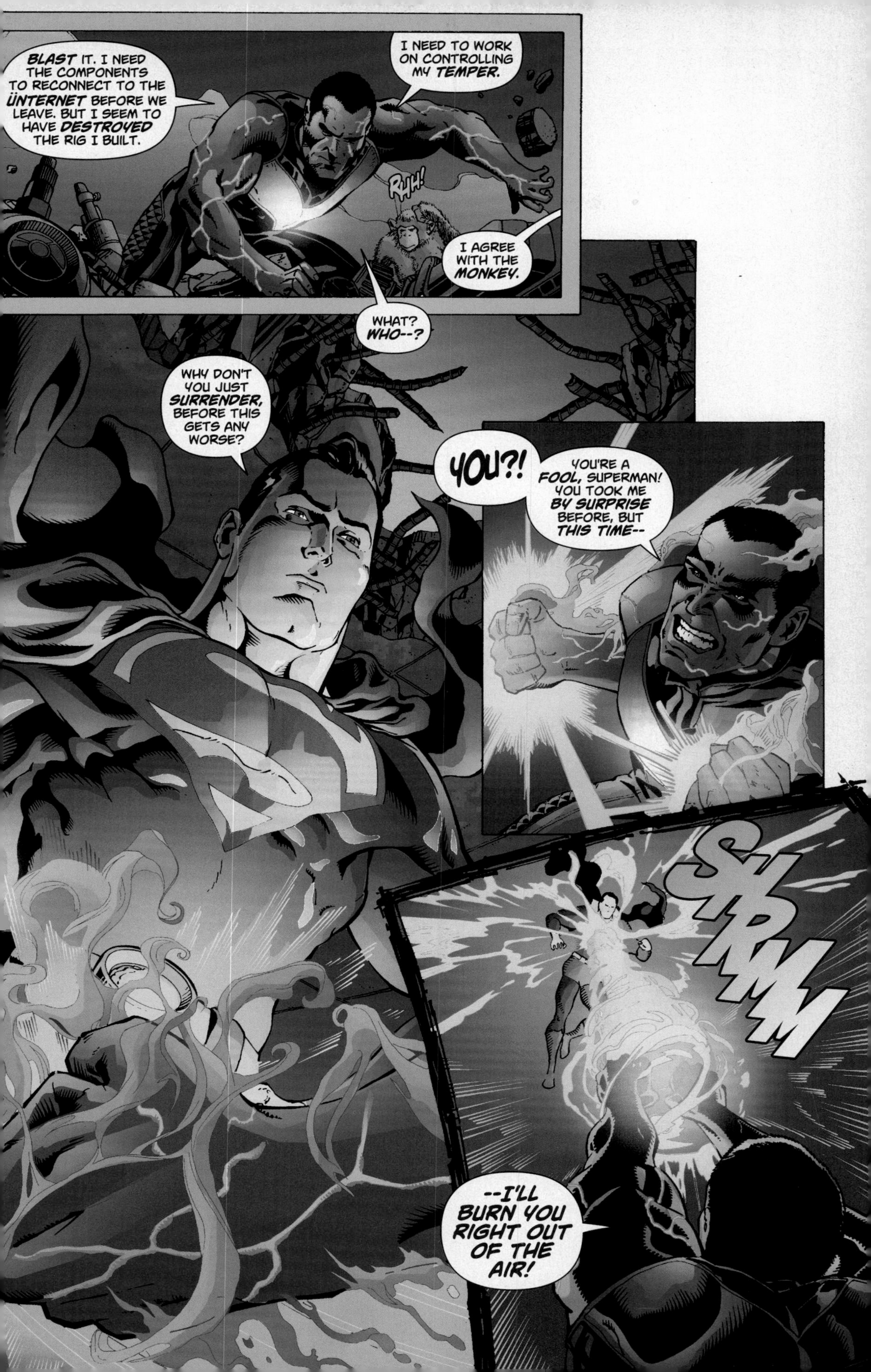

BLAST IT. I NEED THE COMPONENTS TO RECONNECT TO THE ÜNTERNET BEFORE WE LEAVE. BUT I SEEM TO HAVE DESTROYED THE RIG I BUILT.
I NEED TO WORK ON CONTROLLING MY TEMPER.
RHH!
I AGREE WITH THE MONKEY.
WHAT? WHO--?
WHY DON'T YOU JUST SURRENDER, BEFORE THIS GETS ANY WORSE?
YOU?!
YOU'RE A FOOL, SUPERMAN! YOU TOOK ME BY SURPRISE BEFORE, BUT THIS TIME--
SHRMM
--I'LL BURN YOU RIGHT OUT OF THE AIR!

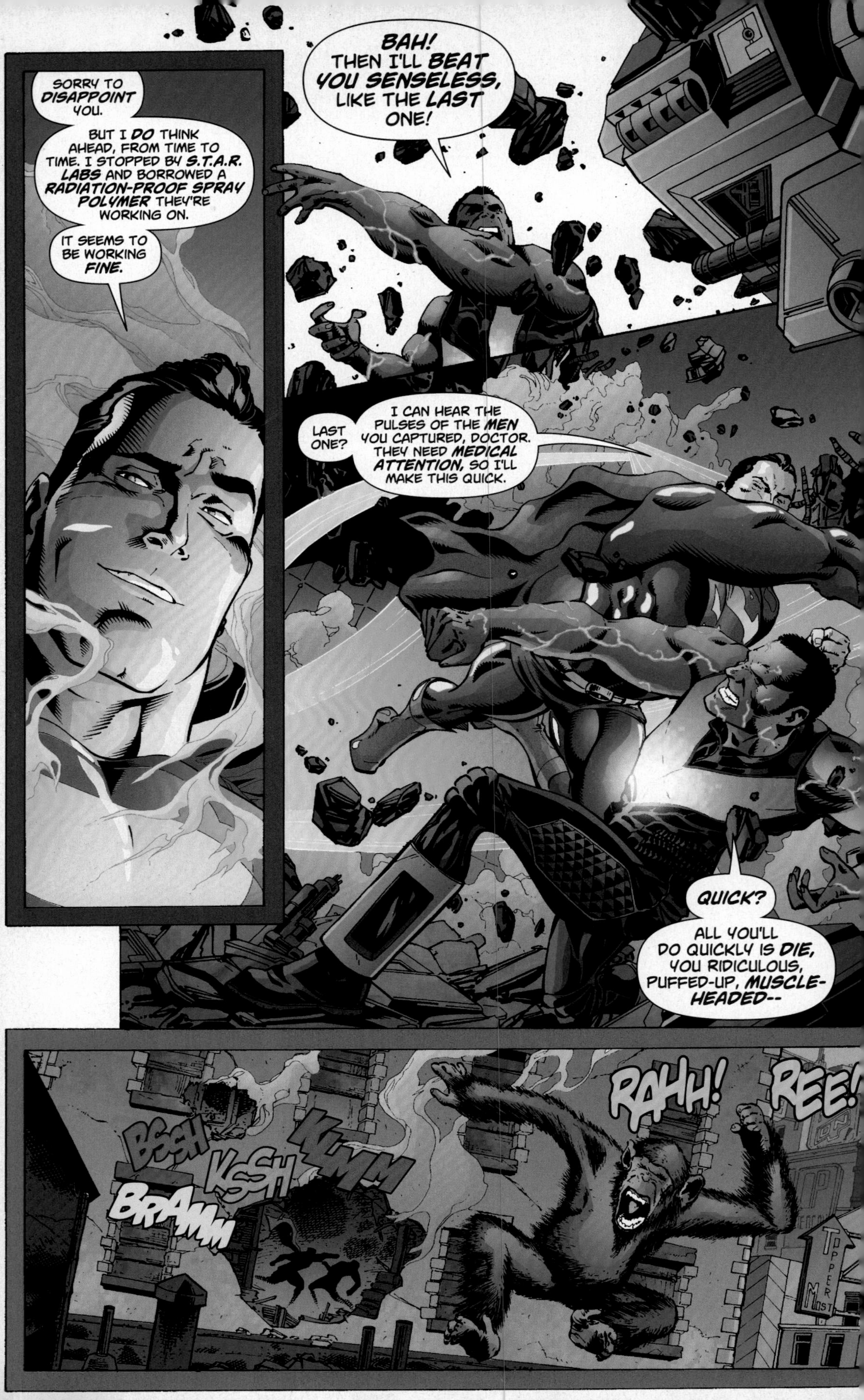

SORRY TO DISAPPOINT YOU.
BUT I DO THINK AHEAD, FROM TIME TO TIME. I STOPPED BY S.T.A.R. LABS AND BORROWED A RADIATION-PROOF SPRAY POLYMER THEY'RE WORKING ON.
IT SEEMS TO BE WORKING FINE.
BAH! THEN I'LL BEAT YOU SENSELESS, LIKE THE LAST ONE!
LAST ONE?
I CAN HEAR THE PULSES OF THE MEN YOU CAPTURED, DOCTOR. THEY NEED MEDICAL ATTENTION, SO I'LL MAKE THIS QUICK.
QUICK?
ALL YOU'LL DO QUICKLY IS DIE, YOU RIDICULOUS, PUFFED-UP, MUSCLE-HEADED--
BSSH
KSSH
WUMM
BRAMM
RAHH!
REE!
TOPPER MOST

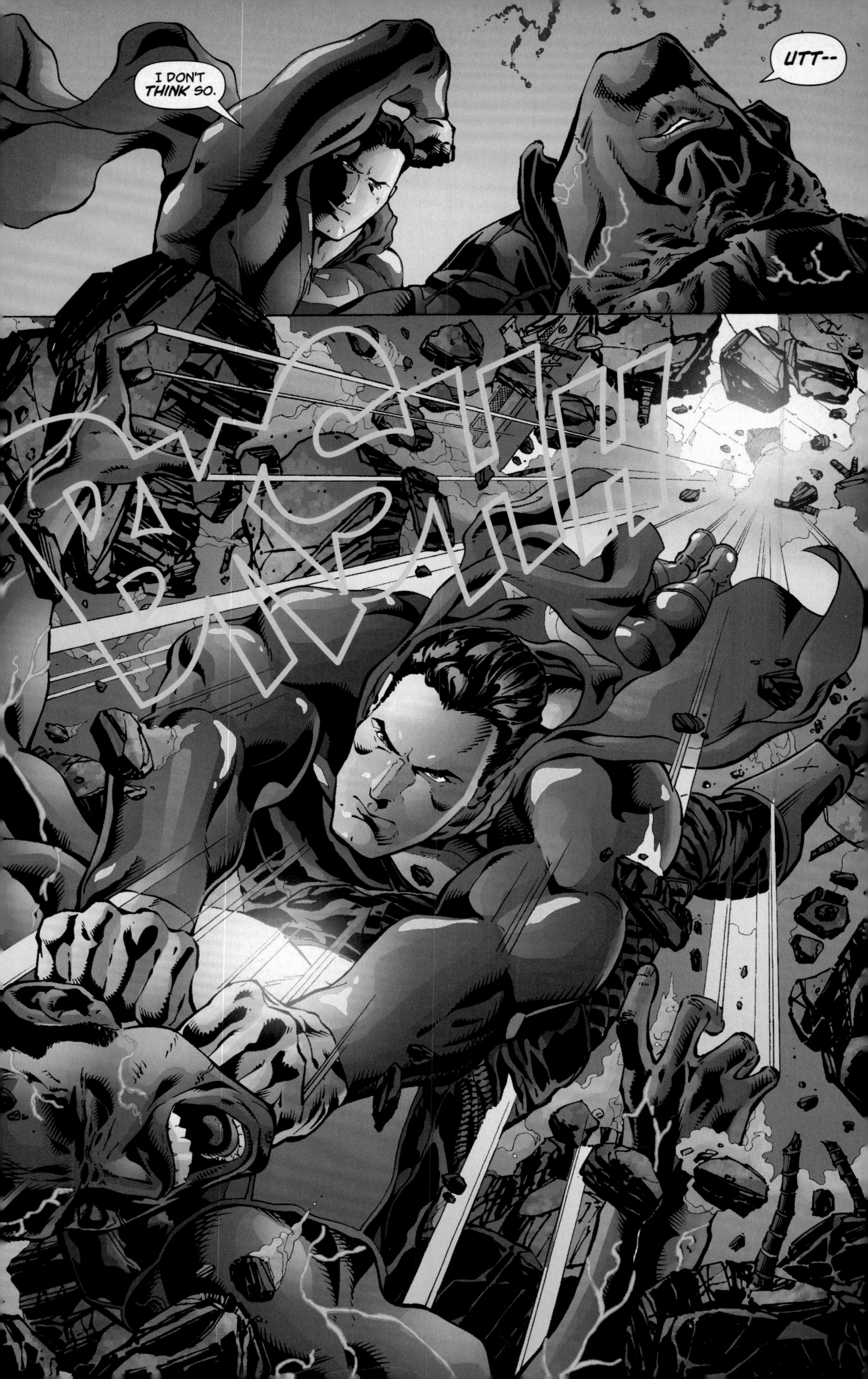
I DON'T THINK SO.
UTT--

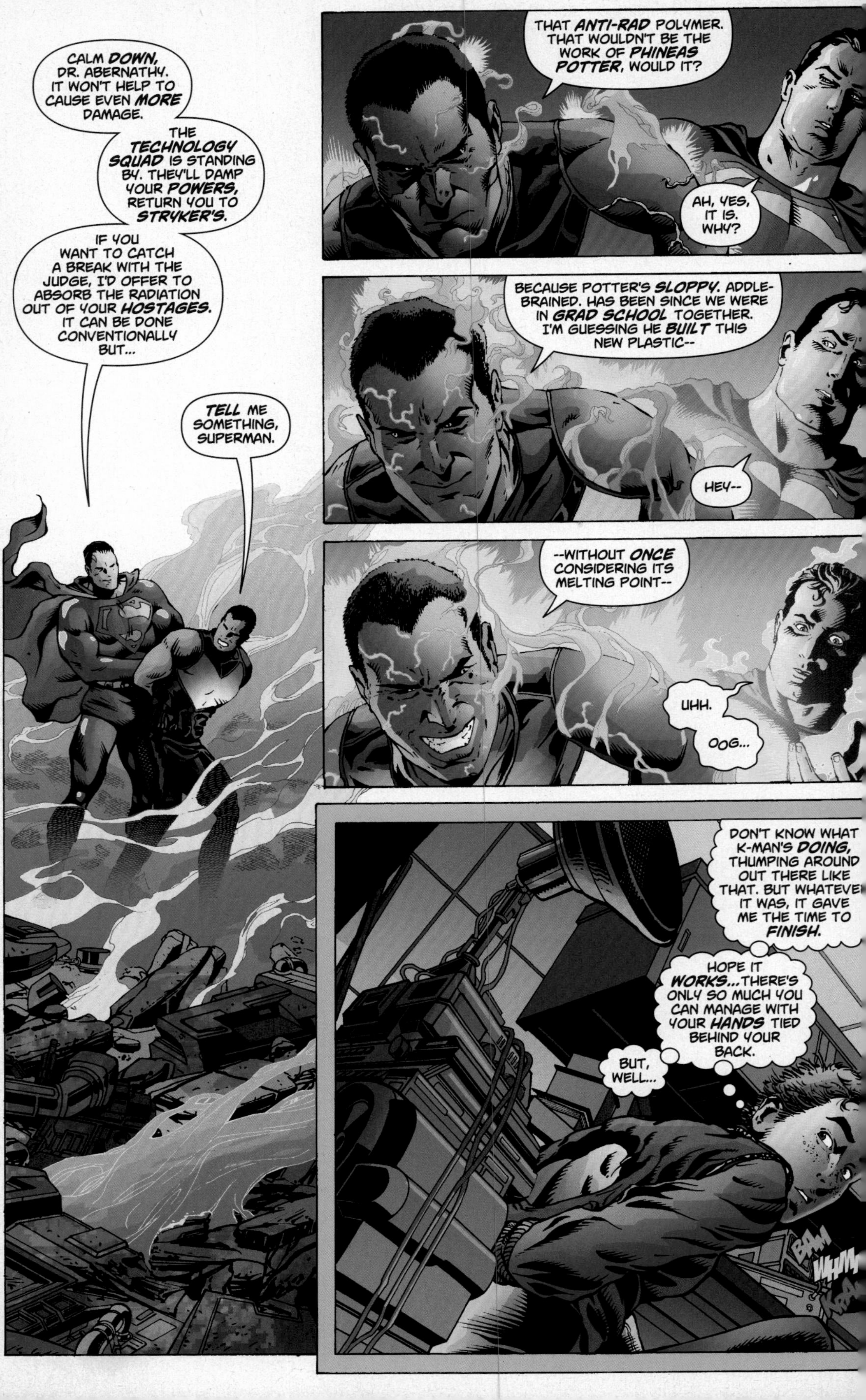

CALM DOWN, DR. ABERNATHY. IT WON'T HELP TO CAUSE EVEN MORE DAMAGE.
THE TECHNOLOGY SQUAD IS STANDING BY. THEY'LL DAMP YOUR POWERS, RETURN YOU TO STRYKER'S.
IF YOU WANT TO CATCH A BREAK WITH THE JUDGE, I'D OFFER TO ABSORB THE RADIATION OUT OF YOUR HOSTAGES. IT CAN BE DONE CONVENTIONALLY BUT...
TELL ME SOMETHING, SUPERMAN.
THAT ANTI-RAD POLYMER. THAT WOULDN'T BE THE WORK OF PHINEAS POTTER, WOULD IT?
AH, YES, IT IS. WHY?
BECAUSE POTTER'S SLOPPY. ADDLE-BRAINED. HAS BEEN SINCE WE WERE IN GRAD SCHOOL TOGETHER. I'M GUESSING HE BUILT THIS NEW PLASTIC--
HEY--
--WITHOUT ONCE CONSIDERING ITS MELTING POINT--
UHH.
OOG...
DON'T KNOW WHAT K-MAN'S DOING, THUMPING AROUND OUT THERE LIKE THAT. BUT WHATEVE IT WAS, IT GAVE ME THE TIME TO FINISH.
HOPE IT WORKS... THERE'S ONLY SO MUCH YOU CAN MANAGE WITH YOUR HANDS TIED BEHIND YOUR BACK.
BUT, WELL...
BAM

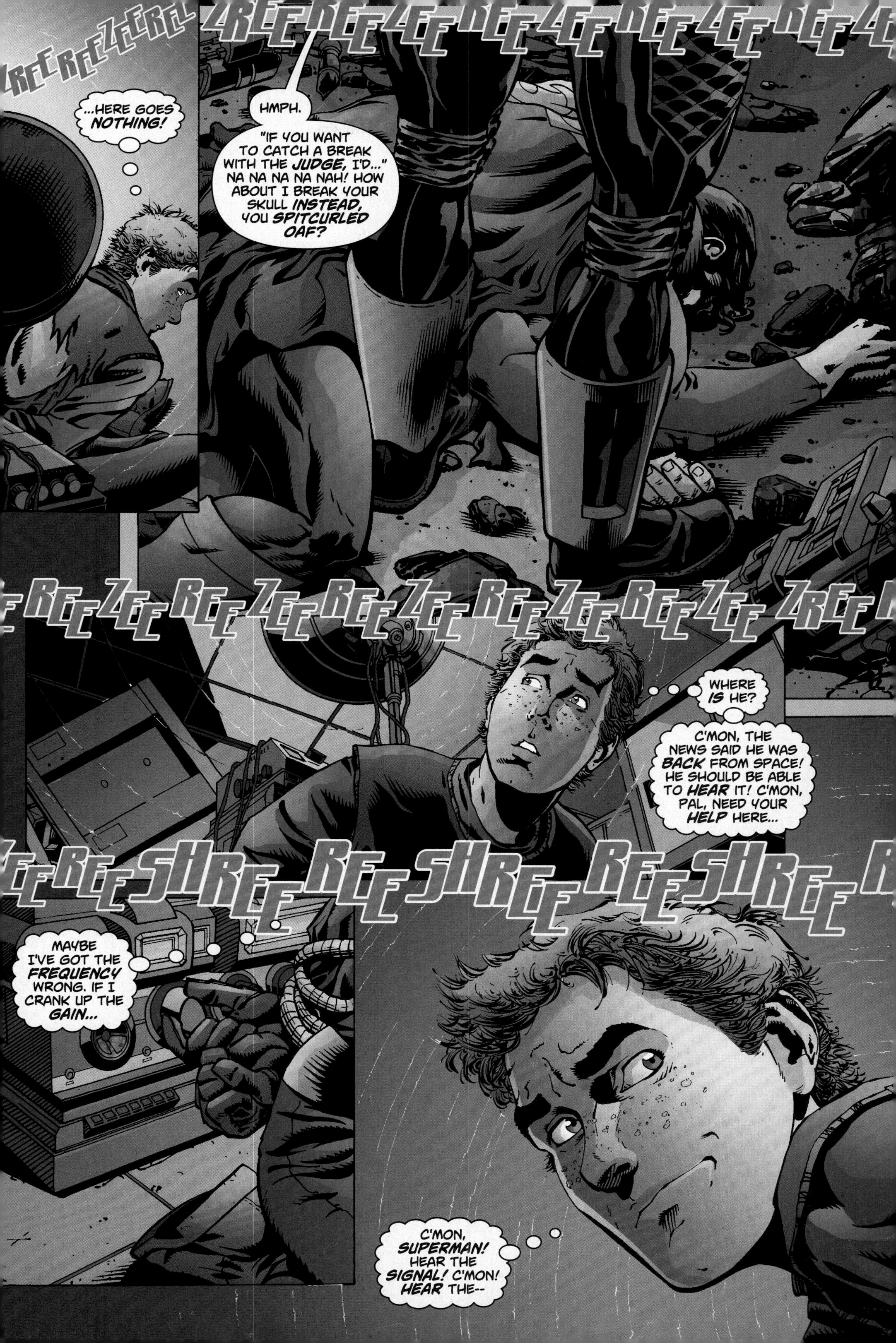
...HERE GOES NOTHING!
HMPH.
"IF YOU WANT TO CATCH A BREAK WITH THE JUDGE, I'D..." NA NA NA NA NAH! HOW ABOUT I BREAK YOUR SKULL INSTEAD, YOU SPITCURLED OAF?
WHERE IS HE?
C'MON, THE NEWS SAID HE WAS BACK FROM SPACE! HE SHOULD BE ABLE TO HEAR IT! C'MON, PAL, NEED YOUR HELP HERE...
MAYBE I'VE GOT THE FREQUENCY WRONG. IF I CRANK UP THE GAIN...
C'MON, SUPERMAN! HEAR THE SIGNAL! C'MON! HEAR THE--

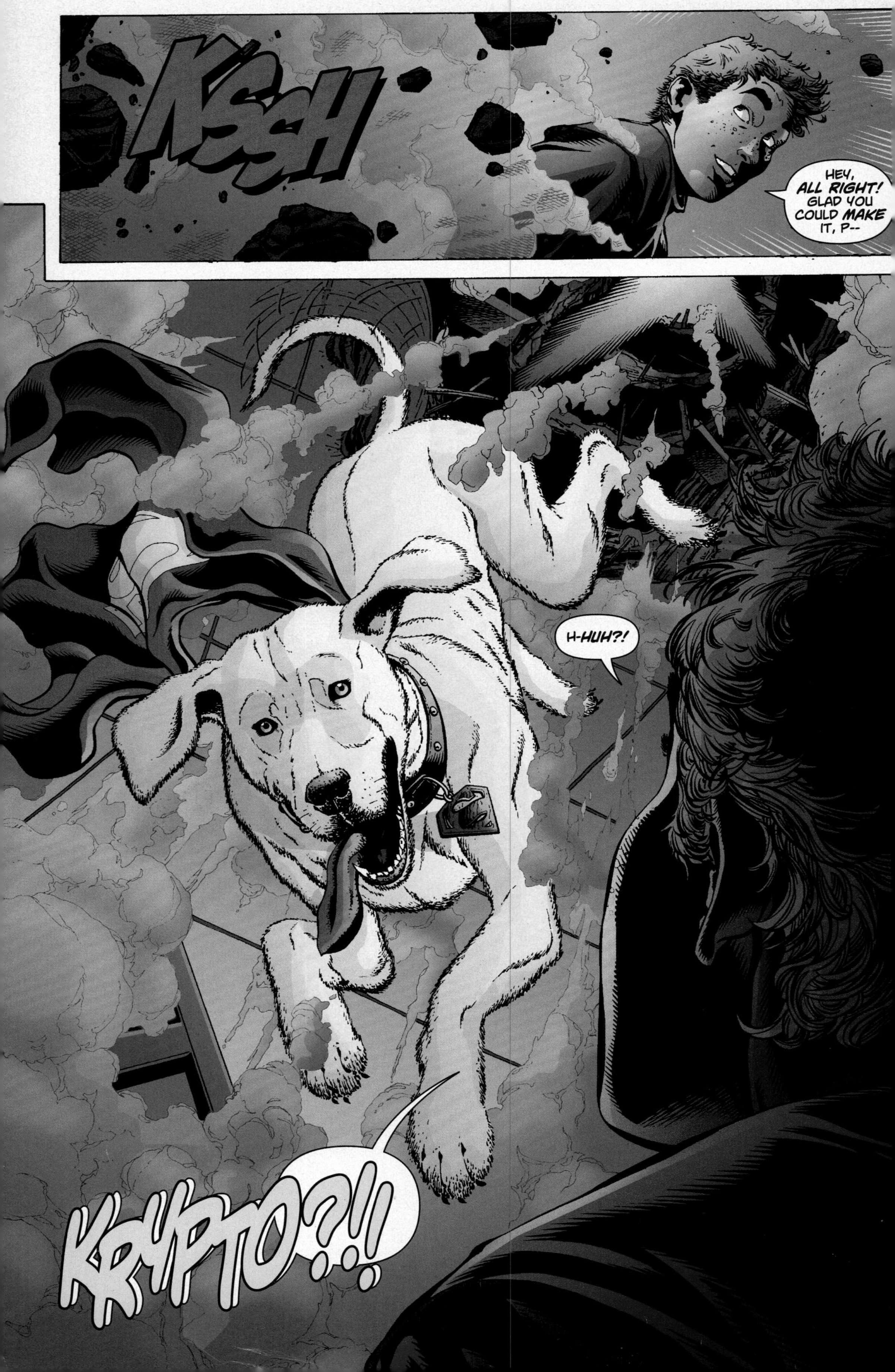
KSSH
HEY, ALL RIGHT! GLAD YOU COULD MAKE IT, P--
H-HUH?!
KRYPTO?!!

ON COMICS 854 Cover art by Brad Walker and John Livesay Coloring by Pete Pantazis

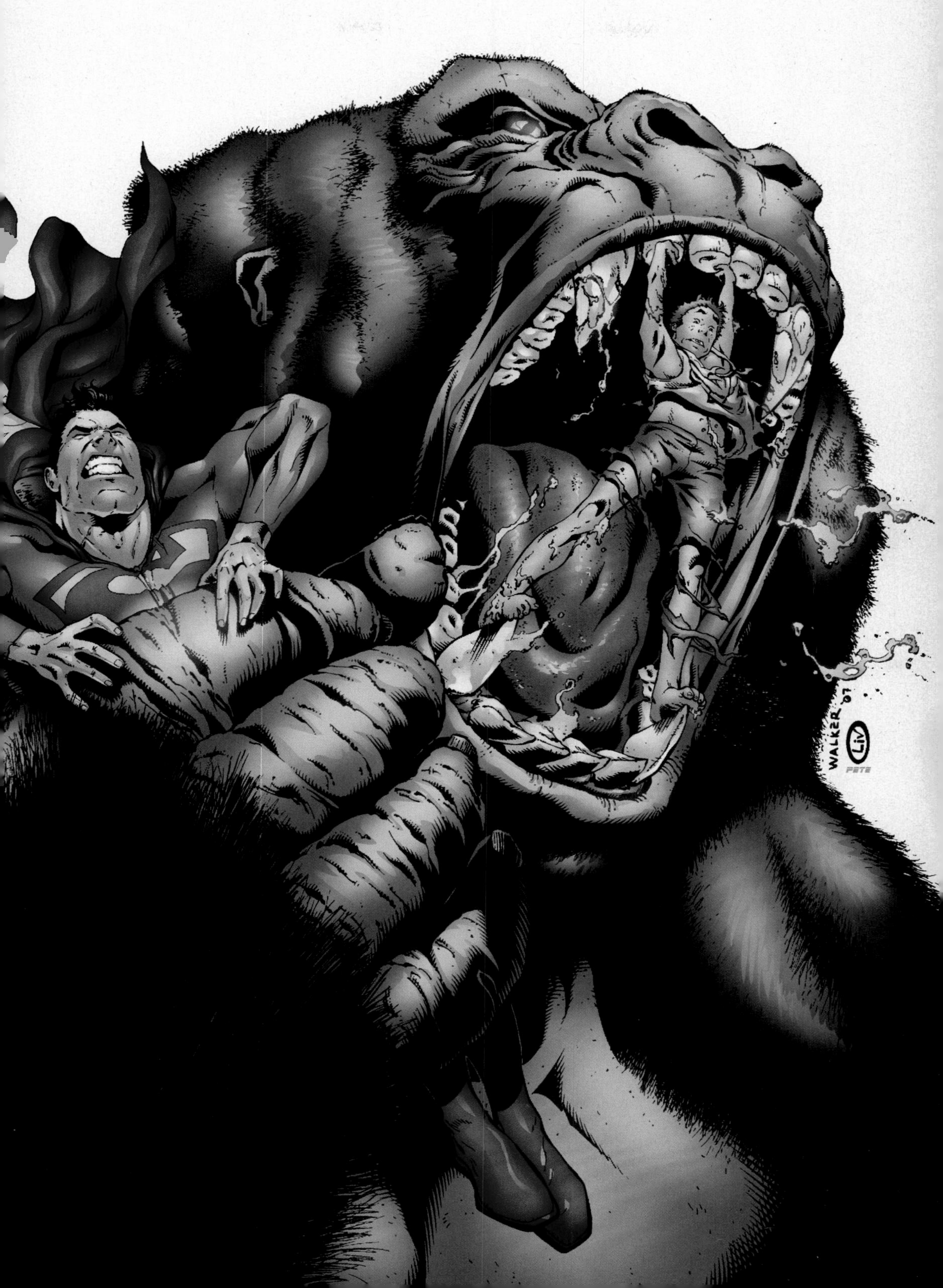
WALKER '07
LIV
PETE

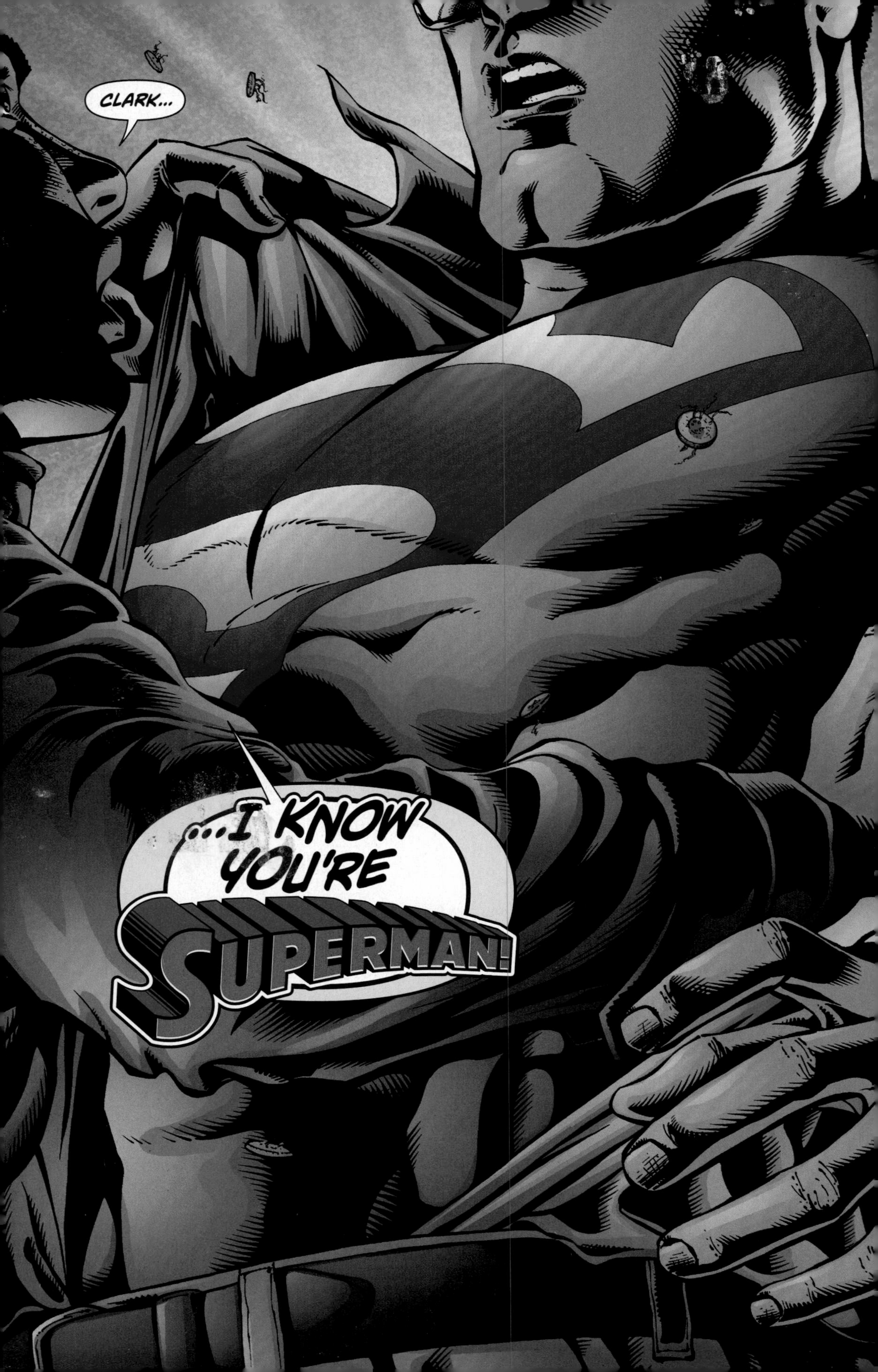
CLARK...
...I KNOW YOU'RE SUPERMAN!

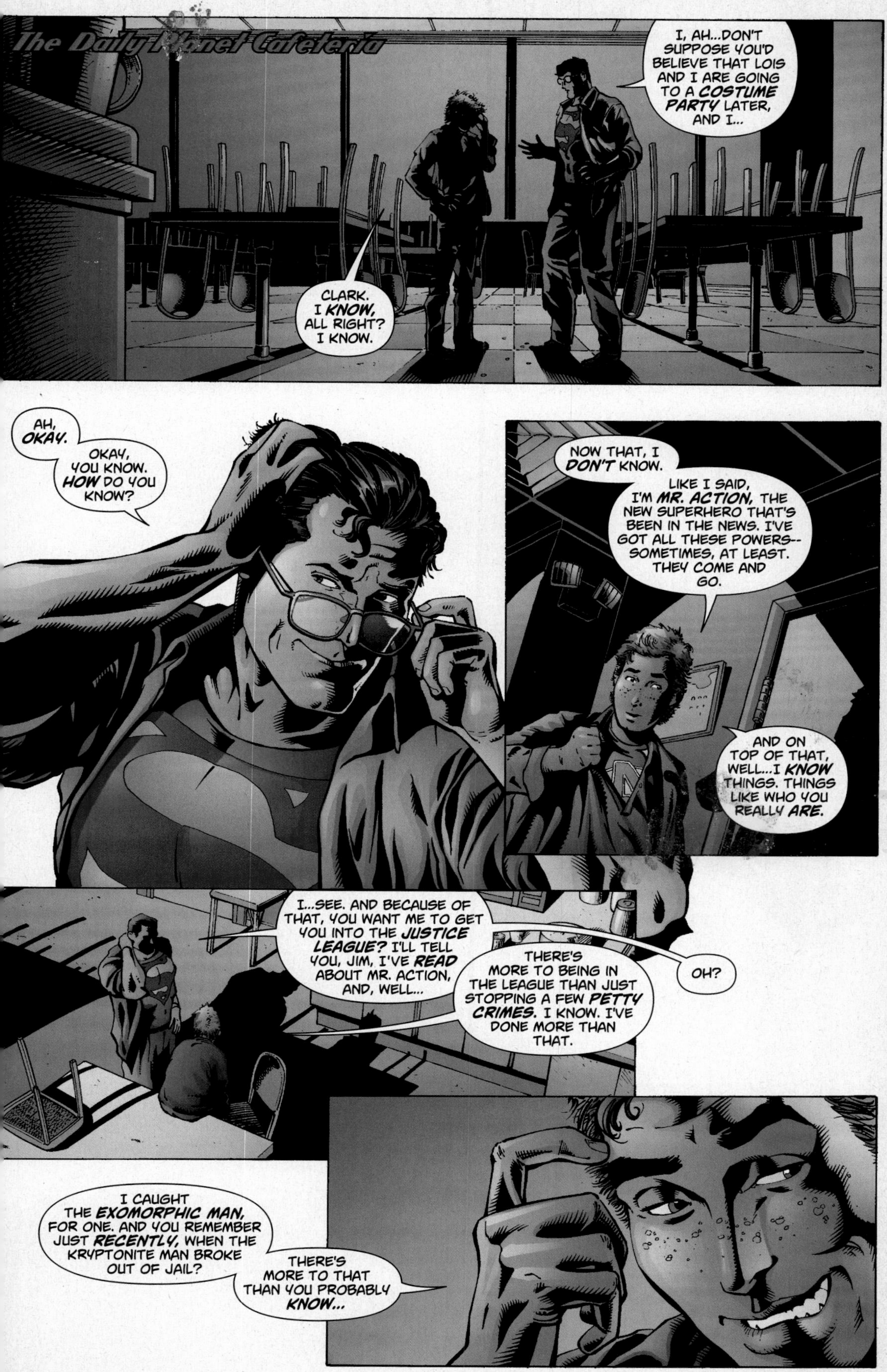
The Daily Planet Cafeteria
I, AH...DON'T SUPPOSE YOU'D BELIEVE THAT LOIS AND I ARE GOING TO A COSTUME PARTY LATER, AND I...
CLARK. I KNOW, ALL RIGHT? I KNOW.
AH, OKAY.
OKAY, YOU KNOW. HOW DO YOU KNOW?
NOW THAT, I DON'T KNOW.
LIKE I SAID, I'M MR. ACTION, THE NEW SUPERHERO THAT'S BEEN IN THE NEWS. I'VE GOT ALL THESE POWERS-- SOMETIMES, AT LEAST. THEY COME AND GO.
AND ON TOP OF THAT, WELL...I KNOW THINGS. THINGS LIKE WHO YOU REALLY ARE.
I...SEE. AND BECAUSE OF THAT, YOU WANT ME TO GET YOU INTO THE JUSTICE LEAGUE? I'LL TELL YOU, JIM, I'VE READ ABOUT MR. ACTION, AND, WELL...
THERE'S MORE TO BEING IN THE LEAGUE THAN JUST STOPPING A FEW PETTY CRIMES. I KNOW. I'VE DONE MORE THAN THAT.
OH?
I CAUGHT THE EXOMORPHIC MAN, FOR ONE. AND YOU REMEMBER JUST RECENTLY, WHEN THE KRYPTONITE MAN BROKE OUT OF JAIL?
THERE'S MORE TO THAT THAN YOU PROBABLY KNOW...

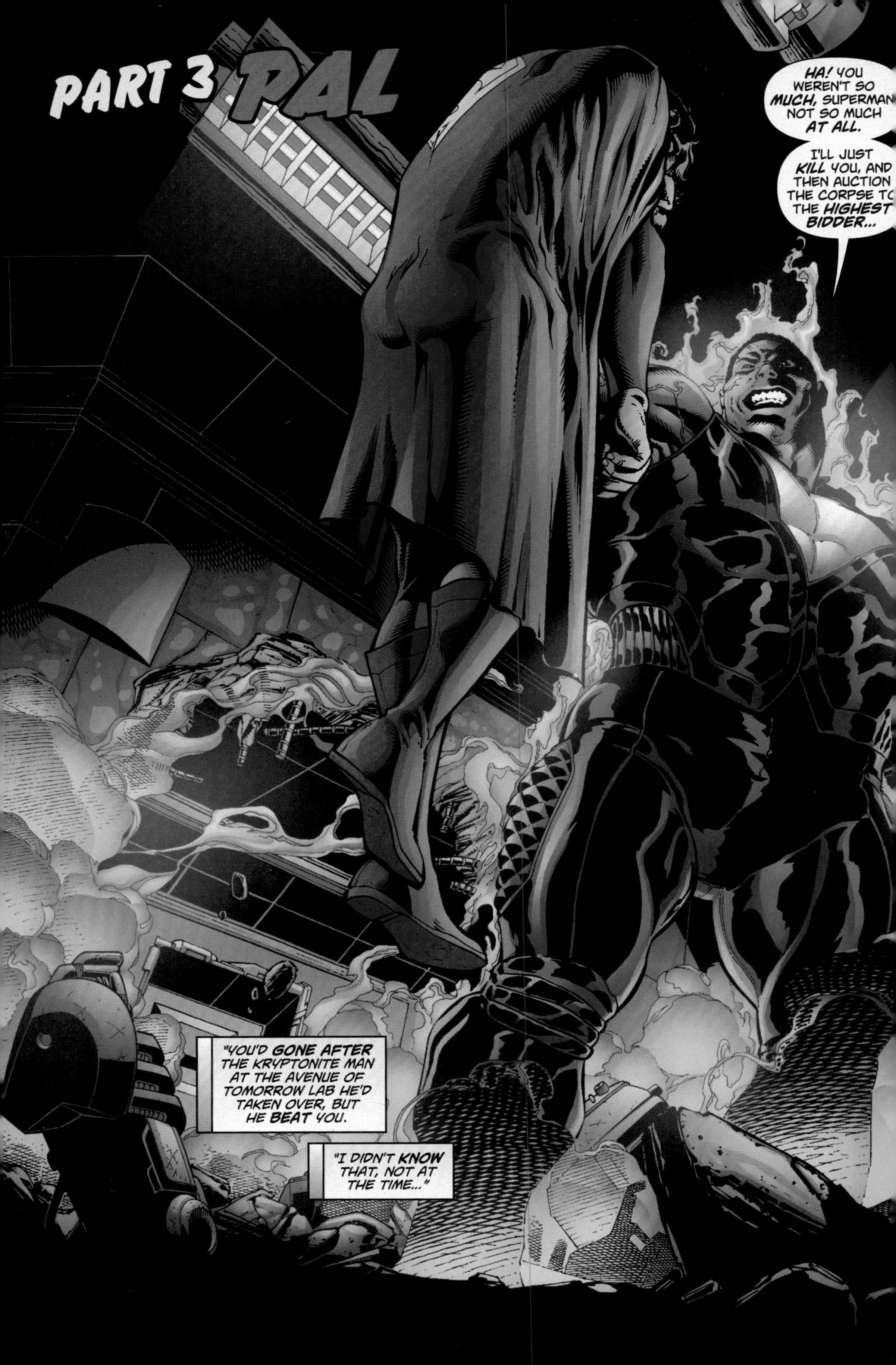
PART 3 PAL
HA! YOU WEREN'T SO MUCH, SUPERMAN NOT SO MUCH AT ALL.
I'LL JUST KILL YOU, AND THEN AUCTION THE CORPSE TO THE HIGHEST BIDDER...
"YOU'D GONE AFTER THE KRYPTONITE MAN AT THE AVENUE OF TOMORROW LAB HE'D TAKEN OVER, BUT HE BEAT YOU.
"I DIDN'T KNOW THAT, NOT AT THE TIME..."

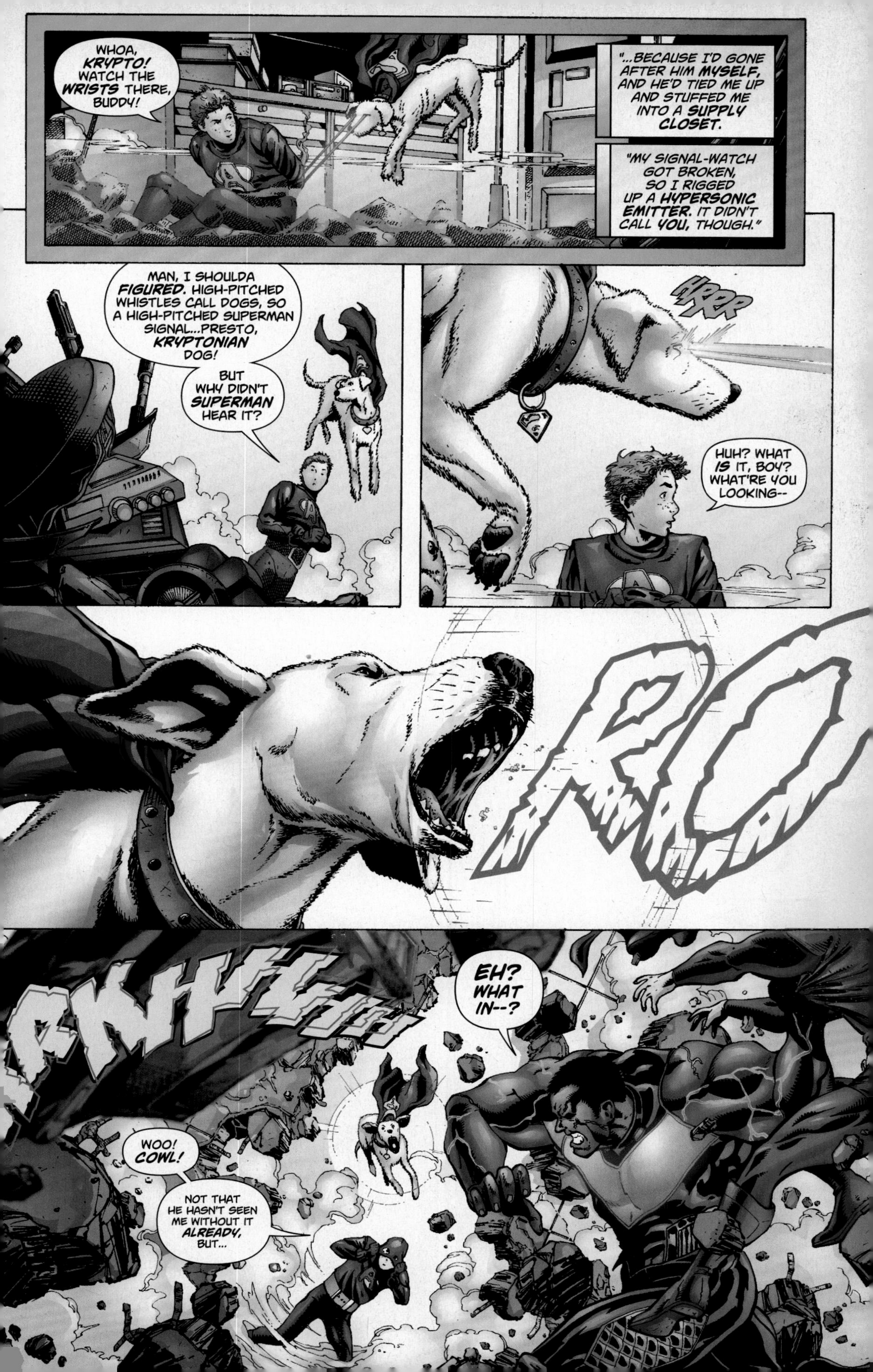

WHOA, KRYPTO! WATCH THE WRISTS THERE, BUDDY!
"...BECAUSE I'D GONE AFTER HIM MYSELF, AND HE'D TIED ME UP AND STUFFED ME INTO A SUPPLY CLOSET.
"MY SIGNAL-WATCH GOT BROKEN, SO I RIGGED UP A HYPERSONIC EMITTER. IT DIDN'T CALL YOU, THOUGH."
MAN, I SHOULDA FIGURED. HIGH-PITCHED WHISTLES CALL DOGS, SO A HIGH-PITCHED SUPERMAN SIGNAL...PRESTO, KRYPTONIAN DOG!
BUT WHY DIDN'T SUPERMAN HEAR IT?
HRRR
HUH? WHAT IS IT, BOY? WHAT'RE YOU LOOKING--
RO
EH? WHAT IN--?
WOO! COWL!
NOT THAT HE HASN'T SEEN ME WITHOUT IT ALREADY, BUT...

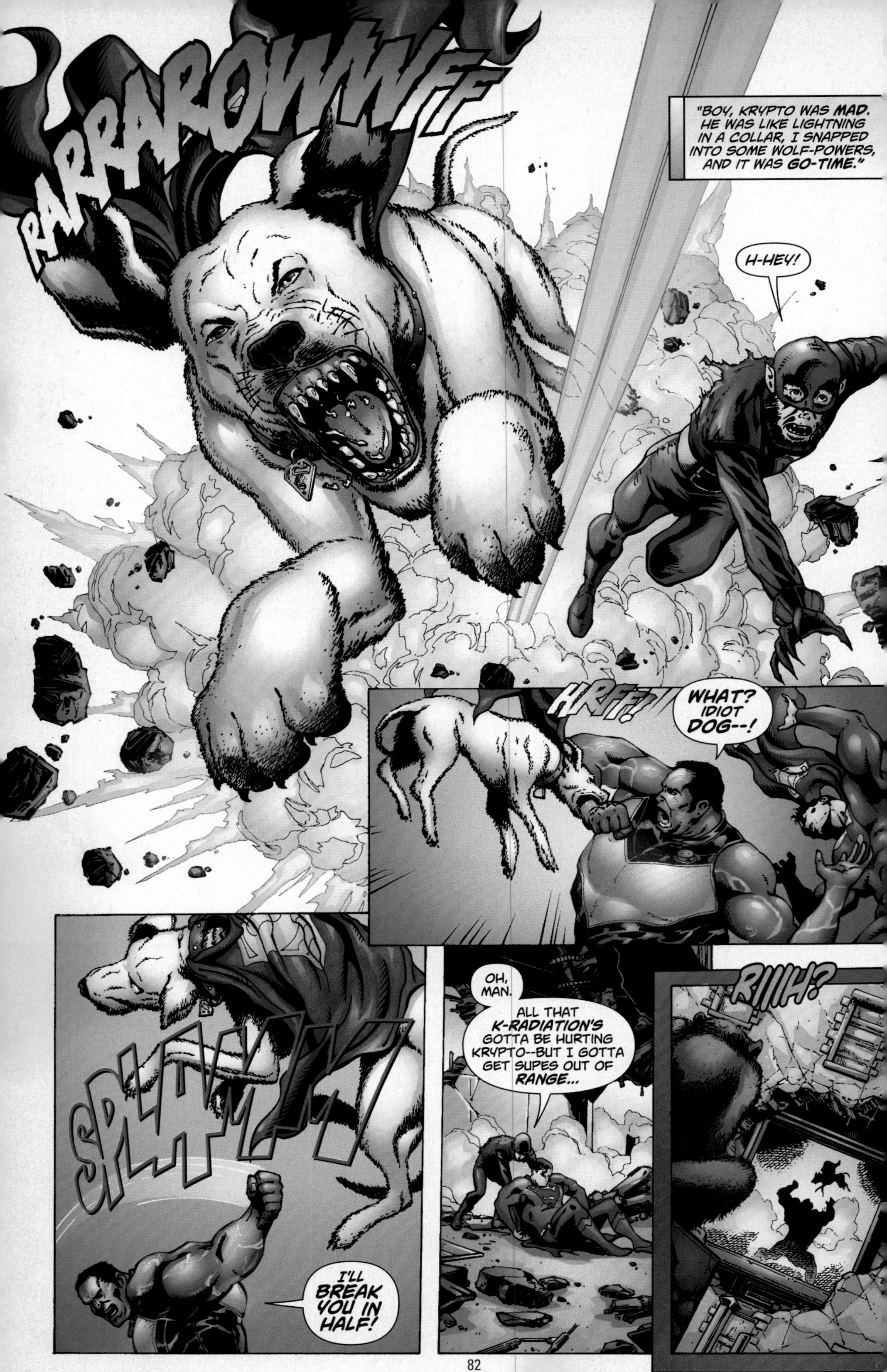
RARRROWWFF
"BOY, KRYPTO WAS MAD. HE WAS LIKE LIGHTNING IN A COLLAR, I SNAPPED INTO SOME WOLF-POWERS, AND IT WAS GO-TIME."
H-HEY!
HRFF!
WHAT? IDIOT DOG--!
SPLAMM
I'LL BREAK YOU IN HALF!
OH, MAN.
ALL THAT K-RADIATION'S GOTTA BE HURTING KRYPTO--BUT I GOTTA GET SUPES OUT OF RANGE...
RIIIH?

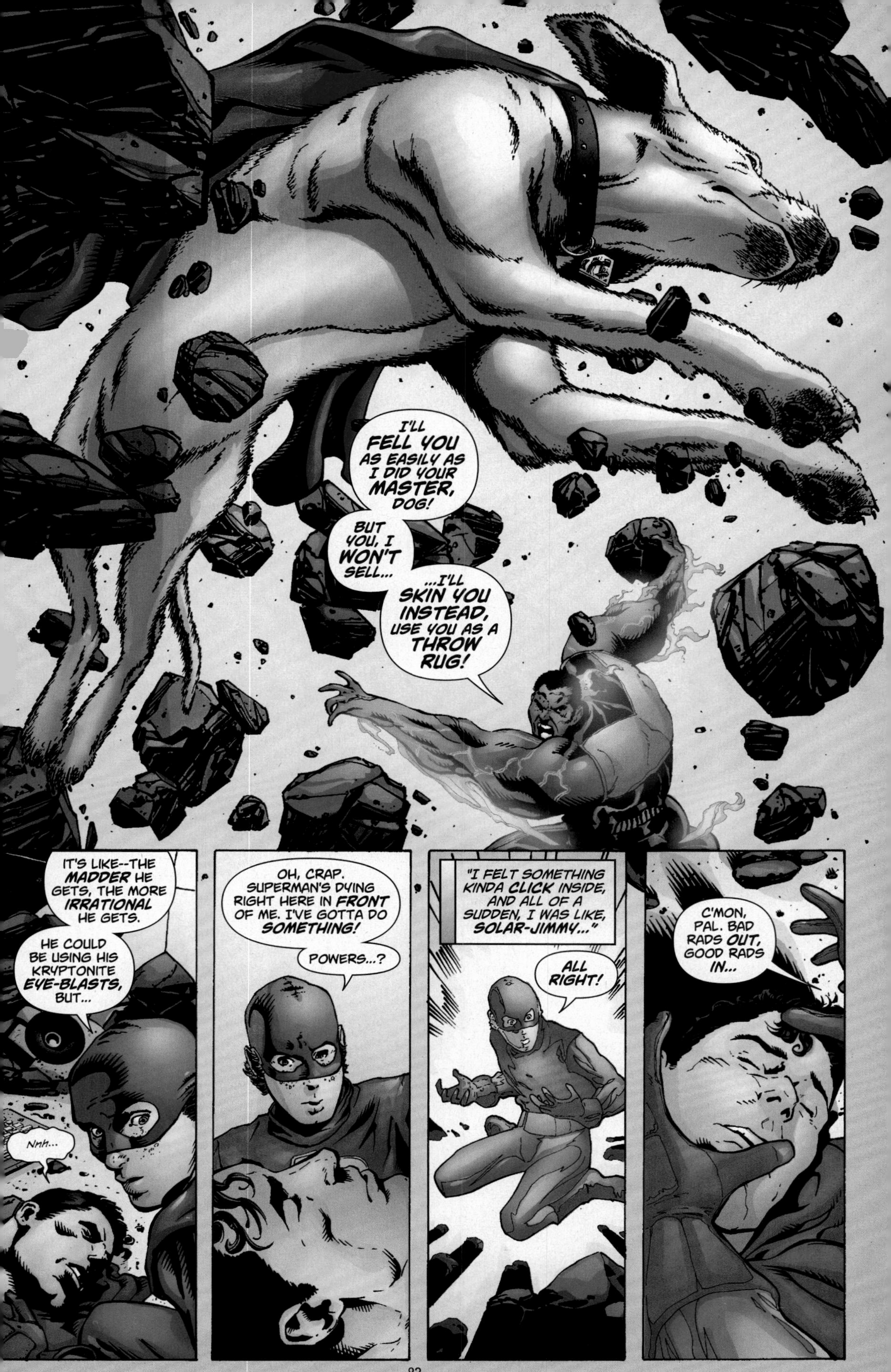
I'LL FELL YOU AS EASILY AS I DID YOUR MASTER, DOG!
BUT YOU, I WON'T SELL...
...I'LL SKIN YOU INSTEAD, USE YOU AS A THROW RUG!
IT'S LIKE--THE MADDER HE GETS, THE MORE IRRATIONAL HE GETS.
HE COULD BE USING HIS KRYPTONITE EYE-BLASTS, BUT...
Nnh...
OH, CRAP. SUPERMAN'S DYING RIGHT HERE IN FRONT OF ME. I'VE GOTTA DO SOMETHING!
POWERS...?
"I FELT SOMETHING KINDA CLICK INSIDE, AND ALL OF A SUDDEN, I WAS LIKE, SOLAR-JIMMY..."
ALL RIGHT!
C'MON, PAL. BAD RADS OUT, GOOD RADS IN...

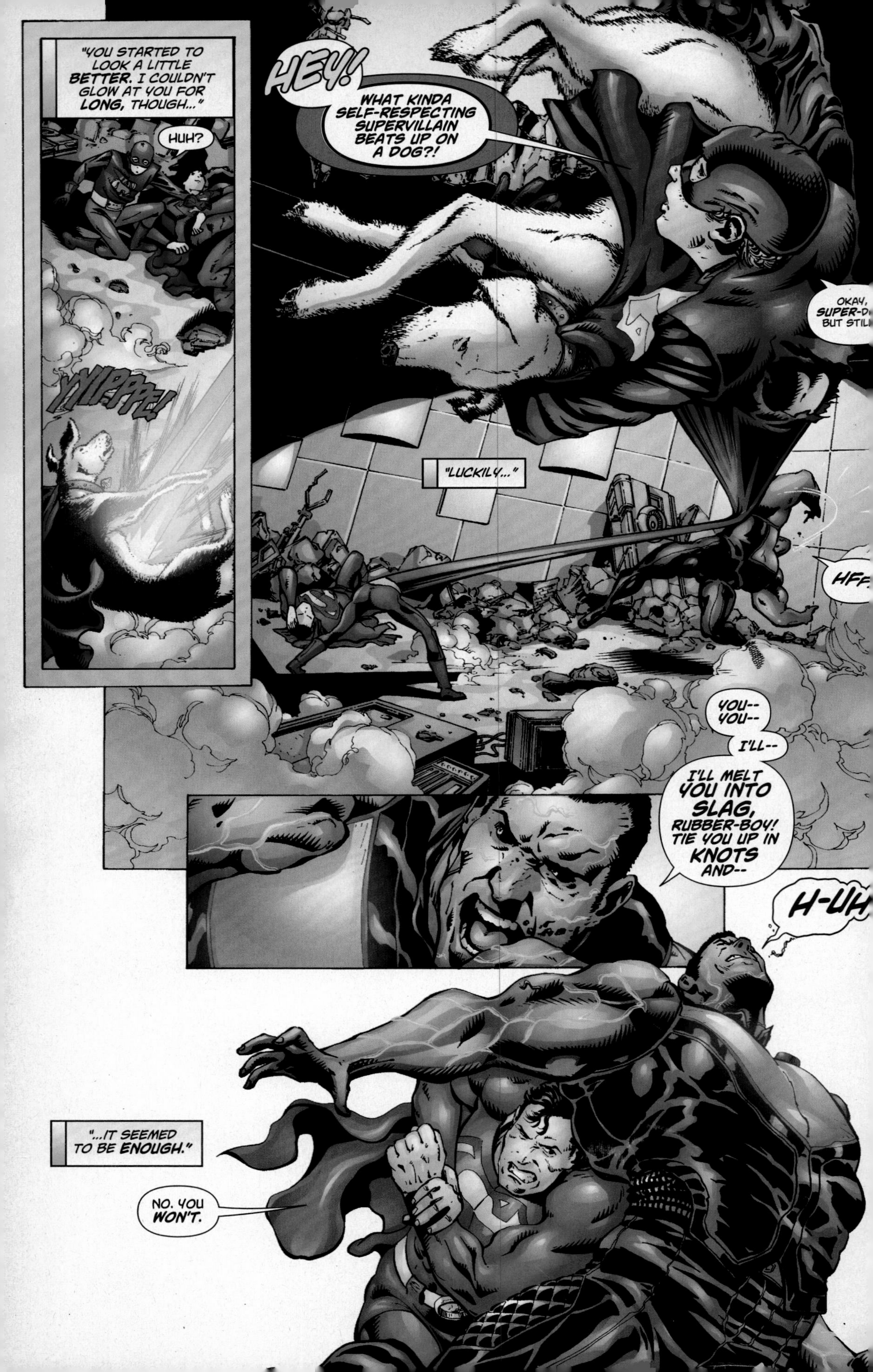
"YOU STARTED TO LOOK A LITTLE BETTER. I COULDN'T GLOW AT YOU FOR LONG, THOUGH..."
HUH?
YIPPE!
HEY!
WHAT KINDA SELF-RESPECTING SUPERVILLAIN BEATS UP ON A DOG?!
"LUCKILY..."
YOU-- YOU--
I'LL--
I'LL MELT YOU INTO SLAG, RUBBER-BOY! TIE YOU UP IN KNOTS AND--
"...IT SEEMED TO BE ENOUGH."
NO. YOU WON'T.

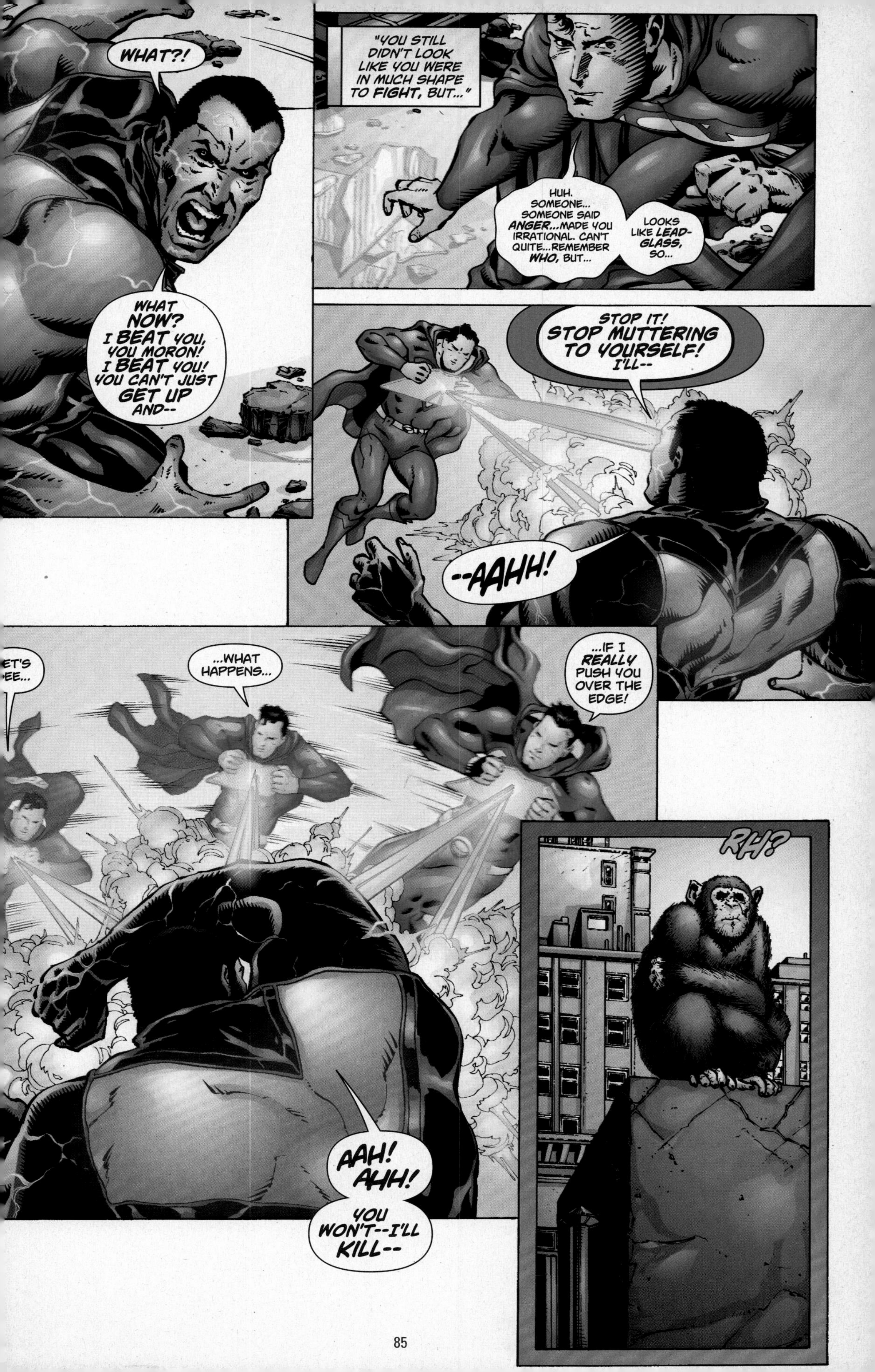

WHAT?!
WHAT NOW? I BEAT YOU, YOU MORON! I BEAT YOU! YOU CAN'T JUST GET UP AND--
"YOU STILL DIDN'T LOOK LIKE YOU WERE IN MUCH SHAPE TO FIGHT, BUT..."
HUH. SOMEONE... SOMEONE SAID ANGER...MADE YOU IRRATIONAL. CAN'T QUITE...REMEMBER WHO, BUT...
LOOKS LIKE LEAD-GLASS, SO...
STOP IT! STOP MUTTERING TO YOURSELF! I'LL--
--AAHH!
...WHAT HAPPENS...
...IF I REALLY PUSH YOU OVER THE EDGE!
AAH! AHH! YOU WON'T--I'LL KILL--
RH?

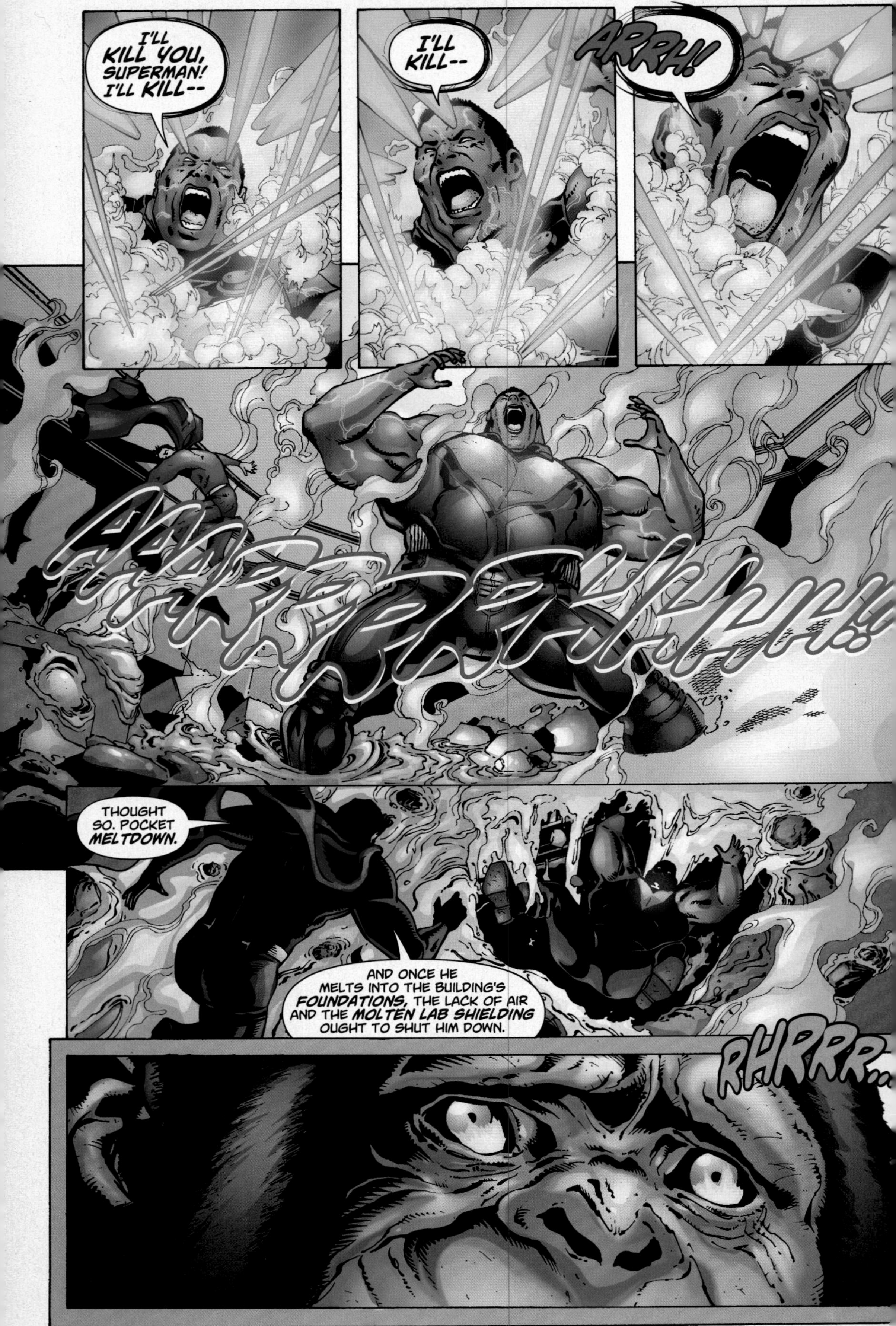
I'LL KILL YOU, SUPERMAN! I'LL KILL--
I'LL KILL--
ARRH!
THOUGHT SO. POCKET MELTDOWN.
AND ONCE HE MELTS INTO THE BUILDING'S FOUNDATIONS, THE LACK OF AIR AND THE MOLTEN LAB SHIELDING OUGHT TO SHUT HIM DOWN.
RHRRR..

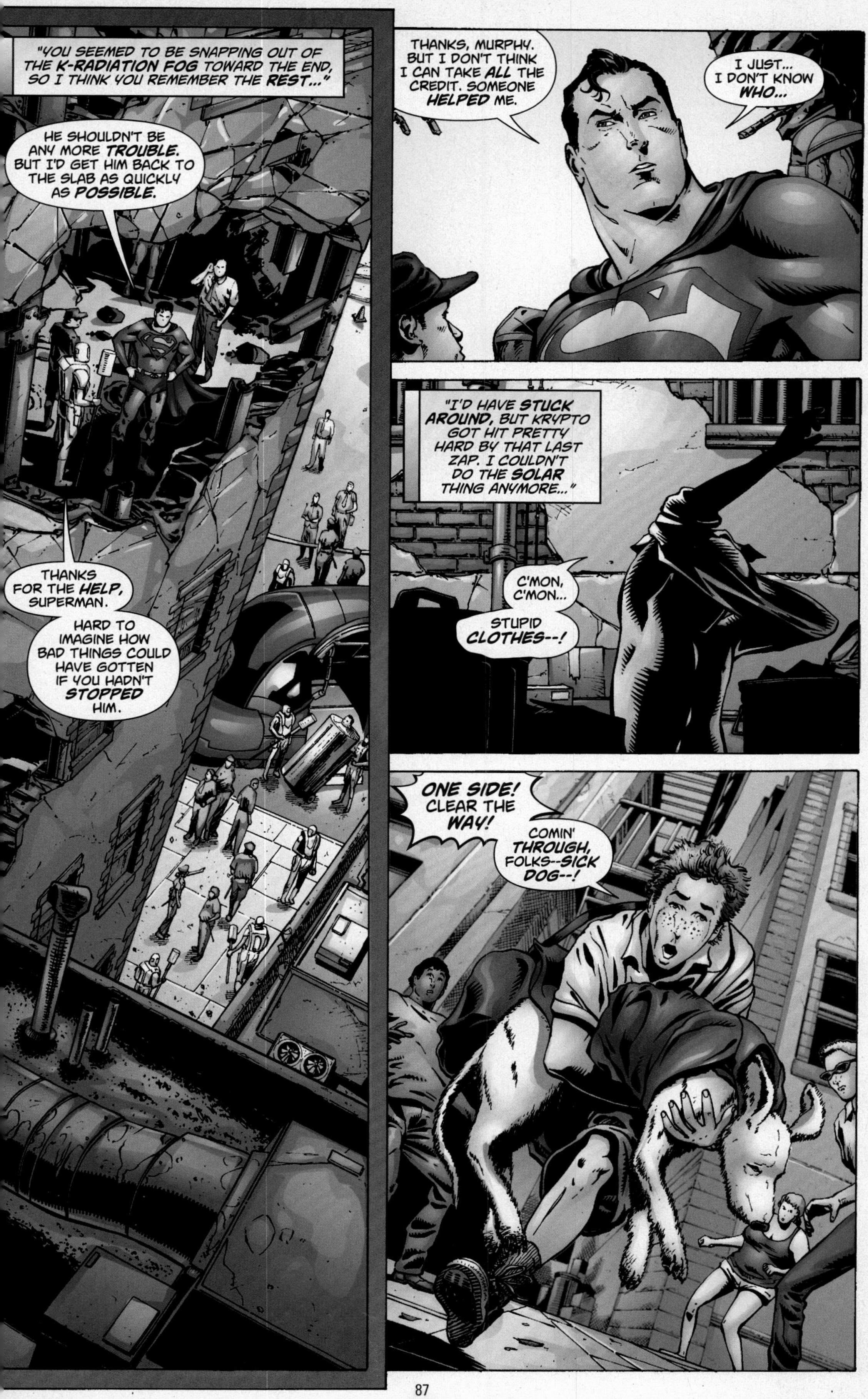
"YOU SEEMED TO BE SNAPPING OUT OF THE K-RADIATION FOG TOWARD THE END, SO I THINK YOU REMEMBER THE REST..."
HE SHOULDN'T BE ANY MORE TROUBLE. BUT I'D GET HIM BACK TO THE SLAB AS QUICKLY AS POSSIBLE.
THANKS FOR THE HELP, SUPERMAN.
HARD TO IMAGINE HOW BAD THINGS COULD HAVE GOTTEN IF YOU HADN'T STOPPED HIM.
THANKS, MURPHY. BUT I DON'T THINK I CAN TAKE ALL THE CREDIT. SOMEONE HELPED ME.
I JUST... I DON'T KNOW WHO...
"I'D HAVE STUCK AROUND, BUT KRYPTO GOT HIT PRETTY HARD BY THAT LAST ZAP. I COULDN'T DO THE SOLAR THING ANYMORE..."
C'MON, C'MON...
STUPID CLOTHES--!
ONE SIDE! CLEAR THE WAY!
COMIN' THROUGH, FOLKS--SICK DOG--!

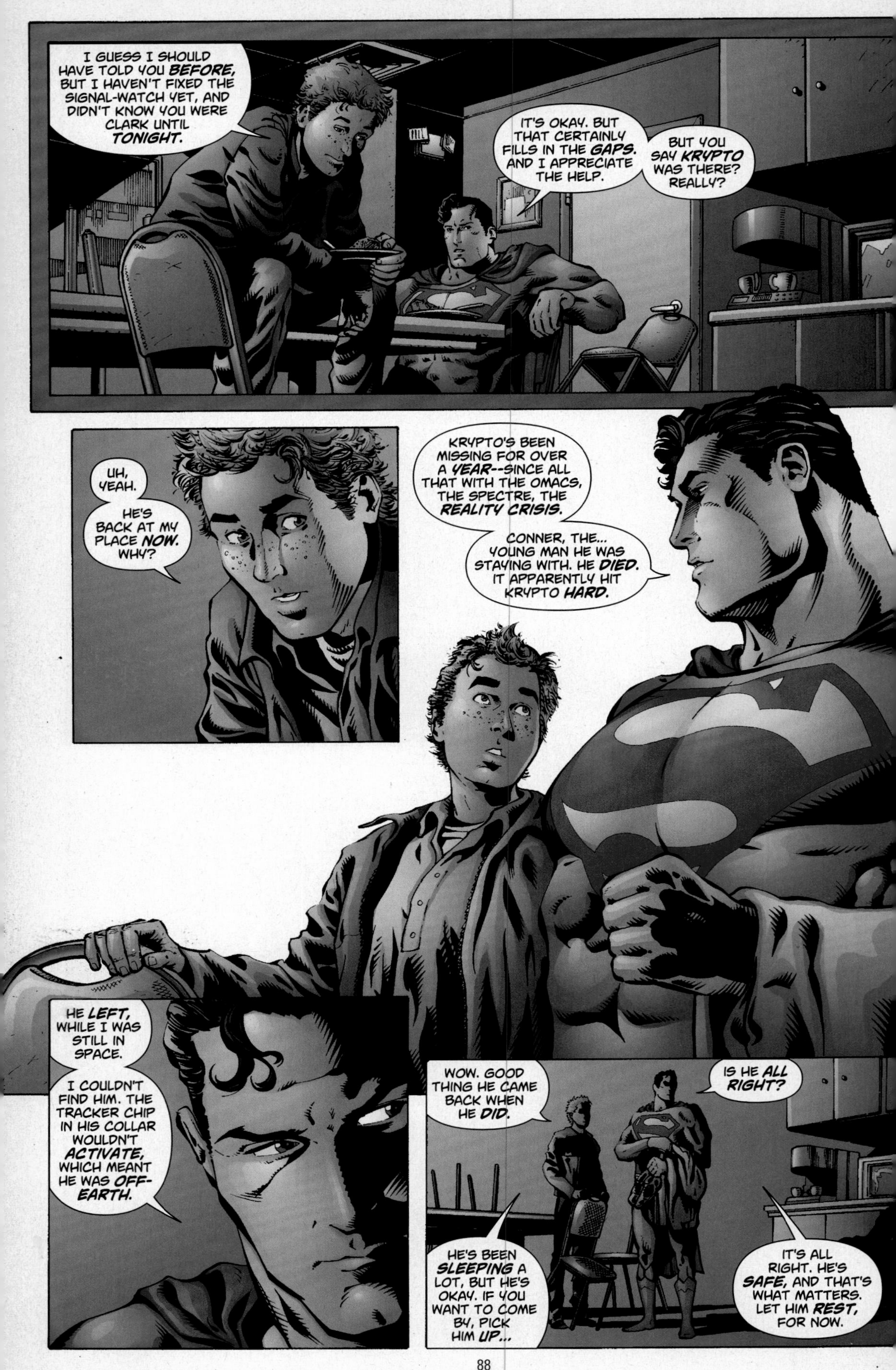
I GUESS I SHOULD HAVE TOLD YOU BEFORE, BUT I HAVEN'T FIXED THE SIGNAL-WATCH YET, AND DIDN'T KNOW YOU WERE CLARK UNTIL TONIGHT.
IT'S OKAY. BUT THAT CERTAINLY FILLS IN THE GAPS. AND I APPRECIATE THE HELP.
BUT YOU SAY KRYPTO WAS THERE? REALLY?
UH, YEAH.
HE'S BACK AT MY PLACE NOW. WHY?
KRYPTO'S BEEN MISSING FOR OVER A YEAR--SINCE ALL THAT WITH THE OMACS, THE SPECTRE, THE REALITY CRISIS.
CONNER, THE... YOUNG MAN HE WAS STAYING WITH. HE DIED. IT APPARENTLY HIT KRYPTO HARD.
HE LEFT, WHILE I WAS STILL IN SPACE.
I COULDN'T FIND HIM. THE TRACKER CHIP IN HIS COLLAR WOULDN'T ACTIVATE, WHICH MEANT HE WAS OFF-EARTH.
WOW. GOOD THING HE CAME BACK WHEN HE DID.
IS HE ALL RIGHT?
HE'S BEEN SLEEPING A LOT, BUT HE'S OKAY. IF YOU WANT TO COME BY, PICK HIM UP...
IT'S ALL RIGHT. HE'S SAFE, AND THAT'S WHAT MATTERS. LET HIM REST, FOR NOW.

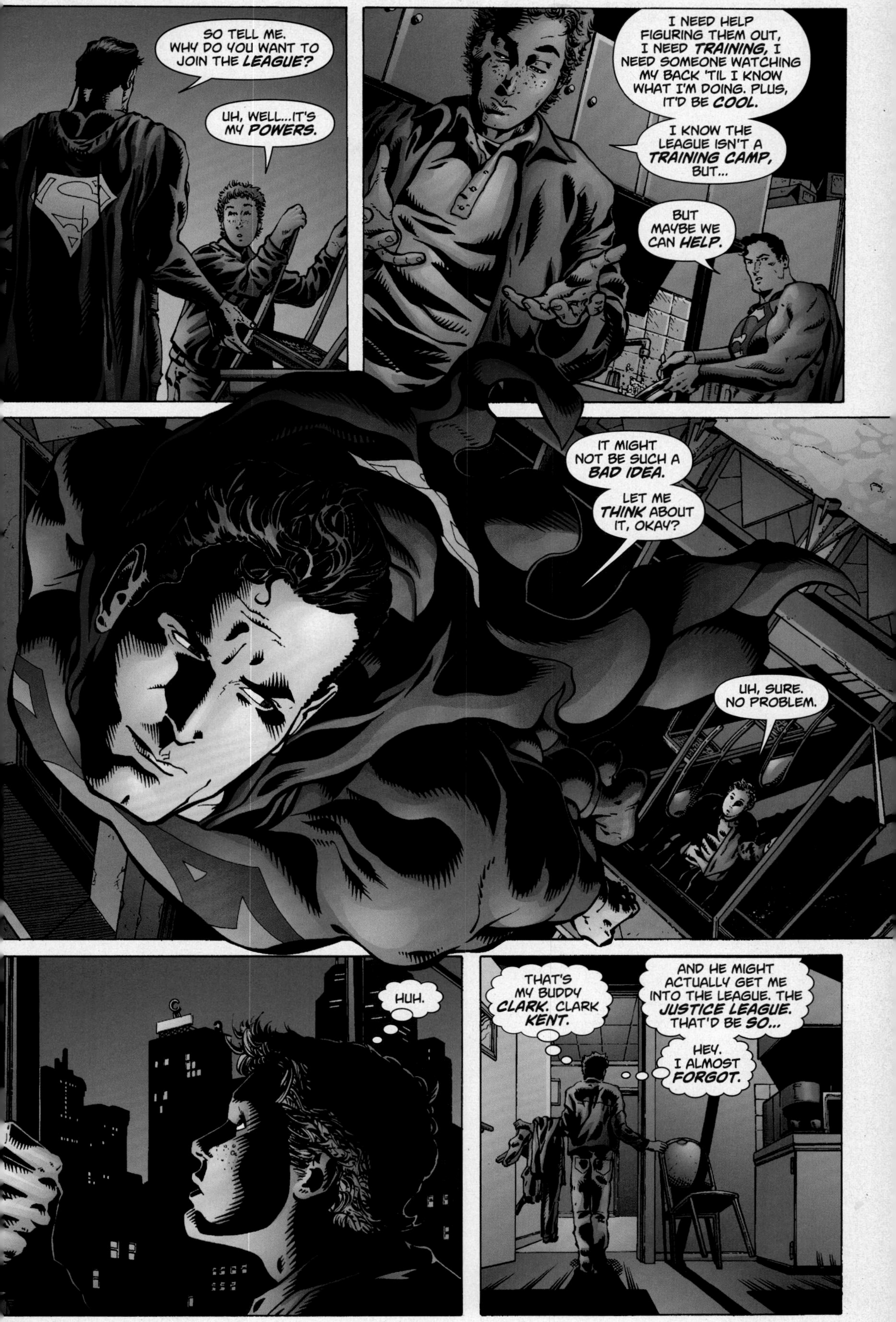
SO TELL ME. WHY DO YOU WANT TO JOIN THE LEAGUE?
UH, WELL...IT'S MY POWERS.
I NEED HELP FIGURING THEM OUT, I NEED TRAINING, I NEED SOMEONE WATCHING MY BACK 'TIL I KNOW WHAT I'M DOING. PLUS, IT'D BE COOL.
I KNOW THE LEAGUE ISN'T A TRAINING CAMP, BUT...
BUT MAYBE WE CAN HELP.
IT MIGHT NOT BE SUCH A BAD IDEA.
LET ME THINK ABOUT IT, OKAY?
UH, SURE. NO PROBLEM.
HUH.
THAT'S MY BUDDY CLARK. CLARK KENT.
AND HE MIGHT ACTUALLY GET ME INTO THE LEAGUE. THE JUSTICE LEAGUE. THAT'D BE SO...
HEY. I ALMOST FORGOT.

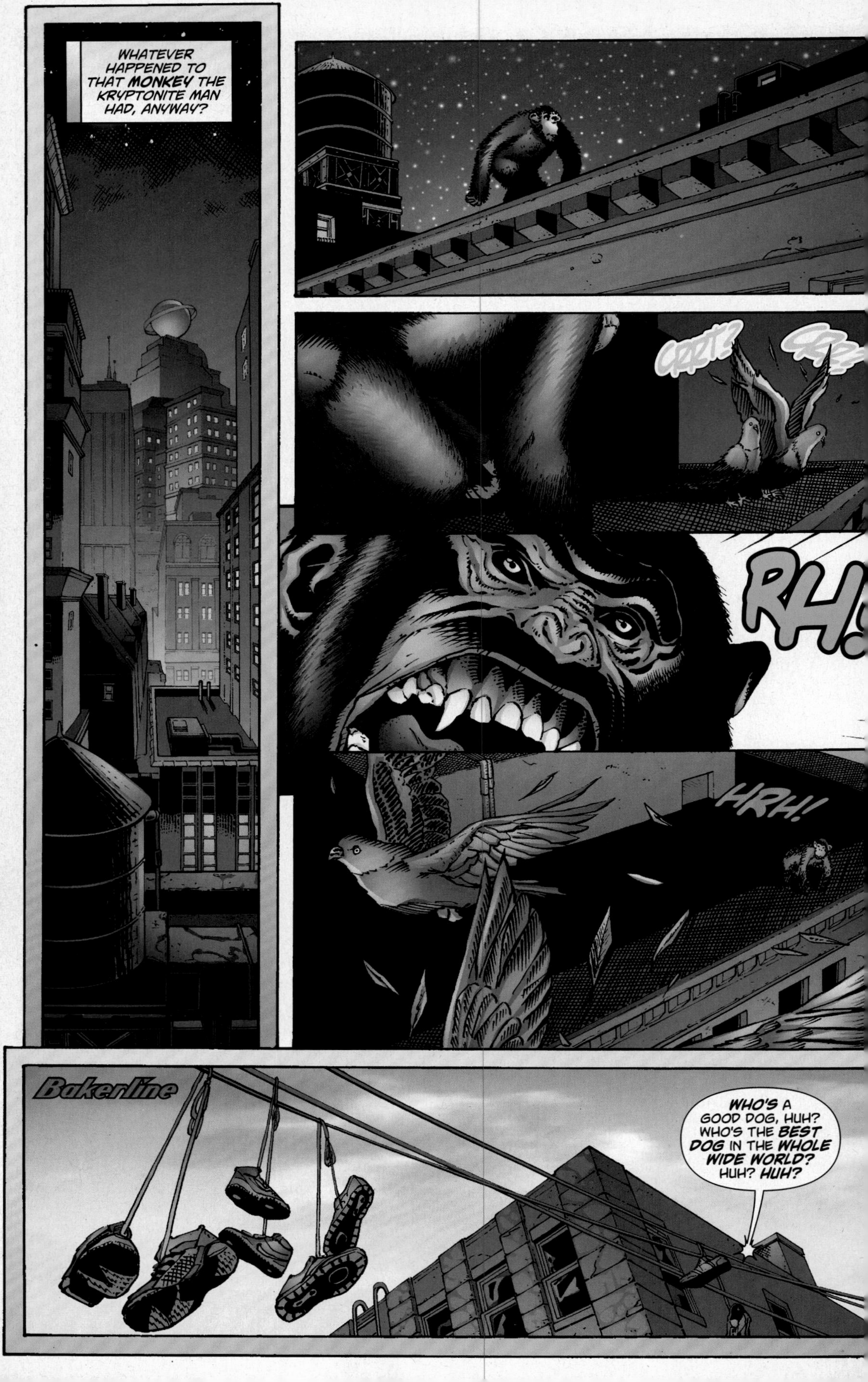
WHATEVER HAPPENED TO THAT MONKEY THE KRYPTONITE MAN HAD, ANYWAY?
CRRT?
RH
HRH!
Bakerline
WHO'S A GOOD DOG, HUH? WHO'S THE BEST DOG IN THE WHOLE WIDE WORLD? HUH? HUH?

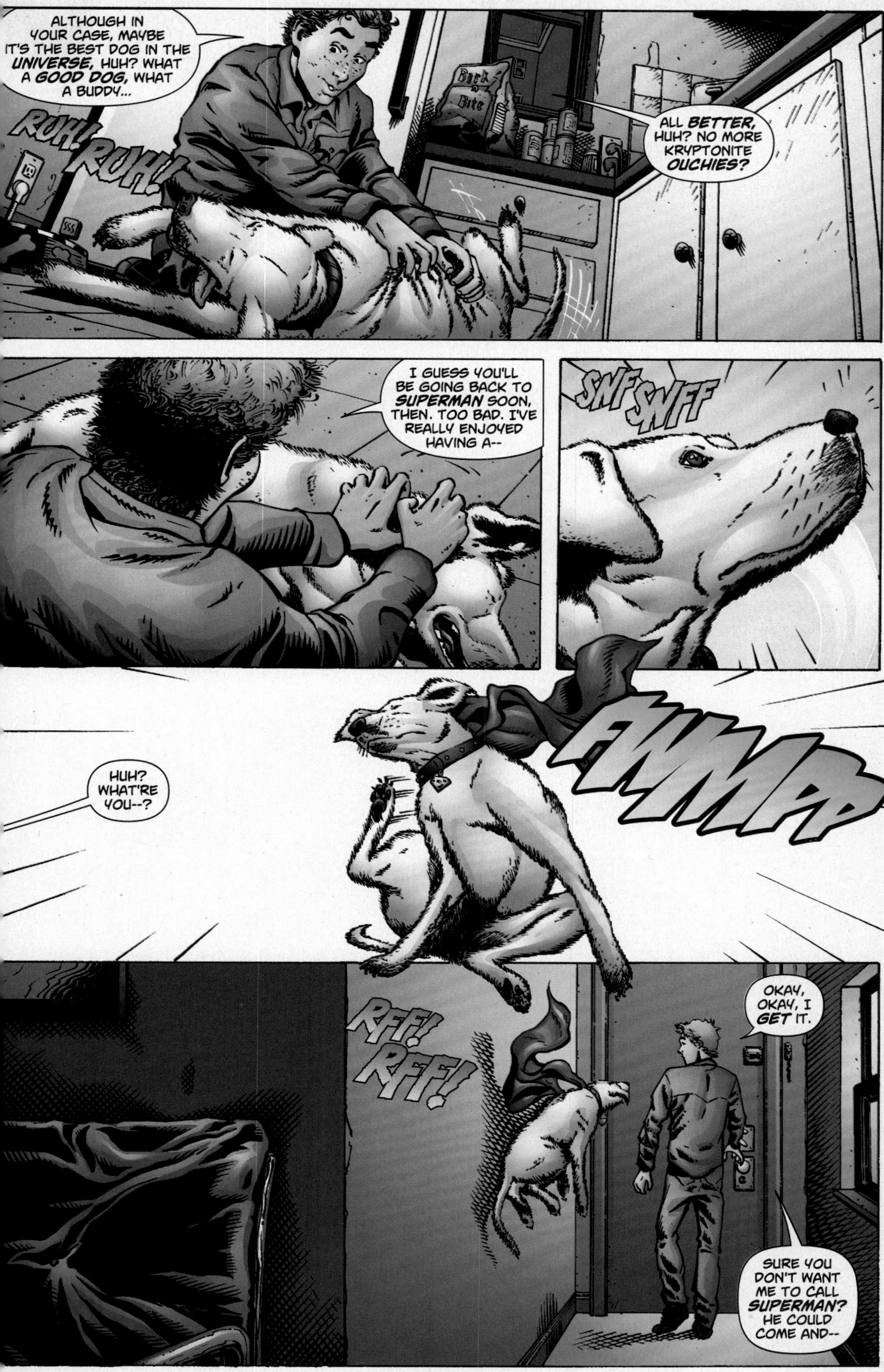

ALTHOUGH IN YOUR CASE, MAYBE IT'S THE BEST DOG IN THE UNIVERSE, HUH? WHAT A GOOD DOG, WHAT A BUDDY...
RUH! RUH!
ALL BETTER, HUH? NO MORE KRYPTONITE OUCHIES?
I GUESS YOU'LL BE GOING BACK TO SUPERMAN SOON, THEN. TOO BAD. I'VE REALLY ENJOYED HAVING A--
SNF SNFF
HUH? WHAT'RE YOU--?
FWMPP
RFF! RFF!
OKAY, OKAY, I GET IT.
SURE YOU DON'T WANT ME TO CALL SUPERMAN? HE COULD COME AND--

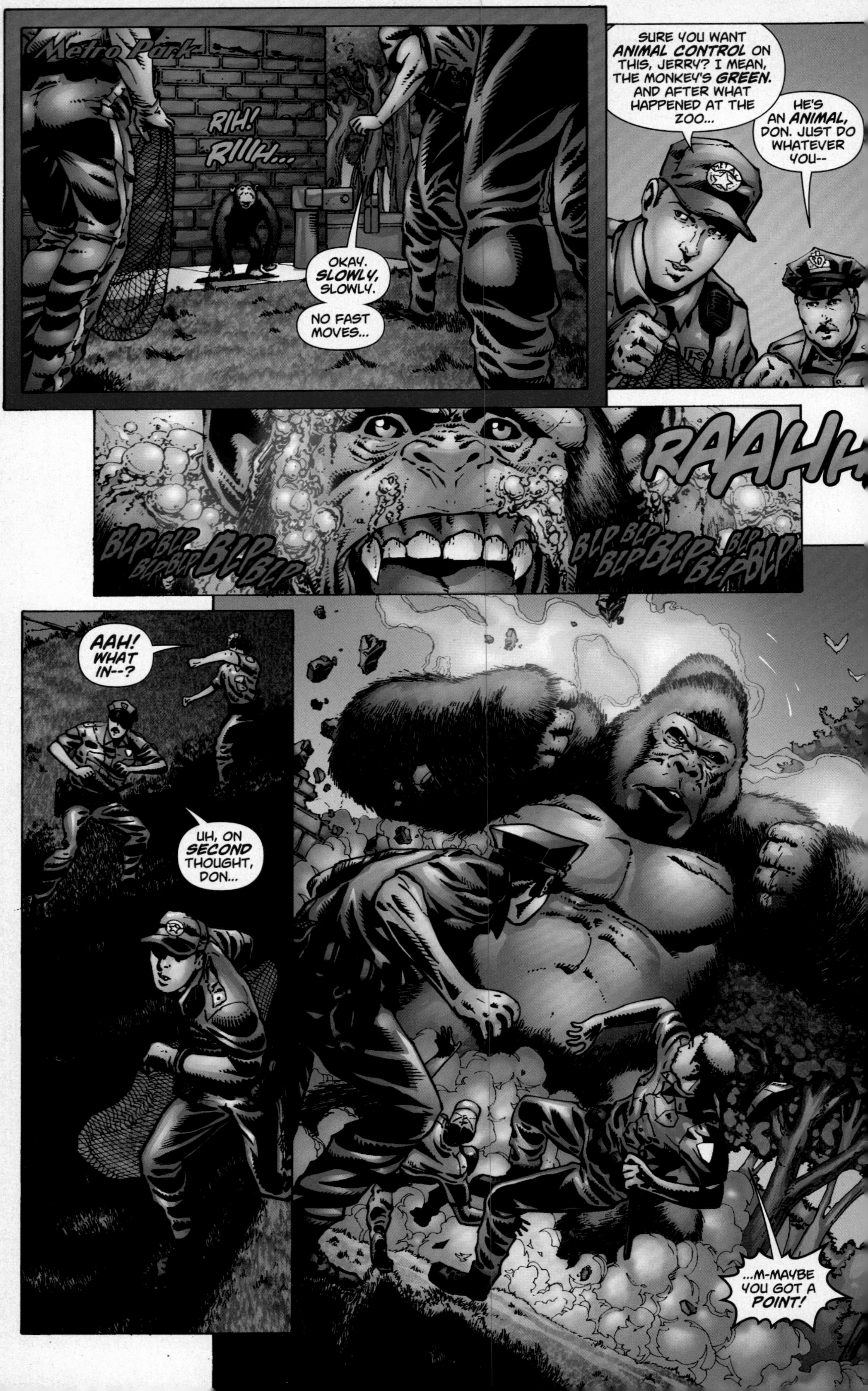
Metro Park
RIH! RIIIH...
OKAY. SLOWLY, SLOWLY.
NO FAST MOVES...
SURE YOU WANT ANIMAL CONTROL ON THIS, JERRY? I MEAN, THE MONKEY'S GREEN. AND AFTER WHAT HAPPENED AT THE ZOO...
HE'S AN ANIMAL, DON. JUST DO WHATEVER YOU--
RAAHH
BLP BLP BLP BLP BLP BLP
BLP BLP BLP BLP BLP BLP BLP BLP
AAH! WHAT IN--?
UH, ON SECOND THOUGHT, DON...
...M-MAYBE YOU GOT A POINT!

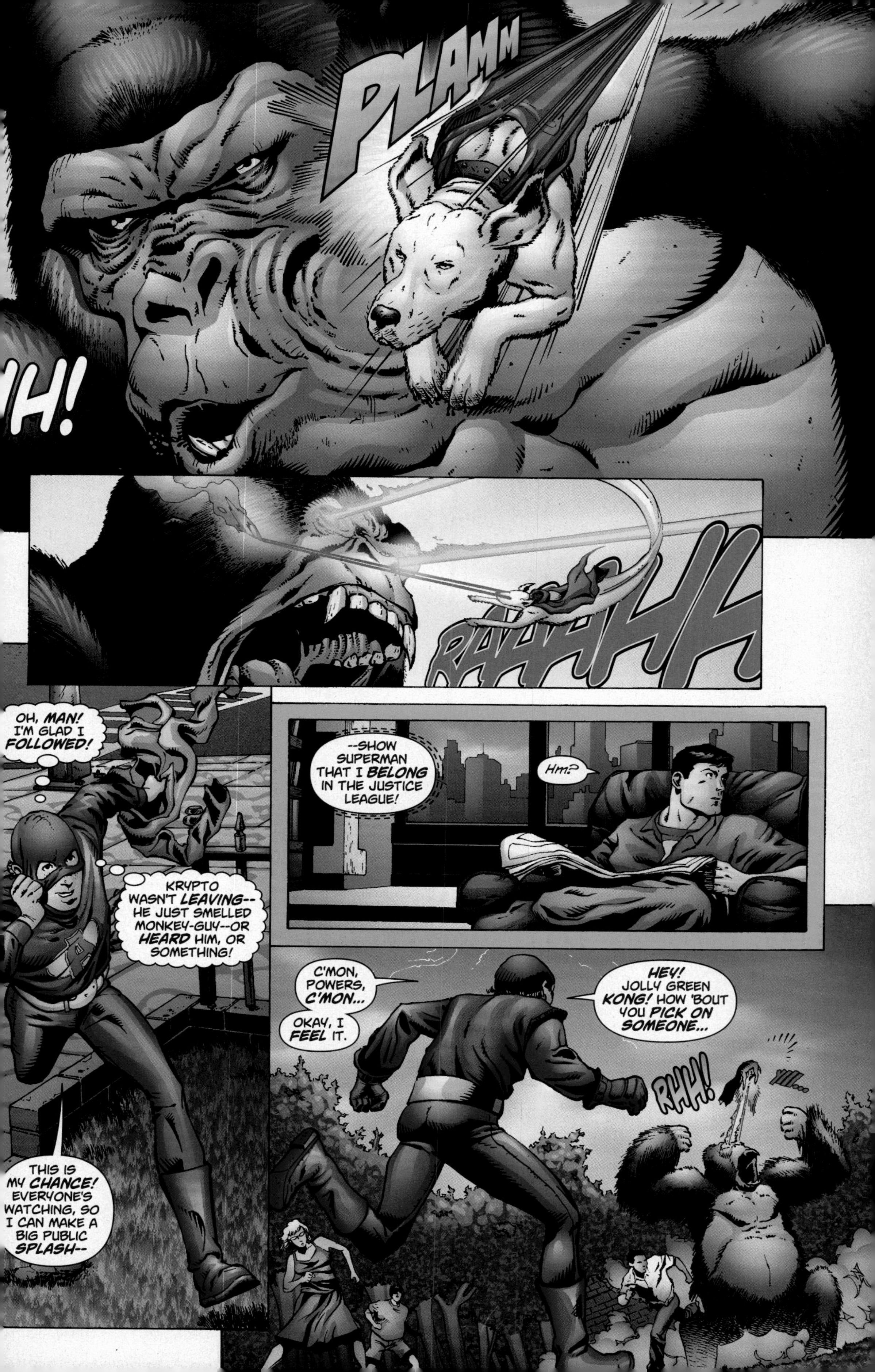
PLAMM
H!
RAAAHH
OH, MAN! I'M GLAD I FOLLOWED!
KRYPTO WASN'T LEAVING-- HE JUST SMELLED MONKEY-GUY--OR HEARD HIM, OR SOMETHING!
THIS IS MY CHANCE! EVERYONE'S WATCHING, SO I CAN MAKE A BIG PUBLIC SPLASH--
--SHOW SUPERMAN THAT I BELONG IN THE JUSTICE LEAGUE!
Hm?
C'MON, POWERS, C'MON...
OKAY, I FEEL IT.
HEY! JOLLY GREEN KONG! HOW 'BOUT YOU PICK ON SOMEONE...
RHH!
YIII...

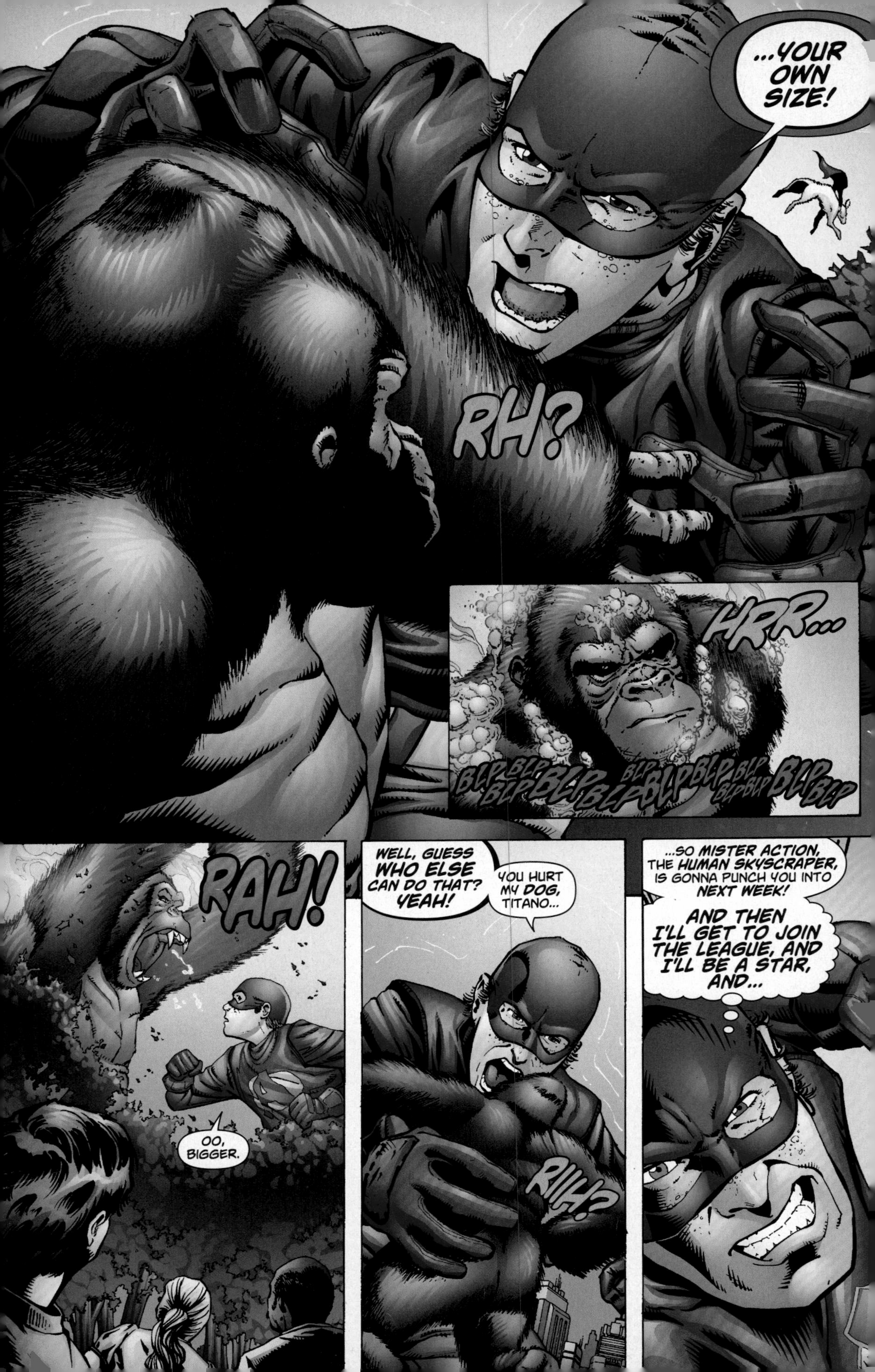
...YOUR OWN SIZE!
RH?
HRR...
BLP BLP BLP BLP BLP BLP BLP BLP BLP BLP BLP BLP BLP BLP
RAH!
OO, BIGGER.
WELL, GUESS WHO ELSE CAN DO THAT? YEAH!
YOU HURT MY DOG, TITANO...
RHH?
...SO MISTER ACTION, THE HUMAN SKYSCRAPER, IS GONNA PUNCH YOU INTO NEXT WEEK!
AND THEN I'LL GET TO JOIN THE LEAGUE, AND I'LL BE A STAR, AND...

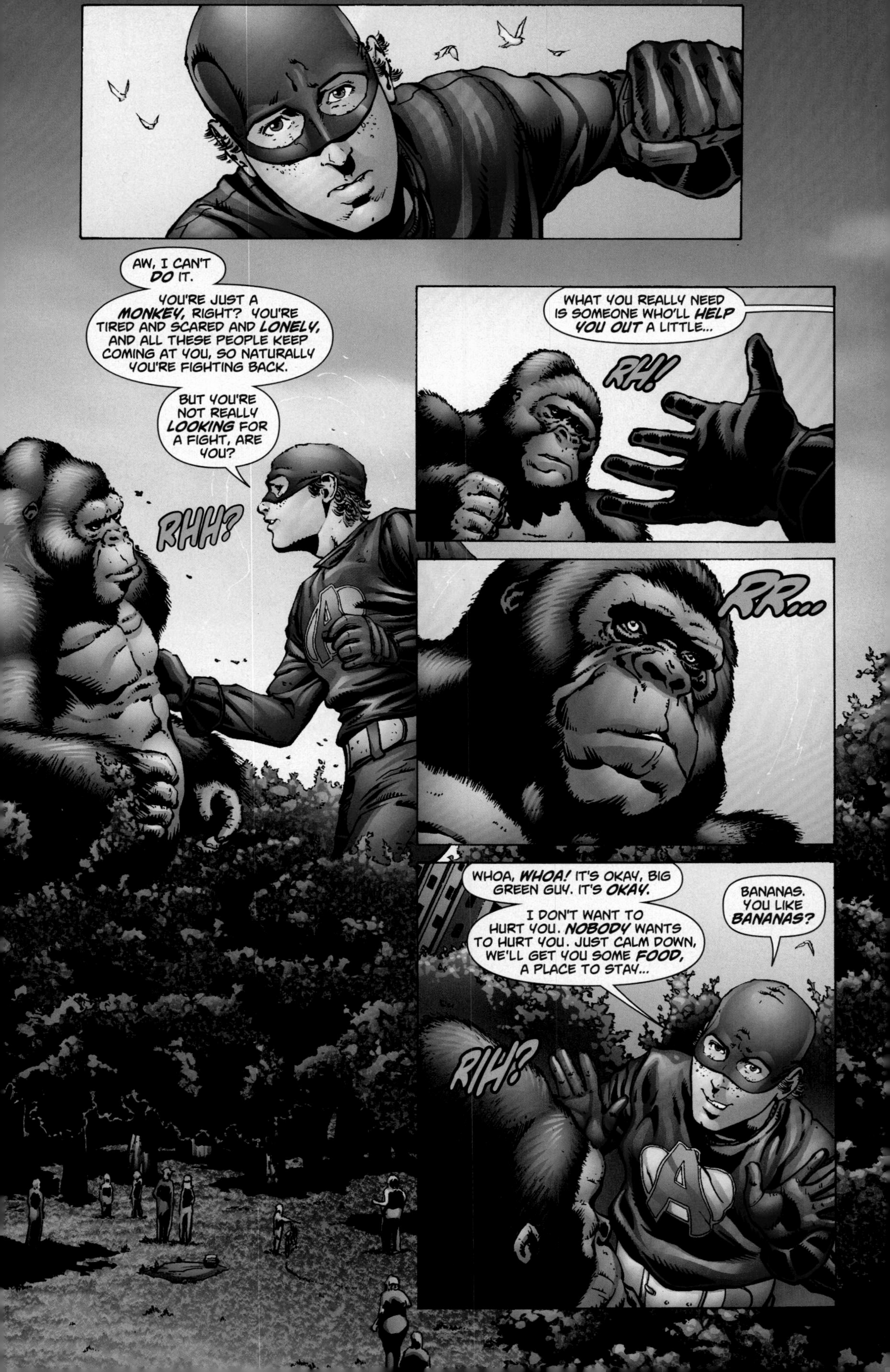
AW, I CAN'T DO IT.
YOU'RE JUST A MONKEY, RIGHT? YOU'RE TIRED AND SCARED AND LONELY, AND ALL THESE PEOPLE KEEP COMING AT YOU, SO NATURALLY YOU'RE FIGHTING BACK.
BUT YOU'RE NOT REALLY LOOKING FOR A FIGHT, ARE YOU?
RHH?
WHAT YOU REALLY NEED IS SOMEONE WHO'LL HELP YOU OUT A LITTLE...
RH!
RR...
WHOA, WHOA! IT'S OKAY, BIG GREEN GUY. IT'S OKAY.
I DON'T WANT TO HURT YOU. NOBODY WANTS TO HURT YOU. JUST CALM DOWN, WE'LL GET YOU SOME FOOD, A PLACE TO STAY...
BANANAS. YOU LIKE BANANAS?
RH?

BLIR BIP BIP BLIRBLIP BIP BLIR BLIP BLIP BIP BLIR BLIR BLIP

RIIIIK!

IT'S ALL GOING TO BE *OKAY*, LITTLE GUY. NO MORE TROUBLE.

BUT, UH--I'M WILLING TO BET THAT PLAYING *SNUGGLIES*™ WITH A MONKEY DOESN'T GET *ANYONE* INTO THE LEAGUE...

YOU MIGHT BE *SURPRISED*, J--AH, MISTER ACTION.

SOLVING A PROBLEM WITHOUT *UNNECESSARY VIOLENCE* OR *DESTRUCTION* MEANS A LOT. WE DON'T SEE NEARLY ENOUGH OF IT.

NICE WOR

SSRPERMPH?

I WAS CONFIDENT YOU COULD *HANDLE* THIS--

"--SO I TOOK THE TIME TO CALL IN A *FRIEND*."

C'MERE, LITTLE FELLA. WE'LL TAKE CARE OF EVERYTHING...

THIS IS *JENET KLYBURN,* OF S.T.A.R. LABS.

THANKS. WE'LL SEE THAT HE'S TREATED *WELL*...

SHE'LL BE ABLE TO GIVE THE MONKEY A *GOOD HOME,* AND STUDY HIS POWERS, SEE WHAT CAN BE *DONE* ABOUT THEM.

JENET, THIS IS *MR. ACTION.* HE'S A...*COLLEAGUE* OF MINE. NOW, IF YOU'LL EXCUSE US...

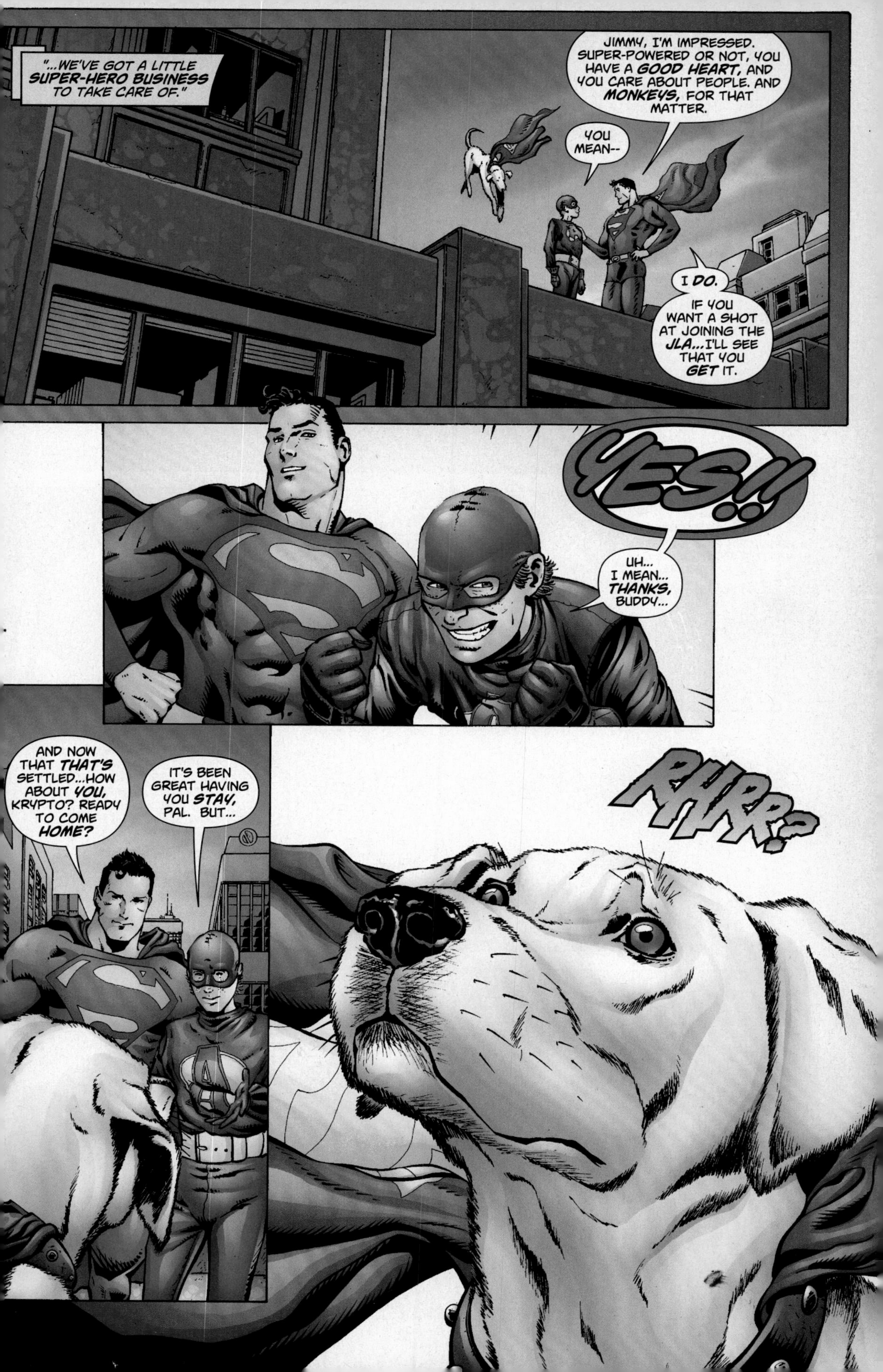
"...WE'VE GOT A LITTLE SUPER-HERO BUSINESS TO TAKE CARE OF."
JIMMY, I'M IMPRESSED. SUPER-POWERED OR NOT, YOU HAVE A GOOD HEART, AND YOU CARE ABOUT PEOPLE. AND MONKEYS, FOR THAT MATTER.
YOU MEAN--
I DO.
IF YOU WANT A SHOT AT JOINING THE JLA...I'LL SEE THAT YOU GET IT.
YES!!
UH... I MEAN... THANKS, BUDDY...
AND NOW THAT THAT'S SETTLED...HOW ABOUT YOU, KRYPTO? READY TO COME HOME?
IT'S BEEN GREAT HAVING YOU STAY, PAL. BUT...
RHRR?

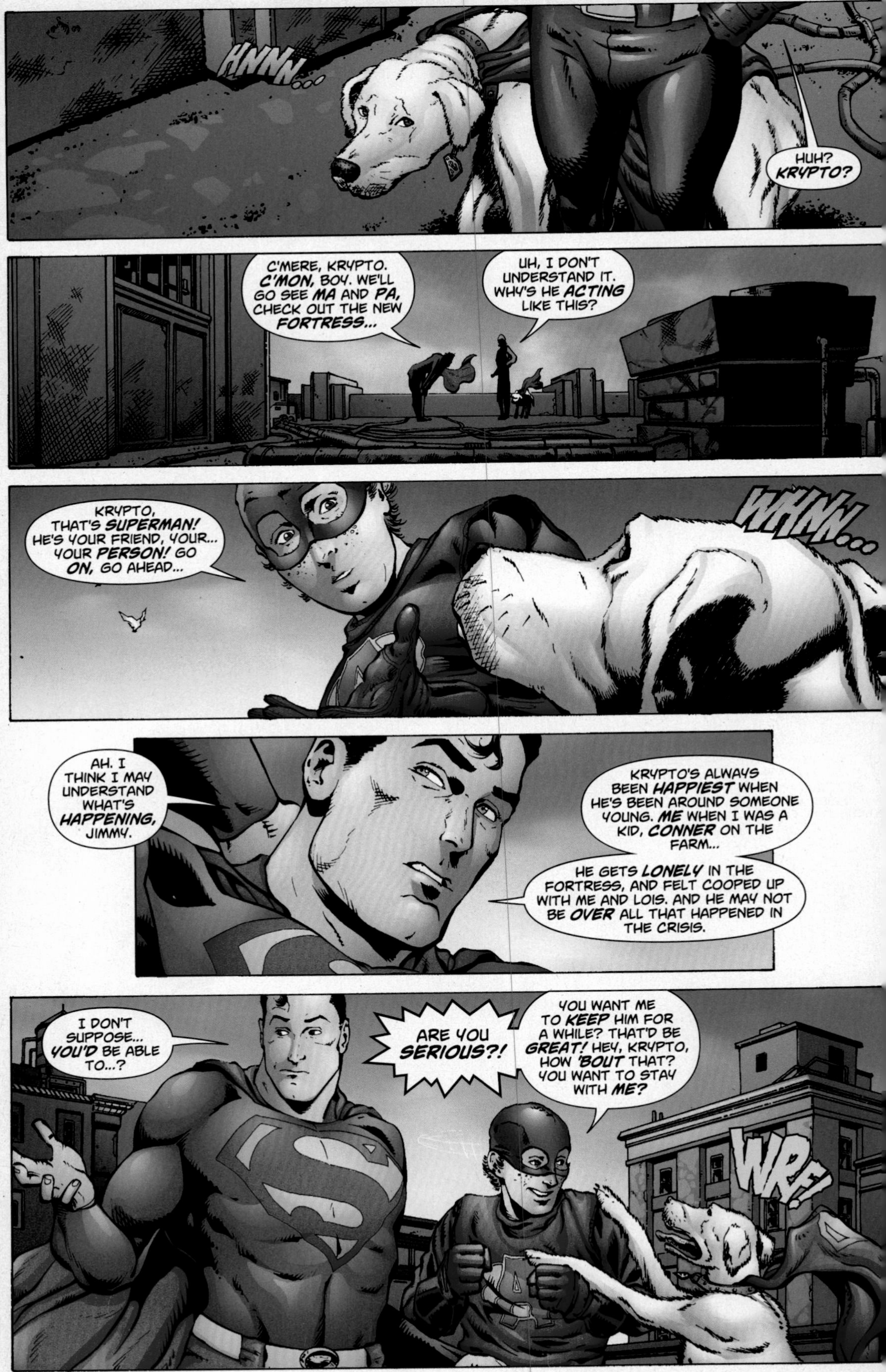
HNNN...
HUH? KRYPTO?
C'MERE, KRYPTO. C'MON, BOY. WE'LL GO SEE MA AND PA, CHECK OUT THE NEW FORTRESS...
UH, I DON'T UNDERSTAND IT. WHY'S HE ACTING LIKE THIS?
KRYPTO, THAT'S SUPERMAN! HE'S YOUR FRIEND, YOUR... YOUR PERSON! GO ON, GO AHEAD...
WHNN...
AH. I THINK I MAY UNDERSTAND WHAT'S HAPPENING, JIMMY.
KRYPTO'S ALWAYS BEEN HAPPIEST WHEN HE'S BEEN AROUND SOMEONE YOUNG. ME WHEN I WAS A KID, CONNER ON THE FARM...
HE GETS LONELY IN THE FORTRESS, AND FELT COOPED UP WITH ME AND LOIS. AND HE MAY NOT BE OVER ALL THAT HAPPENED IN THE CRISIS.
I DON'T SUPPOSE... YOU'D BE ABLE TO...?
ARE YOU SERIOUS?!
YOU WANT ME TO KEEP HIM FOR A WHILE? THAT'D BE GREAT! HEY, KRYPTO, HOW 'BOUT THAT? YOU WANT TO STAY WITH ME?
WRF!

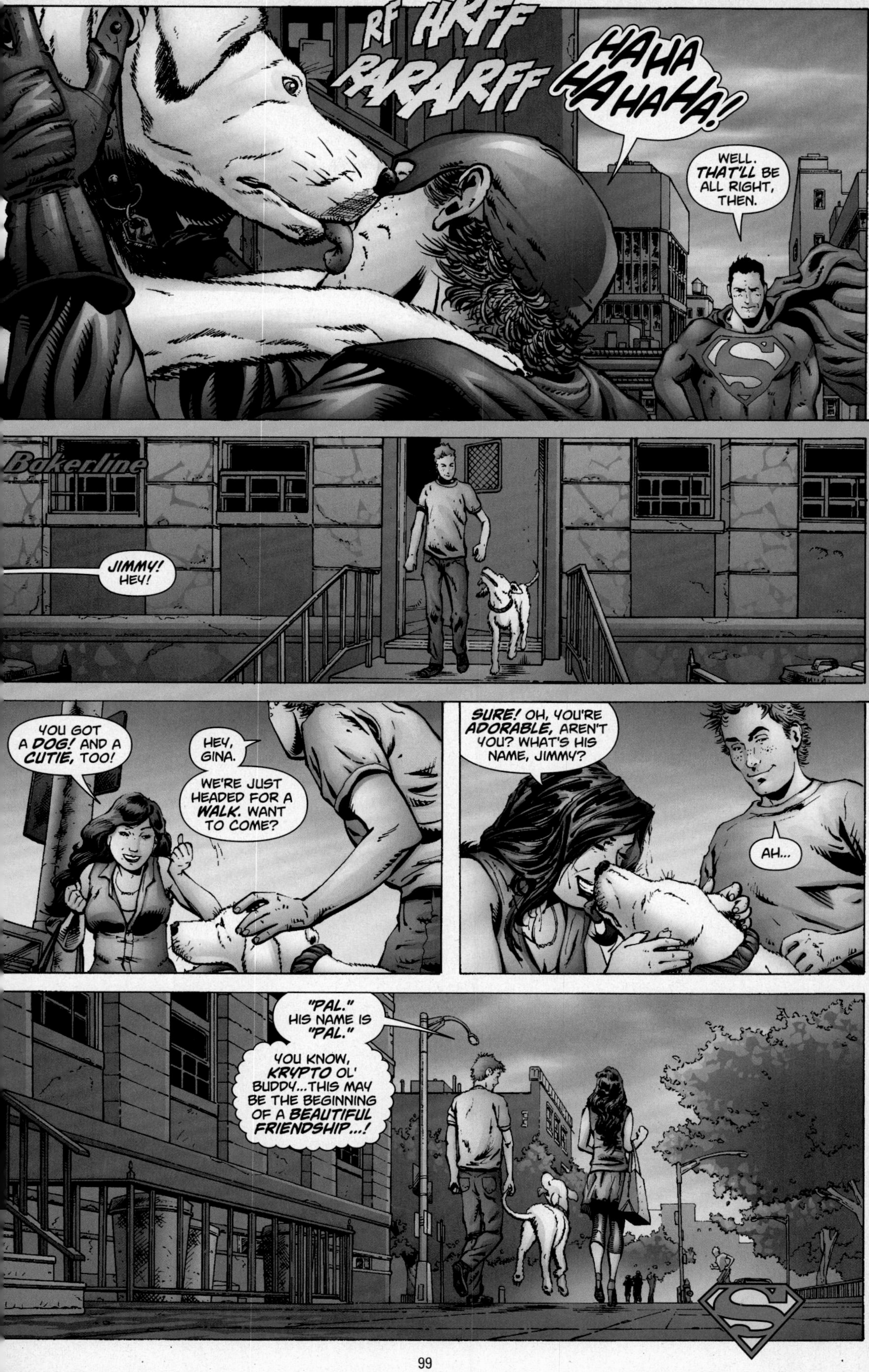
RF HRFF
RARARFF
HAHA HAHAHA!
WELL. THAT'LL BE ALL RIGHT, THEN.
Bakerline
JIMMY! HEY!
YOU GOT A DOG! AND A CUTIE, TOO!
HEY, GINA.
WE'RE JUST HEADED FOR A WALK. WANT TO COME?
SURE! OH, YOU'RE ADORABLE, AREN'T YOU? WHAT'S HIS NAME, JIMMY?
AH...
"PAL." HIS NAME IS "PAL."
YOU KNOW, KRYPTO OL' BUDDY...THIS MAY BE THE BEGINNING OF A BEAUTIFUL FRIENDSHIP...!

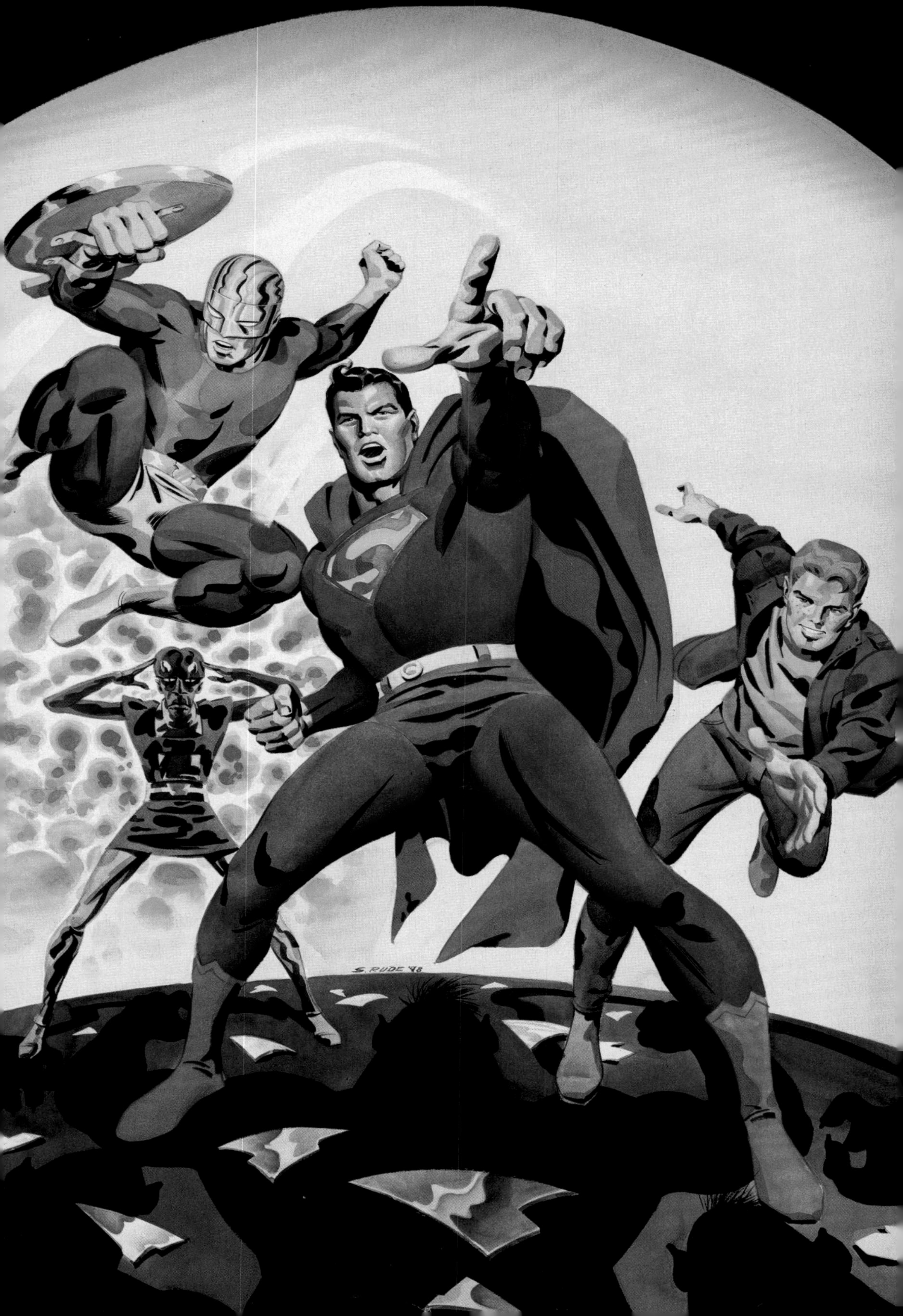
S. RUDE '98

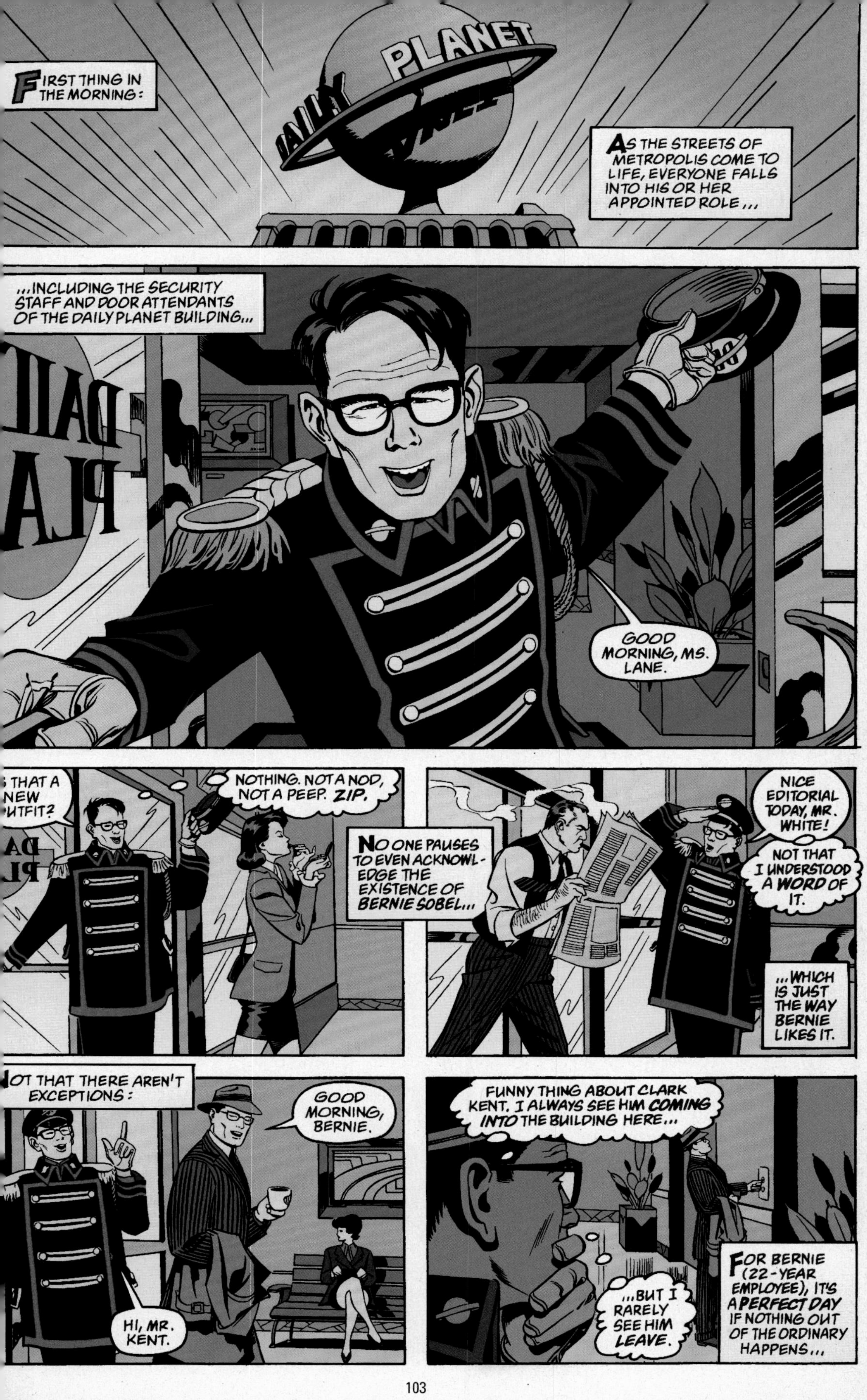
FIRST THING IN THE MORNING:
DAILY PLANET
AS THE STREETS OF METROPOLIS COME TO LIFE, EVERYONE FALLS INTO HIS OR HER APPOINTED ROLE...
...INCLUDING THE SECURITY STAFF AND DOOR ATTENDANTS OF THE DAILY PLANET BUILDING...
GOOD MORNING, MS. LANE.
S THAT A NEW UTFIT?
NOTHING. NOT A NOD, NOT A PEEP. ZIP.
NO ONE PAUSES TO EVEN ACKNOWLEDGE THE EXISTENCE OF BERNIE SOBEL...
NICE EDITORIAL TODAY, MR. WHITE!
NOT THAT I UNDERSTOOD A WORD OF IT.
...WHICH IS JUST THE WAY BERNIE LIKES IT.
OT THAT THERE AREN'T EXCEPTIONS:
GOOD MORNING, BERNIE.
HI, MR. KENT.
FUNNY THING ABOUT CLARK KENT. I ALWAYS SEE HIM COMING INTO THE BUILDING HERE...
...BUT I RARELY SEE HIM LEAVE.
FOR BERNIE (22-YEAR EMPLOYEE), IT'S A PERFECT DAY IF NOTHING OUT OF THE ORDINARY HAPPENS...

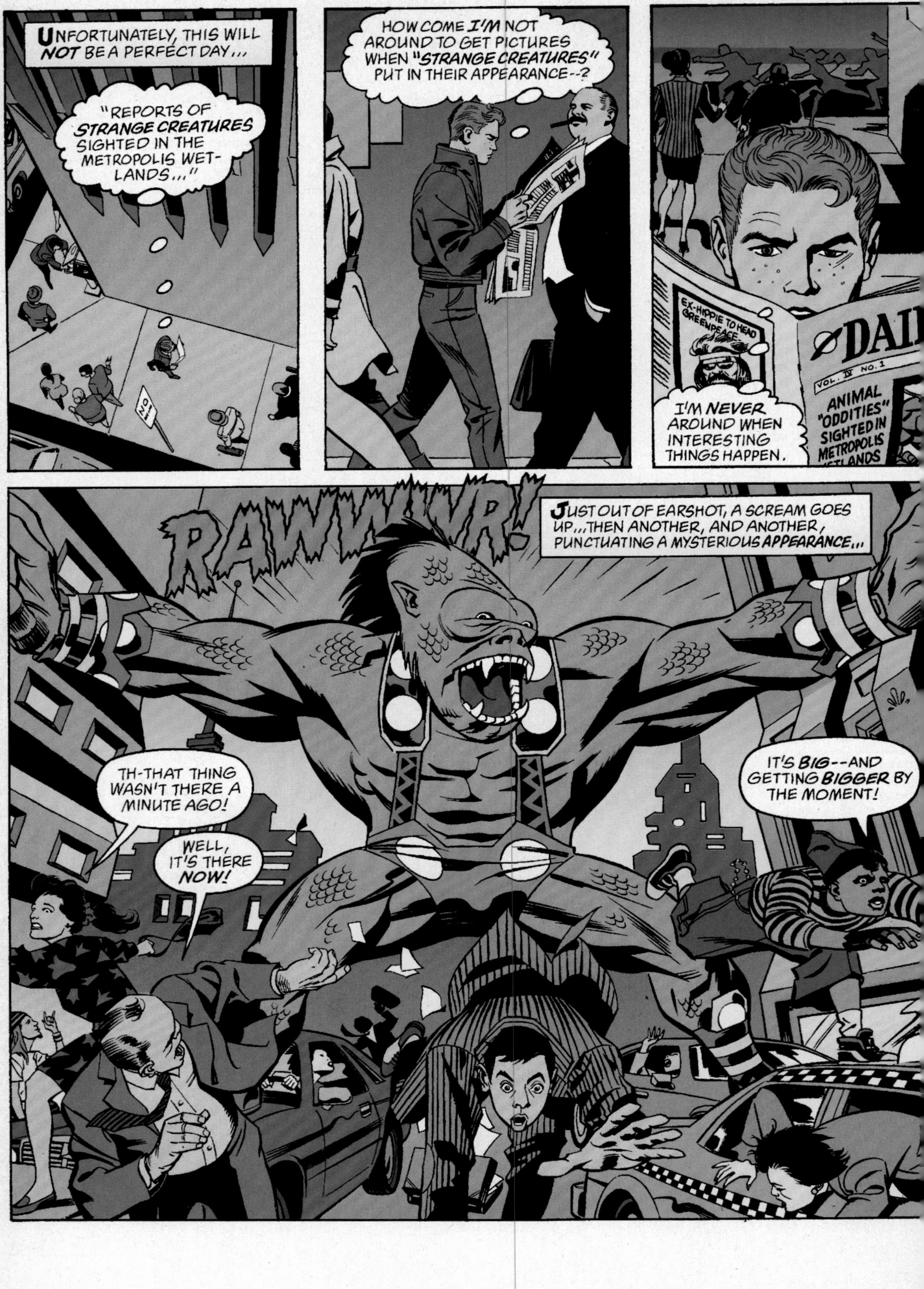
UNFORTUNATELY, THIS WILL NOT BE A PERFECT DAY...
"REPORTS OF STRANGE CREATURES SIGHTED IN THE METROPOLIS WET-LANDS..."
HOW COME I'M NOT AROUND TO GET PICTURES WHEN "STRANGE CREATURES" PUT IN THEIR APPEARANCE--?
EX-HIPPIE TO HEAD GREENPEACE
DAIL
VOL. IV NO. 1
ANIMAL "ODDITIES" SIGHTED IN METROPOLIS WETLANDS
I'M NEVER AROUND WHEN INTERESTING THINGS HAPPEN.
RAWWWR!
JUST OUT OF EARSHOT, A SCREAM GOES UP...THEN ANOTHER, AND ANOTHER, PUNCTUATING A MYSTERIOUS APPEARANCE...
TH-THAT THING WASN'T THERE A MINUTE AGO!
WELL, IT'S THERE NOW!
IT'S BIG--AND GETTING BIGGER BY THE MOMENT!

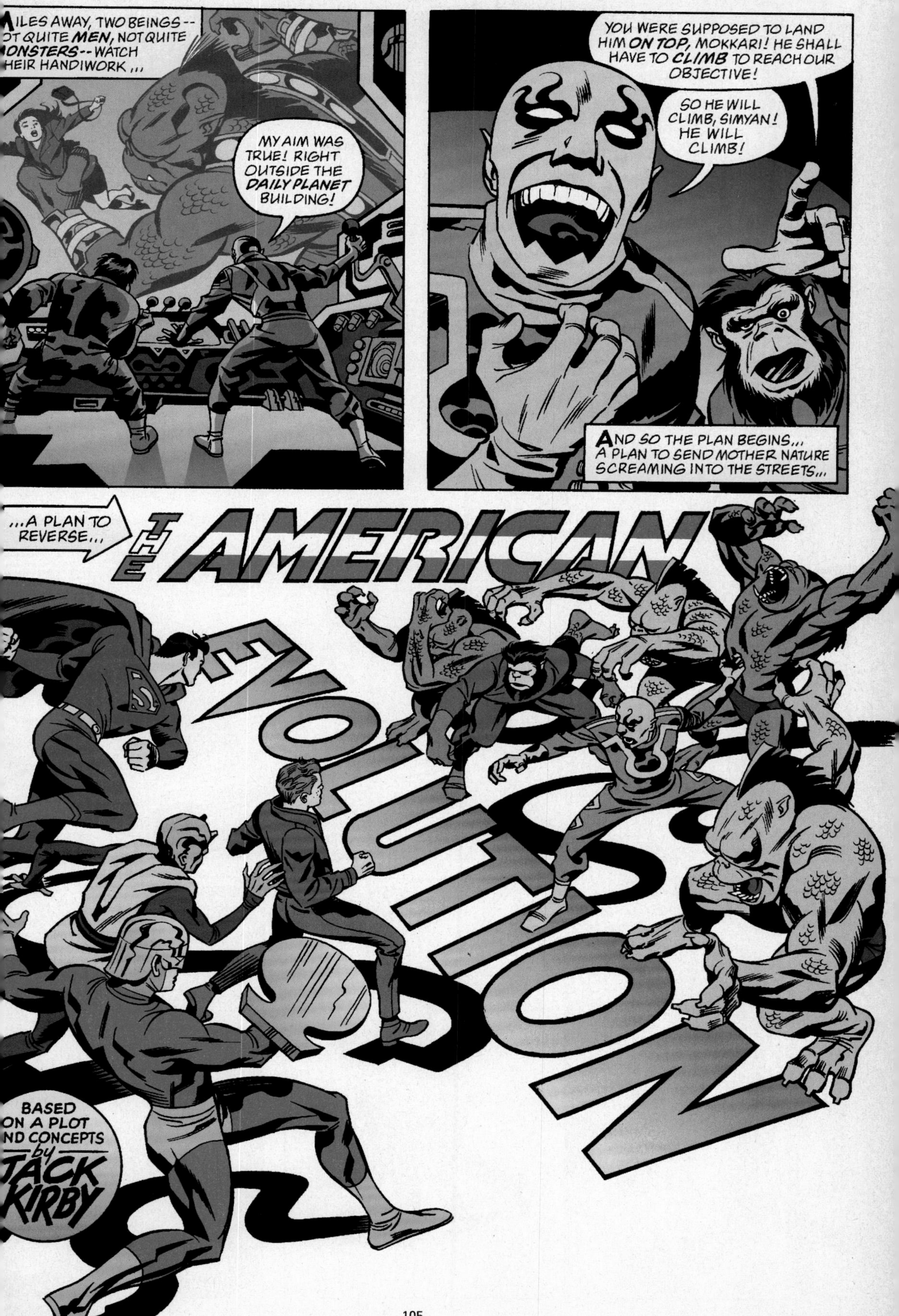
MILES AWAY, TWO BEINGS -- NOT QUITE MEN, NOT QUITE MONSTERS -- WATCH THEIR HANDIWORK ...
MY AIM WAS TRUE! RIGHT OUTSIDE THE DAILY PLANET BUILDING!
YOU WERE SUPPOSED TO LAND HIM ON TOP, MOKKARI! HE SHALL HAVE TO CLIMB TO REACH OUR OBJECTIVE!
SO HE WILL CLIMB, SIMYAN! HE WILL CLIMB!
AND SO THE PLAN BEGINS... A PLAN TO SEND MOTHER NATURE SCREAMING INTO THE STREETS...
...A PLAN TO REVERSE...
THE AMERICAN EVOLUTION
BASED ON A PLOT AND CONCEPTS by JACK KIRBY

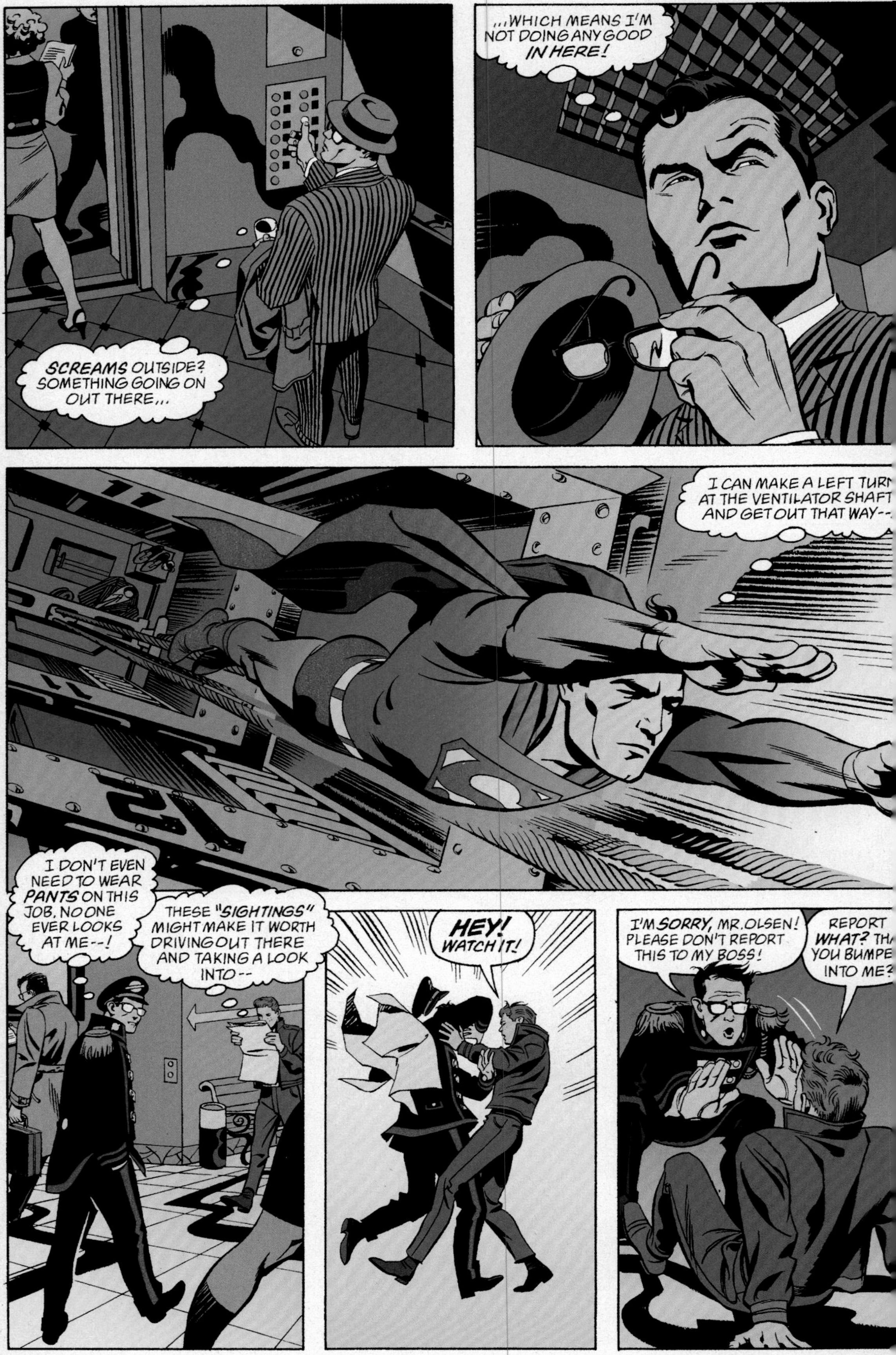
SCREAMS OUTSIDE? SOMETHING GOING ON OUT THERE...
...WHICH MEANS I'M NOT DOING ANY GOOD IN HERE!
I CAN MAKE A LEFT TURN AT THE VENTILATOR SHAFT AND GET OUT THAT WAY--
I DON'T EVEN NEED TO WEAR PANTS ON THIS JOB. NO ONE EVER LOOKS AT ME--!
THESE "SIGHTINGS" MIGHT MAKE IT WORTH DRIVING OUT THERE AND TAKING A LOOK INTO--
HEY! WATCH IT!
I'M SORRY, MR. OLSEN! PLEASE DON'T REPORT THIS TO MY BOSS!
REPORT WHAT? THA YOU BUMPE INTO ME?

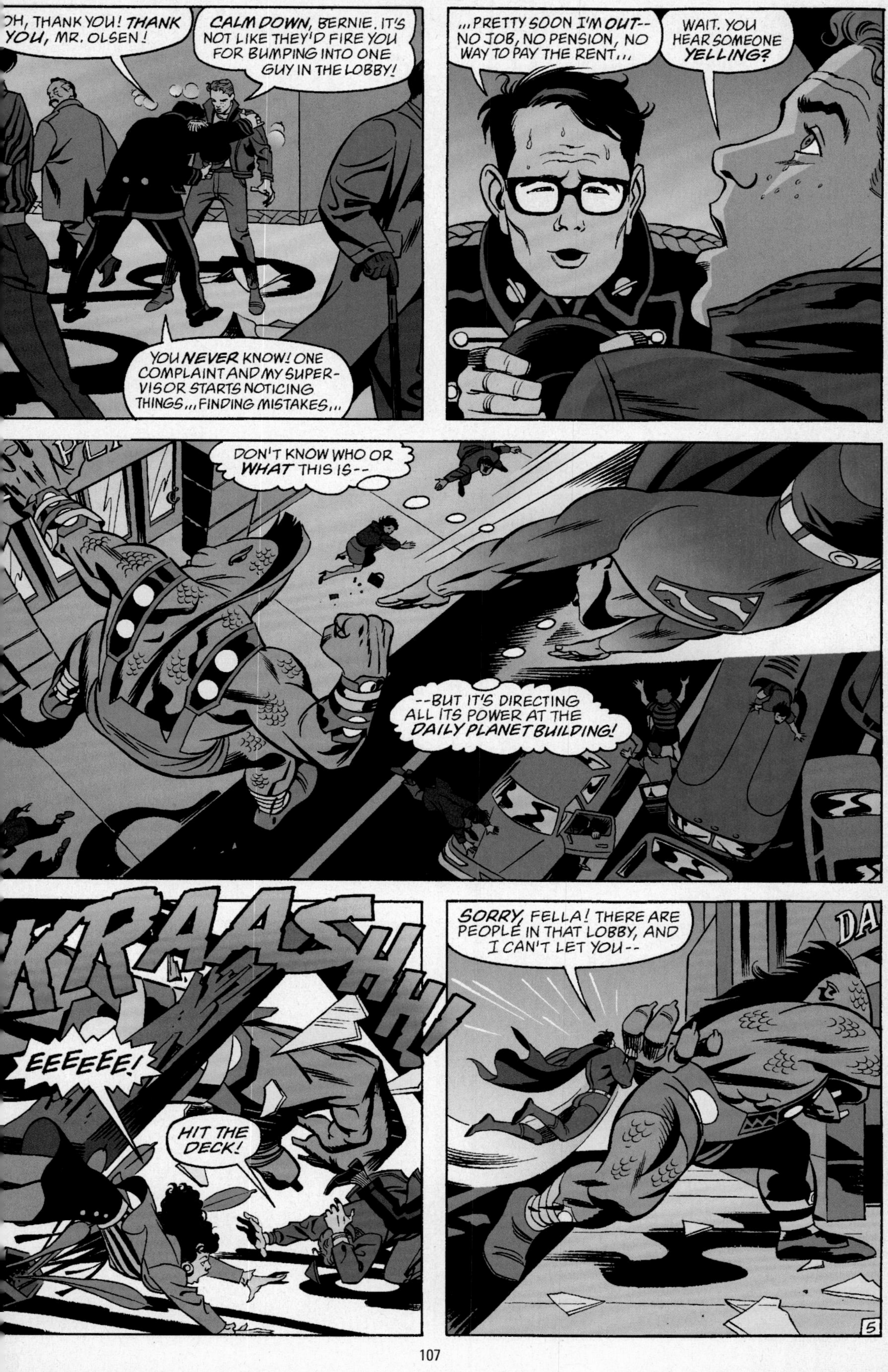
OH, THANK YOU! THANK YOU, MR. OLSEN!
CALM DOWN, BERNIE. IT'S NOT LIKE THEY'D FIRE YOU FOR BUMPING INTO ONE GUY IN THE LOBBY!
YOU NEVER KNOW! ONE COMPLAINT AND MY SUPERVISOR STARTS NOTICING THINGS... FINDING MISTAKES...
...PRETTY SOON I'M OUT-- NO JOB, NO PENSION, NO WAY TO PAY THE RENT...
WAIT. YOU HEAR SOMEONE YELLING?
DON'T KNOW WHO OR WHAT THIS IS--
--BUT IT'S DIRECTING ALL ITS POWER AT THE DAILY PLANET BUILDING!
KRAASHH!
EEEEEE!
HIT THE DECK!
SORRY, FELLA! THERE ARE PEOPLE IN THAT LOBBY, AND I CAN'T LET YOU--
5

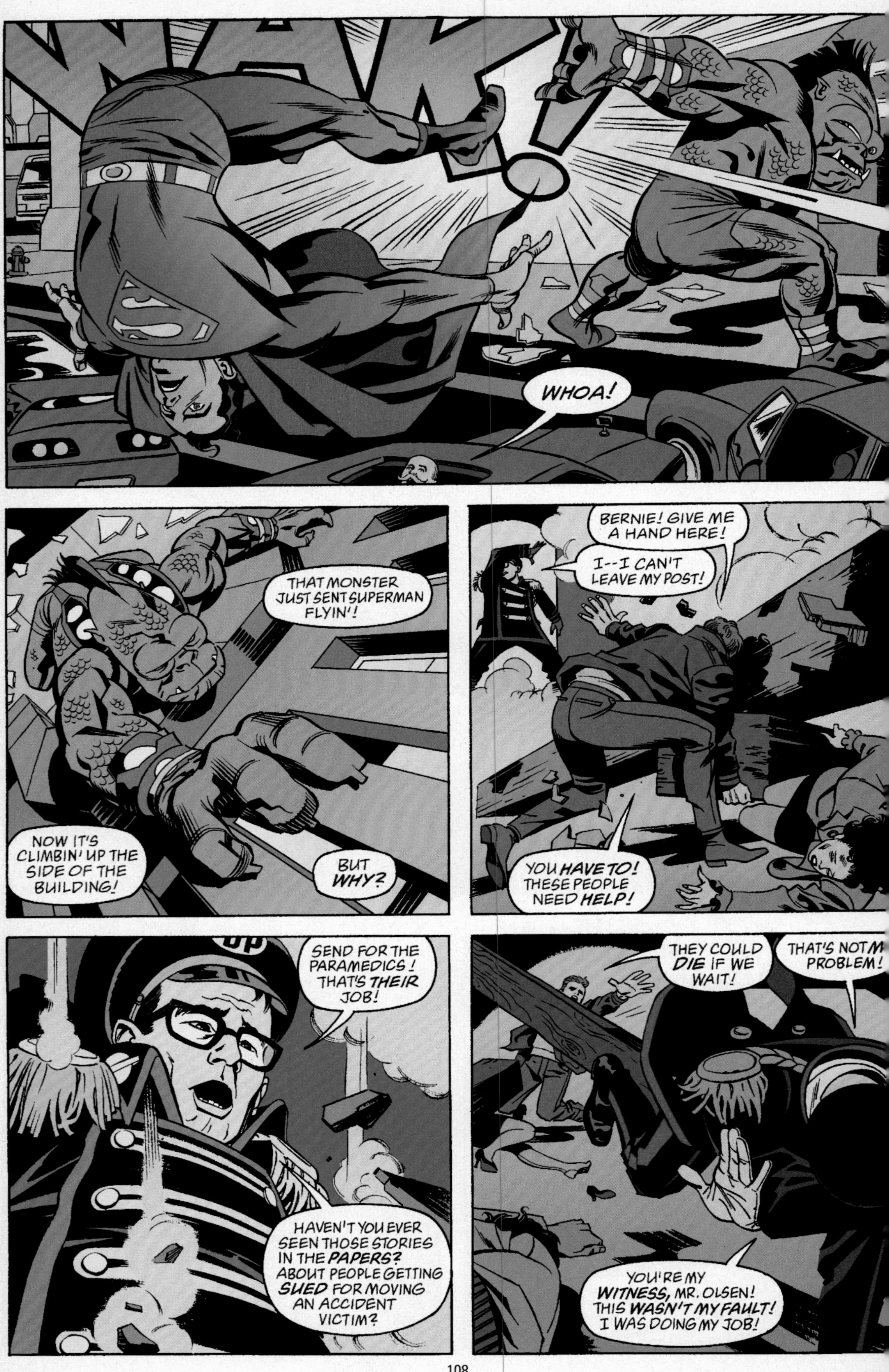
WAK
WHOA!
THAT MONSTER JUST SENT SUPERMAN FLYIN'!
NOW IT'S CLIMBIN' UP THE SIDE OF THE BUILDING!
BUT WHY?
BERNIE! GIVE ME A HAND HERE!
I--I CAN'T LEAVE MY POST!
YOU HAVE TO! THESE PEOPLE NEED HELP!
SEND FOR THE PARAMEDICS! THAT'S THEIR JOB!
HAVEN'T YOU EVER SEEN THOSE STORIES IN THE PAPERS? ABOUT PEOPLE GETTING SUED FOR MOVING AN ACCIDENT VICTIM?
THEY COULD DIE IF WE WAIT!
THAT'S NOT M PROBLEM!
YOU'RE MY WITNESS, MR. OLSEN! THIS WASN'T MY FAULT! I WAS DOING MY JOB!

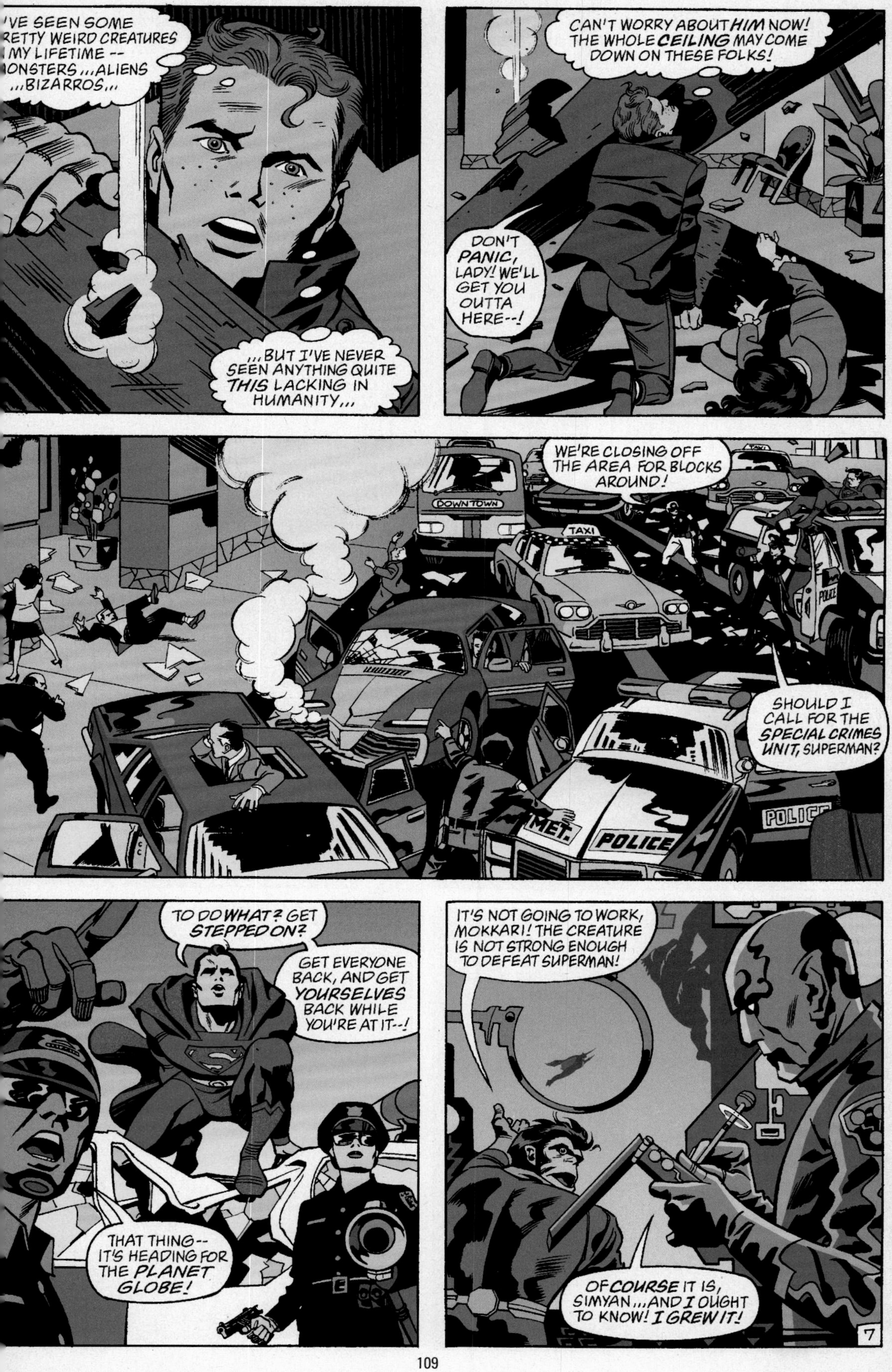
'VE SEEN SOME RETTY WEIRD CREATURES MY LIFETIME -- ONSTERS ... ALIENS ... BIZARROS ...
... BUT I'VE NEVER SEEN ANYTHING QUITE THIS LACKING IN HUMANITY ...
CAN'T WORRY ABOUT HIM NOW! THE WHOLE CEILING MAY COME DOWN ON THESE FOLKS!
DON'T PANIC, LADY! WE'LL GET YOU OUTTA HERE--!
WE'RE CLOSING OFF THE AREA FOR BLOCKS AROUND!
SHOULD I CALL FOR THE SPECIAL CRIMES UNIT, SUPERMAN?
DOWNTOWN
TAXI
MET.
POLICE
TO DO WHAT? GET STEPPED ON?
GET EVERYONE BACK, AND GET YOURSELVES BACK WHILE YOU'RE AT IT--!
THAT THING-- IT'S HEADING FOR THE PLANET GLOBE!
IT'S NOT GOING TO WORK, MOKKARI! THE CREATURE IS NOT STRONG ENOUGH TO DEFEAT SUPERMAN!
OF COURSE IT IS, SIMYAN ... AND I OUGHT TO KNOW! I GREW IT!
7

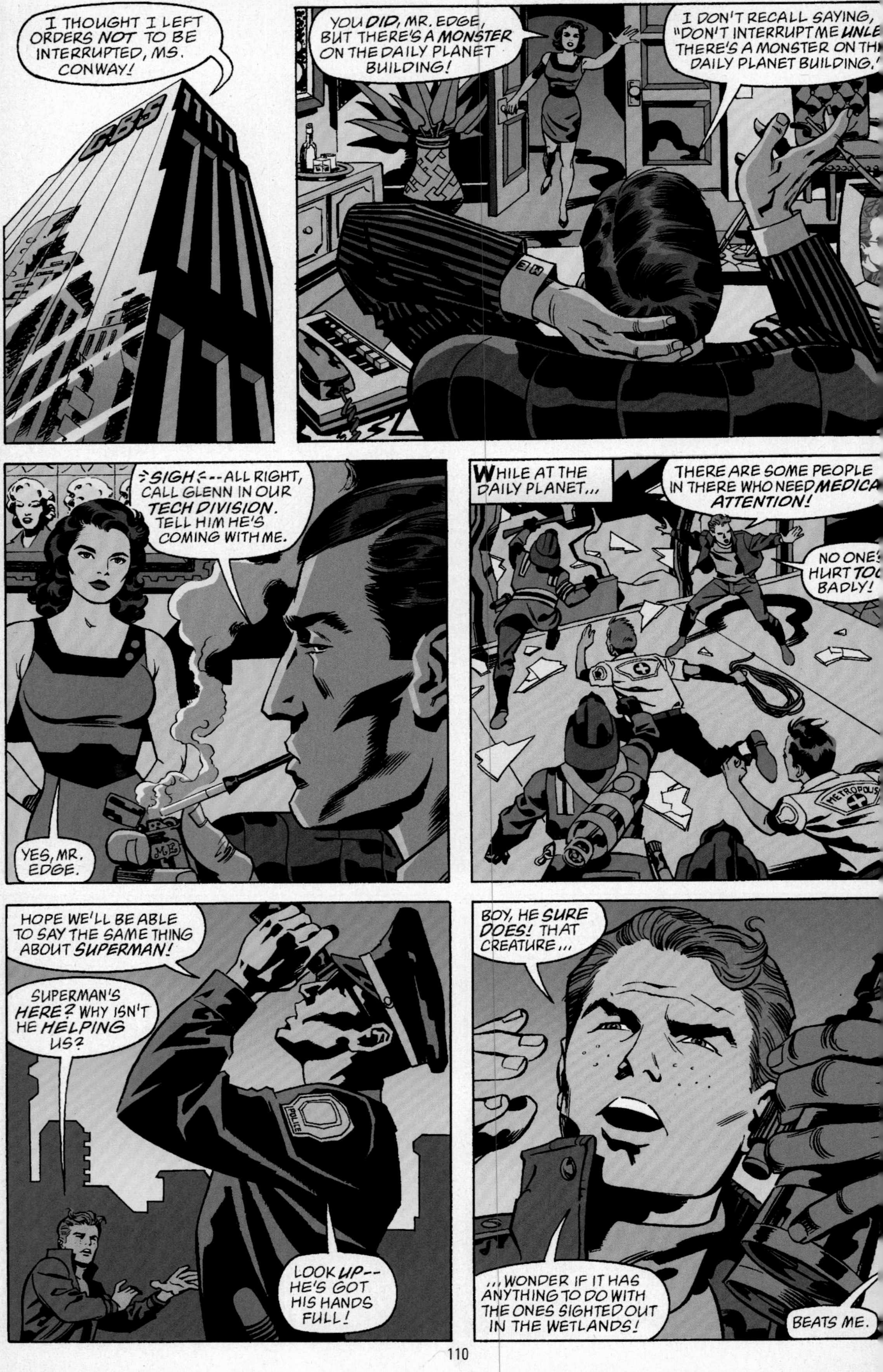

I THOUGHT I LEFT ORDERS NOT TO BE INTERRUPTED, MS. CONWAY!
YOU DID, MR. EDGE, BUT THERE'S A MONSTER ON THE DAILY PLANET BUILDING!
I DON'T RECALL SAYING, "DON'T INTERRUPT ME UNLE THERE'S A MONSTER ON TH DAILY PLANET BUILDING."
SIGH --ALL RIGHT, CALL GLENN IN OUR TECH DIVISION. TELL HIM HE'S COMING WITH ME.
YES, MR. EDGE.
WHILE AT THE DAILY PLANET...
THERE ARE SOME PEOPLE IN THERE WHO NEED MEDICA ATTENTION!
NO ONE'S HURT TOO BADLY!
HOPE WE'LL BE ABLE TO SAY THE SAME THING ABOUT SUPERMAN!
SUPERMAN'S HERE? WHY ISN'T HE HELPING US?
LOOK UP-- HE'S GOT HIS HANDS FULL!
BOY, HE SURE DOES! THAT CREATURE...
...WONDER IF IT HAS ANYTHING TO DO WITH THE ONES SIGHTED OUT IN THE WETLANDS!
BEATS ME.

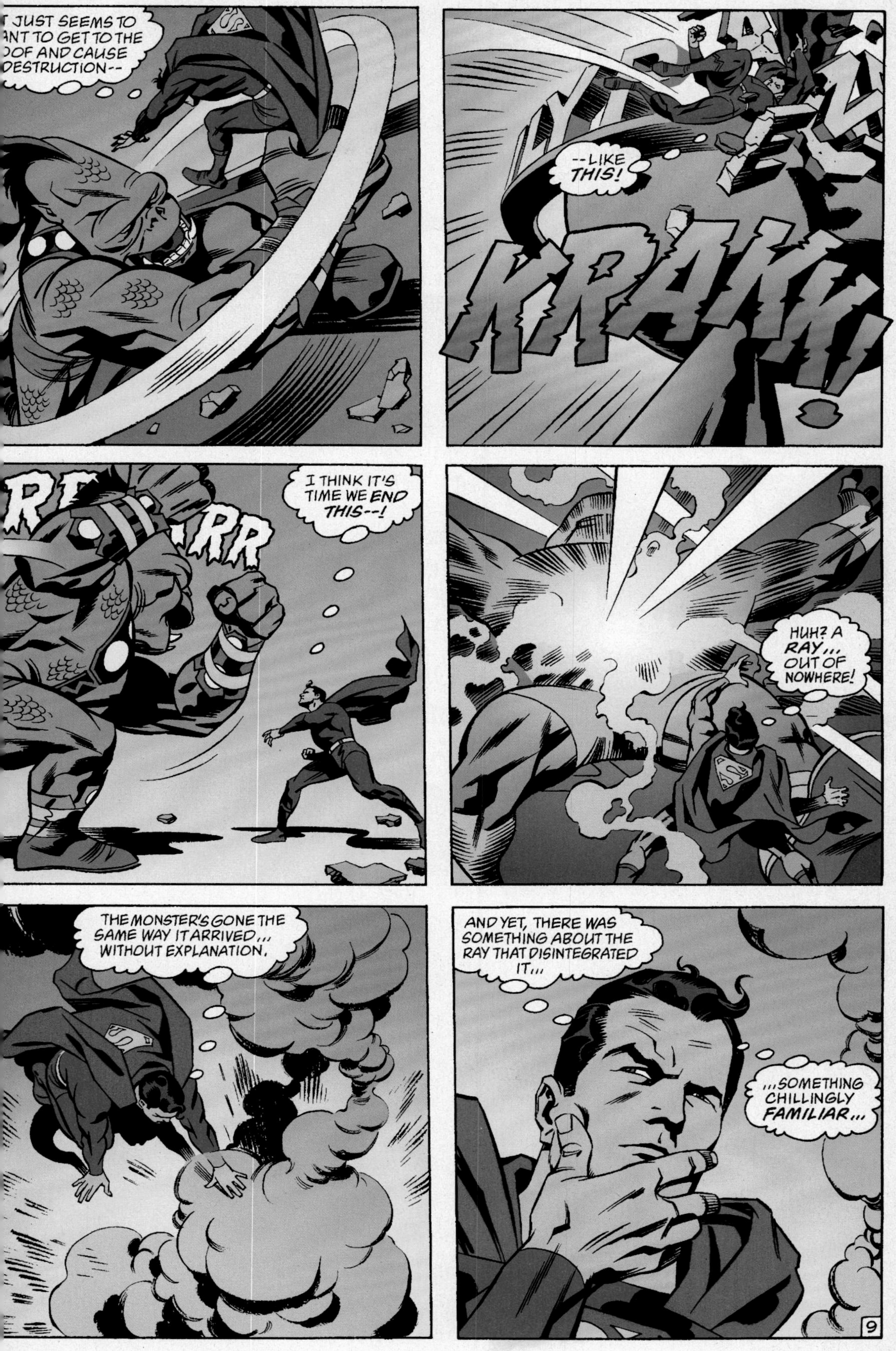
T JUST SEEMS TO
ANT TO GET TO THE
OOF AND CAUSE
DESTRUCTION--
--LIKE THIS!
KRAKK!
I THINK IT'S TIME WE END THIS--!
HUH? A RAY... OUT OF NOWHERE!
THE MONSTER'S GONE THE SAME WAY IT ARRIVED... WITHOUT EXPLANATION.
AND YET, THERE WAS SOMETHING ABOUT THE RAY THAT DISINTEGRATED IT...
...SOMETHING CHILLINGLY FAMILIAR...
9

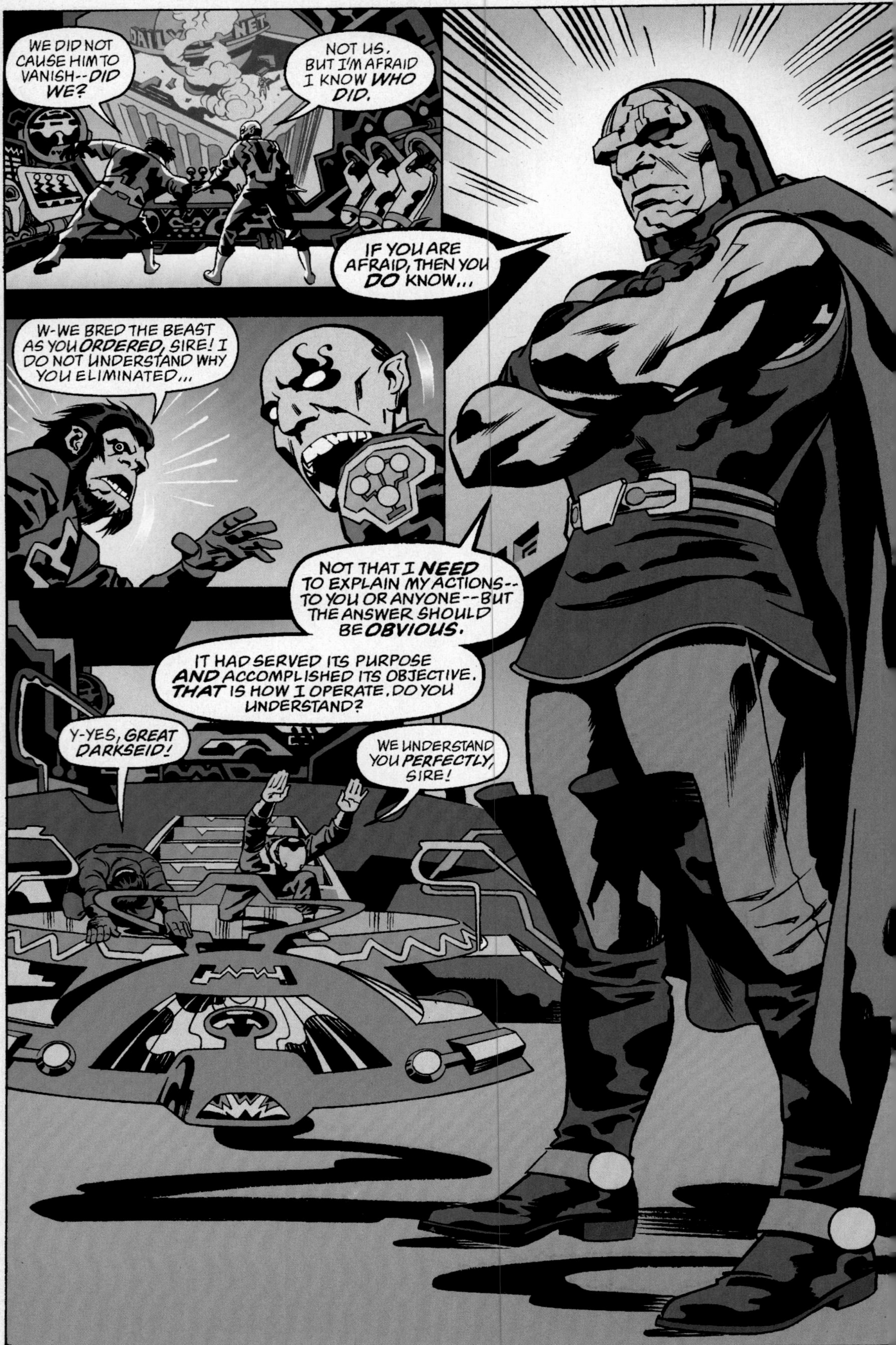
WE DID NOT CAUSE HIM TO VANISH--DID WE?
NOT US. BUT I'M AFRAID I KNOW WHO DID.
IF YOU ARE AFRAID, THEN YOU DO KNOW...
W-WE BRED THE BEAST AS YOU ORDERED, SIRE! I DO NOT UNDERSTAND WHY YOU ELIMINATED...
NOT THAT I NEED TO EXPLAIN MY ACTIONS--TO YOU OR ANYONE--BUT THE ANSWER SHOULD BE OBVIOUS.
IT HAD SERVED ITS PURPOSE AND ACCOMPLISHED ITS OBJECTIVE. THAT IS HOW I OPERATE. DO YOU UNDERSTAND?
Y-YES, GREAT DARKSEID!
WE UNDERSTAND YOU PERFECTLY, SIRE!

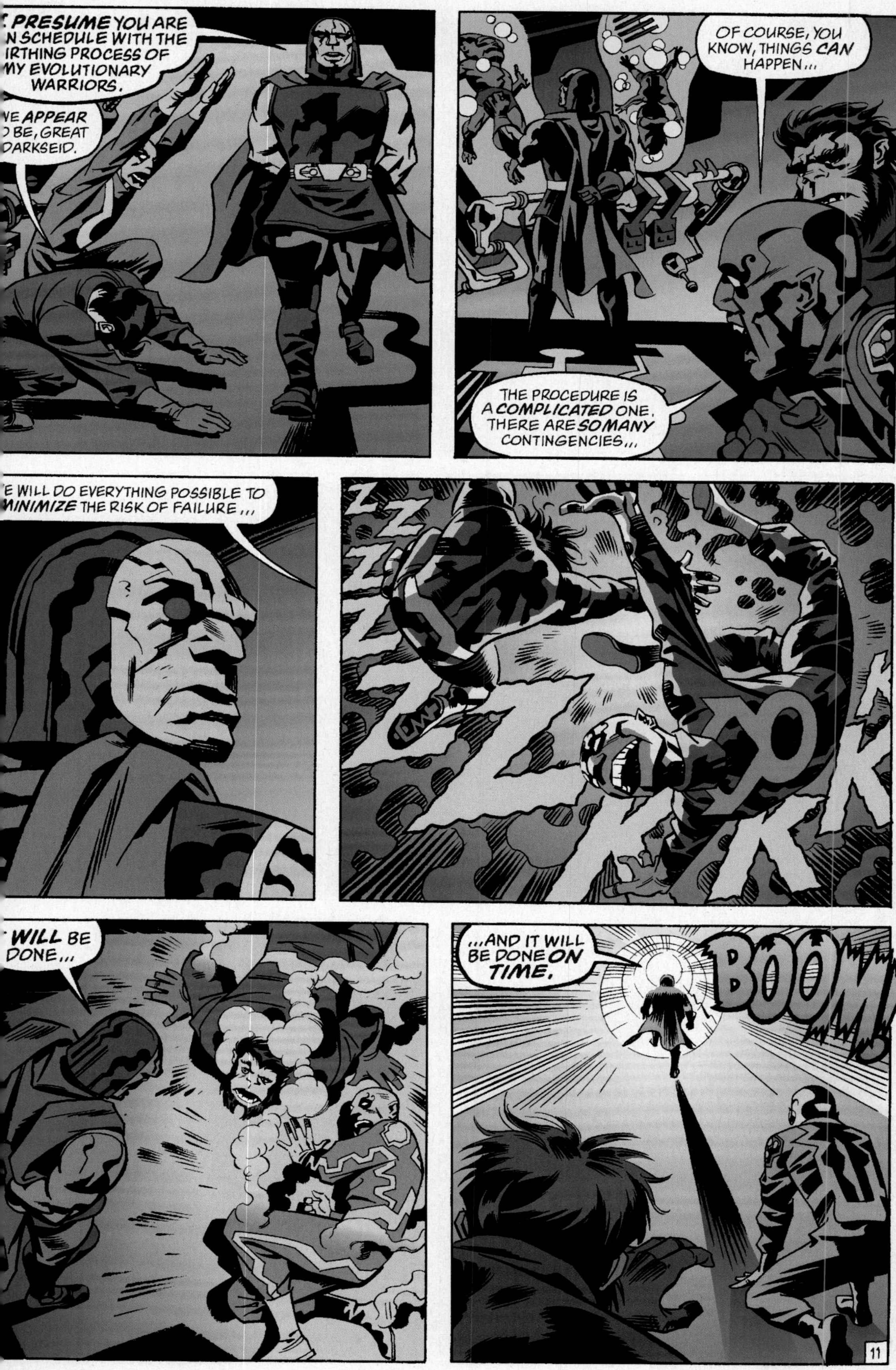

I PRESUME YOU ARE ON SCHEDULE WITH THE BIRTHING PROCESS OF MY EVOLUTIONARY WARRIORS.
WE APPEAR TO BE, GREAT DARKSEID.
OF COURSE, YOU KNOW, THINGS CAN HAPPEN...
THE PROCEDURE IS A COMPLICATED ONE. THERE ARE SO MANY CONTINGENCIES...
WE WILL DO EVERYTHING POSSIBLE TO MINIMIZE THE RISK OF FAILURE...
IT WILL BE DONE...
...AND IT WILL BE DONE ON TIME.
BOOM!
11

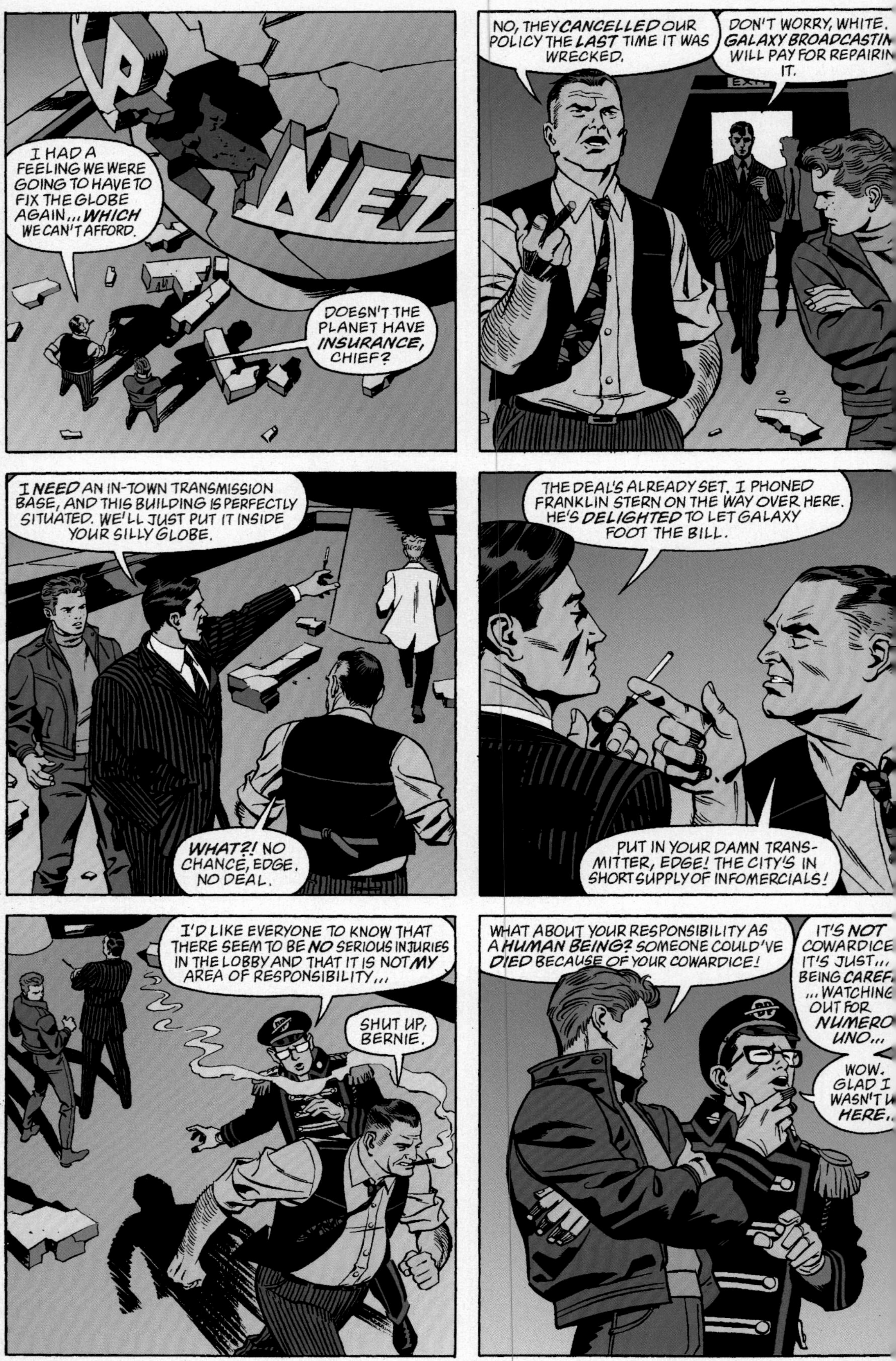
I HAD A FEELING WE WERE GOING TO HAVE TO FIX THE GLOBE AGAIN... WHICH WE CAN'T AFFORD.
DOESN'T THE PLANET HAVE INSURANCE, CHIEF?
NO, THEY CANCELLED OUR POLICY THE LAST TIME IT WAS WRECKED.
DON'T WORRY, WHITE. GALAXY BROADCASTIN WILL PAY FOR REPAIRIN IT.
I NEED AN IN-TOWN TRANSMISSION BASE, AND THIS BUILDING IS PERFECTLY SITUATED. WE'LL JUST PUT IT INSIDE YOUR SILLY GLOBE.
WHAT?! NO CHANCE, EDGE. NO DEAL.
THE DEAL'S ALREADY SET. I PHONED FRANKLIN STERN ON THE WAY OVER HERE. HE'S DELIGHTED TO LET GALAXY FOOT THE BILL.
PUT IN YOUR DAMN TRANS-MITTER, EDGE! THE CITY'S IN SHORT SUPPLY OF INFOMERCIALS!
I'D LIKE EVERYONE TO KNOW THAT THERE SEEM TO BE NO SERIOUS INJURIES IN THE LOBBY AND THAT IT IS NOT MY AREA OF RESPONSIBILITY...
SHUT UP, BERNIE.
WHAT ABOUT YOUR RESPONSIBILITY AS A HUMAN BEING? SOMEONE COULD'VE DIED BECAUSE OF YOUR COWARDICE!
IT'S NOT COWARDICE IT'S JUST... BEING CAREF ...WATCHING OUT FOR NUMERO UNO...
WOW. GLAD I WASN'T HERE.

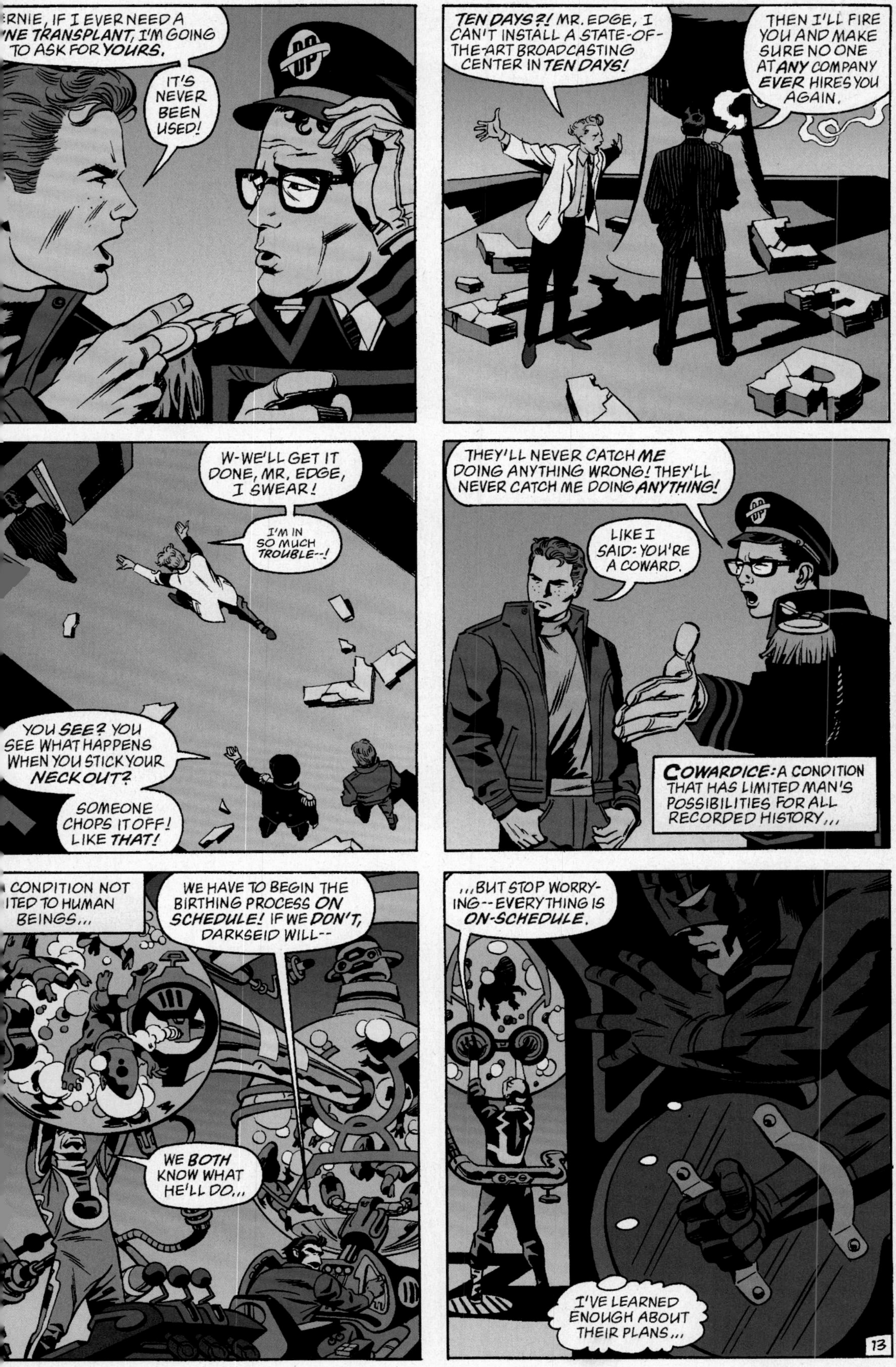
ERNIE, IF I EVER NEED A
NE TRANSPLANT, I'M GOING
TO ASK FOR YOURS.
IT'S NEVER BEEN USED!
TEN DAYS?! MR. EDGE, I CAN'T INSTALL A STATE-OF-THE-ART BROADCASTING CENTER IN TEN DAYS!
THEN I'LL FIRE YOU AND MAKE SURE NO ONE AT ANY COMPANY EVER HIRES YOU AGAIN.
W-WE'LL GET IT DONE, MR. EDGE, I SWEAR!
I'M IN SO MUCH TROUBLE--!
YOU SEE? YOU SEE WHAT HAPPENS WHEN YOU STICK YOUR NECK OUT?
SOMEONE CHOPS IT OFF! LIKE THAT!
THEY'LL NEVER CATCH ME DOING ANYTHING WRONG! THEY'LL NEVER CATCH ME DOING ANYTHING!
LIKE I SAID: YOU'RE A COWARD.
COWARDICE: A CONDITION THAT HAS LIMITED MAN'S POSSIBILITIES FOR ALL RECORDED HISTORY...
CONDITION NOT ITED TO HUMAN BEINGS...
WE HAVE TO BEGIN THE BIRTHING PROCESS ON SCHEDULE! IF WE DON'T, DARKSEID WILL--
WE BOTH KNOW WHAT HE'LL DO...
...BUT STOP WORRYING--EVERYTHING IS ON-SCHEDULE.
I'VE LEARNED ENOUGH ABOUT THEIR PLANS...
13

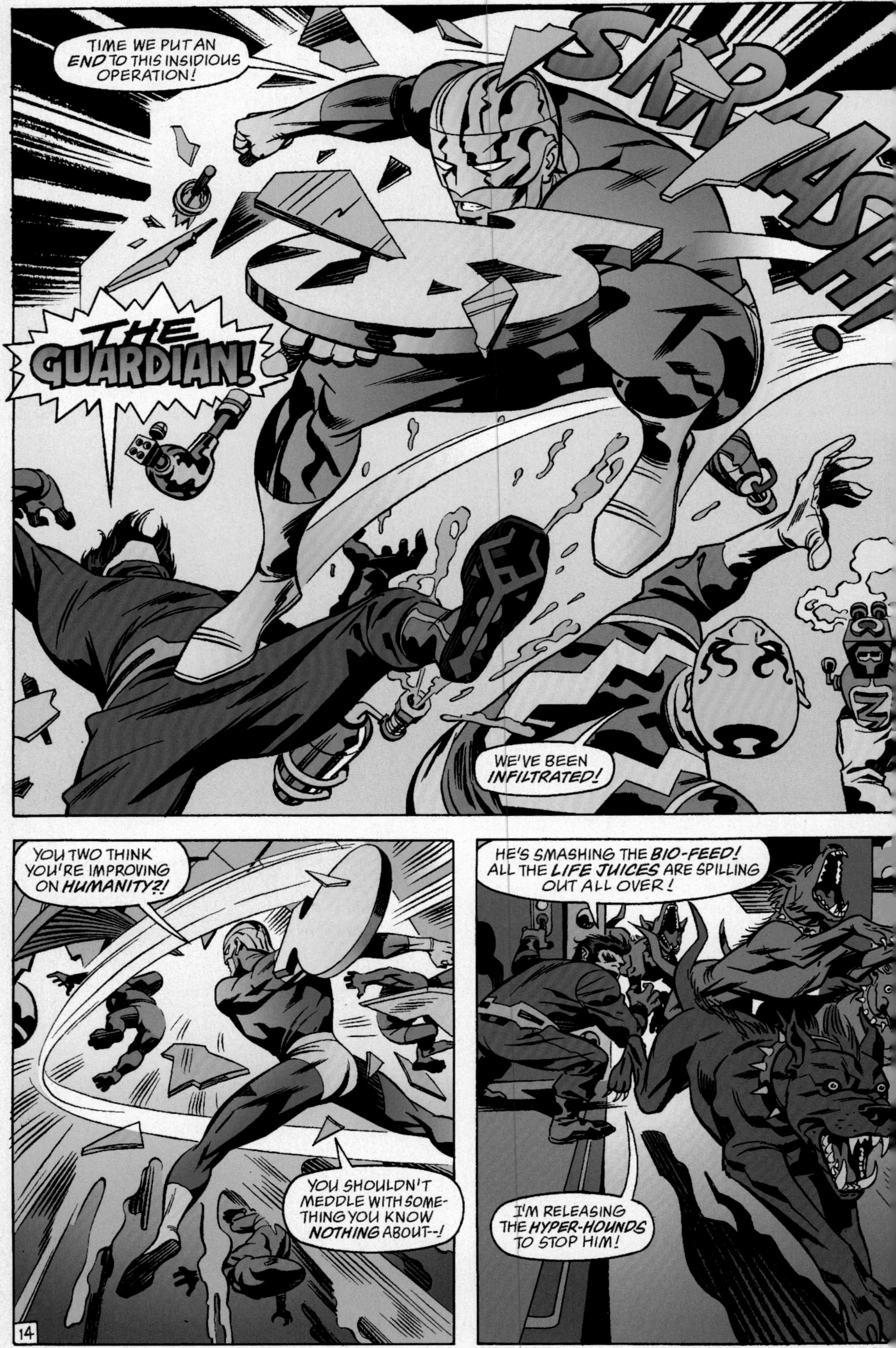
TIME WE PUT AN END TO THIS INSIDIOUS OPERATION!
SKRASH!
THE GUARDIAN!
WE'VE BEEN INFILTRATED!
YOU TWO THINK YOU'RE IMPROVING ON HUMANITY?!
YOU SHOULDN'T MEDDLE WITH SOMETHING YOU KNOW NOTHING ABOUT--!
HE'S SMASHING THE BIO-FEED! ALL THE LIFE JUICES ARE SPILLING OUT ALL OVER!
I'M RELEASING THE HYPER-HOUNDS TO STOP HIM!
14

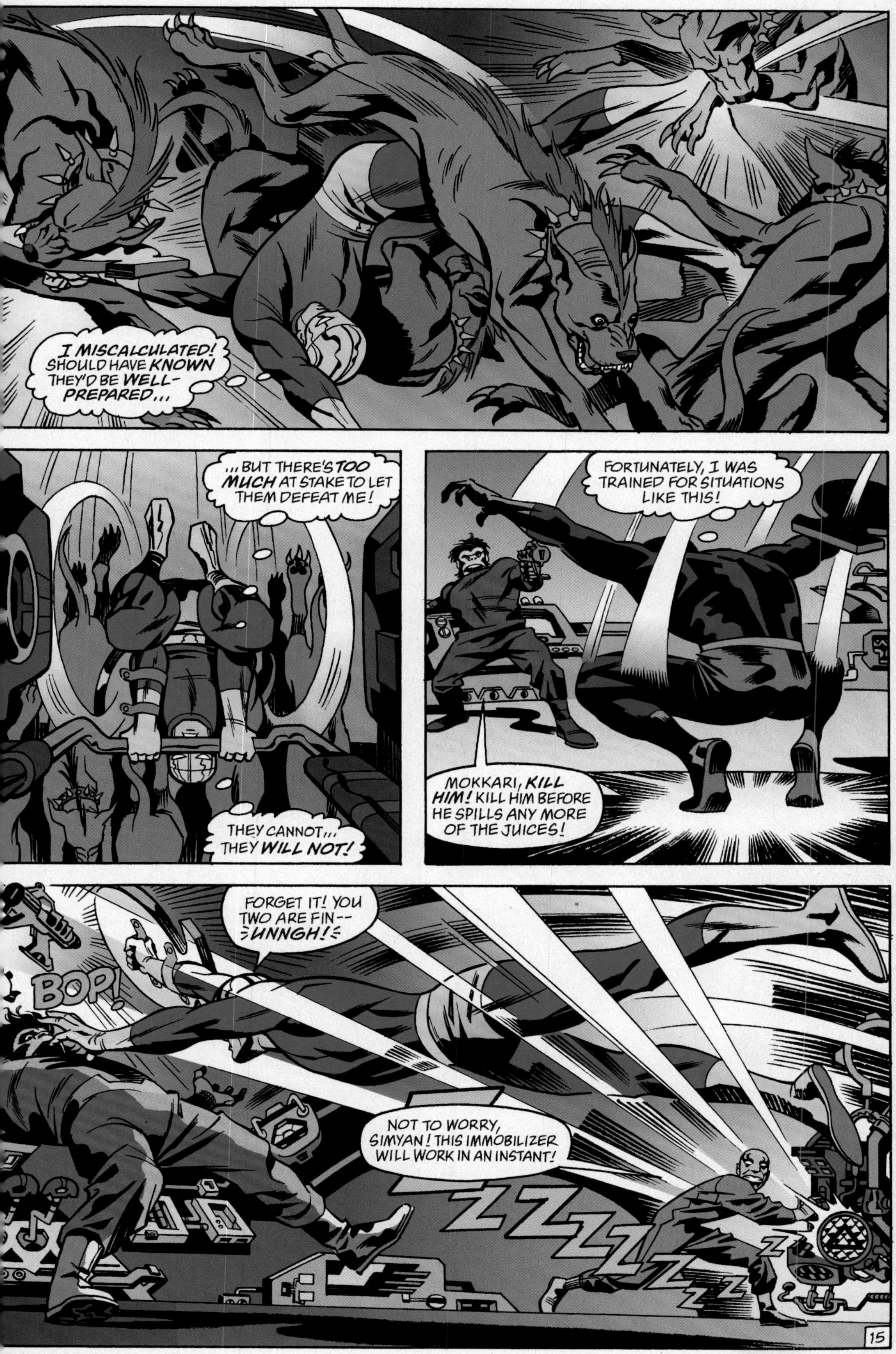
I MISCALCULATED! SHOULD HAVE KNOWN THEY'D BE WELL-PREPARED...
...BUT THERE'S TOO MUCH AT STAKE TO LET THEM DEFEAT ME!
THEY CANNOT... THEY WILL NOT!
FORTUNATELY, I WAS TRAINED FOR SITUATIONS LIKE THIS!
MOKKARI, KILL HIM! KILL HIM BEFORE HE SPILLS ANY MORE OF THE JUICES!
FORGET IT! YOU TWO ARE FIN-- UNNGH!
BOP!
NOT TO WORRY, SIMYAN! THIS IMMOBILIZER WILL WORK IN AN INSTANT!
15

IS HE...?

NO. THERE IS STILL AN *IOTA* OF ENERGY LEFT WITHIN HIM.

WE MAY NEED HIM,...FOR SPARE PARTS OR STUDY. I DRAINED ALL THE *LIFE* FROM HIM,...ALL BUT THE *ABSOLUTE MINIMUM* HE NEEDS TO SUBSIST.

PUT HIM IN THE *LIVING CELL* FOR NOW! WE HAVE MORE *PRESSING* MATTERS TO TEND TO.

HE SPILLED SO MUCH OF THE *JUICE* WE HAVEN'T ENOUGH! IF WE ARE TO CREATE *MORE*...

"...SOMEONE MUST OBTAIN THE MATERIALS FOR US!"

GIVE ME ONE GOOD REASON WHY MY *INTER-GANG* GUYS SHOULD RISK OUR BUTTS TO GET YOU WHAT YOU NEED.

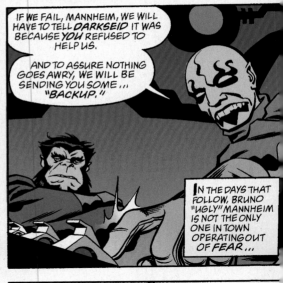

IF WE FAIL, MANNHEIM, WE WILL HAVE TO TELL *DARKSEID* IT WAS BECAUSE *YOU* REFUSED TO HELP US.

AND TO ASSURE NOTHING GOES AWRY, WE WILL BE SENDING YOU SOME... *"BACKUP."*

IN THE DAYS THAT FOLLOW, BRUNO "UGLY" MANNHEIM IS NOT THE ONLY ONE IN TOWN OPERATING OUT OF *FEAR*...

THE RENOVATION OF THE PLANET GLOBE IS DONE UNDER MUCH THE SAME ANXIETY...

THIS EQUIPMENT... I'VE NEVER HEARD OF THESE BRANDS OR SOME OF THESE PARTS!

NEITHER HAVE I, BUT THEY GAVE ME THE SPECS AND WE HAVE TO FOLLOW THEM.

YOU *REALLY* THINK EDGE'LL BE MAD IF THIS AIN'T DONE ON TIME?

THEY SAY HE ONCE FIRED A WOMAN FOR SPILLING HIS CAPPUCCINO, *TWO DAYS* BEFORE HER RETIREMENT. AND THAT WAS HIS *MOTHER*.

DOES *THAT* ANSWER YOUR QUESTION?

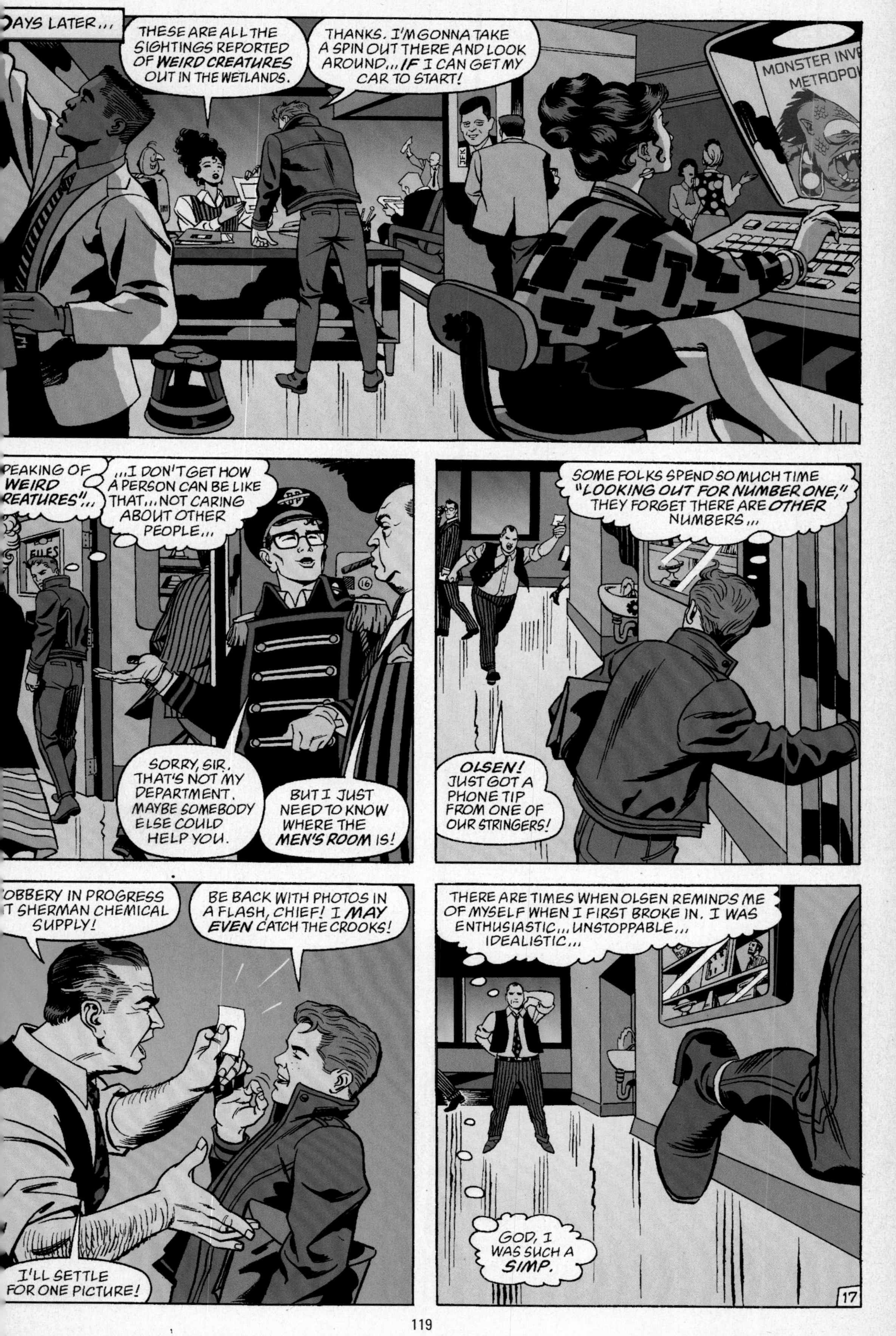
AYS LATER...
THESE ARE ALL THE SIGHTINGS REPORTED OF WEIRD CREATURES OUT IN THE WETLANDS.
THANKS. I'M GONNA TAKE A SPIN OUT THERE AND LOOK AROUND... IF I CAN GET MY CAR TO START!
MONSTER INV
METROPO
PEAKING OF WEIRD REATURES"...
...I DON'T GET HOW A PERSON CAN BE LIKE THAT... NOT CARING ABOUT OTHER PEOPLE...
FILES
SORRY, SIR. THAT'S NOT MY DEPARTMENT. MAYBE SOMEBODY ELSE COULD HELP YOU.
BUT I JUST NEED TO KNOW WHERE THE MEN'S ROOM IS!
SOME FOLKS SPEND SO MUCH TIME "LOOKING OUT FOR NUMBER ONE," THEY FORGET THERE ARE OTHER NUMBERS...
OLSEN! JUST GOT A PHONE TIP FROM ONE OF OUR STRINGERS!
OBBERY IN PROGRESS T SHERMAN CHEMICAL SUPPLY!
BE BACK WITH PHOTOS IN A FLASH, CHIEF! I MAY EVEN CATCH THE CROOKS!
I'LL SETTLE FOR ONE PICTURE!
THERE ARE TIMES WHEN OLSEN REMINDS ME OF MYSELF WHEN I FIRST BROKE IN. I WAS ENTHUSIASTIC... UNSTOPPABLE... IDEALISTIC...
GOD, I WAS SUCH A SIMP.
17

I DON'T GET IT! "UGLY" GIVES US ALL THESE SUPER-WEAPONS TO STEAL *WHAT*--? GOLD? DIAMONDS? NO,... CHEMICALS!

SHUT UP! THE GUY'S PAYING US GOOD MONEY!

YEAH,...

...BUT NOT ENOUGH TO FACE *HIM!*

INTERGANG THUGS! WHAT ARE THEY AFTER IN *THIS* PLACE?

AND WHAT KIND OF FUN TOYS DO THEY HAVE TO TRY TO STOP ME *THIS TIME*--?

THIS THING TOTALED A *BUICK* IN OUR PRACTICE SESSION,...

JUST KEEP SUPERMAN *DISTRACTED* WHILE I RADIO THE TRUCK TO PICK UP THE CARGO!

BETTER TELL THEM TO HURRY--!

VLOOOOOM!

INTERGANG MAY ARM THESE CROOKS WITH THE MOST ADVANCED *WEAPONS,* BUT THEY DON'T TEACH THEM A LOT ABOUT *AIM.*

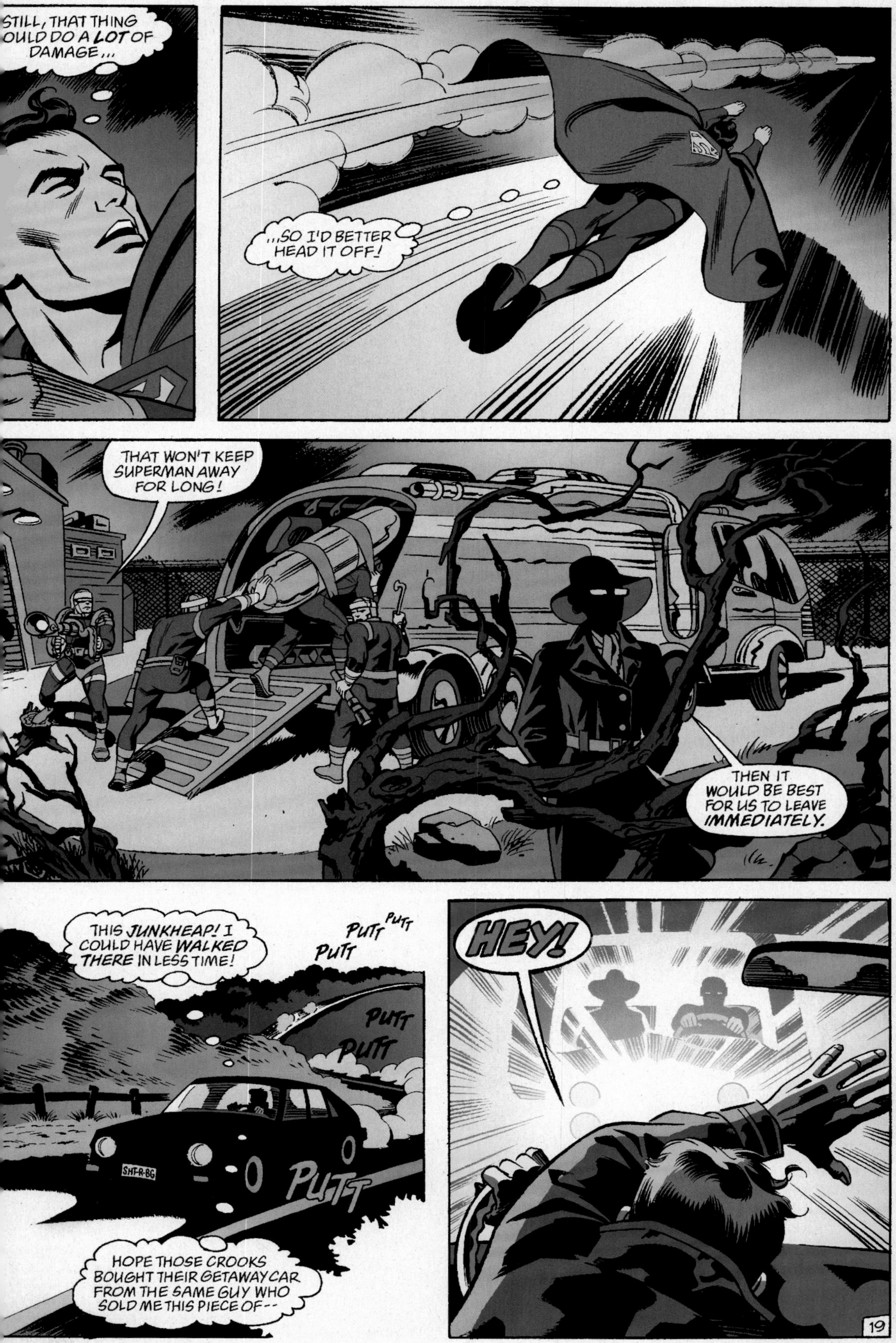

STILL, THAT THING OULD DO A LOT OF DAMAGE...
...SO I'D BETTER HEAD IT OFF!
THAT WON'T KEEP SUPERMAN AWAY FOR LONG!
THEN IT WOULD BE BEST FOR US TO LEAVE IMMEDIATELY.
THIS JUNKHEAP! I COULD HAVE WALKED THERE IN LESS TIME!
PUTT PUTT PUTT
PUTT PUTT
SHT-R-BG
PUTT
HOPE THOSE CROOKS BOUGHT THEIR GETAWAY CAR FROM THE SAME GUY WHO SOLD ME THIS PIECE OF--
HEY!
19

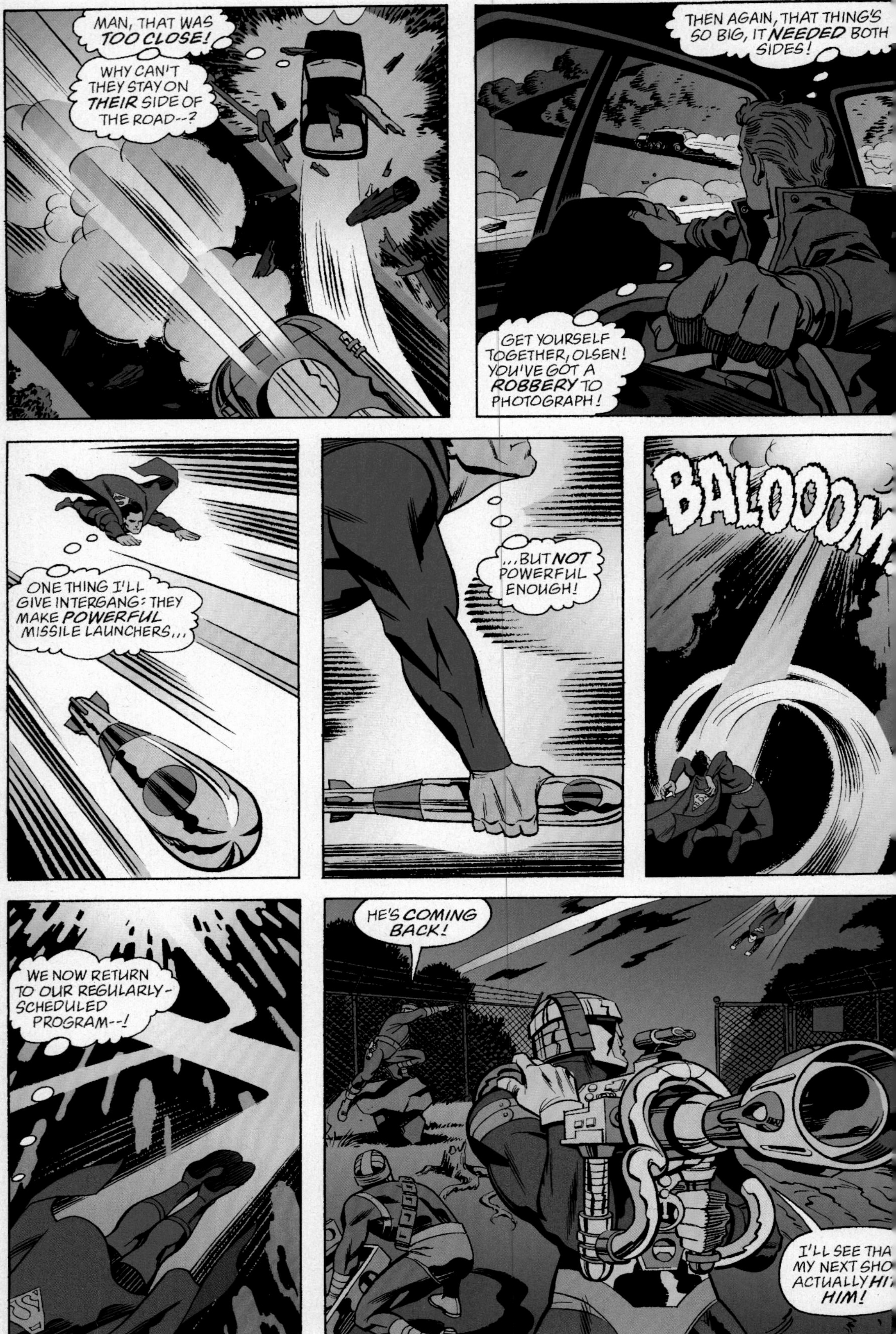
MAN, THAT WAS TOO CLOSE!
WHY CAN'T THEY STAY ON THEIR SIDE OF THE ROAD--?
THEN AGAIN, THAT THING'S SO BIG, IT NEEDED BOTH SIDES!
GET YOURSELF TOGETHER, OLSEN! YOU'VE GOT A ROBBERY TO PHOTOGRAPH!
ONE THING I'LL GIVE INTERGANG: THEY MAKE POWERFUL MISSILE LAUNCHERS...
...BUT NOT POWERFUL ENOUGH!
BALOOOM
WE NOW RETURN TO OUR REGULARLY-SCHEDULED PROGRAM--!
HE'S COMING BACK!
I'LL SEE THA MY NEXT SHO ACTUALLY HI HIM!

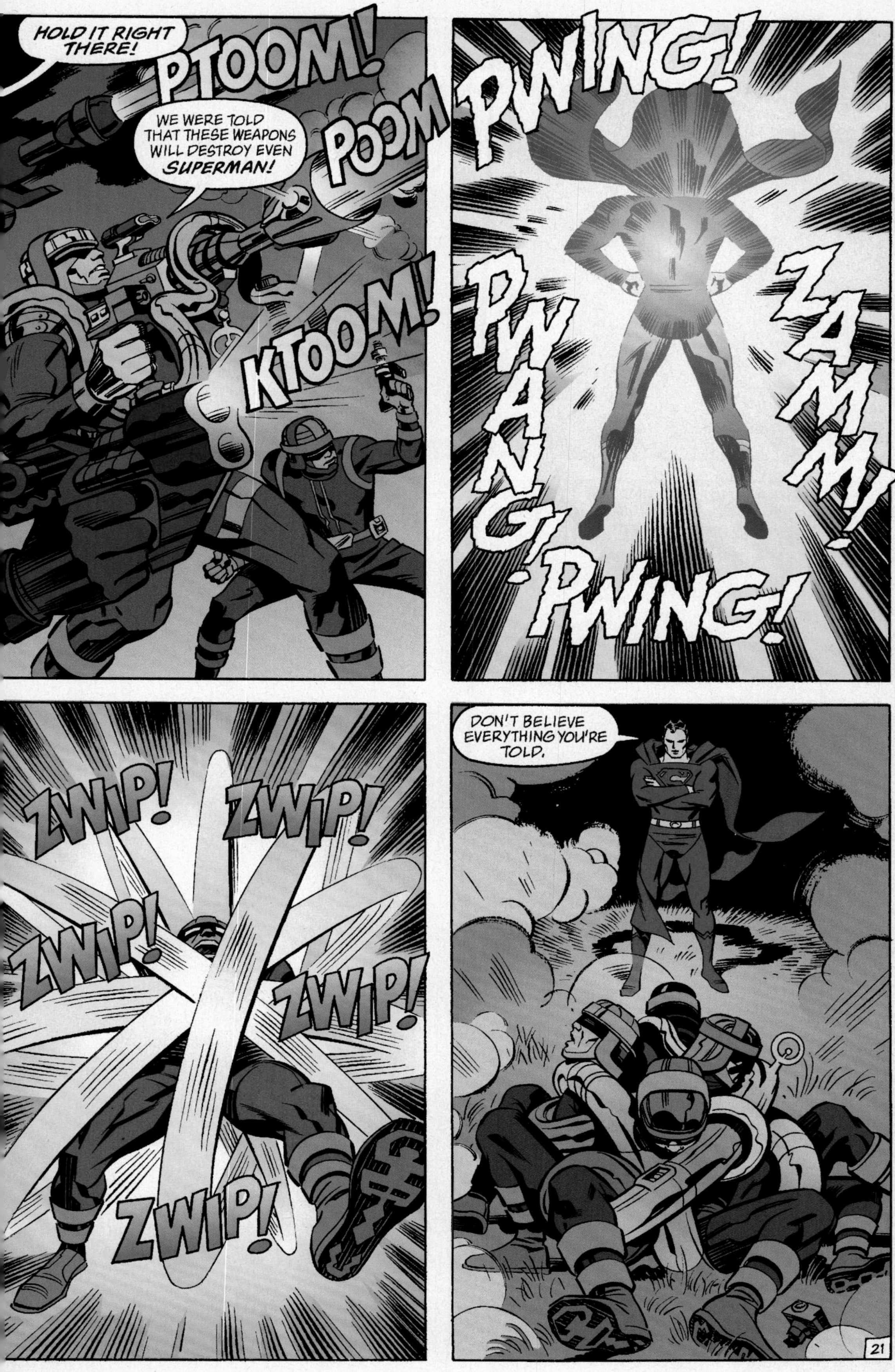
HOLD IT RIGHT THERE!
PTOOM!
WE WERE TOLD THAT THESE WEAPONS WILL DESTROY EVEN SUPERMAN!
POOM
KTOOM!
PWING!
PWANG!
ZAMM!
PWING!
ZWIP!
ZWIP!
ZWIP!
ZWIP!
ZWIP!
DON'T BELIEVE EVERYTHING YOU'RE TOLD.
21

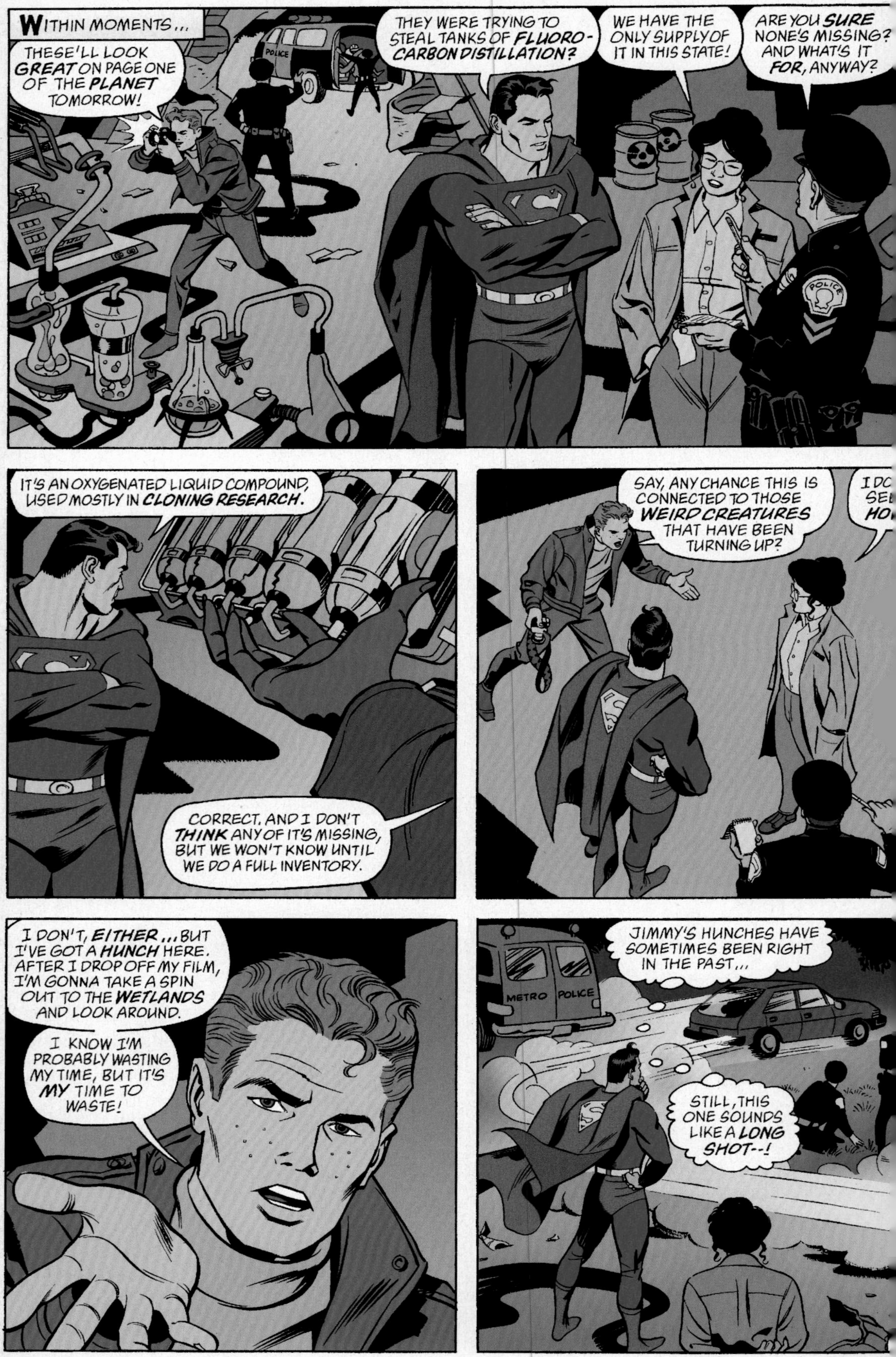
WITHIN MOMENTS...
THESE'LL LOOK GREAT ON PAGE ONE OF THE PLANET TOMORROW!
POLICE
THEY WERE TRYING TO STEAL TANKS OF FLUORO-CARBON DISTILLATION?
WE HAVE THE ONLY SUPPLY OF IT IN THIS STATE!
ARE YOU SURE NONE'S MISSING? AND WHAT'S IT FOR, ANYWAY?
POLICE
IT'S AN OXYGENATED LIQUID COMPOUND, USED MOSTLY IN CLONING RESEARCH.
CORRECT. AND I DON'T THINK ANY OF IT'S MISSING, BUT WE WON'T KNOW UNTIL WE DO A FULL INVENTORY.
SAY, ANY CHANCE THIS IS CONNECTED TO THOSE WEIRD CREATURES THAT HAVE BEEN TURNING UP?
I DON'T, EITHER... BUT I'VE GOT A HUNCH HERE. AFTER I DROP OFF MY FILM, I'M GONNA TAKE A SPIN OUT TO THE WETLANDS AND LOOK AROUND.
I KNOW I'M PROBABLY WASTING MY TIME, BUT IT'S MY TIME TO WASTE!
JIMMY'S HUNCHES HAVE SOMETIMES BEEN RIGHT IN THE PAST...
METRO POLICE
STILL, THIS ONE SOUNDS LIKE A LONG SHOT--!

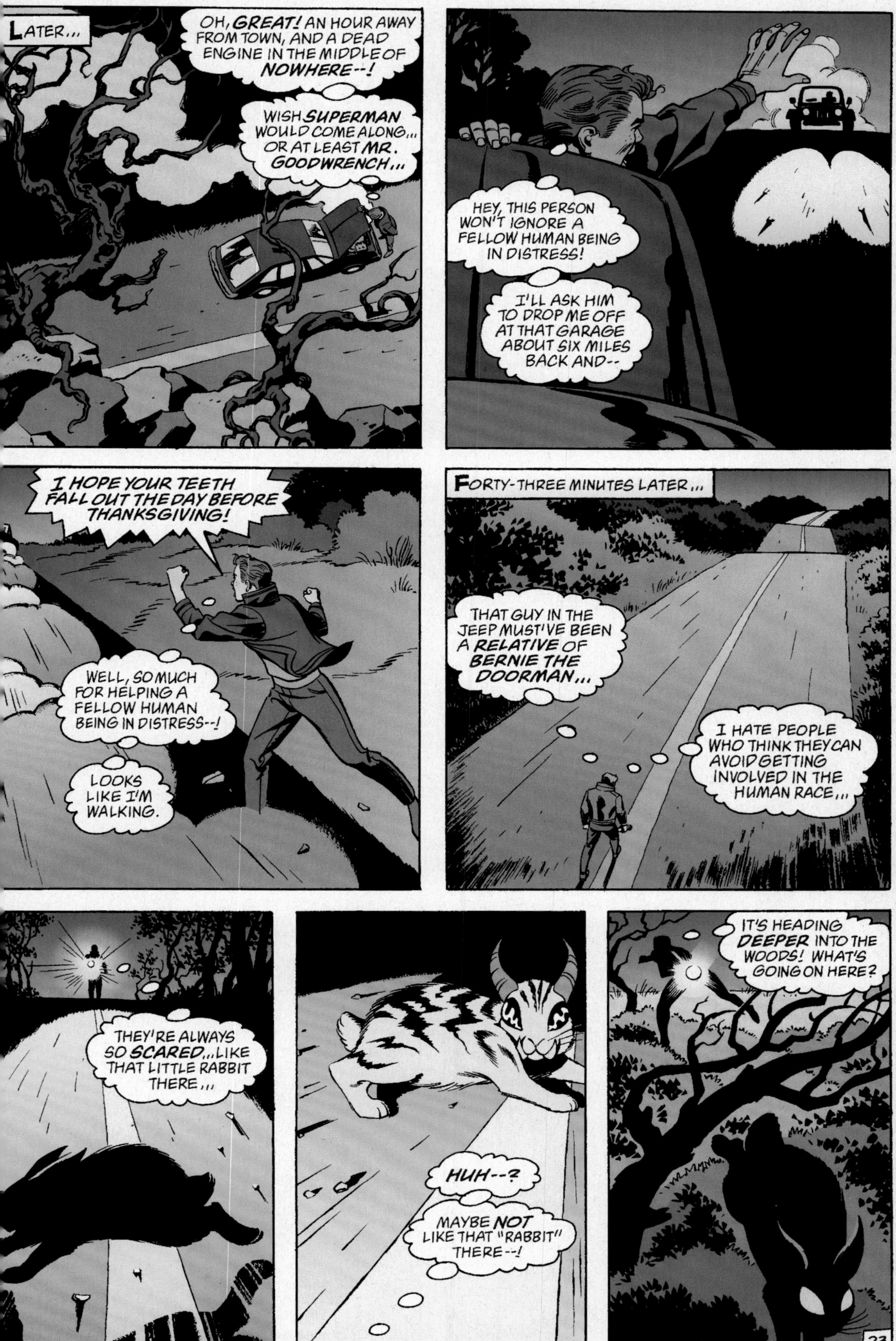
LATER...
OH, GREAT! AN HOUR AWAY FROM TOWN, AND A DEAD ENGINE IN THE MIDDLE OF NOWHERE--!
WISH SUPERMAN WOULD COME ALONG... OR AT LEAST MR. GOODWRENCH...
HEY, THIS PERSON WON'T IGNORE A FELLOW HUMAN BEING IN DISTRESS!
I'LL ASK HIM TO DROP ME OFF AT THAT GARAGE ABOUT SIX MILES BACK AND--
I HOPE YOUR TEETH FALL OUT THE DAY BEFORE THANKSGIVING!
WELL, SO MUCH FOR HELPING A FELLOW HUMAN BEING IN DISTRESS--!
LOOKS LIKE I'M WALKING.
FORTY-THREE MINUTES LATER...
THAT GUY IN THE JEEP MUST'VE BEEN A RELATIVE OF BERNIE THE DOORMAN...
I HATE PEOPLE WHO THINK THEY CAN AVOID GETTING INVOLVED IN THE HUMAN RACE...
THEY'RE ALWAYS SO SCARED... LIKE THAT LITTLE RABBIT THERE...
HUH--?
MAYBE NOT LIKE THAT "RABBIT" THERE--!
IT'S HEADING DEEPER INTO THE WOODS! WHAT'S GOING ON HERE?
WLMMN
23

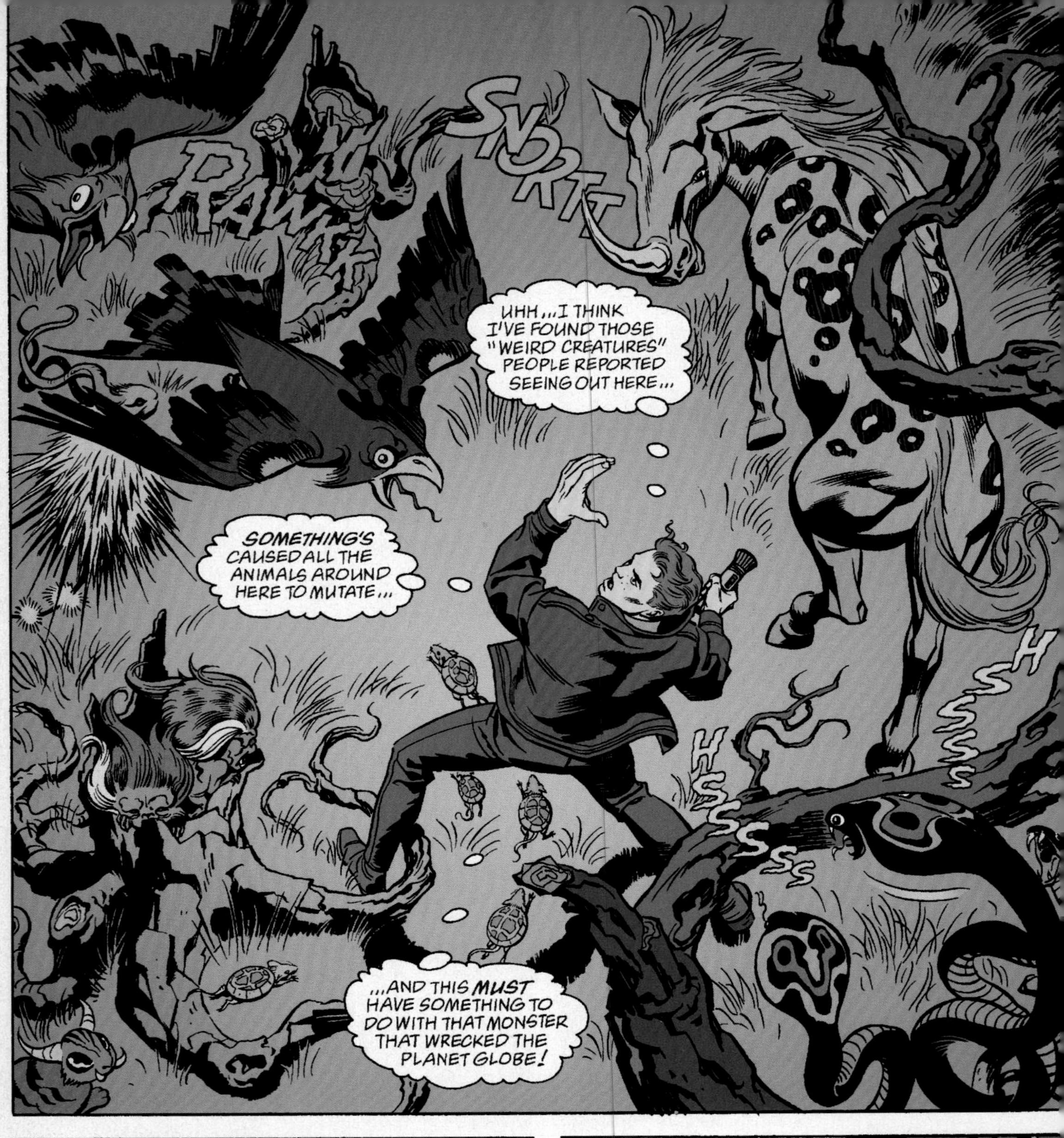
RAWWK
SNORTT
UHH...I THINK I'VE FOUND THOSE "WEIRD CREATURES" PEOPLE REPORTED SEEING OUT HERE...
SOMETHING'S CAUSED ALL THE ANIMALS AROUND HERE TO MUTATE...
HSSSSS
HSSSSS
...AND THIS MUST HAVE SOMETHING TO DO WITH THAT MONSTER THAT WRECKED THE PLANET GLOBE!

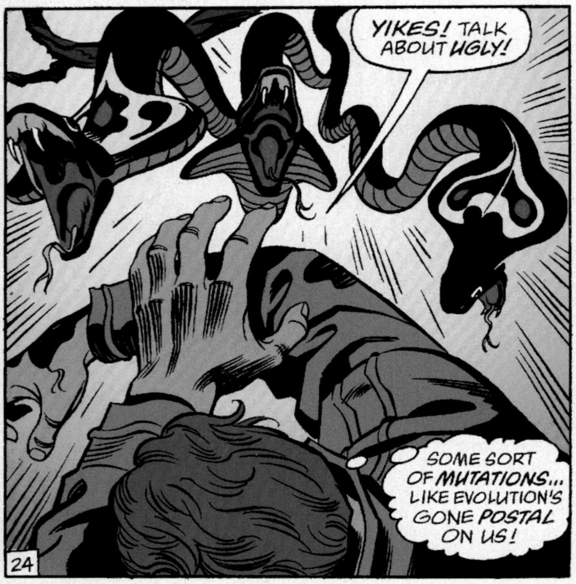
YIKES! TALK ABOUT UGLY!
SOME SORT OF MUTATIONS... LIKE EVOLUTION'S GONE POSTAL ON US!
24

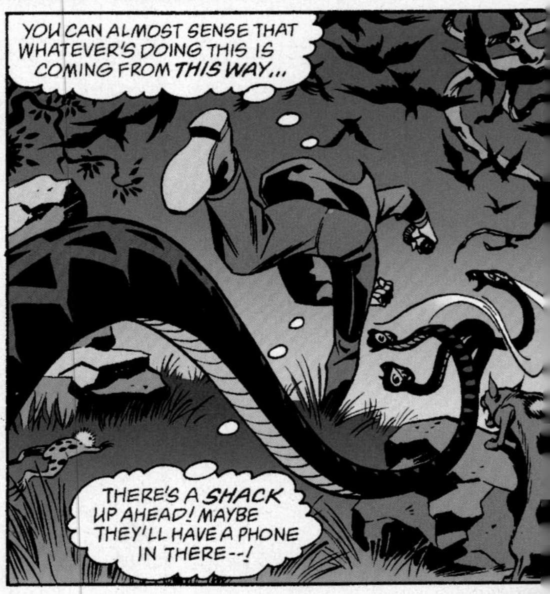
YOU CAN ALMOST SENSE THAT WHATEVER'S DOING THIS IS COMING FROM THIS WAY...
THERE'S A SHACK UP AHEAD! MAYBE THEY'LL HAVE A PHONE IN THERE--!

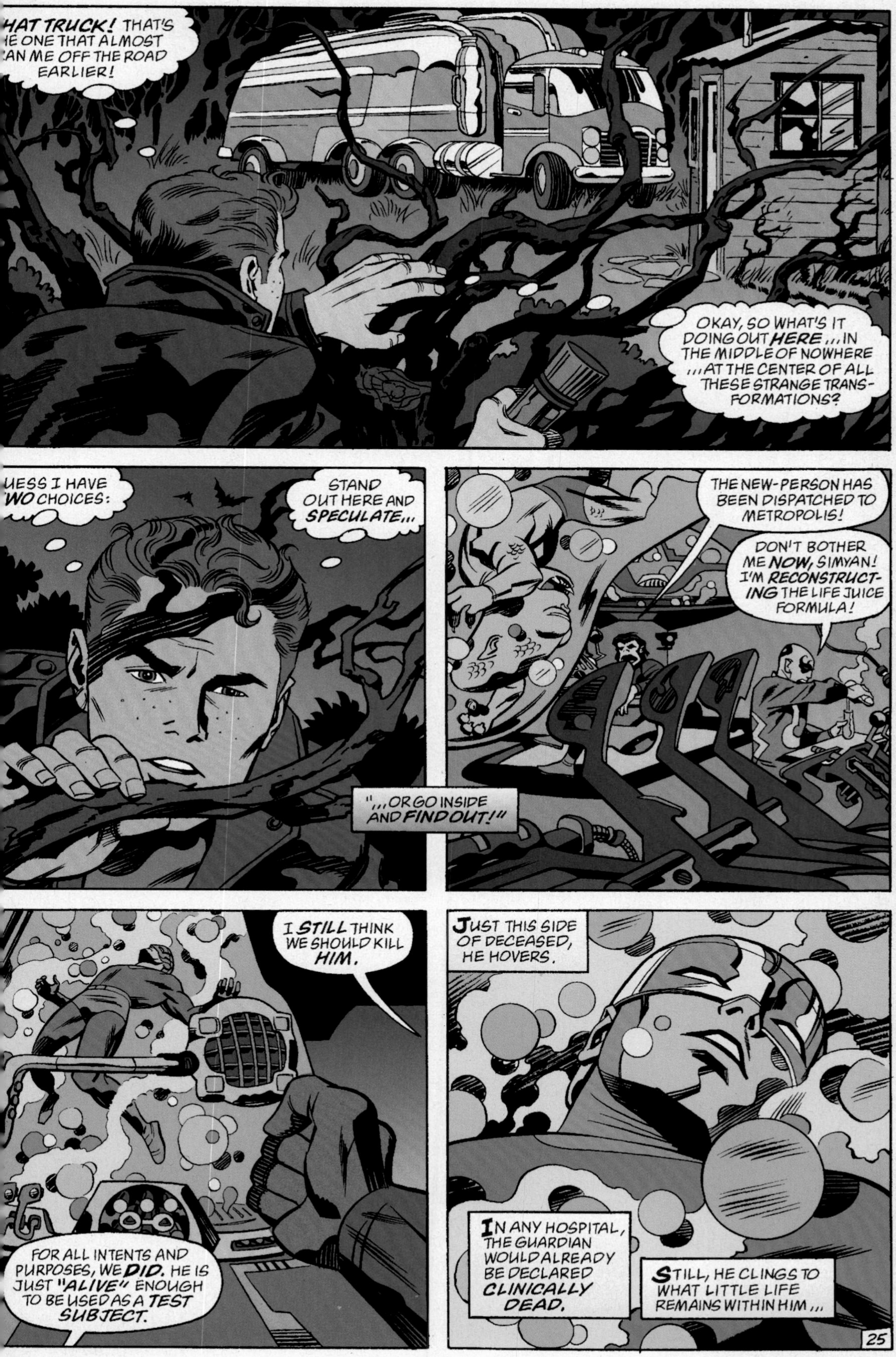

HAT TRUCK! THAT'S
HE ONE THAT ALMOST
RAN ME OFF THE ROAD
EARLIER!
OKAY, SO WHAT'S IT DOING OUT HERE... IN THE MIDDLE OF NOWHERE ...AT THE CENTER OF ALL THESE STRANGE TRANS-FORMATIONS?
UESS I HAVE TWO CHOICES:
STAND OUT HERE AND SPECULATE...
"...OR GO INSIDE AND FIND OUT!"
THE NEW-PERSON HAS BEEN DISPATCHED TO METROPOLIS!
DON'T BOTHER ME NOW, SIMYAN! I'M RECONSTRUCT-ING THE LIFE JUICE FORMULA!
I STILL THINK WE SHOULD KILL HIM.
FOR ALL INTENTS AND PURPOSES, WE DID. HE IS JUST "ALIVE" ENOUGH TO BE USED AS A TEST SUBJECT.
JUST THIS SIDE OF DECEASED, HE HOVERS.
IN ANY HOSPITAL, THE GUARDIAN WOULD ALREADY BE DECLARED CLINICALLY DEAD.
STILL, HE CLINGS TO WHAT LITTLE LIFE REMAINS WITHIN HIM...
25

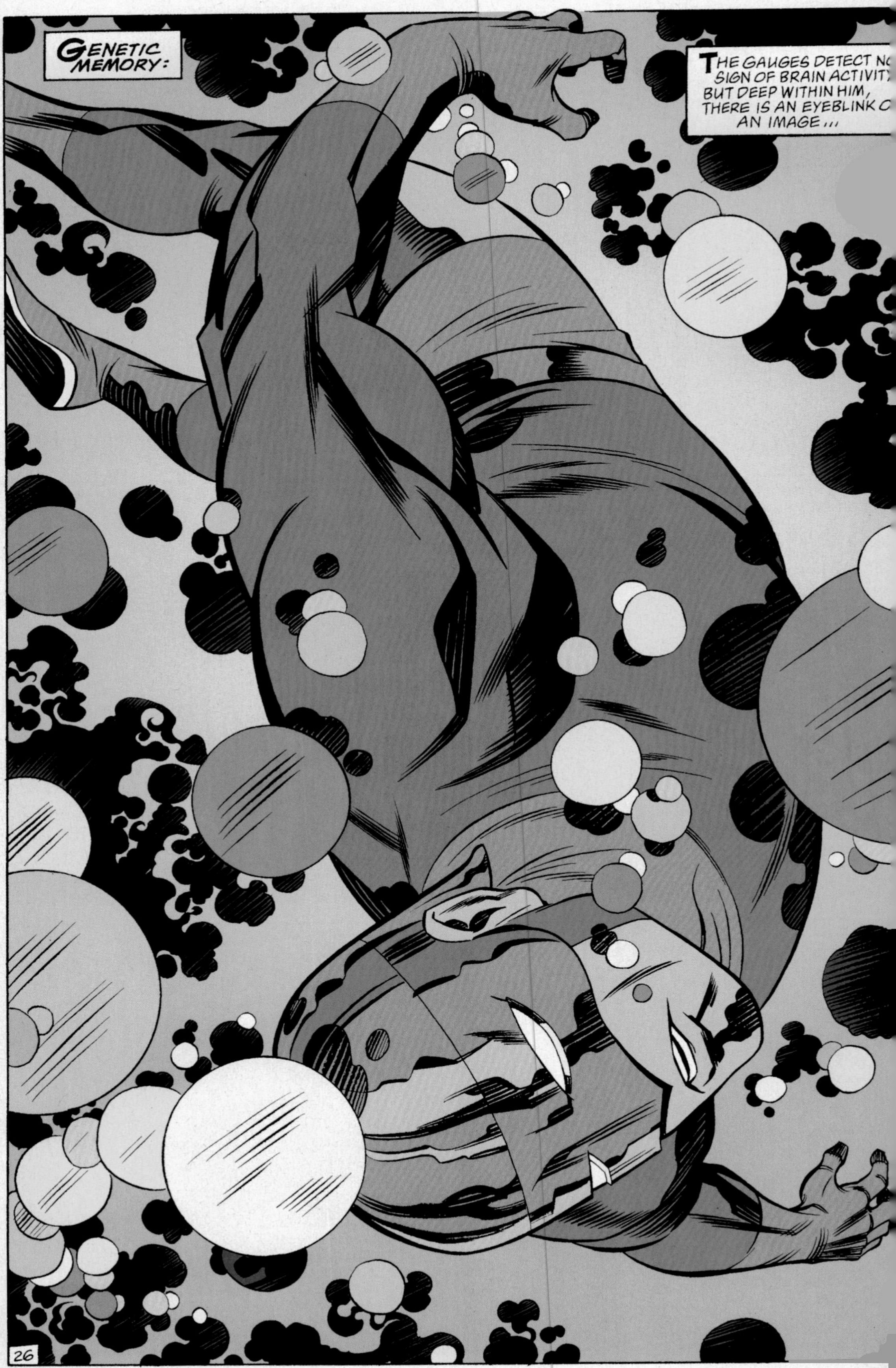
GENETIC MEMORY:
THE GAUGES DETECT NO SIGN OF BRAIN ACTIVITY BUT DEEP WITHIN HIM, THERE IS AN EYEBLINK OF AN IMAGE...
26

...AN IMAGE OF A MAN NAMED **JIM HARPER**, WHO WANTED NOTHING MORE THAN TO BE A POLICEMAN.

HARPER WALKED A BEAT KNOWN (RIGHTFULLY) AS **SUICIDE SLUM**, WHERE HE LEARNED THAT IDEALISM AND A BADGE WERE **NOT** ENOUGH.

THAT REALIZATION HAD STOPPED MOST OTHER COPS. IT DIDN'T STOP HARPER...

IF I'M GOING TO PROTECT PEOPLE, I'M GOING TO HAVE TO DO IT **MY** WAY...

JIM HARPER SOON BECAME THE LEGAL GUARDIAN OF FOUR **NEWSBOYS** WHO ASSISTED IN HIS EFFORTS...

THOCK!

WAK!

BONK!

AND WHILE SUICIDE SLUM NEVER **QUITE** BECAME "UPTOWN," LIFE WAS BETTER THERE FOR ALL, THANKS TO THE **NEWSBOY LEGION** AND THE **GUARDIAN**.

[TH]E GUARDIAN [DIS]APPEARED [WH]EN HARPER [WA]S TRANS-[FE]RRED TO THE [DE]TECTIVE [DI]VISION IN [AN]OTHER [P]RECINCT.

HE DID SUCH A GOOD JOB THAT INTERGANG PUT OUT A CONTRACT ON HIM...

THE CONTRACT AND ITS SUBJECT WERE SOON MARKED "CANCELLED."

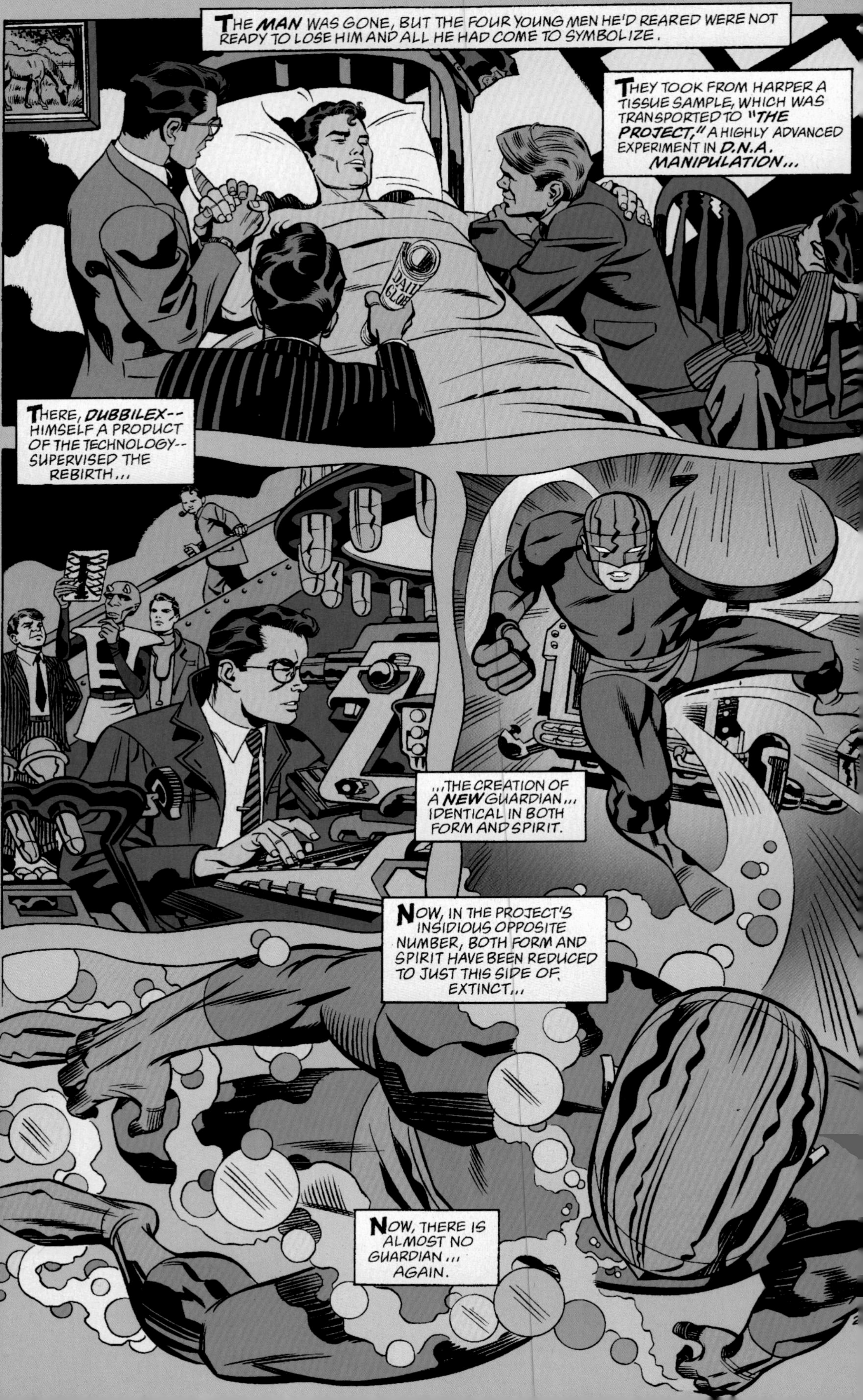
THE MAN WAS GONE, BUT THE FOUR YOUNG MEN HE'D REARED WERE NOT READY TO LOSE HIM AND ALL HE HAD COME TO SYMBOLIZE.
THEY TOOK FROM HARPER A TISSUE SAMPLE, WHICH WAS TRANSPORTED TO "THE PROJECT," A HIGHLY ADVANCED EXPERIMENT IN D.N.A. MANIPULATION...
DAILY GLOBE
THERE, DUBBILEX--HIMSELF A PRODUCT OF THE TECHNOLOGY--SUPERVISED THE REBIRTH...
...THE CREATION OF A NEW GUARDIAN... IDENTICAL IN BOTH FORM AND SPIRIT.
NOW, IN THE PROJECT'S INSIDIOUS OPPOSITE NUMBER, BOTH FORM AND SPIRIT HAVE BEEN REDUCED TO JUST THIS SIDE OF EXTINCT...
NOW, THERE IS ALMOST NO GUARDIAN... AGAIN.

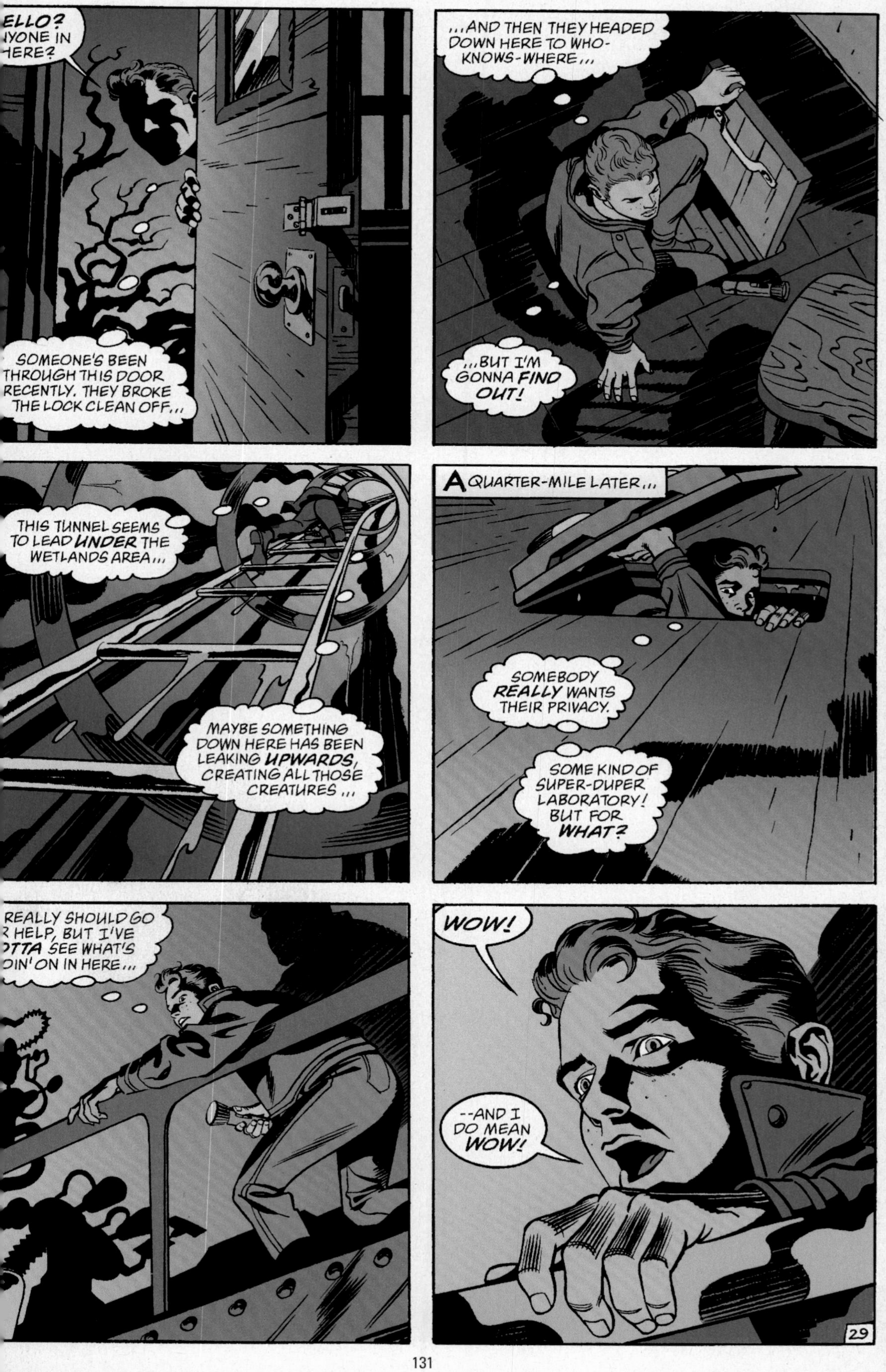
ELLO? NYONE IN HERE?
SOMEONE'S BEEN THROUGH THIS DOOR RECENTLY. THEY BROKE THE LOCK CLEAN OFF...
...AND THEN THEY HEADED DOWN HERE TO WHO-KNOWS-WHERE...
...BUT I'M GONNA FIND OUT!
THIS TUNNEL SEEMS TO LEAD UNDER THE WETLANDS AREA...
MAYBE SOMETHING DOWN HERE HAS BEEN LEAKING UPWARDS, CREATING ALL THOSE CREATURES...
A QUARTER-MILE LATER...
SOMEBODY REALLY WANTS THEIR PRIVACY.
SOME KIND OF SUPER-DUPER LABORATORY! BUT FOR WHAT?
REALLY SHOULD GO R HELP, BUT I'VE OTTA SEE WHAT'S OIN' ON IN HERE...
WOW!
--AND I DO MEAN WOW!
29

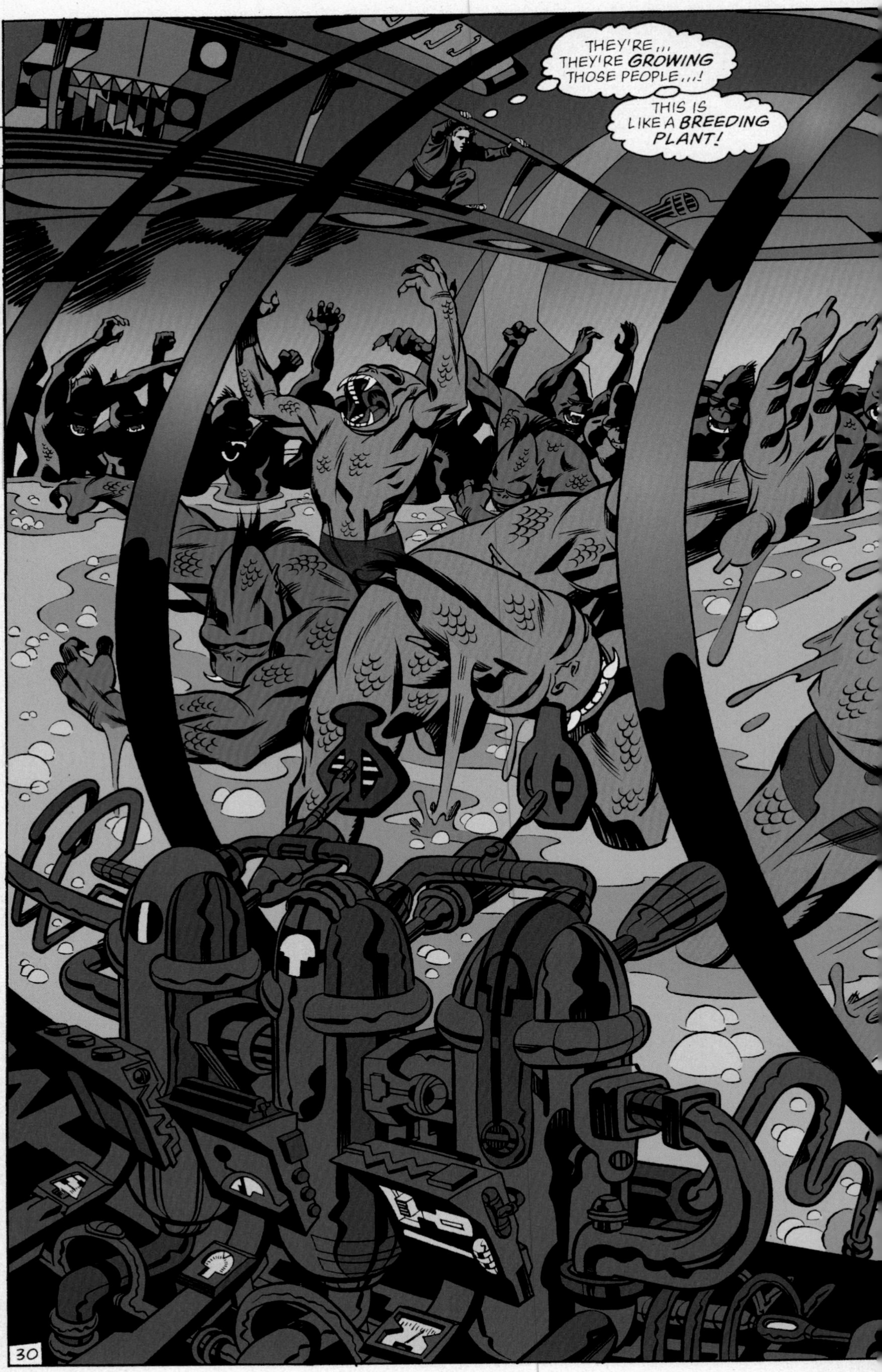
THEY'RE... THEY'RE GROWING THOSE PEOPLE...!
THIS IS LIKE A BREEDING PLANT!
30

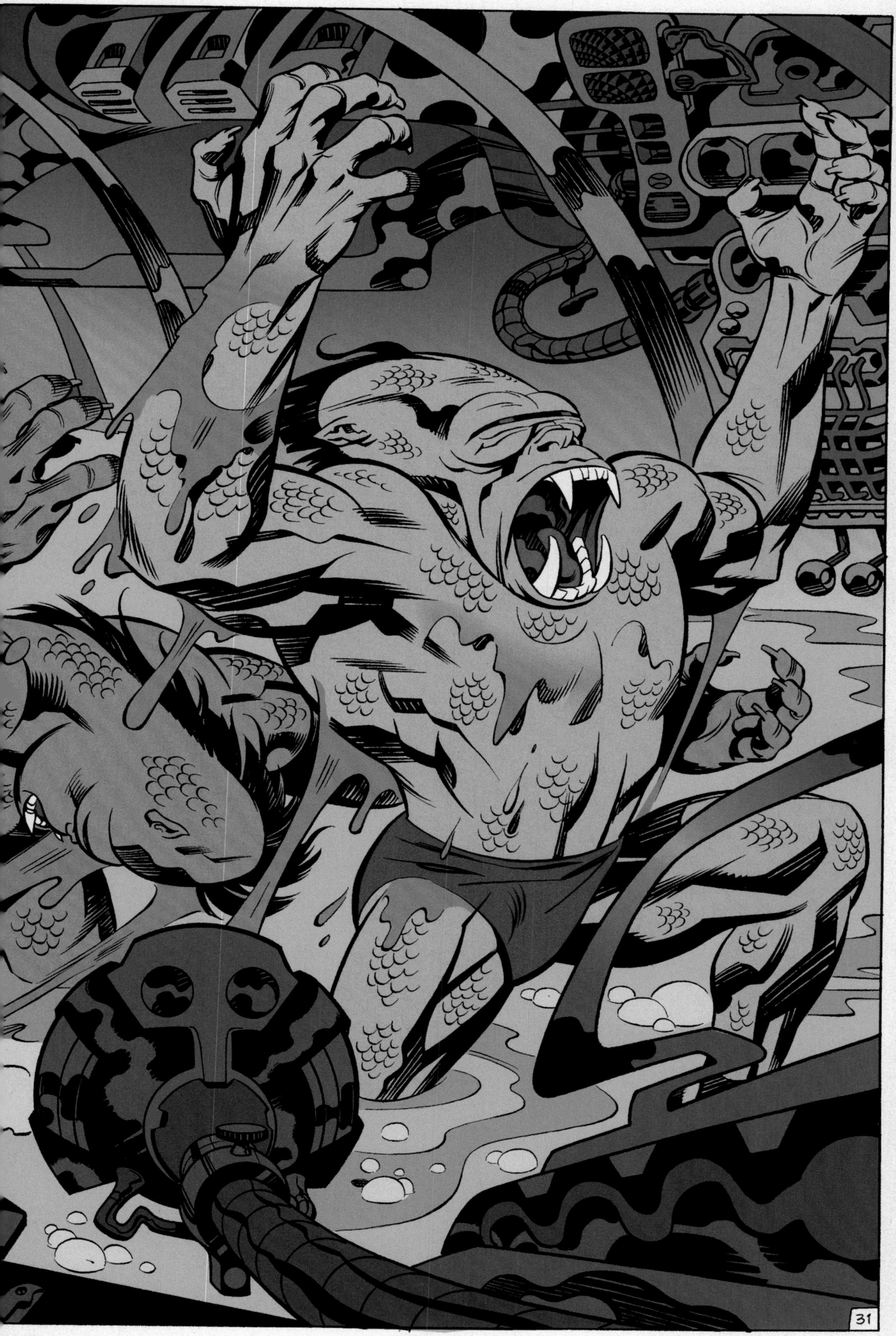
31

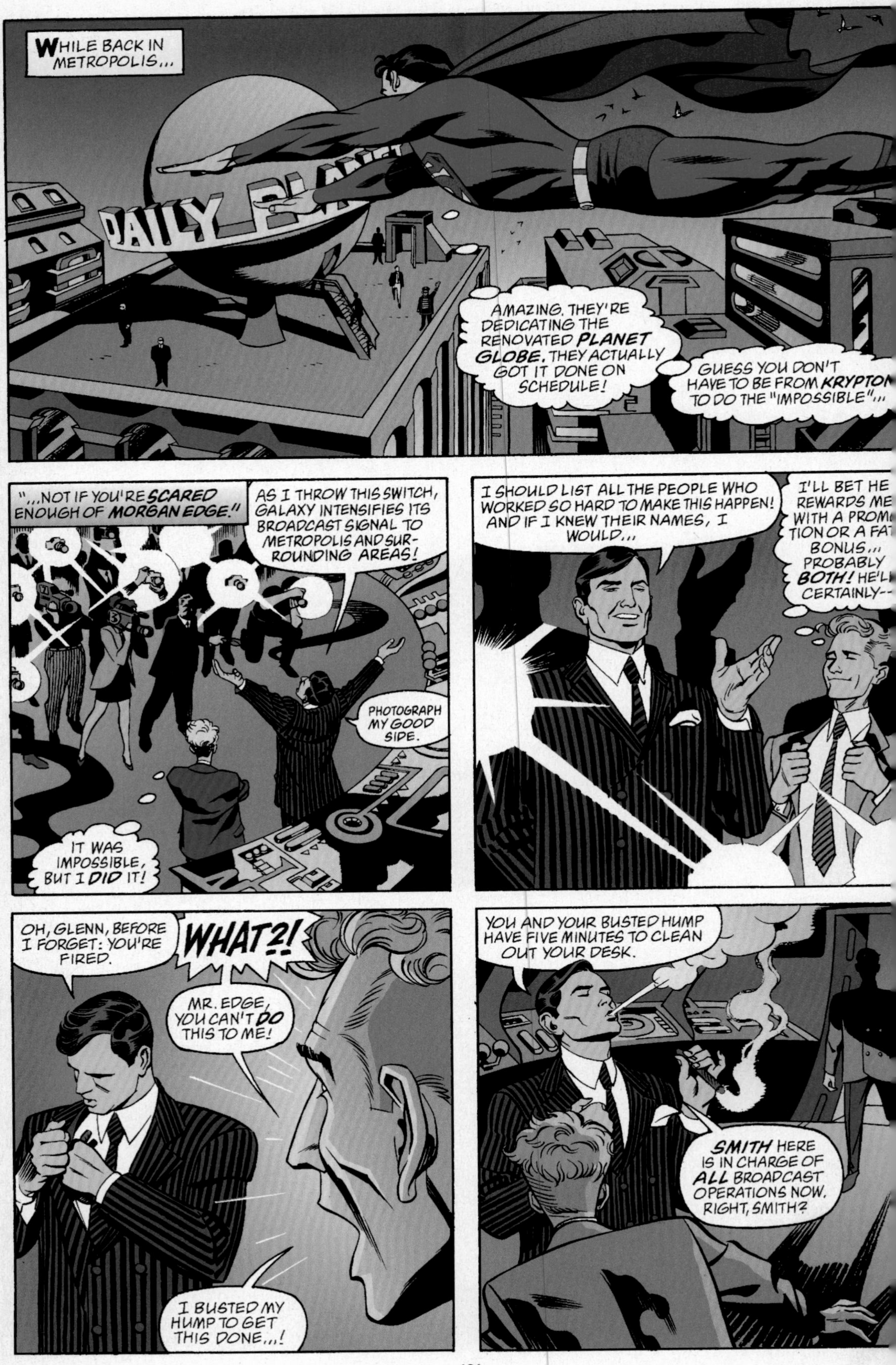
WHILE BACK IN METROPOLIS...
DAILY PLANET
AMAZING. THEY'RE DEDICATING THE RENOVATED PLANET GLOBE. THEY ACTUALLY GOT IT DONE ON SCHEDULE!
GUESS YOU DON'T HAVE TO BE FROM KRYPTON TO DO THE "IMPOSSIBLE"...
"...NOT IF YOU'RE SCARED ENOUGH OF MORGAN EDGE."
AS I THROW THIS SWITCH, GALAXY INTENSIFIES ITS BROADCAST SIGNAL TO METROPOLIS AND SURROUNDING AREAS!
PHOTOGRAPH MY GOOD SIDE.
IT WAS IMPOSSIBLE, BUT I DID IT!
I SHOULD LIST ALL THE PEOPLE WHO WORKED SO HARD TO MAKE THIS HAPPEN! AND IF I KNEW THEIR NAMES, I WOULD...
I'LL BET HE REWARDS ME WITH A PROMO TION OR A FAT BONUS... PROBABLY BOTH! HE'LL CERTAINLY--
OH, GLENN, BEFORE I FORGET: YOU'RE FIRED.
WHAT?!
MR. EDGE, YOU CAN'T DO THIS TO ME!
I BUSTED MY HUMP TO GET THIS DONE...!
YOU AND YOUR BUSTED HUMP HAVE FIVE MINUTES TO CLEAN OUT YOUR DESK.
SMITH HERE IS IN CHARGE OF ALL BROADCAST OPERATIONS NOW. RIGHT, SMITH?

HATEVER
I SAY, MR.
EDGE.

THAT'S THE
WAY I LIKE MY
EMPLOYEES TO
THINK.

PLEASE! YOU HAVE TO GIVE ME ANOTHER CHANCE--AT LEAST AN EXPLANATION!

FLIK

I'M THE BOSS, I DON'T "HAVE TO" DO ANYTHING I DON'T WANT TO.

NOW, IF YOU'LL EXCUSE ME, I NEED TO PREPARE MY SPEECH FOR THE GUILD AWARD PROGRAM TONIGHT.

THAT'S HOW IT ALWAYS HAPPENS! THE SQUEAKY WHEEL IS THE FIRST ONE THAT GETS REPLACED!

WELL, THAT'S NEVER GONNA HAPPEN TO ME...NEVER! LET 'EM CALL ME A COWARD... AN UNDERACHIEVER...

AT LEAST I'LL HAVE MY JOB.

A STUDY IN CONTRASTS: A MAN WHO NEVER TAKES CHANCES...

AND ONE WHO CANNOT SEEM TO AVOID THEM.

THIS IS LIKE A BIG ASSEMBLY LINE... BIRTHING THOSE CREATURES WHO, IN TURN, BIRTH MORE...

...AND MORE AND MORE AND MORE...

MOKKARI! WE'VE HAD ANOTHER SECURITY BREACH! THE ALARM SENSES AN INTRUDER!

THE OCTOPOD WILL HAVE TO DEAL WITH IT! THIS IS A VITAL MOMENT IN THE PROCEDURE!

33

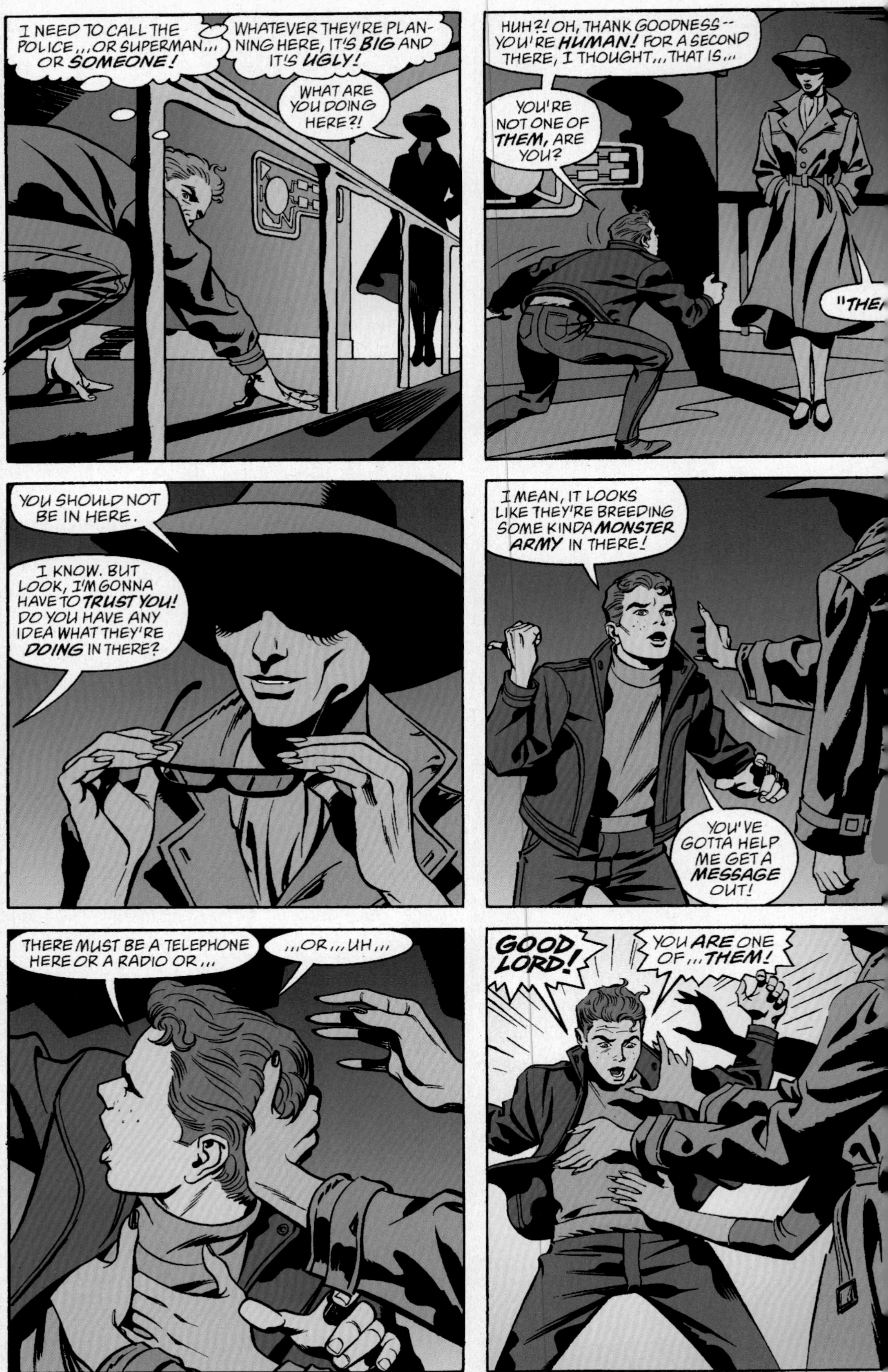
I NEED TO CALL THE POLICE,,,OR SUPERMAN,,, OR SOMEONE!
WHATEVER THEY'RE PLANNING HERE, IT'S BIG AND IT'S UGLY!
WHAT ARE YOU DOING HERE?!
HUH?! OH, THANK GOODNESS-- YOU'RE HUMAN! FOR A SECOND THERE, I THOUGHT,,,THAT IS,,,
YOU'RE NOT ONE OF THEM, ARE YOU?
"THEM
YOU SHOULD NOT BE IN HERE.
I KNOW. BUT LOOK, I'M GONNA HAVE TO TRUST YOU! DO YOU HAVE ANY IDEA WHAT THEY'RE DOING IN THERE?
I MEAN, IT LOOKS LIKE THEY'RE BREEDING SOME KINDA MONSTER ARMY IN THERE!
YOU'VE GOTTA HELP ME GET A MESSAGE OUT!
THERE MUST BE A TELEPHONE HERE OR A RADIO OR,,,
,,,OR,,,UH,,,
GOOD LORD!
YOU ARE ONE OF,,,THEM!

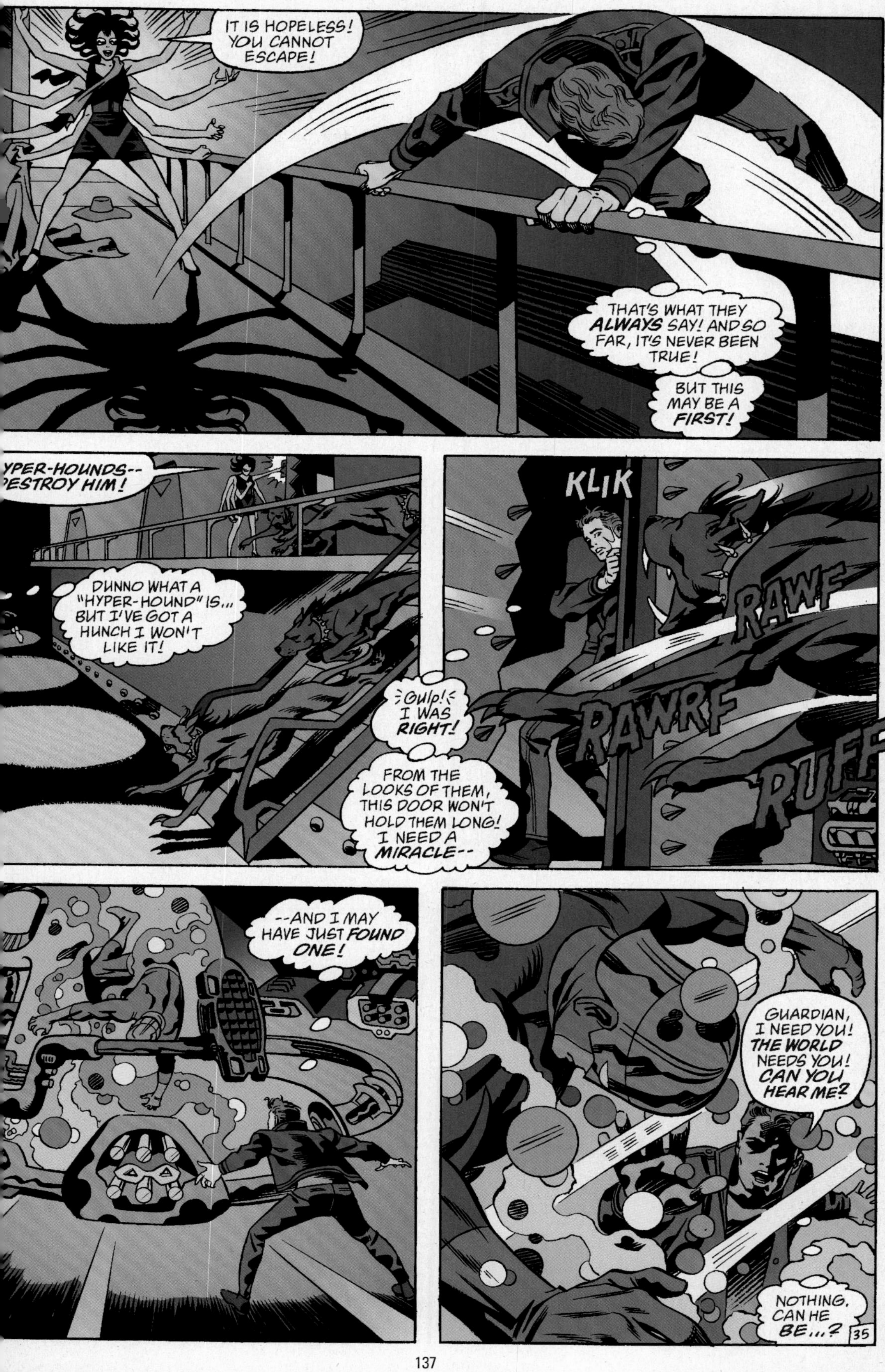
IT IS HOPELESS! YOU CANNOT ESCAPE!
THAT'S WHAT THEY ALWAYS SAY! AND SO FAR, IT'S NEVER BEEN TRUE!
BUT THIS MAY BE A FIRST!
YPER-HOUNDS-- ESTROY HIM!
DUNNO WHAT A "HYPER-HOUND" IS... BUT I'VE GOT A HUNCH I WON'T LIKE IT!
KLIK
RAWF
RAWRF
RUFF
Gulp! I WAS RIGHT!
FROM THE LOOKS OF THEM, THIS DOOR WON'T HOLD THEM LONG! I NEED A MIRACLE--
--AND I MAY HAVE JUST FOUND ONE!
GUARDIAN, I NEED YOU! THE WORLD NEEDS YOU! CAN YOU HEAR ME?
NOTHING. CAN HE BE...?
35

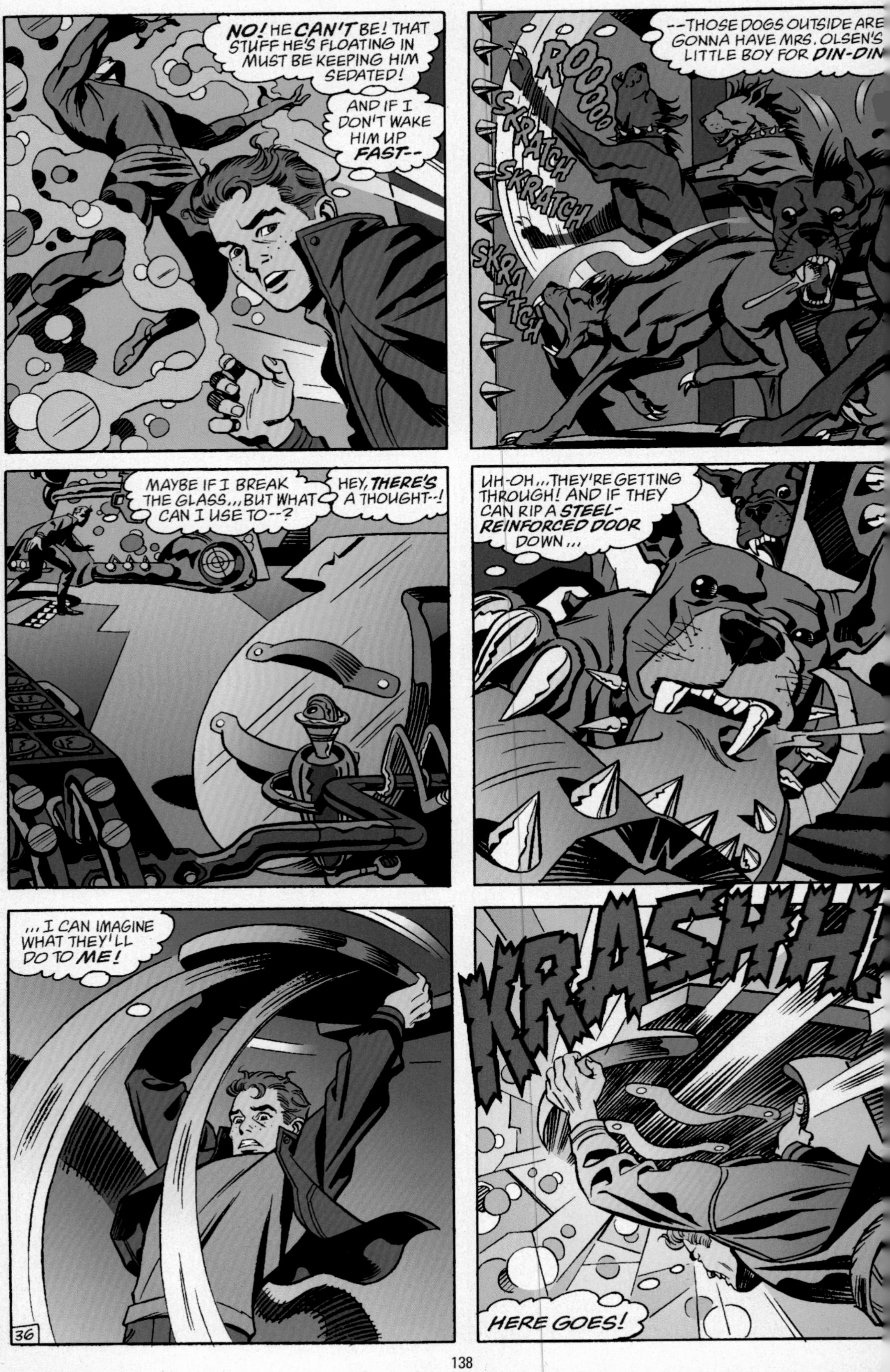
NO! HE CAN'T BE! THAT STUFF HE'S FLOATING IN MUST BE KEEPING HIM SEDATED!
AND IF I DON'T WAKE HIM UP FAST--
--THOSE DOGS OUTSIDE ARE GONNA HAVE MRS. OLSEN'S LITTLE BOY FOR DIN-DIN
ROOOOO
SKRATCH
SKRATCH
SKRATCH
SKRATCH
MAYBE IF I BREAK THE GLASS... BUT WHAT CAN I USE TO--?
HEY, THERE'S A THOUGHT--!
UH-OH... THEY'RE GETTING THROUGH! AND IF THEY CAN RIP A STEEL-REINFORCED DOOR DOWN...
...I CAN IMAGINE WHAT THEY'LL DO TO ME!
36
KRASH!
HERE GOES!

I'M TOAST... OR KIBBLE...OR SOMETHING!

KLOOSHHH

DON'T WORRY... JIMMY! I HEARD YOU...

I ALWAYS HEAR...WHEN I'M NEEDED...

OKKARI! THE GUARDIAN HAS BROKEN OUT OF THE TANK! YOU AND WE DRAINED EVERY BIT OF LIFE FROM HIM!

HE SHOULD NOT EVEN BE ABLE TO MOVE!

GUARDIAN! MAN, AM I GLAD TO SEE YOU!

GET OUT OF HERE! I'LL HOLD THEM OFF WHILE YOU LOOK FOR AN ESCAPE ROUTE!

37

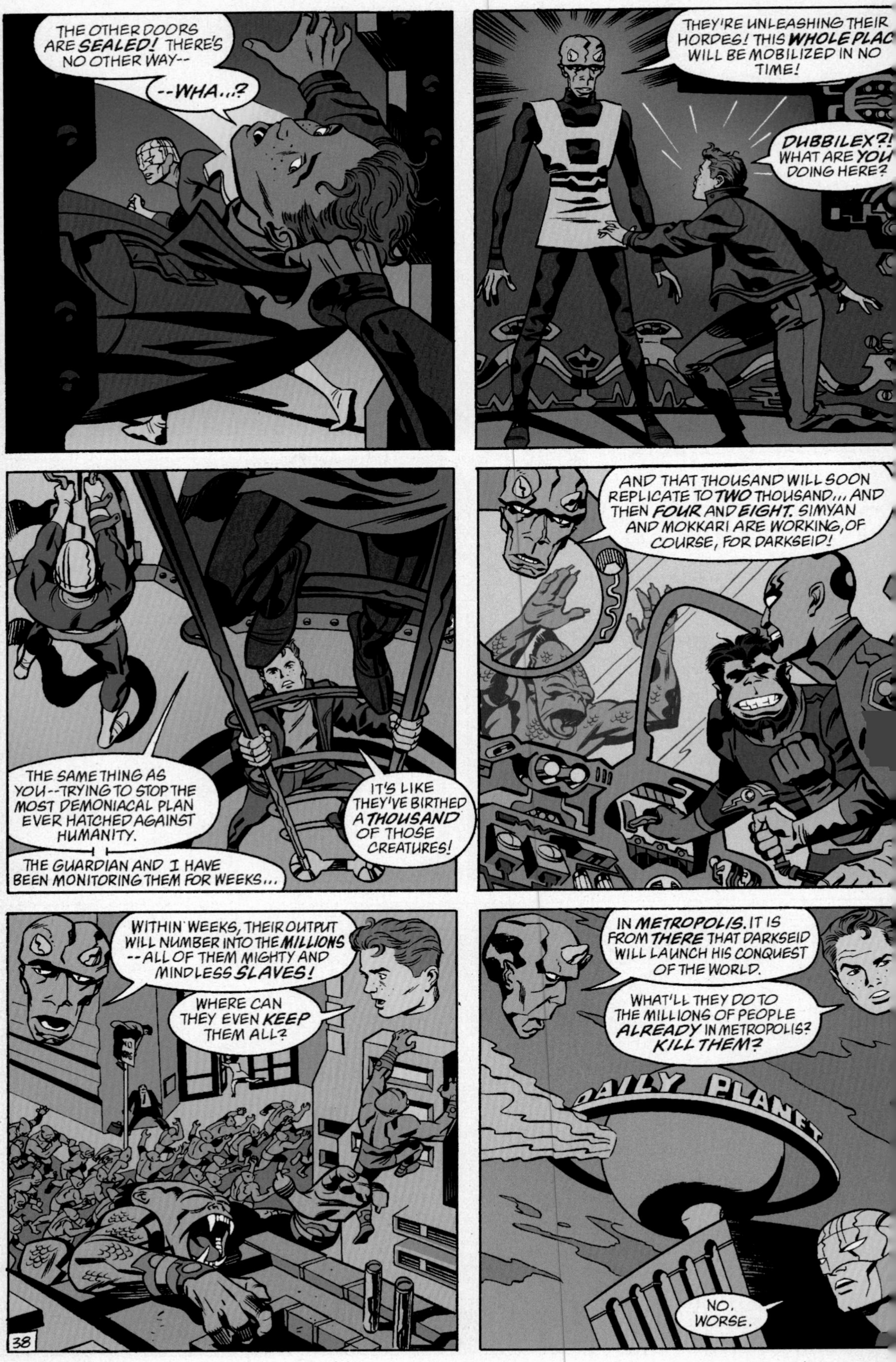

THE OTHER DOORS ARE SEALED! THERE'S NO OTHER WAY--
--WHA...?
THEY'RE UNLEASHING THEIR HORDES! THIS WHOLE PLAC WILL BE MOBILIZED IN NO TIME!
DUBBILEX?! WHAT ARE YOU DOING HERE?
THE SAME THING AS YOU--TRYING TO STOP THE MOST DEMONIACAL PLAN EVER HATCHED AGAINST HUMANITY.
THE GUARDIAN AND I HAVE BEEN MONITORING THEM FOR WEEKS...
IT'S LIKE THEY'VE BIRTHED A THOUSAND OF THOSE CREATURES!
AND THAT THOUSAND WILL SOON REPLICATE TO TWO THOUSAND... AND THEN FOUR AND EIGHT. SIMYAN AND MOKKARI ARE WORKING, OF COURSE, FOR DARKSEID!
WITHIN WEEKS, THEIR OUTPUT WILL NUMBER INTO THE MILLIONS --ALL OF THEM MIGHTY AND MINDLESS SLAVES!
WHERE CAN THEY EVEN KEEP THEM ALL?
IN METROPOLIS. IT IS FROM THERE THAT DARKSEID WILL LAUNCH HIS CONQUEST OF THE WORLD.
WHAT'LL THEY DO TO THE MILLIONS OF PEOPLE ALREADY IN METROPOLIS? KILL THEM?
DAILY PLANET
NO. WORSE.
38

THE SAME ENERGY THEY USE TO ADVANCE THE DEVELOPMENT PROCESS CAN BE *REVERSED*. IT CAN LITERALLY INVERT THE *EVOLUTIONARY PROCESS...*

'RIGHT NOW IN METROPOLIS, A *REGRESSION DEVICE* IS SENDING OUT THESE ENERGY WAVES, STARTING TO DEVOLVE HUMANS TO THEIR PRIMAL ANCESTRY...

"...TRANSFORMING THEM INTO *BEASTS OF BURDEN* FOR DARKSEID'S LEGIONS!"

WE'VE GOTTA GET TO THAT DEVICE AND *DESTROY IT!* I WISH I'D SOMEHOW CONTACTED SUPERMAN BEFORE I CAME IN HERE!

I DID.

WELL THEN, LET'S HOPE HE GETS HERE *SOON!*

39

141

KRASH!

THIS SOON ENOUGH FOR YOU?

IT'LL DO!

I TRUST YOU RECEIVED MY MESSAGE, SUPERMAN.

THAT I DID, *DUBBILEX!* NOW YOU AND JIMMY FIND YOUR WAY OUT OF HERE! WE'LL HOLD THEM OFF!

WORKS FOR ME!

THESE CREATUR HAVE GRE POWER BUT *NO* MIND--

I BELIEVE I KNOW THE LOCATION OF THE DE-EVOLUTIONARY TRANS-MITTER IN METROPOLIS!

IF I SENSE CORRECTLY, WE HAVE LESS THAN *TWENTY MINUTES* TO REACH AND DISARM IT!

MY CAR'S GONE *KABLOOEY* ON ME--SO I HOPE *YOU* BROUGHT WHEELS!

WHAT I BROUGHT--

--WOULD QUALIF AS A BIT MORE THAN "*WHEELS*"

IT SURE DOES!

THE **WHIZ WAGON!** THE **NEWSBOY LEGION'S** SUPER-SOUPED-UP VEHICLE!

I WAS **WONDERING** WHAT BECAME OF IT! **YOU'VE** BEEN CRUISING AROUND IN IT LATELY?

I WOULD SUGGEST WE GET **IN** AND DISCUSS MATTERS **ON THE WAY**...

"... THE SURVIVAL OF YOUR SPECIES S, AFTER ALL, **AT STAKE!**"

NTERGANG SAYS TO GET UT OF THE CITY **NOW**, EDGE! UR 'COPTER'S WAITIN' ON YOUR BUILDING'S ROOF!

DARKSEID TAKES CARE OF HIS OWN...

GONNA DANDY UP FOR THE BIG **GUILD AWARD** PROGRAM, EH, MR. **EDGE?**

I MUST FORGO THE PLEASURE, FRIENDS! CHOOSE ONE AMONG **YOU** TO STAND IN FOR ME TONIGHT!

T'S YOU, THE **ITTLE PEOPLE**" WHO'VE HELPED MAKE **GALAXY** WHAT IT IS!

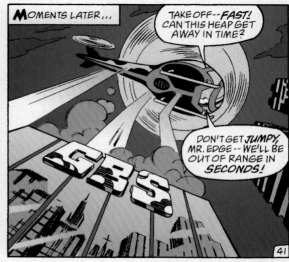

MOMENTS LATER...

TAKE OFF--**FAST!** CAN THIS HEAP GET AWAY IN TIME?

DON'T GET **JUMPY**, MR. EDGE -- WE'LL BE OUT OF RANGE IN **SECONDS!**

GBS

41

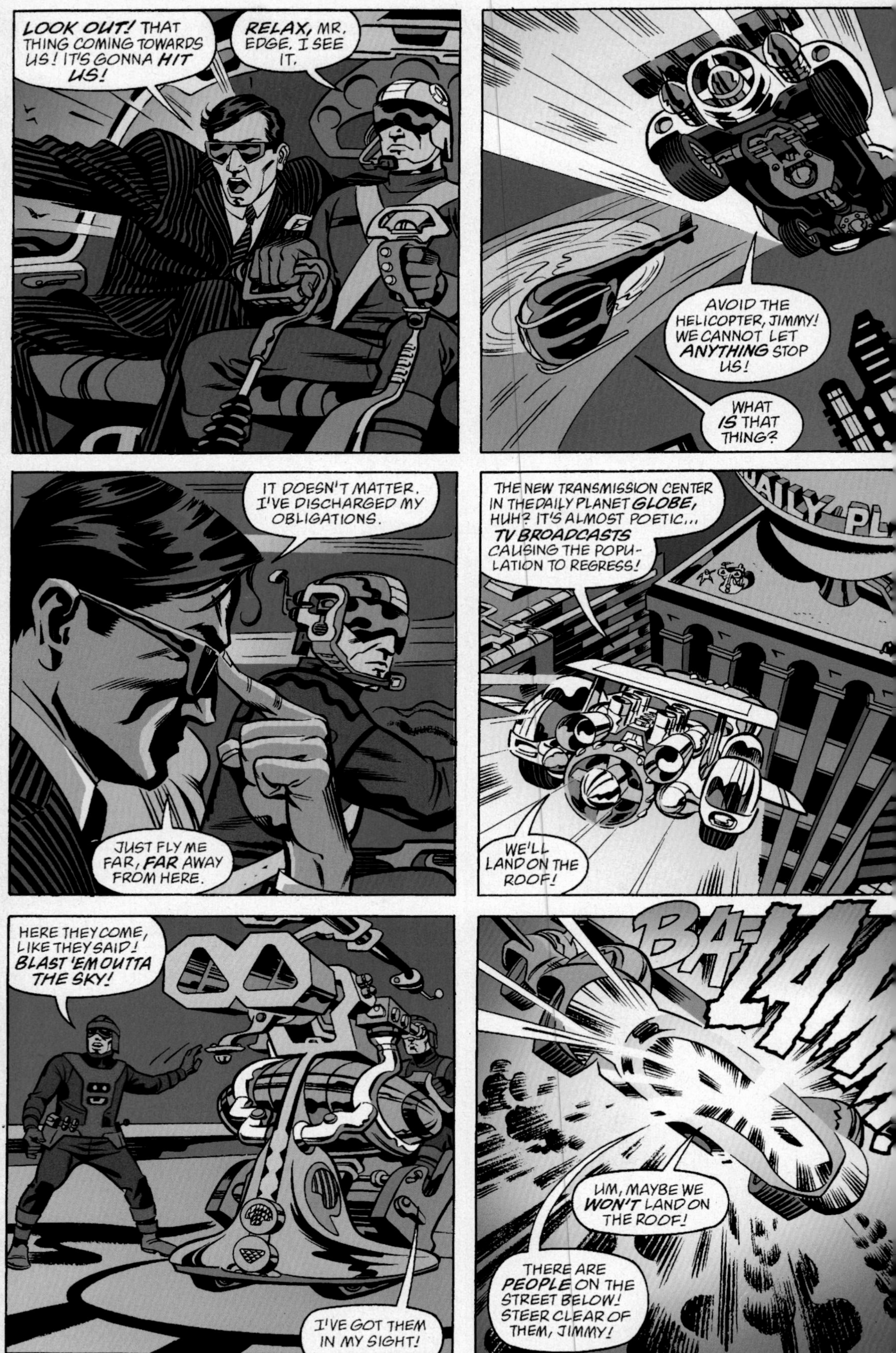

LOOK OUT! THAT THING COMING TOWARDS US! IT'S GONNA HIT US!
RELAX, MR. EDGE. I SEE IT.
AVOID THE HELICOPTER, JIMMY! WE CANNOT LET ANYTHING STOP US!
WHAT IS THAT THING?
IT DOESN'T MATTER. I'VE DISCHARGED MY OBLIGATIONS.
JUST FLY ME FAR, FAR AWAY FROM HERE.
THE NEW TRANSMISSION CENTER IN THE DAILY PLANET GLOBE, HUH? IT'S ALMOST POETIC... TV BROADCASTS CAUSING THE POPULATION TO REGRESS!
WE'LL LAND ON THE ROOF!
HERE THEY COME, LIKE THEY SAID! BLAST 'EM OUTTA THE SKY!
I'VE GOT THEM IN MY SIGHT!
UM, MAYBE WE WON'T LAND ON THE ROOF!
THERE ARE PEOPLE ON THE STREET BELOW! STEER CLEAR OF THEM, JIMMY!

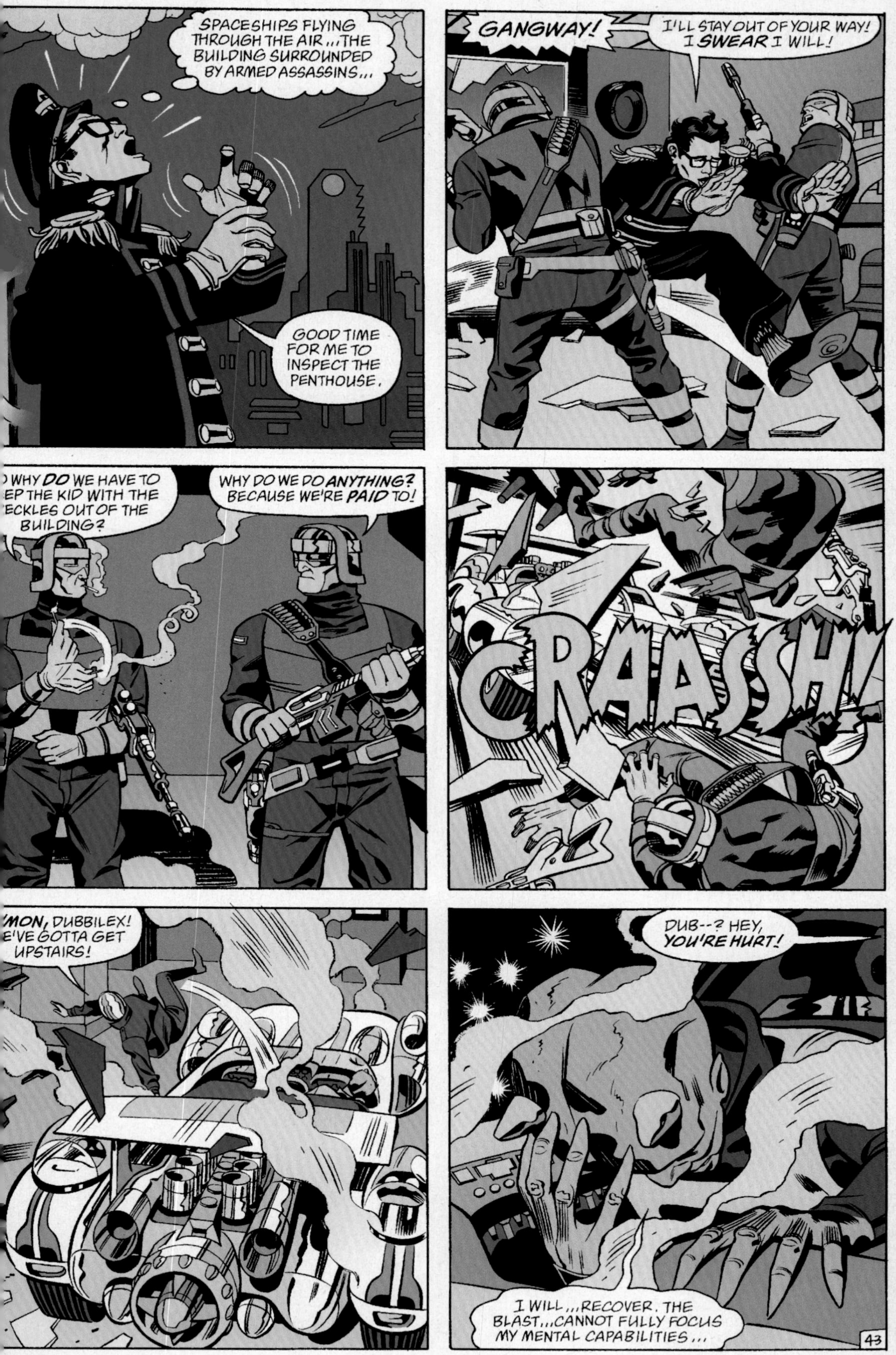
SPACESHIPS FLYING THROUGH THE AIR... THE BUILDING SURROUNDED BY ARMED ASSASSINS...
GOOD TIME FOR ME TO INSPECT THE PENTHOUSE.
GANGWAY!
I'LL STAY OUT OF YOUR WAY! I SWEAR I WILL!
WHY DO WE HAVE TO
EP THE KID WITH THE
ECKLES OUT OF THE
BUILDING?
WHY DO WE DO ANYTHING? BECAUSE WE'RE PAID TO!
CRAASH!
MON, DUBBILEX!
E'VE GOTTA GET UPSTAIRS!
DUB--? HEY, YOU'RE HURT!
I WILL... RECOVER. THE BLAST... CANNOT FULLY FOCUS MY MENTAL CAPABILITIES...
43

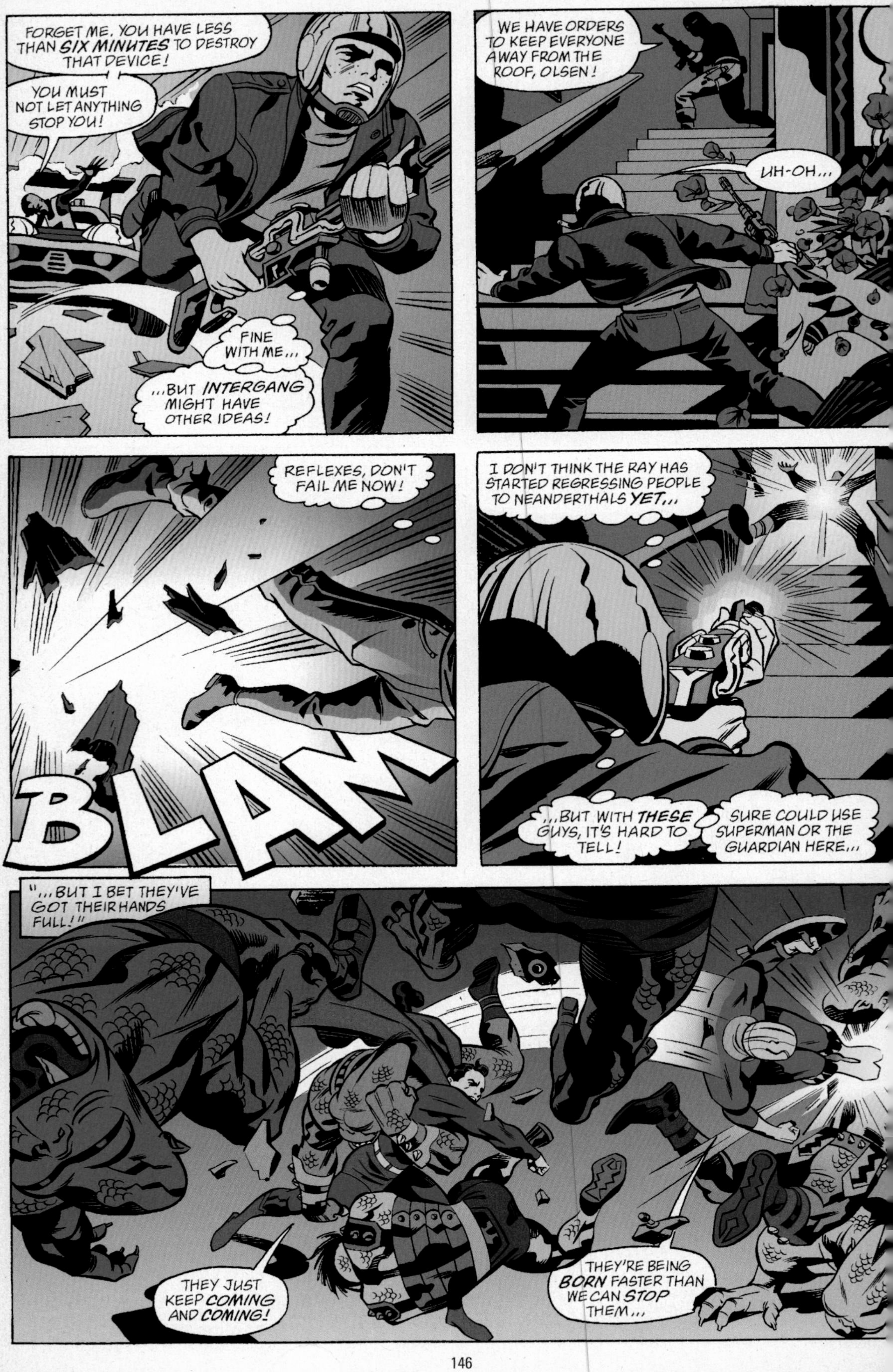
FORGET ME. YOU HAVE LESS THAN SIX MINUTES TO DESTROY THAT DEVICE!
YOU MUST NOT LET ANYTHING STOP YOU!
FINE WITH ME...
...BUT INTERGANG MIGHT HAVE OTHER IDEAS!
WE HAVE ORDERS TO KEEP EVERYONE AWAY FROM THE ROOF, OLSEN!
UH-OH...
REFLEXES, DON'T FAIL ME NOW!
BLAM
I DON'T THINK THE RAY HAS STARTED REGRESSING PEOPLE TO NEANDERTHALS YET...
...BUT WITH THESE GUYS, IT'S HARD TO TELL!
SURE COULD USE SUPERMAN OR THE GUARDIAN HERE...
"...BUT I BET THEY'VE GOT THEIR HANDS FULL!"
THEY JUST KEEP COMING AND COMING!
THEY'RE BEING BORN FASTER THAN WE CAN STOP THEM...

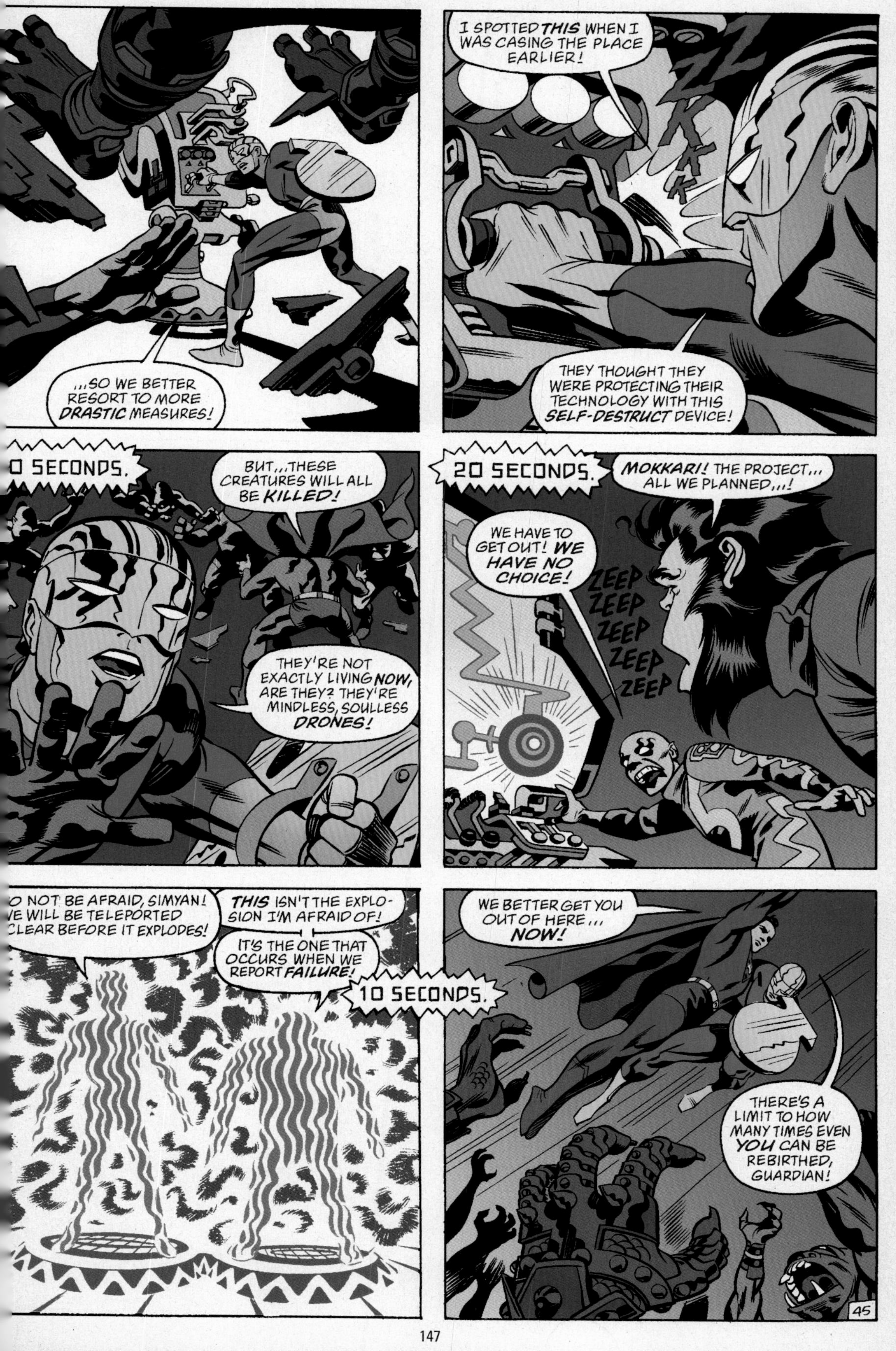
...SO WE BETTER RESORT TO MORE DRASTIC MEASURES!
I SPOTTED THIS WHEN I WAS CASING THE PLACE EARLIER!
KKKK
THEY THOUGHT THEY WERE PROTECTING THEIR TECHNOLOGY WITH THIS SELF-DESTRUCT DEVICE!
0 SECONDS.
BUT... THESE CREATURES WILL ALL BE KILLED!
THEY'RE NOT EXACTLY LIVING NOW, ARE THEY? THEY'RE MINDLESS, SOULLESS DRONES!
20 SECONDS.
MOKKARI! THE PROJECT... ALL WE PLANNED...!
WE HAVE TO GET OUT! WE HAVE NO CHOICE!
ZEEP ZEEP ZEEP ZEEP ZEEP
O NOT BE AFRAID, SIMYAN! VE WILL BE TELEPORTED CLEAR BEFORE IT EXPLODES!
THIS ISN'T THE EXPLOSION I'M AFRAID OF!
IT'S THE ONE THAT OCCURS WHEN WE REPORT FAILURE!
10 SECONDS.
WE BETTER GET YOU OUT OF HERE... NOW!
THERE'S A LIMIT TO HOW MANY TIMES EVEN YOU CAN BE REBIRTHED, GUARDIAN!
45

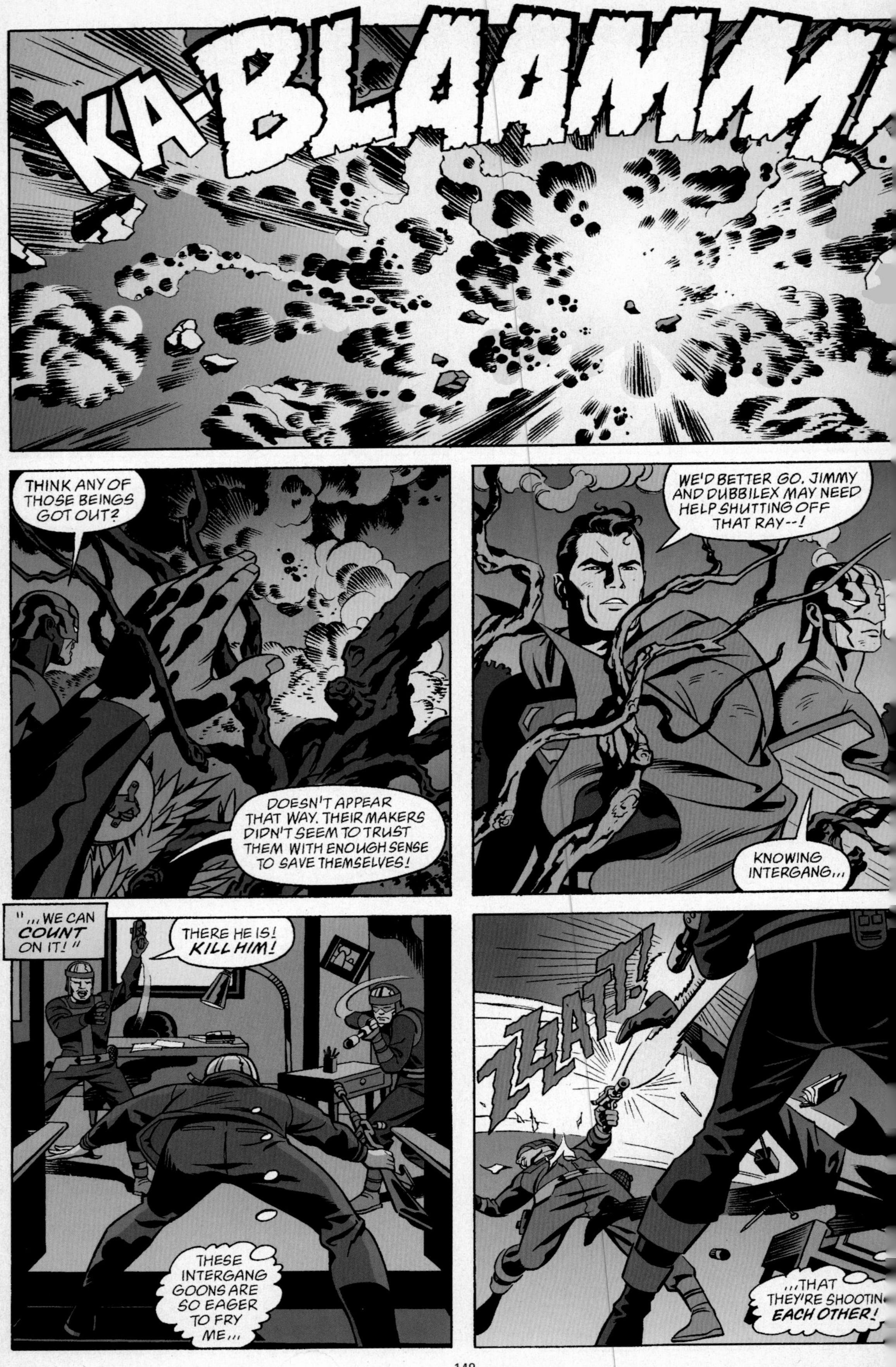
KA-BLAMM!
THINK ANY OF THOSE BEINGS GOT OUT?
DOESN'T APPEAR THAT WAY. THEIR MAKERS DIDN'T SEEM TO TRUST THEM WITH ENOUGH SENSE TO SAVE THEMSELVES!
WE'D BETTER GO. JIMMY AND DUBBILEX MAY NEED HELP SHUTTING OFF THAT RAY--!
KNOWING INTERGANG,,,
",,, WE CAN COUNT ON IT!"
THERE HE IS! KILL HIM!
THESE INTERGANG GOONS ARE SO EAGER TO FRY ME,,,
ZZZATT!
,,,THAT THEY'RE SHOOTIN EACH OTHER!

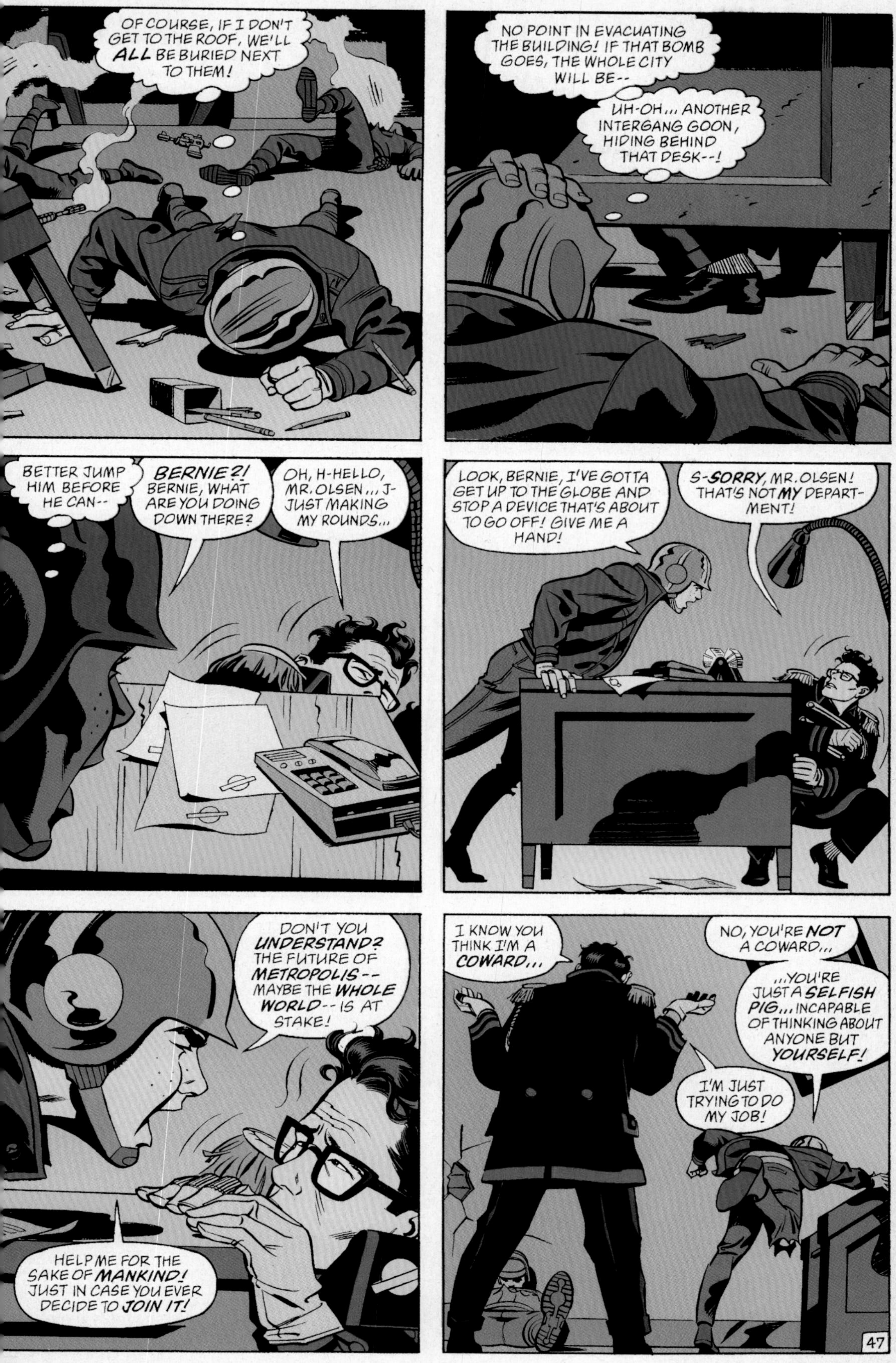
OF COURSE, IF I DON'T GET TO THE ROOF, WE'LL ALL BE BURIED NEXT TO THEM!
NO POINT IN EVACUATING THE BUILDING! IF THAT BOMB GOES, THE WHOLE CITY WILL BE--
UH-OH... ANOTHER INTERGANG GOON, HIDING BEHIND THAT DESK--!
BETTER JUMP HIM BEFORE HE CAN--
BERNIE?! BERNIE, WHAT ARE YOU DOING DOWN THERE?
OH, H-HELLO, MR. OLSEN... J-JUST MAKING MY ROUNDS...
LOOK, BERNIE, I'VE GOTTA GET UP TO THE GLOBE AND STOP A DEVICE THAT'S ABOUT TO GO OFF! GIVE ME A HAND!
S-SORRY, MR. OLSEN! THAT'S NOT MY DEPARTMENT!
DON'T YOU UNDERSTAND? THE FUTURE OF METROPOLIS-- MAYBE THE WHOLE WORLD-- IS AT STAKE!
HELP ME FOR THE SAKE OF MANKIND! JUST IN CASE YOU EVER DECIDE TO JOIN IT!
I KNOW YOU THINK I'M A COWARD...
NO, YOU'RE NOT A COWARD...
...YOU'RE JUST A SELFISH PIG... INCAPABLE OF THINKING ABOUT ANYONE BUT YOURSELF!
I'M JUST TRYING TO DO MY JOB!
47

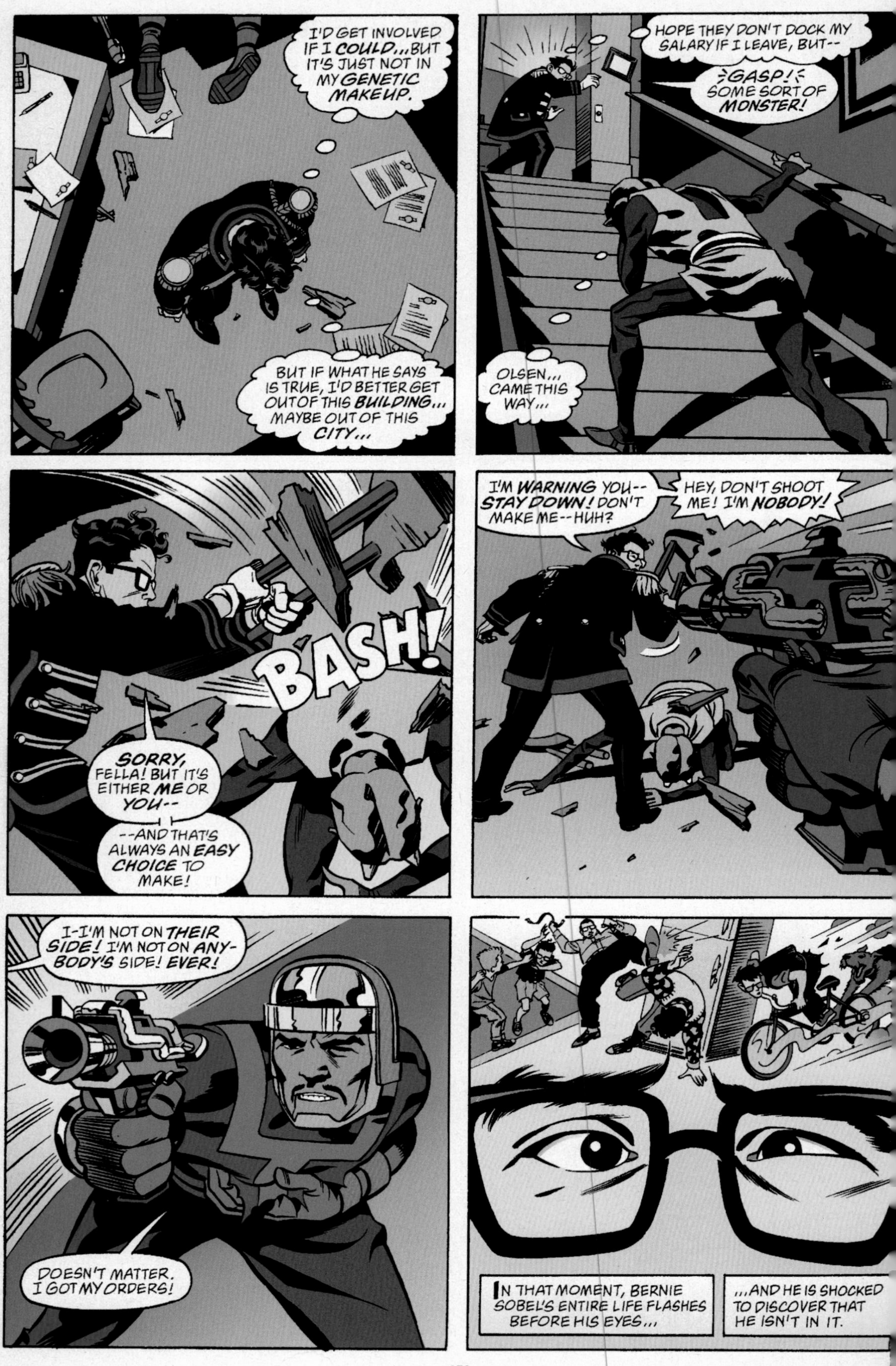
I'D GET INVOLVED IF I COULD... BUT IT'S JUST NOT IN MY GENETIC MAKEUP.
BUT IF WHAT HE SAYS IS TRUE, I'D BETTER GET OUT OF THIS BUILDING... MAYBE OUT OF THIS CITY...
HOPE THEY DON'T DOCK MY SALARY IF I LEAVE, BUT--
GASP! SOME SORT OF MONSTER!
OLSEN... CAME THIS WAY...
BASH!
SORRY, FELLA! BUT IT'S EITHER ME OR YOU--
--AND THAT'S ALWAYS AN EASY CHOICE TO MAKE!
I'M WARNING YOU-- STAY DOWN! DON'T MAKE ME--HUH?
HEY, DON'T SHOOT ME! I'M NOBODY!
I-I'M NOT ON THEIR SIDE! I'M NOT ON ANYBODY'S SIDE! EVER!
DOESN'T MATTER. I GOT MY ORDERS!
IN THAT MOMENT, BERNIE SOBEL'S ENTIRE LIFE FLASHES BEFORE HIS EYES...
...AND HE IS SHOCKED TO DISCOVER THAT HE ISN'T IN IT.

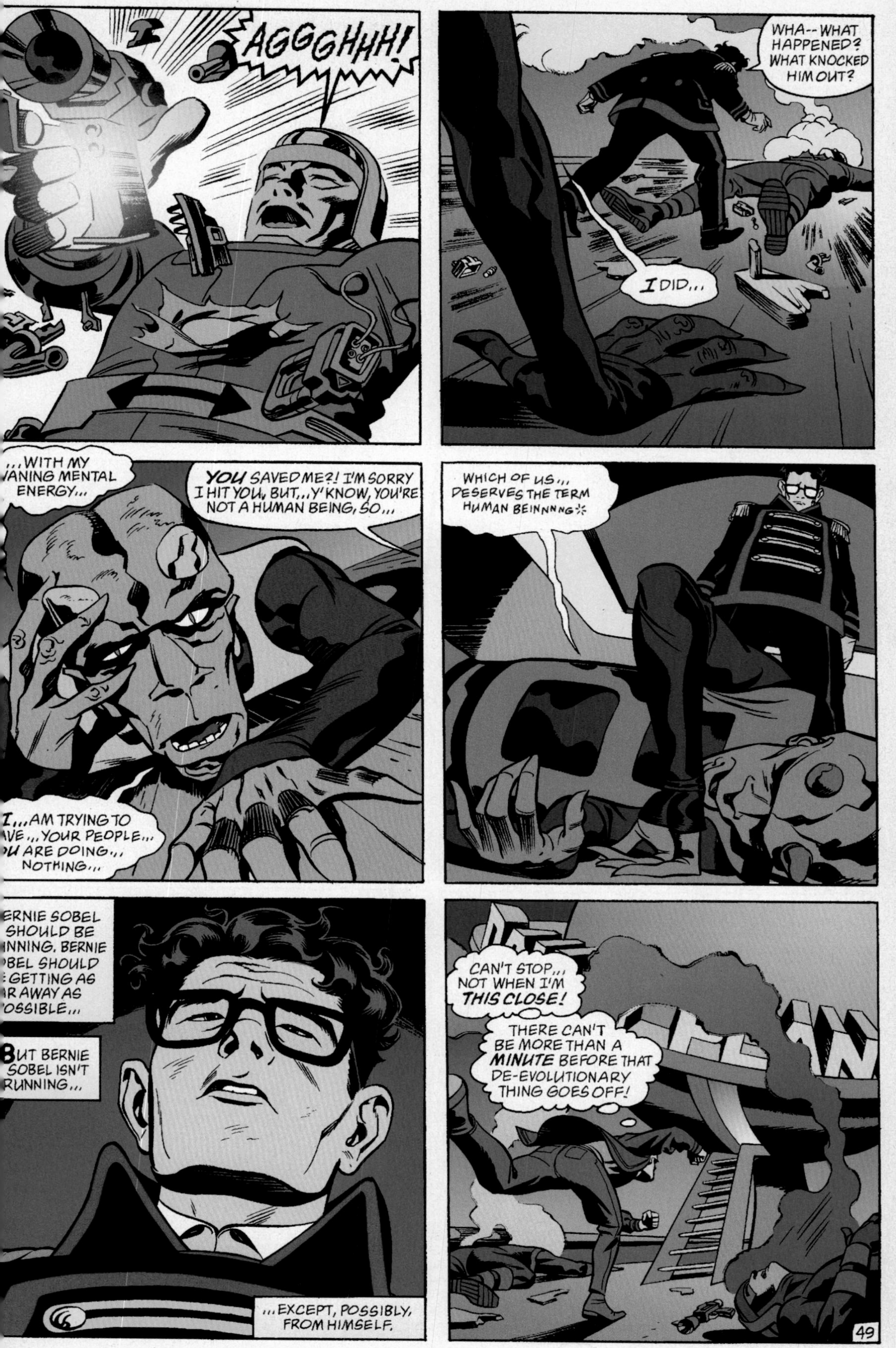
AGGGHHH!
WHA--WHAT HAPPENED? WHAT KNOCKED HIM OUT?
I DID...
...WITH MY WANING MENTAL ENERGY...
YOU SAVED ME?! I'M SORRY I HIT YOU, BUT...Y'KNOW, YOU'RE NOT A HUMAN BEING, SO...
I...AM TRYING TO SAVE...YOUR PEOPLE... YOU ARE DOING... NOTHING...
WHICH OF US... DESERVES THE TERM HUMAN BEINNNNG*
BERNIE SOBEL SHOULD BE RUNNING. BERNIE SOBEL SHOULD BE GETTING AS FAR AWAY AS POSSIBLE...
BUT BERNIE SOBEL ISN'T RUNNING...
...EXCEPT, POSSIBLY, FROM HIMSELF.
CAN'T STOP... NOT WHEN I'M THIS CLOSE!
THERE CAN'T BE MORE THAN A MINUTE BEFORE THAT DE-EVOLUTIONARY THING GOES OFF!
49

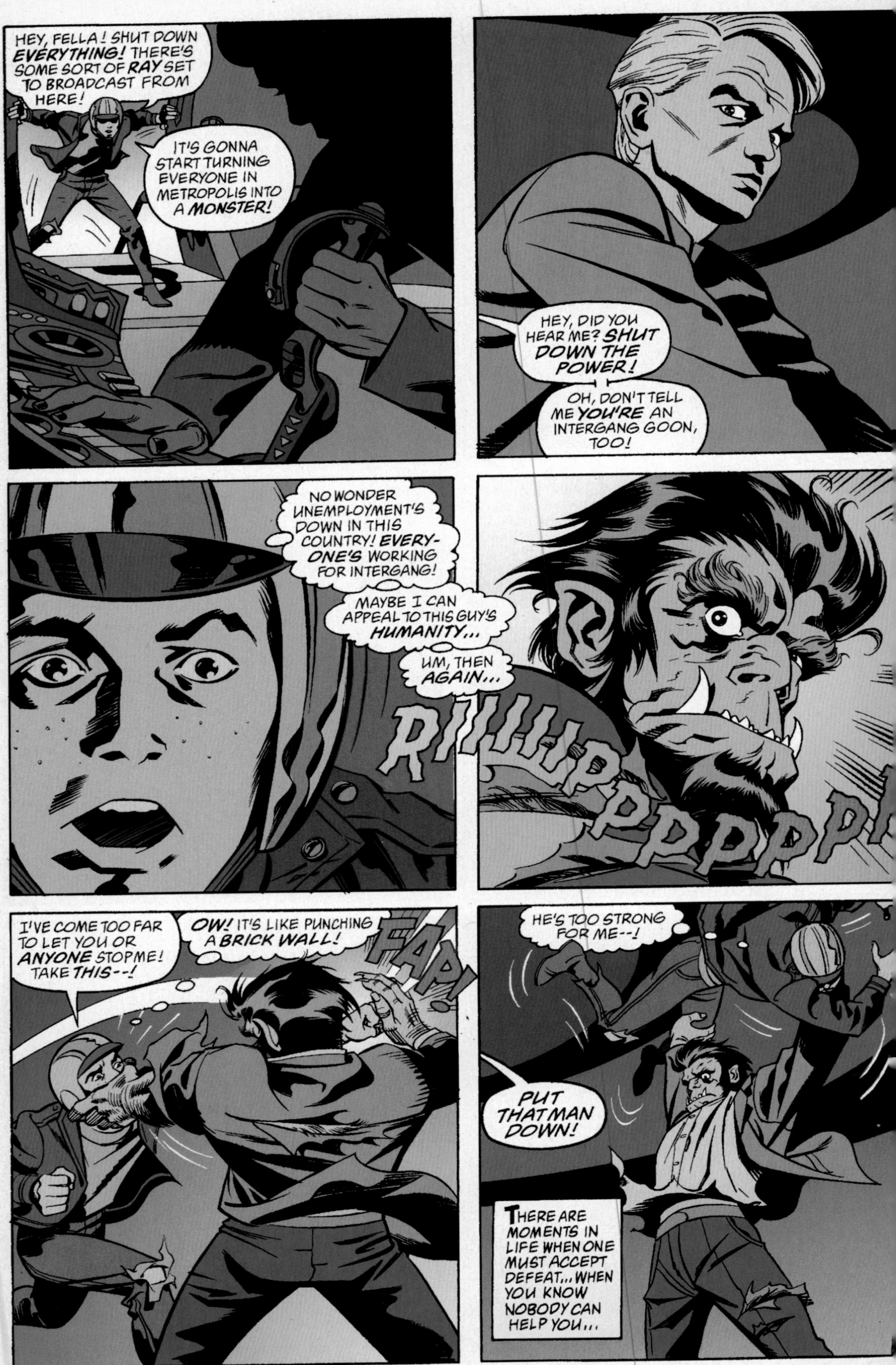
HEY, FELLA! SHUT DOWN EVERYTHING! THERE'S SOME SORT OF RAY SET TO BROADCAST FROM HERE!
IT'S GONNA START TURNING EVERYONE IN METROPOLIS INTO A MONSTER!
HEY, DID YOU HEAR ME? SHUT DOWN THE POWER!
OH, DON'T TELL ME YOU'RE AN INTERGANG GOON, TOO!
NO WONDER UNEMPLOYMENT'S DOWN IN THIS COUNTRY! EVERY-ONE'S WORKING FOR INTERGANG!
MAYBE I CAN APPEAL TO THIS GUY'S HUMANITY...
UM, THEN AGAIN...
RIIIIPPPPPP
I'VE COME TOO FAR TO LET YOU OR ANYONE STOP ME! TAKE THIS--!
OW! IT'S LIKE PUNCHING A BRICK WALL!
FAP!
HE'S TOO STRONG FOR ME--!
PUT THAT MAN DOWN!
THERE ARE MOMENTS IN LIFE WHEN ONE MUST ACCEPT DEFEAT... WHEN YOU KNOW NOBODY CAN HELP YOU...

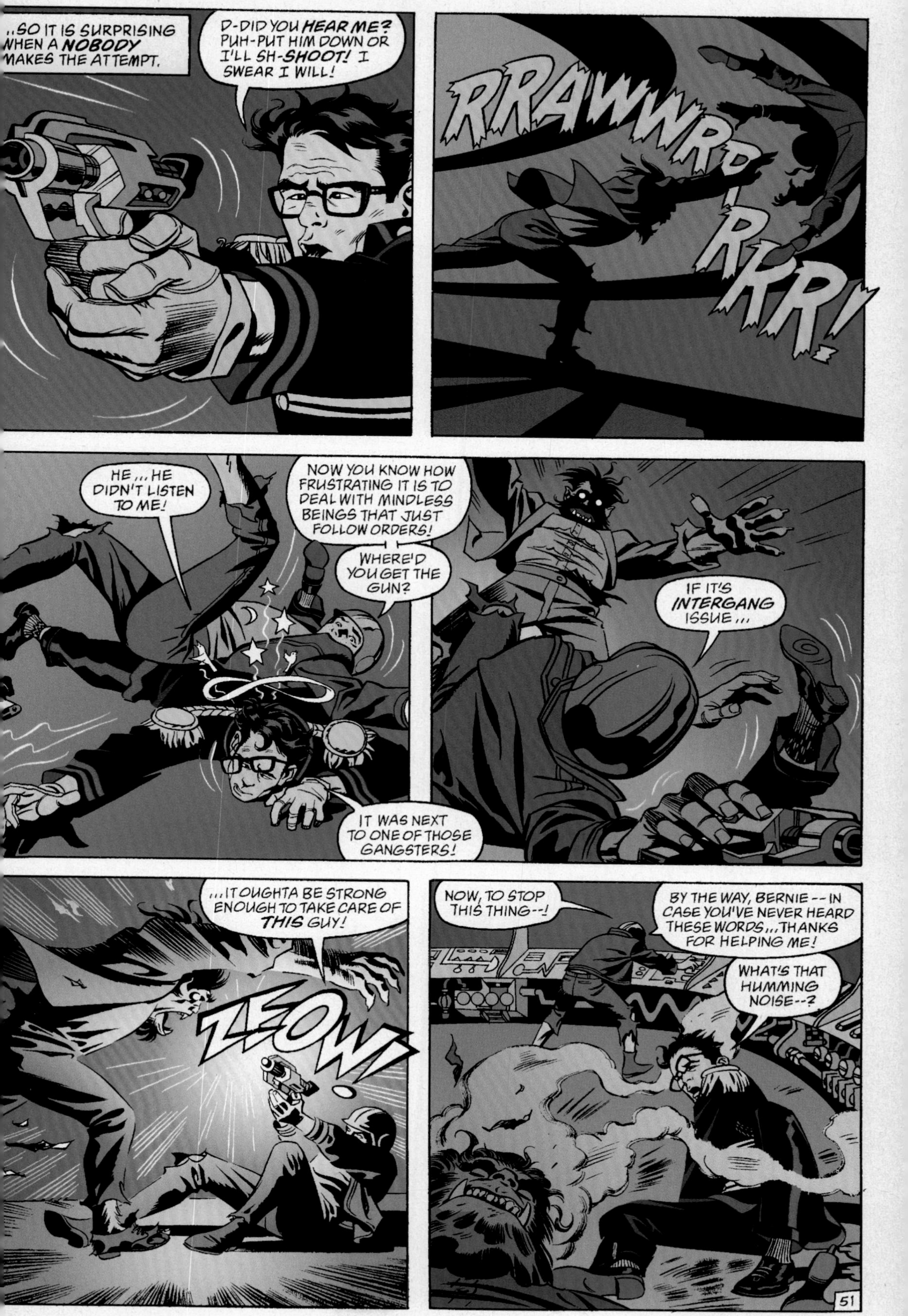
..SO IT IS SURPRISING WHEN A NOBODY MAKES THE ATTEMPT.
D-DID YOU HEAR ME? PUH-PUT HIM DOWN OR I'LL SH-SHOOT! I SWEAR I WILL!
RRAWWRD RRKR!
HE... HE DIDN'T LISTEN TO ME!
NOW YOU KNOW HOW FRUSTRATING IT IS TO DEAL WITH MINDLESS BEINGS THAT JUST FOLLOW ORDERS!
WHERE'D YOU GET THE GUN?
IT WAS NEXT TO ONE OF THOSE GANGSTERS!
IF IT'S INTERGANG ISSUE...
...IT OUGHTA BE STRONG ENOUGH TO TAKE CARE OF THIS GUY!
ZEOW!
NOW, TO STOP THIS THING--!
BY THE WAY, BERNIE -- IN CASE YOU'VE NEVER HEARD THESE WORDS... THANKS FOR HELPING ME!
WHAT'S THAT HUMMING NOISE--?
51

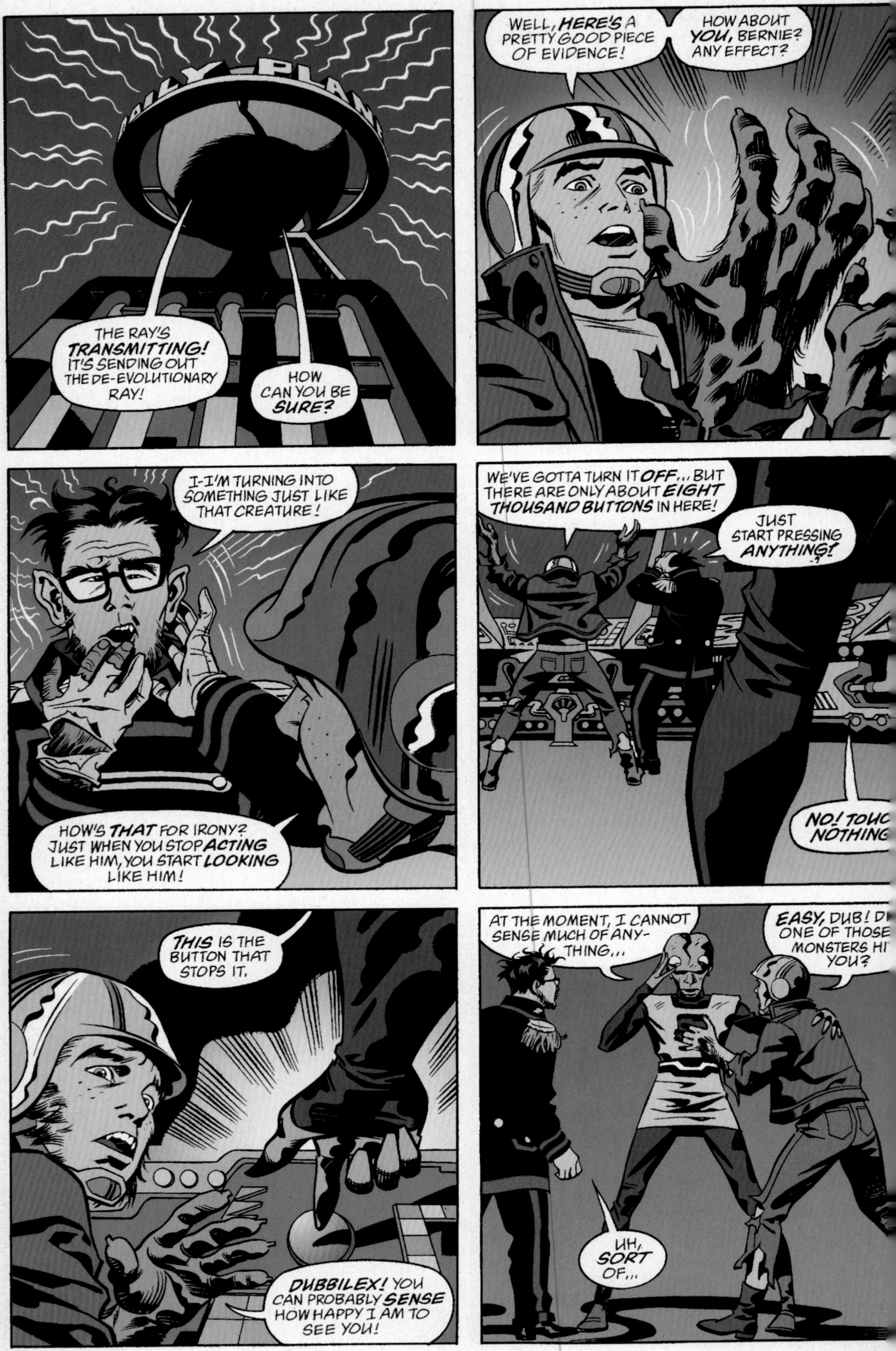
DAILY PLANE
THE RAY'S TRANSMITTING! IT'S SENDING OUT THE DE-EVOLUTIONARY RAY!
HOW CAN YOU BE SURE?
WELL, HERE'S A PRETTY GOOD PIECE OF EVIDENCE!
HOW ABOUT YOU, BERNIE? ANY EFFECT?
I-I'M TURNING INTO SOMETHING JUST LIKE THAT CREATURE!
HOW'S THAT FOR IRONY? JUST WHEN YOU STOP ACTING LIKE HIM, YOU START LOOKING LIKE HIM!
WE'VE GOTTA TURN IT OFF... BUT THERE ARE ONLY ABOUT EIGHT THOUSAND BUTTONS IN HERE!
JUST START PRESSING ANYTHING!
NO! TOUC NOTHING
THIS IS THE BUTTON THAT STOPS IT.
DUBBILEX! YOU CAN PROBABLY SENSE HOW HAPPY I AM TO SEE YOU!
AT THE MOMENT, I CANNOT SENSE MUCH OF ANY-THING...
EASY, DUB! D ONE OF THOSE MONSTERS HI YOU?
UH, SORT OF...

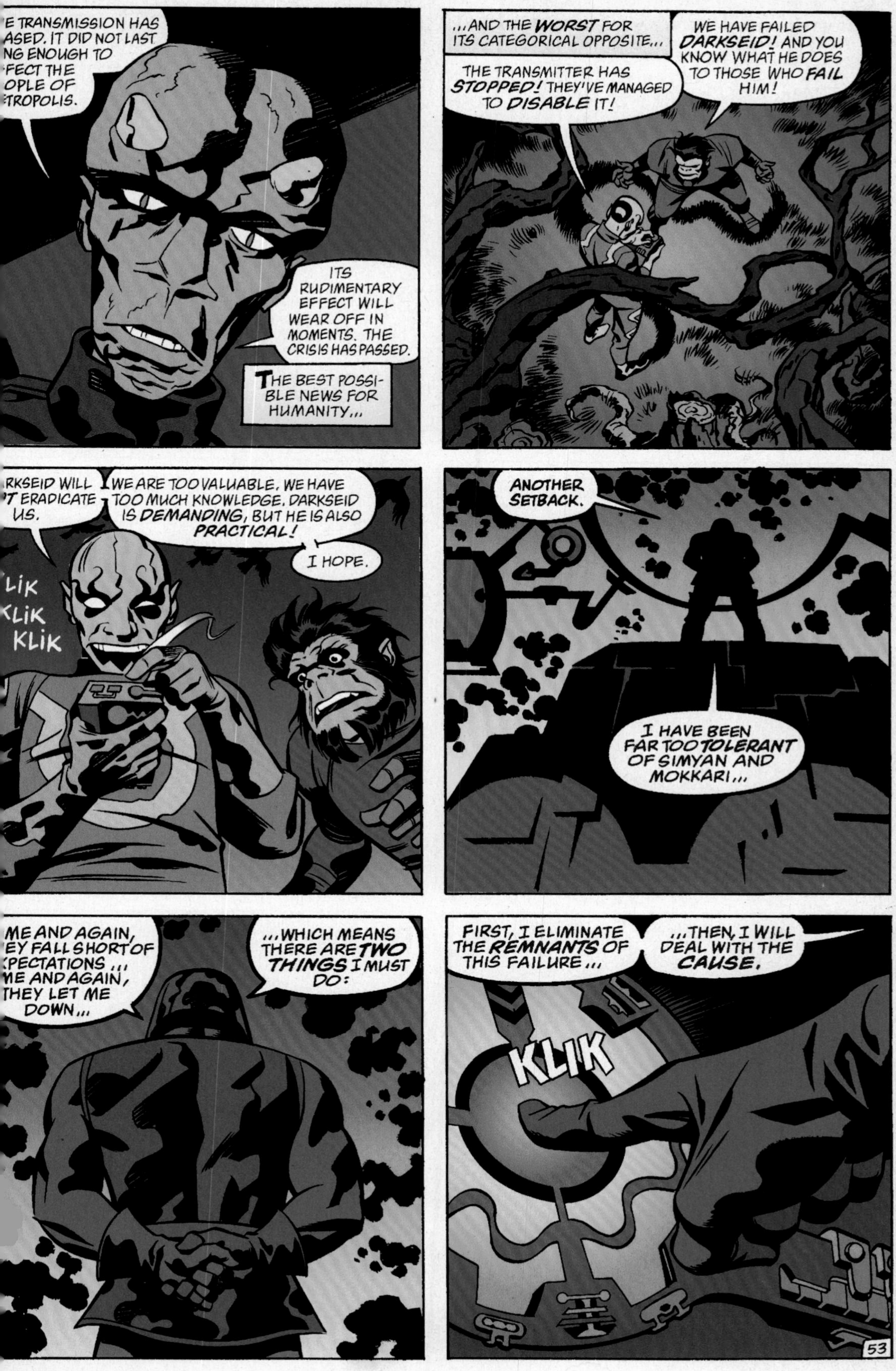
E TRANSMISSION HAS ASED. IT DID NOT LAST NG ENOUGH TO FECT THE OPLE OF TROPOLIS.
ITS RUDIMENTARY EFFECT WILL WEAR OFF IN MOMENTS. THE CRISIS HAS PASSED.
THE BEST POSSIBLE NEWS FOR HUMANITY...
...AND THE WORST FOR ITS CATEGORICAL OPPOSITE...
THE TRANSMITTER HAS STOPPED! THEY'VE MANAGED TO DISABLE IT!
WE HAVE FAILED DARKSEID! AND YOU KNOW WHAT HE DOES TO THOSE WHO FAIL HIM!
RKSEID WILL T ERADICATE US.
WE ARE TOO VALUABLE. WE HAVE TOO MUCH KNOWLEDGE. DARKSEID IS DEMANDING, BUT HE IS ALSO PRACTICAL!
I HOPE.
LIK
KLIK
KLIK
ANOTHER SETBACK.
I HAVE BEEN FAR TOO TOLERANT OF SIMYAN AND MOKKARI...
ME AND AGAIN, EY FALL SHORT OF PECTATIONS... ME AND AGAIN, THEY LET ME DOWN...
...WHICH MEANS THERE ARE TWO THINGS I MUST DO:
FIRST, I ELIMINATE THE REMNANTS OF THIS FAILURE...
...THEN, I WILL DEAL WITH THE CAUSE.
KLIK
53

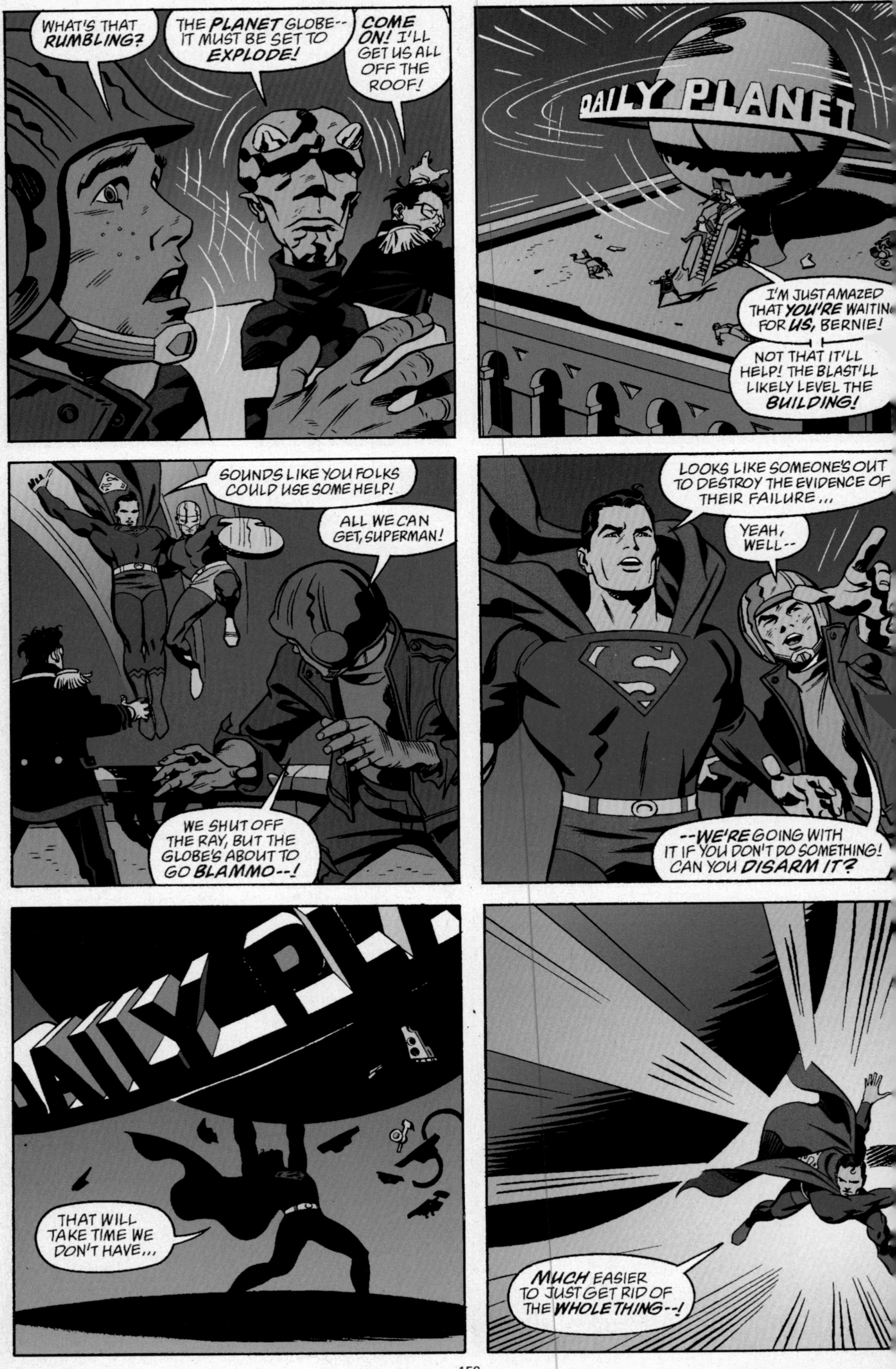
WHAT'S THAT RUMBLING?
THE PLANET GLOBE-- IT MUST BE SET TO EXPLODE!
COME ON! I'LL GET US ALL OFF THE ROOF!
DAILY PLANET
I'M JUST AMAZED THAT YOU'RE WAITING FOR US, BERNIE!
NOT THAT IT'LL HELP! THE BLAST'LL LIKELY LEVEL THE BUILDING!
SOUNDS LIKE YOU FOLKS COULD USE SOME HELP!
ALL WE CAN GET, SUPERMAN!
WE SHUT OFF THE RAY, BUT THE GLOBE'S ABOUT TO GO BLAMMO--!
LOOKS LIKE SOMEONE'S OUT TO DESTROY THE EVIDENCE OF THEIR FAILURE...
YEAH, WELL--
--WE'RE GOING WITH IT IF YOU DON'T DO SOMETHING! CAN YOU DISARM IT?
THAT WILL TAKE TIME WE DON'T HAVE...
MUCH EASIER TO JUST GET RID OF THE WHOLE THING--!

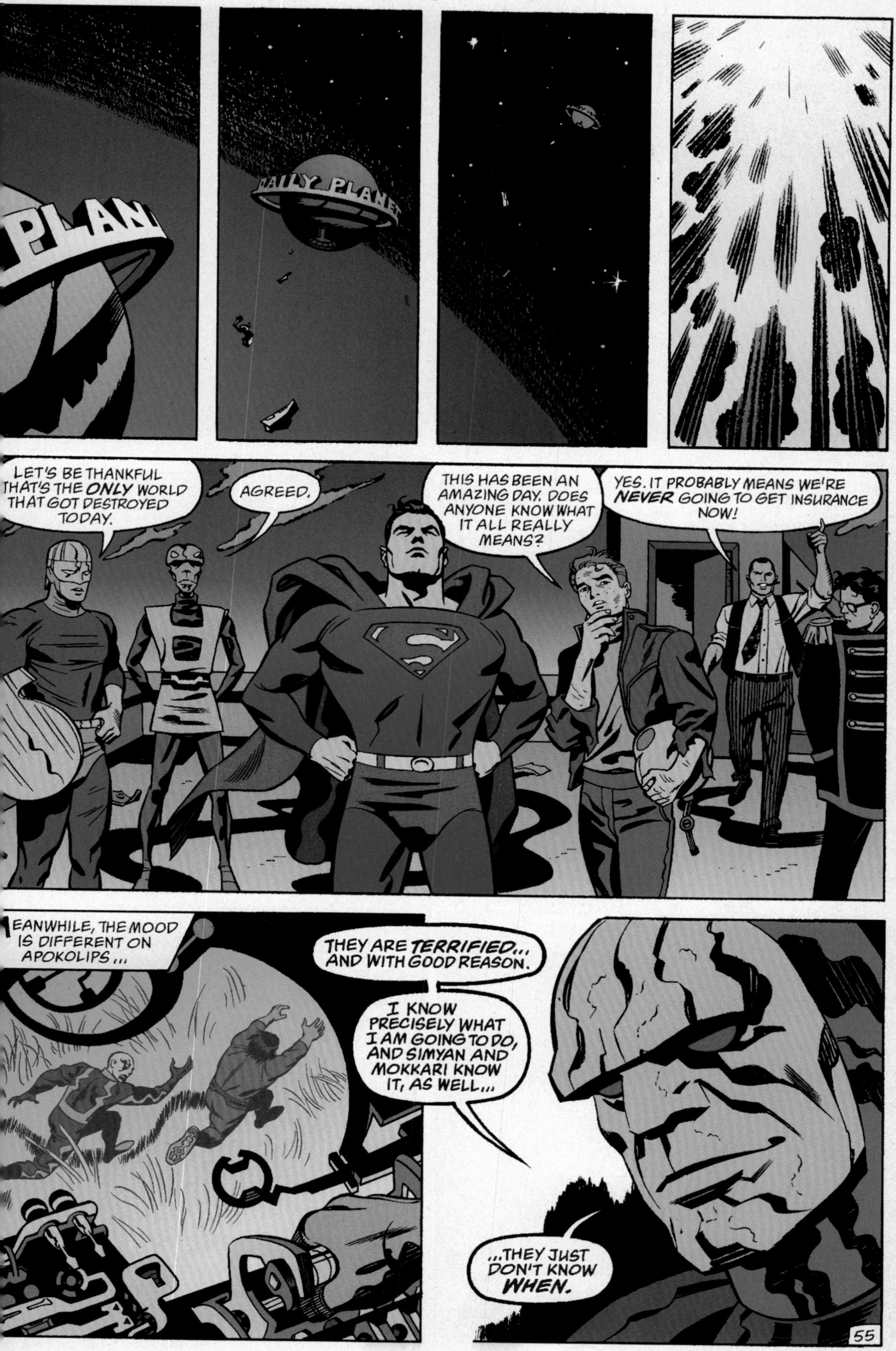
PLAN
DAILY PLANET
LET'S BE THANKFUL THAT'S THE ONLY WORLD THAT GOT DESTROYED TODAY.
AGREED.
THIS HAS BEEN AN AMAZING DAY. DOES ANYONE KNOW WHAT IT ALL REALLY MEANS?
YES. IT PROBABLY MEANS WE'RE NEVER GOING TO GET INSURANCE NOW!
EANWHILE, THE MOOD IS DIFFERENT ON APOKOLIPS...
THEY ARE TERRIFIED... AND WITH GOOD REASON.
I KNOW PRECISELY WHAT I AM GOING TO DO, AND SIMYAN AND MOKKARI KNOW IT, AS WELL...
...THEY JUST DON'T KNOW WHEN.
55

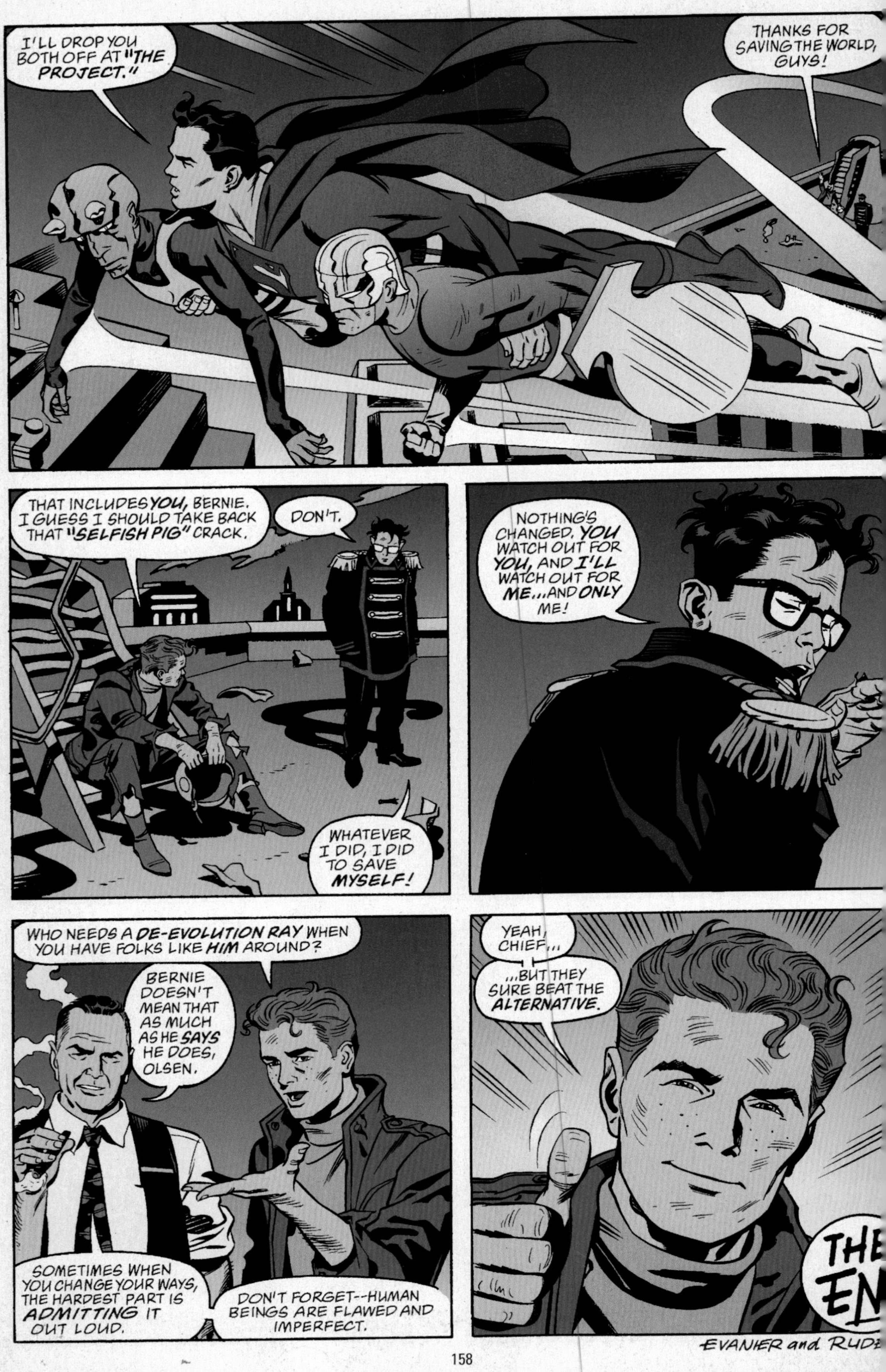
I'LL DROP YOU BOTH OFF AT "THE PROJECT."
THANKS FOR SAVING THE WORLD, GUYS!
THAT INCLUDES YOU, BERNIE. I GUESS I SHOULD TAKE BACK THAT "SELFISH PIG" CRACK.
DON'T.
WHATEVER I DID, I DID TO SAVE MYSELF!
NOTHING'S CHANGED. YOU WATCH OUT FOR YOU, AND I'LL WATCH OUT FOR ME... AND ONLY ME!
WHO NEEDS A DE-EVOLUTION RAY WHEN YOU HAVE FOLKS LIKE HIM AROUND?
BERNIE DOESN'T MEAN THAT AS MUCH AS HE SAYS HE DOES, OLSEN.
SOMETIMES WHEN YOU CHANGE YOUR WAYS, THE HARDEST PART IS ADMITTING IT OUT LOUD.
DON'T FORGET--HUMAN BEINGS ARE FLAWED AND IMPERFECT.
YEAH, CHIEF...
...BUT THEY SURE BEAT THE ALTERNATIVE.
EVANIER and RUDE

EAD MORE OF THE
AN OF STEEL'S
OVENTURES IN
HESE COLLECTIONS
ROM DC COMICS:

SUPERMAN

UPERMAN: OR TOMORROW OLUME 1

rian Azzarello, Jim Lee and **cott Williams** tell the epic le of a cataclysmic event at strikes the Earth, affecting illions – including those osest to the Man of Steel.

DC
BRIAN AZZARELLO JIM LEE SCOTT WILLIAMS
SUPERMAN
FOR TOMORROW
VOLUME ONE

BIG HERO NEEDS A BIG STORY, D THIS TEAM DOESN'T DISAPPOINT."
THE WASHINGTON POST

SUPERMAN: THE MAN OF STEEL VOLUME 1

DC
JOHN BYRNE DICK GIORDANO
SUPERMAN
THE MAN OF STEEL

SUPERMAN FOR ALL SEASONS

DC
Superman
For All Seasons
Jeph Loeb
Tim Sale
with Bjarne Hansen

THE DEATH OF SUPERMAN

THE BEST-SELLING GRAPHIC NOVEL OF ALL TIME!
THE DEATH OF
SUPERMAN
Dan JURGENS
Jerry ORDWAY
Louise SIMONSON
Roger STERN
Jon BOGDANOVE
Tom GRUMMETT
Jackson GUICE
Brett BREEDING
Rick BURCHETT
Doug HAZLEWOOD
Dennis JANKE
Denis RODIER
DC

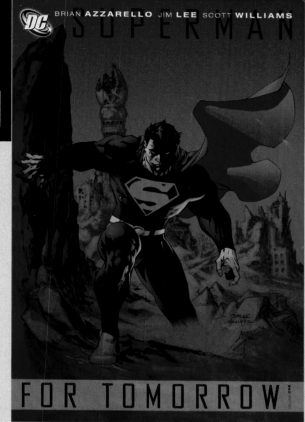

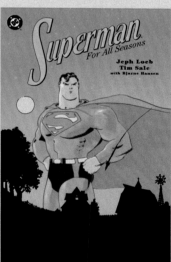